M000289061

PRAISE FOR
COLD WAR 2.0

"George S. Takach has convinced me: we are in the midst of a new cold war with autocratic governments around the globe. This war, Takach argues, will be won or lost not on human reaction to unfolding events, but on a people's mastery of artificial intelligence. This mastery is fueled by human innovation, usually embraced in the United States. *Cold War 2.0* is a superbly researched treatise on the imminent danger we find ourselves in, and a roadmap to our only route to victory."

—**Lis Wiehl, author of** *A Spy in Plain Sight*

"This comprehensive, clear, and compelling book argues convincingly that the U.S.-led democracies will win the current Cold War 2.0 against the China-led authoritarian powers. Drawing on rich evidence and ideas from the past 2,500 years, Takach adds his personal experience and an impressive array of current detail to make his case. Moving smoothly from an analysis of countries' key relative capabilities, through current flashpoints, to policy prescriptions and practical solutions, he identifies what they can and should do now to ensure that the democratic powers win this second cold war. It is a must-read for the many policymakers, scholars, and citizens afflicted by the current tidal wave of crises, uncertainties, and doubts, as it offers a message of hope—and shows why and how this hope can come true for the world as a whole."

—**John Kirton, professor emeritus of political science,**
University of Toronto

"George Takach has made a compelling and fascinating argument in taking on the crucial question of how cutting-edge technology, particularly AI, semiconductors, quantum computing, biotech, cloud computing, and fusion energy will impact the upcoming cold war with China. Technological innovation, as a process, has been the subject of constant evolution since the end of the nineteenth century, and its careful manipulation by the democracies played a decisive role in ending the first cold war. Takach explores these dynamics, including what he terms hyper-innovation, and the decisive role played by gender-inclusion and the particular advantages possessed by democracies in innovation. An insightful examination."

—**Professor Julian Spencer-Churchill,**
Concordia University

"A fascinating, timely, and chilling assessment of how AI will shape the looming struggle between China and the US over the battlefield of Taiwan. Key decision makers in Washington, DC, need to read George S. Takach's compelling study before it's too late."

—**Saul David, author of** *Devil Dogs: From Guadalcanal to the*
Shores of Japan, **Operation** *Thunderbolt,* **Crucible** *of Hell,*
and *The Force.*

"Russian aggression in Ukraine and Chinese designs on Taiwan rightly worry the citizens of Western democracies. Add the uncertainty of innovations such as AI and biotech, and the future feels destined to be a dystopian science fiction political thriller. Takach, however, soberly analyzes the geopolitical and technological dangers and offers a hopeful message: the political strength of democracy and the innovative potential of market economies are more than enough to defeat our autocratic adversaries—if we understand the nature of Cold War 2.0."

—**David Head, author of** *A Republic of Scoundrels: The Schemers,*
Intriguers, and Adventurers Who Created a New American Nation
and *A Crisis of Peace: George Washington, the Newburgh Conspiracy,*
and the Fall of the American Revolution

COLD WAR 2.0

ARTIFICIAL INTELLIGENCE IN THE NEW BATTLE
BETWEEN CHINA, RUSSIA, AND AMERICA

GEORGE S. TAKACH

PEGASUS BOOKS
NEW YORK LONDON

COLD WAR 2.0

Pegasus Books, Ltd.
148 West 37th Street, 13th Floor
New York, NY 10018

Copyright © 2024 by George S. Takach

First Pegasus Books cloth edition March 2024

Interior design by Maria Fernandez

All rights reserved. No part of this book may be reproduced in whole or in part without written permission from the publisher, except by reviewers who may quote brief excerpts in connection with a review in a newspaper, magazine, or electronic publication; nor may any part of this book be reproduced, stored in a retrieval system, or transmitted in any form or by any means electronic, mechanical, photocopying, recording, or other, without written permission from the publisher.

Library of Congress Cataloging-in-Publication Data is available.

ISBN: 978-1-63936-563-0

10 9 8 7 6 5 4 3 2 1

Printed in the United States of America
Distributed by Simon & Schuster
www.pegasusbooks.com

For Barb

CONTENTS

GLOSSARY

ADS: air defense system

AI: artificial intelligence

BT: biotechnology

C4: command, control, communication, and computers

CCP: Chinese Communist Party

Cheka, NKVD, KGB, FSB: different terms for the state security police of the Soviet Union and Russia from 1917 to the present

CSTO: Collective Security Treaty Organization

DPP: the Democratic Progressive Party of Taiwan

EDA: electronic design automation

EGM: ectogenesis machine

EU: European Union

EUL: Extreme Ultraviolet Lithography

GATO: Global Alliance Treaty Organization (a proposed collective defense alliance, like NATO, but among willing democracies all around the world)

GRU: Soviet and Russian military intelligence

KMT: the Kuomintang

MIC: military-industrial complex

NATO: North Atlantic Treaty Organization

OECD: Organization of Economic Co-operation and Development

PATO: Pacific Alliance Treaty Organization (a proposed collective defense alliance, like NATO, but among willing democracies in the Pacific)

People's Republic of China: "mainland/Communist" China

PLA: People's Liberation Army

QC: quantum computer

RCP: Russian Communist Party

Republic of China: Taiwan

SC: semiconductor chip

SCO: Shanghai Cooperation Organization

SCS: South China Sea

SME: semiconductor manufacturing equipment

STEM: science, technology, engineering, and mathematics

TRA: Taiwan Relations Act

TSMC: Taiwan Semiconductor Manufacturing Corporation

UNCLOS: United Nations Convention on the Law of the Sea

UNSC: United Nations Security Council

WHO: World Health Organization

INTRODUCTION

C hina's autocrat Xi Jinping, the leader of a country of 1.4 billion people, has stated clearly that Taiwan, a democracy of 23 million people, must become a part of China. China is 265 times larger than Taiwan geographically, and has 61 times as many people. Yet Xi has made the continued independent existence of Taiwan an existential threat to China. Autocrats detest democracies as neighbors, lest the urge to democratize infect the autocrat's own citizens and unseat the autocrat from power. The tension between autocracy and democracy is a central theme of Cold War 2.0.

Xi's preference would be to have Taiwan surrender to China peacefully, but the likely election in January 2024 of another Democratic Progressive Party president of Taiwan, who wants to keep Taiwan separate from China, as it has been since 1949, virtually ensures that Beijing will now move to take Taiwan by military force. China intends to attack Taiwan, much as Russia invaded Ukraine in 2022. All that remains to be seen is when and how.

In terms of timing, Xi doesn't wish to leave to his successor the task of subduing Taiwan, as Xi has woven into his persona the subjugation of the Taiwanese people. In the best autocratic tradition, Xi has also engineered himself into the "leader-for-life" position atop the Chinese Communist

Party, the only political party permitted in China, which not only runs the government but also controls all aspects of Chinese society. Nevertheless, assuming he wants to repatriate Taiwan while he is in his seventies (he was born in 1953), Xi's likely outside date for the takeover of Taiwan is 2034. All that remains, therefore, is the precise attack plan.

Military analysts anticipate that China will implement one of two attack plans for the takeover of Taiwan. China's People's Liberation Army (PLA) could carry out a military invasion of the island or China could opt for blockading the island with the PLA's navy and air force in order to pressure Taiwan into submission. Frankly, even the blockade scenario will likely turn violent quickly when the Taiwanese or United States armed forces act to break the blockade, given that Taiwan only has eight days of energy stockpiled on the island.

Assume China elects the invasion option. In such a Chinese attack, suddenly on the radar screens of military Command, Control, Communication, and Computers (C4) posts in Taiwan, on Taiwanese and American naval vessels in the waters around the island, and in many other American C4 centers around the world, several hundred blips will appear all at once. Each blip represents a precision-guided missile or drone launched by China from hundreds of aircraft, ships, and land bases on the east coast of China. The launch of these missiles and drones will be detected by a number of Taiwanese and American radar and sensor systems: Taiwan's Bee Eye radar stations; the American-built Precision Acquisition Vehicle Entry Phased Array Warning System (PAVE PAWS) radar system located in Taiwan; the radars of the Taiwanese and American air defense systems (ADS) on Taiwan and on ships around the island, including the Taiwanese Tien-Kung (Sky Bow), Tien Chien 2 (Sky Sword), and Avenger air defense batteries. Also alerted would be the American Patriot and Aegis ADS batteries; the American Space-Based Infrared System (SBIRS) of twelve geostationary satellites, with its C4 center at the North American Aerospace Defense Command and U.S. Space Command (NORAD/SPACECOM) facility in Colorado; and the Solid State Phased Array Radar System (SSPARS) located in Alaska. Detecting the massive Chinese missile and drone attack will not be a problem. Dealing with it effectively and in time will be the challenge for the Taiwanese and American defenders.

At the moment China launches this unprecedented deluge of missiles and drones, time will cease to be Taiwan's friend. The Taiwan Strait, the body of water separating the principal island of Taiwan from mainland China, is only 160 kilometers (100 miles) wide. The hundreds of cruise missiles fired from batteries on the Chinese coast will reach Taiwan in twelve minutes. Those fired from Chinese naval vessels and aircraft would hit Taiwan in only a few minutes. China's hypersonic missiles would be detected by Taiwan and American radar/satellites earlier at the C4 facilities noted above, but because of their incredible speed (6 kilometers per second), intercepting them with return fire will present a challenge of a different magnitude. Moreover, the objective is to shoot down the incoming missiles in a "missile engagement zone" that is well out in the middle of the Taiwan Strait, and not over Taiwan itself, and especially not over one of its heavily populated cities. The bottom line, for the Taiwanese and American militaries hoping to respond effectively to the first wave of the Chinese attack, is that time will be of the essence.

In this attack the fate of Taiwan, and the future of the global balance of power between the leading autocracies and the principal democracies (especially between the United States and China), will depend on the Avenger, Sky Bow, Sky Sword, Patriot, and Aegis air defense systems noted above. These ADS are built by the Taiwanese and American defense industries, and are operated by the Taiwanese and American militaries. The core computers of these ADS weapons are driven by an artificial intelligence (AI) software that receives information about enemy missiles and drones instantaneously from their own and other radars, satellites, and other sensors as soon as these enemy weapons are launched. It then determines and tracks the trajectories of the incoming missiles and drones, and then at the appropriate moment the ADS launches its own missiles to intercept the enemy's missiles and drones. But that's not all this AI software has to do.

The AI software of each ADS also has to communicate with the AI software of all the other ADS units to make sure that every enemy missile and drone is being dealt with methodically and thoroughly. It would be extremely unfortunate if two or more defensive interceptor missiles were tasked to take out the same incoming missile, and thus let a second incoming missile hit its target unimpeded. This is complicated work. One type of ADS interceptor missile can only hit relatively slow-flying drones. Another specializes in intercepting the fastest hypersonic missiles of the enemy. The AI system, therefore, must figure out what each blip on the C4 screen is, and which ADS to assign to its destruction. Hovering over the complex and critical workload of the AI system—and its human handlers—is the cruel logic of missile battles: the attacker doesn't need to achieve 100 percent success (which is why they launch so many missiles and drones), while the defender does have to achieve 100 percent success. It seems hardly a fair fight.

There's more to cause angst for the Taiwanese and American militaries. Taiwan is located in a region of incredibly busy commercial air traffic. A brief scan of flightaware.com shows dozens of flights coming into and leaving from Taiwan during most working hours of the day. The AI system underpinning the defense of Taiwan has to factor in these aircraft in an effort to reduce, ideally to zero, the downing of civilian planes during what will become known as the Battle of the Taiwan Strait. The memories of the USS *Vincennes* (an American naval vessel that in 1988 shot down an Iranian civilian aircraft during the Iran-Iraq War, killing 290) and Malaysia Airlines Flight 17 (shot down in 2014 by Russian-backed rebels in Ukraine using a Russian missile, killing 298) will make the concern around civilian friendly fire very real for the Taiwanese and American defenders.

Military doctrine in the democracies allows three modes of operation for the AI software when it comes to target allocation. *Manual* means the AI collects and processes the data, but always requires the human operator to make the actual decision about the target and its timing. *Semi-automatic* means the AI will select the target (the incoming missile or drone), but the human operator has a short period (i.e., fifteen seconds) to override or delay the computer's decision. *Automatic mode* allows the AI system to select the targets with no opportunity for human operator intervention.

Chances are, on that fateful day when China launches the opening shower of missiles and drones on Taiwan, the AI will quickly be set to automatic mode. Why? For the simple reason that there will be insufficient time to permit Taiwanese and American military personnel to effectively insert themselves into target selection and approval activities. Human eyes and ears cannot meaningfully absorb sufficient data points in this battle scenario quickly enough, and the human brain cannot digest and process information fast enough to know rationally what to do in the case of hundreds of missiles and drones coming at them, most of which will hit their intended targets a few minutes after launch. Ironically, the previous handicap of the military leader, the so-called fog of war (where the leader knew too little of what was going on in the battle space), has been replaced in this Taiwan attack scenario by the equally problematic "overwhelming clarity of war" (the leader has all the data points, just doesn't know what to do with them all in a timely manner). The only chance of success here for the democracies is that the AI underpinning all the different defensive ADS weapons does its job spectacularly well, *autonomously.*

This autonomous setting for the AI system constitutes the most psychologically, emotionally, and operationally fraught deployment of AI in human affairs to date. The AI system in the ADS is huge, when viewed as lines of computer code. It has to be able to process millions of scenarios in real time, simultaneously. It is the most complex software ever written. This battle scenario over the future of Taiwan represents the epitome of the human/technology conundrum of our time. Human innovation has created precision-guided attack missiles (which also use AI) that are so fast and effective that to counter them human defenders need to harness technology that removes human oversight from the core processes of the combat. What could possibly go wrong? Still, this critical autonomy-in-defense design feature of the ADS—no human in the loop—is absolutely necessary. In this extremely time-constrained, pressure-filled situation, people, even experienced military technical experts, just get in the way. There is simply no time for humans to get involved.

In essence, the survival of Taiwan as an independent democracy depends on the AI in the Taiwanese and American ADS weapons operating blazingly fast. Fortunately, it turns out that a few years before, the ADS computer infrastructure for these ADS weapons systems was upgraded to operate centrally and remotely (by means of the "cloud") on a quantum computer (QC). A QC operates about 200 million times faster than the quickest classical computer. In the military a QC is well suited to inhaling huge volumes of attack data, determining a course of action, and then distributing instructions to individual defensive ADS missile batteries to which it is networked. In the Battle of the Taiwan Strait, this compelling capability of the QC-based ADS network software ensures that each and every missile launched by China will be met by an adequate and timely response, at least in theory; the tricky part about wide-area missile defense systems is that they cannot be fully tested on a large scale—the first time they are used in combat against hundreds of incoming missiles is also their first real test.

The instructions issued by the ADS AI (running on the QC) are distributed to the hundreds of hardware control devices responsible for firing each interceptor missile from the ADS weapons. This hardware sits inside the ADS control equipment, right beside the actual missile about to be fired. This hardware can then perform at breakneck speed the instructions received from the AI C4 unit because the hardware runs on the world's most powerful semiconductor chips (SCs). Irony of ironies, these SCs were manufactured not in the United States, but rather in Taiwan by the world's leading SC maker, Taiwan Semiconductor Manufacturing Corporation (TSMC). The TSMC plant in Taiwan where these SCs are made contains the most complex manufacturing process known to humankind. Altogether, several hundred companies in a dozen democracies contributed equipment, or component parts for such equipment, so that TSMC could produce an SC the size of a thumbnail that contains about 15 billion transistors, which collectively allow the SC to perform about 16 trillion operations a second. The democracies' arsenal of technology for manufacturing today's leading weapons systems is spread around the world; for example, the most important piece of equipment used in the TSMC plant, costing a cool $500 million for one unit, is made in the Netherlands. TSMC then specializes in pulling all the pieces together to make an SC device that is the equivalent of modern magic, and that cause the ADS weapons to unleash their defensive missiles in time against the Chinese missiles and drones.

As anticipated by Taiwan and the US, fifteen minutes after China starts hostilities it releases a second wave of missiles. Unexpectedly, though, this second round of Chinese projectiles is not armed with explosive warheads. Rather, it contains canisters filled with a biological virus that, within minutes of releasing their active agent in Taiwan and on naval vessels, will cause millions of Taiwanese and thousands of American sailors and other service members to double over in pain with intense stomach cramps, essentially disabling them for two days. These victims will not die (at least not from the biological agent), but they will be unable to perform their military duties for what will be the most uncomfortable forty-eight hours of their lives. When, a few hours after these second missiles deliver their biological payload, Chinese paratroopers begin to land on the island, followed by several hundred thousand Chinese amphibious troops, they will be immune to the viral agent because they have all taken the required antidote in the week leading up to the attack.

Victory in what history will call the Battle of the Taiwan Strait will be determined by the degree of each side's mastery over four critical technologies: artificial intelligence, semiconductor chips, quantum computers, and biotechnology. In turn, the success (or failure) of these four technologies will depend on two factors: first, the quality of the science, technology, engineering, and mathematics (STEM) graduates that have been coming out of master's and PhD programs in the autocracies and the democracies, respectively, over the twenty-five years prior to the battle, and second, how well the military-industrial complex in both camps has integrated these innovations into their respective weapons systems and defense ecosystems. Fusing civilian and military innovation is very hard work. Never before will so much depend on so few college grads.

No one relishes a war between China (on the one hand) and Taiwan, the United States, and their allies (on the other). Indeed, a hot war can be avoided over Taiwan, but only if the democracies can persuade China that its success in such a kinetic conflict is not certain and that the cost to China of pursuing such an unprovoked adventure will prove to be enormous, likely putting at risk the stability of Chinese society as massive unemployment follows the imposition of draconian economic sanctions on China by a large group of democracies after the initial attack by the Chinese. In effect, the democracies must convince China that its planned military campaign for Taiwan will prove to be as serious a failure as Russian president Vladimir Putin's fiasco in Ukraine.

The best way for the democracies to convey this urgent message to autocratic leaders is to declare that the autocracies and the democracies are already in a cold war. Then, by taking measures appropriate for such a cold war, the democracies can demonstrate their collective resolve to fend off both cold war and hot war enemies. This is precisely what the democracies failed to do after Russia invaded Ukraine in 2014 and illegally annexed Crimea. The failure of the democracies to declare a cold war in 2014 (and to take steps appropriate for such a cold war) helped convince Putin to launch his full-scale invasion of Ukraine in 2022. That mistake by the democracies in 2014 should not be repeated with Taiwan. Fortunately, Ukraine's counteroffensive in 2023 has achieved sufficient success, and this result can be usefully leveraged by the democracies to demonstrate what awaits China should it attempt to take Taiwan by force. A key goal of the democracies must be to ensure that there will only be one major war for territorial expansion in the 21st century, and not two.

Many citizens in the democracies, particularly some of those old enough to have lived through part of the previous cold war, will not want to hear that we are in a new cold war between the democracies and the autocracies. This is indeed bad news, but the democracies do themselves a great disservice by ignoring this (or other) bad news. There is, however, plenty of good news as well.

BAD NEWS, GOOD NEWS

First, though, the bad news. The principal democracies are indeed once again in a cold war (Cold War 2.0) with the key autocracies. It didn't have to be this way, but the autocrats are determined to overturn the rules-based international order that has brought an unprecedented degree of global peace, prosperity, and social progress for the last eighty years. Moreover, like the last cold war (Cold War 1), Cold War 2.0 also has hot wars. In Europe, in February 2022, Russian autocrat Vladimir Putin launched an unprovoked full-scale war against neighboring Ukraine, a democracy, as a follow-up to his illegal annexation of Ukrainian Crimea in 2014. In this Cold War 2.0 kinetic war, Putin has vowed to destroy the Ukrainian nation, which he sees as threatening his own autocracy by being a shining example to Russian citizens of democracy, personal freedoms, and rule of law, none of which is currently enjoyed in Russia.

Then there are the menacing Cold War 2.0 actions of strongmen short of war with kinetic weapons. In Asia, Chinese autocrat Xi Jinping breached an important international treaty by terminating democracy in Hong Kong twenty-five years early. Xi also nabs nationals of other countries off the streets of Chinese cities and holds them hostage without any legal justification, solely to swap them in prisoner exchanges. Further, paramount leader Xi lays claim to virtually the entire South China/West Philippines Sea to the exclusion of all his Asian neighbors, contrary to the United Nations Law of the Sea Convention (that a predecessor of Xi signed some fifty years ago). Xi also regularly launches missiles over and near Taiwan, a democracy, whenever the leadership of Taiwan meets with a world leader of any importance. While these missiles don't land in Taiwan itself, they are certainly a form of psychological warfare and intense intimidation. These military exercises by China are also serious practice for the "attack on Taiwan" scenario discussed above.

There's more Cold War 2.0 bad news from other less powerful but still important autocrats. In 2018, Saudi Arabia invited *Washington Post* columnist Jamal Khashoggi to pick up some routine travel documents at its embassy in Istanbul. Khashoggi walked into the building and was promptly hacked to death. His dismembered body parts were removed in multiple garbage bags. Saudi Arabia now attempts to "sports launder" the memory of this heinous act by buying the Newcastle football (soccer) club in England, and starting a new golf tour by paying astounding sums (in the range of $50 to $200 million) as signing bonuses to a number of golfers from the democracies who take the money and stare blankly when asked how it feels to be part of the sports-laundering operation for the disgraceful Saudi regime. Another oil-infused autocracy, Venezuela, has a dictator who has driven 7 million citizens out of the country as émigrés, because autocratic president for life Nicolás Maduro has brought man-made famine to what not that long ago was a prosperous country.

There's yet more Cold War 2.0 bad news from the world's autocrats. Theocratic Iran (which with Russia, China, and North Korea now forms an "Arc of Autocracy") over the last few years killed about 500 protesters (including 60 women) because women in that country are demanding the freedom to walk outside their homes without being covered by a hijab. North Korea's third-generation autocrat, Kim Jong Un, leaves his people to starve while he spends enormous amounts building nuclear weapons; like the Chinese do with their missiles over Taiwan, Kim routinely launches test missiles menacingly over South Korea and Japan.

Now the good news. The democracies will prevail in Cold War 2.0 against the leading autocracies (including China and Russia), for many of the reasons they won Cold War 1, most important, the singular ability of the democracies to innovate technology to produce far superior economic, military, and soft power than that generated by the autocracies. Autocracies do innovation in a top-down, government-directed manner, and that simply doesn't produce brilliant, sustained innovation. Moreover, it's not enough that a scientist in China or Russia ideates a novel invention in an academic laboratory. The development of the great next new thing then needs to be funded and operationalized into workable technology, and ultimately developed into useful, rugged, and sought-after commercial (or military) products.

The very structure of an autocracy precludes it from excelling at these innovation-related activities. Critically, when a major new scientific/technological/business model innovation comes along, it must be allowed to *competitively displace* the incumbent technology or business process. This presents an insurmountable challenge to the autocrat, because they, or one of their main enablers, is typically heavily invested in the incumbent. The result is that the next new thing (however great its potential) is squashed and buried. Often, to add insult to injury, the scientist or entrepreneur behind the new innovation escapes to a democracy, where he or she can finally bring it to the marketplace successfully.

Adding to their innovation advantage, the democracies have many more high-performance research universities than the autocracies. These top-tier universities in the democracies then attract the smartest people in the world (many in the STEM domains hail from autocracies), who then produce clusters of scientific breakthroughs and state-of-the-art technologies. Many of these same people also then choose to start businesses (funded by huge pools of private "smart" capital), or join existing private enterprises, that accelerate the big innovation from the lab into the marketplace. This is the most successful innovation model known to humankind, and it only exists fully formed in democracies. This is why the democracies will prevail over the autocracies in Cold War 2.0.

In short, the technology innovation model in autocratic China is nowhere near optimal, while the one in the US is far superior. Other key democracies, including France, Germany, Japan, the Netherlands, South Korea, Taiwan, and the United Kingdom, are not as innovative or entrepreneurial as the US, but still outstrip China when it comes to moving ideas from the science lab to the marketplace. Collectively, the democracies dwarf China in innovation, as shown by the metrics in this book. This advantage will bring home success to the democracies in their Cold War 2.0 contest with the autocracies, provided this innovation superiority is exploited properly—as recommended in this book.

There is even more good news from the democracies. Since the end of Cold War 1 in 1989–1991, the democracies have acquired yet additional advantages over the autocracies when it comes to developing and exploiting technological innovation. One critical new source of strength in the democracies is that they are moving steadily to achieve gender equality. While there remains much to be done in this regard, the progress toward a level playing field between men and women has been significant; in June 2023 the female participation rate in the US economy hit 77.5 percent, an all-time high, and also in America women are getting more college degrees than men.

It is inspiring, for instance, to see Tsai Ing-wen, the female president of Taiwan (a democracy since 1987) rally her fellow citizens to stand up to the bully Xi Jinping, the paramount leader (aka autocrat) of mainland China. In the United States, it is heartening to see many women in senior roles in the country's largest tech and defense companies, including Lisa Su, the CEO of AMD (one of the leading semiconductor chip companies in the world), who came to America from Taiwan when she was three, and Kathy J. Warden, who is the CEO at Northrop Grumman, one of America's leading prime defense contractors. In Canada Chrystia Freeland is minister of finance, deputy prime minister, and one of the most steadfast supporters of Ukraine within the G7; Rita Anand recently served as minister of defense; and Christyn Cianfarani is president and CEO of the Canadian Association of Defence and Security Industries. It is rare to see a woman in a senior leadership position anywhere near the autocrats of China, Russia, Saudi Arabia, Iran, Venezuela, or North Korea. In democracies women now regularly lead governments, and in the United States currently Janet Yellen (treasury secretary) and Gina Raimondo (commerce secretary) are playing critical roles in Cold War 2.0 in the Biden administration.

In a similar vein, social diversity is another important positive differentiator of democracy over autocracy. Incredibly, autocrats see social diversity as a weakness of the democracies. They are dead wrong. Apple Inc. is the world's most valuable company (with a market cap of $2.5 trillion), and arguably the globe's leading tech company. Apple's CEO, Tim Cook, is gay, as are millions of people in all countries around the world, including the autocracies. Unlike the autocracies, which make life very dangerous—and sometimes impossible—for gay people (Russia passed yet another antigay law in 2022), over the past fifty years the democracies have welcomed gay people into the mainstream of their societies, where they are fully participating in science, technology, politics, business, culture, education, and civil society.

The democracies also welcome, support, and celebrate racial diversity, whether they are people with deep family roots in their countries or are recent arrivals through immigration. The US secretary of defense, Lloyd Austin, and the chairman of the joint chiefs of staff, Charles Brown, are African American. Several quick further examples: the CEOs of many public and private tech companies, including IBM, Google (Alphabet), and Microsoft, three giants of the US technology sector, were born in India (as were the current CEOs of less-known US public tech companies Adobe, Micron Technology, NetApp, and VMware).

In contrasting the democracies to the autocracies, this book will discuss in detail a number of the drivers that contribute to national economic, military, and soft power today, particularly the oversized role of technology and technological innovation. Ultimately, though, even technology comes down to people, those individuals who innovate, develop, and deploy leading new technologies to make countries stronger economically and from a national security perspective. Given the prevailing misogynist, homophobic, nationalistic, chauvinistic, and racist attitudes found in autocracies, their countries deny themselves the skills, brains, and hard work of a large proportion of their adult populations. The democracies, by contrast, are able to draw on the effective participation of many more of their citizens, including in senior leadership positions. This is a massive structural advantage for the democracies over the autocracies, and a critical contributor to the outcome of Cold War 2.0.

To be clear, Cold War 2.0 will be a more challenging contest for the democracies than Cold War 1. The autocracies have learned from some of their devastating mistakes in Cold War 1, including that fully autocratic economies are destined for ruin because they just don't work. Fundamentally, Soviet Russia collapsed in the late 1980s because an economy cannot be run in a top-down manner by a central command bureaucracy that sets prices, sets innovation practices, determines production quotas, and decides who gets what products and services based primarily on political decisions. Today, both Russia and China utilize certain open market practices learned from the democracies, and the Chinese economic growth miracle of the last forty years has been the result.

Neither Russia nor China, though, has learned the real secret sauce of democracy—that people who are free to think and speak and collaborate with others as they please are far more innovative and productive than those whose minds, actions, appetites, and horizons are blinkered by the autocratic state. And while the military is not intended to be an exemplar of democracy in terms of its structure and operations, in a democracy the ability of junior officers—and often even soldiers of the lowest rank—to think creatively and independently about many operational decisions again sets them apart from their tightly constrained autocratic counterparts, as exemplified by Ukrainian success in the Russo-Ukrainian War.

Put another way, the single biggest obstacle to successful innovation in the autocracies is the autocrat. This impediment is just as pronounced today in Cold War 2.0 as it was in Cold War 1. Moreover, it is a prominent structural defect of autocratic forms of government. It is possible to have a tight top-down hyper-controlled society enforced by the autocrat and his enablers, or it is possible to have a flourishing bottom-up culture of innovation, but it is impossible to have both at the same time in the same place. By contrast, hyper-innovation in the democracies produces an incredibly dynamic economy, generating a much larger financial surplus that can be used to raise living standards across the population, as well as funding superior national security.

This fundamental distinction between the democracies and the autocracies was true in Cold War 1, but is even more compelling in our current digital age, as immense technological progress is currently underway on multiple innovation fronts simultaneously, with each subdiscipline's breakthrough successes fueling not only its own growth, but also accelerating moonshot-quality achievements in the other areas of research. This environment of hyper-innovation can only be fully realized in a democracy, and is why the democracies will prevail over the autocracies in Cold War 2.0.

While that's the general theme of this book, there are many nuances that are also relevant, especially when implementing various ideas in the real world; while there is a cerebral component to Cold War 2.0, success in it will be measured on the ground. Moreover, even with their nonoptimal innovation structures, the autocrats are still formidable on many fronts. China and some of the other autocracies have amassed great reserves of wealth—not so much from innovating technology, but rather from manufacturing products or commodities produced from or with the assistance of technology developed in the democracies. What they lack in quality of innovation, autocracies will try to make up in quantity of acquired or stolen second-rate technology, and at a certain point quantity has a quality all its own.

There is, however, a fundamental flaw in the autocratic project that invariably leads to its unraveling. The four accelerator technologies highlighted in this book—artificial intelligence, semiconductor chips, quantum computers, and biotechnology—have the potential to be the most liberating, freedom-inducing technologies yet devised by humans. The autocracies, though, are using them to construct the most oppressive system of government control of humans ever devised. This endeavor, a signature development of the autocracies in Cold War 2.0, will ultimately backfire on the autocracies. The precedent for the coming backlash can be seen in the significant protests that broke out in China in the fall of 2022 against the autocratic government's draconian lockdown measures to combat the COVID-19 pandemic. There is a limit to how long a government can keep someone locked up in their own tiny apartment, and it seems thirty days is it. After that, there is a human explosion. In many of the autocracies a similar ignition point will occur against the suffocating system of social control implemented by incredibly intrusive technology systems. The intriguing question is—when?

There is another nuance in Cold War 2.0 that is important to understand and, for the democracies, to address. As painful as it is to admit, the democracies can often be their own worst enemies. Ironically, democracy, due to its essential openness, presents a posture of vulnerability that autocrats are only too happy to exploit. In a world made up solely of democracies, their instinct toward openness would not be a problem. In the real world of Cold War 2.0, though, this reflex of unlimited scientific and technological sharing, coupled with unfettered social media manipulation, present their own significant risks. There is also the supreme irony that the political openness of democracy can allow the growth of autocrats among the democracies. (It can never be forgotten that Putin in 2000, like Hitler in 1933, came to power democratically.) In effect, the democracies continually have to learn from their own shortcomings (including their self-inflicted liabilities), and then they must course-correct to meet new challenges. It is nowhere written on some eternal marble tablet that the democracies are destined to prevail against the autocracies. As much as we hope it might, history in fact will never end. Rather, each generation of citizens who believe fervently in the model of democracy need to recommit themselves to sustaining and improving it. A citizen in a democracy can never arrive at the perfect democracy; they can only pledge to be a great ancestor to those who come after themselves.

A further nuance will be that while the democracies will prevail in Cold War 2.0, Cold War 2.0 will end very differently than Cold War 1. In the first cold war, the democracies did truly "win," and Soviet Russia "lost." Cold War 1 had a very "zero-sum" denouement, one very much in favor of the democracies. It will be different in Cold War 2.0. Given the sheer size of China, and the fact that the democracies actually do an enormous amount of business with China, it is likely that the democracies will not "prevail" in Cold War 2.0 in the sense that there will be regime change or any other defeat of the government in Beijing. Rather, an optimal outcome for both camps will be that much of the current commercial trading between China and the democracies continues, but that in a number of technologically strategic domains there is a partial or complete decoupling of relations, and especially a severing of joint innovation and technology creation and sharing. This will result in a partially technologically bifurcated world, but ideally one that is stable, where democracies can continue to thrive, and where nuclear war, and most conventional wars, can be avoided. It should also allow for a world where the democracies and the autocracies continue to jointly work on global challenges, such as climate change. (Although for reasons discussed in chapter 14, the success of such collaboration—or even its likelihood—in a Cold War 2.0 environment is not at all assured.)

An important exception to this possible scenario for geopolitical stability occurs if or when China invades Taiwan militarily. That would be a major hot war. The United States would be directly involved in that war, and thousands of American service personnel would die in defending Taiwan. At a minimum, thousands of Japanese soldiers likely would die as well. In that case the democracies would shift from a technological decoupling from China to a much broader, and likely overall, decoupling from China. Presumably most members of the coalition of fifty-one democracies that supplied Ukraine with weapons and money in the fight against Russia would reassemble for round two against the autocracies. This support for Taiwan would include deep sanctions against China, but these would really hurt the economies of the democracies, too, much more so then when sanctions were levied on Russia. At the same time, though, these sanctions would be very difficult for China. Partial technological decoupling is one thing, but a full-scale halt to trade between at least the major democracies and China is something else again (currently, the United States is China's largest trading partner, by a long measure). Indeed, it is precisely this prospect of commercial Armageddon that plays such an important part—the *leading* part—in keeping the current peace over Taiwan. *Deterrence*, a critically important and useful word in the lexicon of geopolitics, is not a function of offering peace, but (ironically) rather results from the threat of war and destruction.

Speaking of important words and phrases, the title to this book includes the contentious phrase "cold war." Some will argue that the relationship between the democracies and the autocracies is one of rivalry, but that the intensity of the situation does not rise to the level of a *cold war*. This view is misguided. The relationship between the New York Yankees and the Boston Red Sox in baseball, or Manchester United and Manchester City in English football, or between Hawthorn and Geelong in the Australian

Football League, or between the Toronto Maple Leafs and the Montreal Canadiens in hockey, these are all rivalries. Pepsi and Coke have a rivalry. In stark contrast to each of these contests—however bitter they might be—the confrontation between the principal democracies and the leading autocracies is acutely different because it is deeply profound, ideologically driven, and existential. The current attack by the autocracies on the rules-based international order is sustained, systemic, and global in nature. If the autocracies succeed, they will have life altering impact on the democracies. This is why, empirically speaking, Cold War 2.0 is real, is critically important, and requires serious attention.

Moreover, labeling the current assault of the autocracies on the rules-based international order as Cold War 2.0 is necessary because it signals to populations in the democracies that the present threat from the autocrats is real, very dangerous, widespread, and that it must be resisted because failure to do so could mean a greatly diminished place for democracy in the human condition. As a "cold war" it should grab people's attention. Ideally people will also grasp from the term that this conflict will take some time to resolve, given that Cold War 1 lasted forty-five years. Surely Russia's full-scale invasion of Ukraine, China's weekly threatening of Taiwan with missiles, and China's imperious actions in the South China/West Philippines Sea and its creation of an incredibly oppressive system of citizen control through technological systems make the title of this book uncontroversial, particularly because this work is ultimately a clarion call to action.

As for the "2.0" designation in the title of this book, that's to indicate that technology will play an oversized role in the new cold war. This should not surprise anyone given that high-tech machines, devices, and business models have insinuated themselves into every nook and cranny of modern life. Still, the degree to which technology and innovation fuel national economic, military, and soft power today is truly unprecedented. The future of global geopolitics is to be found as much in an artificial intelligence algorithm, on a tiny semiconductor microchip, inside an unfathomable quantum computer, and in a genome splicer, as anywhere else. Hence, we are in Cold War *2.0*.

OVERVIEW

Chapter 1: Technology and National Power

In 1927 Mao Zedong, China's first communist autocratic dictator, said "Political power grows out of the barrel of a gun." He knew what he was talking about. Twenty-two years later his Chinese Communist Party (CCP) won China's civil war and Mao became the supreme leader of the world's most populous country. His current autocratic successor, Xi Jinping, would probably update Mao's aphorism to "civilian and military power is generated by the semiconductor chip," in response to the embargo certain democracies have placed on the export of semiconductor chips (SCs) to China. A few years ago, Vladimir Putin (Russia's current autocrat) said whoever masters artificial intelligence (AI) will rule the world. Mao and Putin were correct, and Xi would be right to emphasize microelectronics, because today and for the duration of Cold War 2.0, technology innovation is and will be the primary source of economic, military, and soft power.

To fully grasp what Mao, Xi, and Putin were getting at, and thereby to come to grips with the civilian and military global geopolitical power dynamics at play in Cold War 2.0, it is imperative to understand the mechanics of innovation, industrial capacity, hyper-innovation, digital innovation, and the important role played by "competitive displacement." Some consideration, though, also has to be given to the cost of, and value derived from, military innovation, lest an ever-growing defense budget ends up devouring the whole of the rest of government, like a huge black hole. Finally, Japan's experience with economic and military power over the past 150 years, derived largely from technology innovation, is instructive, and could usefully serve as a model for China.

Chapter 2: Cold War 1: Autocracy, Democracy, and Technology

Cold War 1 was the defining geopolitical preoccupation of the world for the better part of forty years (1945–1989). It implicated the vast, globe-spanning ambitions of two divergent ideologies. It was fueled by two very different approaches to the design, development, and deployment of novel industrial, consumer, and military technologies. It spawned space technology and human space travel. It witnessed a divided world struggling to manage the kryptonite of its day—thousands of nuclear weapons. It came close to witnessing the fight of an unimaginable nuclear war. Then, as the leading autocrat in the bipolar tango struggled to maintain technological pace with the leading democracy, many other inherent weaknesses of the autocracies emerged and ultimately took their toll. Finally, the cement wall and Iron Curtain separating the two camps were dismantled by the bare hands of frustrated and hopeful citizens; the East Europeans were freed and the Germanies were reunited (but not the Koreas), all with hardly a burst of violence.

There are many differences between Cold War 2.0 and its predecessor. Nevertheless, there are certainly lessons to be learned from Cold War 1 that can help today's leaders navigate the treacherous waters of Cold War 2.0. A common reality of the two conflicts is that both involved democracies pitted against autocracies. This is important. Most international wars spring from domestic factors. Moreover, an autocrat who refuses to abide by the rule of law at home will never adhere to treaties abroad; it is utter naivete—and dangerous—for the leader of a democracy to think otherwise. At the same time, some leaders in democracies pine to be autocrats. And because they find it difficult to vent their autocratic fantasy domestically, they try to pull off the autocratic playbook in some of their foreign affairs. Hence the usefulness of comparing these two conceptions of life and politics at the very outset.

Chapter 3: The Emergence of China

Except for China's critical intervention in the Korean War, when in 1950 its 700,000 troops swooped in to save the regime of North Korean autocrat Kim Il-Sung, China's role in Cold War 1 was fairly peripheral. Moreover, in the middle of Cold War 1 China and Russia had a major falling-out, and in 1969 the two communist autocracies even fought a border skirmish, with several hundred dead and wounded. Under Mao, China was reluctant to play a meaningful role on the world stage. After Mao's death, China begins to seriously engage with the world. Under Xi Jinping, bolstered by an unwavering commitment to technology development and deployment, China sets out to change the world to its liking.

China, not Russia, is the key autocratic protagonist in Cold War 2.0. Russia is a serious player in Cold War 2.0, given that Russia punches above its weight—largely because it is willing to punch so often. China's enormous population and economy, and its capacity to fund technology development, makes it the prime preoccupation of the democracies in Cold War 2.0. Once the Russo-Ukrainian War is over, Russia will be relegated to China's junior partner. It is therefore important to understand the meteoric rise of China's national economic and military power over the past forty-five years. This has allowed China to foster a great deal of technology design, development, and deployment (and theft where indigenous tech creation had proven particularly challenging). China's model of promoting technology, and translating technology into economic and military power, is not without its (sometimes serious) shortcomings. Cold War 2.0 will be a marathon, not a sprint.

Chapter 4: Storm Clouds and Near Wars

Wars (hot and cold) never simply start. Just as Cold War 1 really began in 1917, but then broke out fully in 1945, the early warning signs of Cold War 2.0 appeared many years before Russia's 2014 annexation of Crimea and China's aggression in the South China Sea around the same time. Putin actually began his descent into autocracy right after he was elected president in 2000. Post-Mao China actually started to bare its autocratic fangs when numerous Beijing leadership hard-liners overruled many fewer reformers and ordered the army to murder several hundred unarmed student political protesters in Tiananmen Square in 1989. A keen observer of these events would have realized in an instant that international cold war behavior was going to follow closely on the heels of these internal stains of autocracy.

In 2012 Xi Jinping further confirmed China's break with the democracies when he declared that China has no interest in pursuing democracy practices, extolling instead the Chinese one-party system led by the glorious Chinese Communist Party. Xi also proceeded to implement the most draconian citizen surveillance and oppression technology on earth, and began to export it to seventy countries. Xi spent huge sums on the largest military buildup program in history, while chronically underfunding the Chinese healthcare system. He also waged economic coercion against half a dozen democracies. Intellectual property theft, such a critical plank in the Cold War 1 playbook, came back in vogue for China and Russia; they both updated their electronic skill sets so they can launch large numbers of cyberattacks against the democracies. The action turned physical when in 2014 Russia annexed Crimea and sent irregular soldiers into Ukraine's Donbas. China used a range of armed ships to make a play for ownership of 90 percent of the South China Sea, thumbing its nose with impunity at the sputtering democracies. Cold War 2.0 has begun.

Chapter 5: The Contest for Artificial Intelligence Supremacy

Artificial intelligence (AI), a software-based capability already being harnessed by businesses, governments, and militaries all around the world, is poised over the next decade to become the most important, valuable, and dangerous technology ever innovated by humans. AI will profoundly impact—and be impacted by—Cold War 2.0. The worst fears of the current cold war, and some of the world's most life-changing hopes, rest with this relatively new technology. There will be constraints put on AI by governments, but these will look very different depending on whether they are levied by the democracies or the autocracies. This will be a critical fault line in Cold War 2.0.

AI is an "accelerator technology," in that it not only progresses at warp speed itself, but it serves as an accelerant turbocharging all other technology innovation as well. The other principal technologies discussed in the next three chapters, namely semiconductor chips, quantum computing, and biotechnology, are also accelerators, with each of them (and especially AI) releasing powerful waves of competitive displacement through the economy and national security structures. Whichever camp—the autocracies or the democracies—can best capture the added value of these accelerators will prevail in Cold War 2.0.

Chapter 6: The Contest for Semiconductor Chip Supremacy

Two events in 2022 profoundly changed the course of Cold War 2.0. The first was Russia's full-scale military invasion of Ukraine. The second was the embargo on high-performance semiconductor chips (SCs) placed by the US on China. Most people understand viscerally the gravity of the hot war in Ukraine. The deep ramifications of the cold war denial of SCs, and especially equipment to make SCs, against China are somewhat more subtle, but just as critical. SCs are the lifeblood of the modern economy and military. Without them there are no functioning electronics. Without high-performance SCs there are no smartphones and no precision-guided weapons, like missiles. It turns out the two most important events of 2022 are crucially intertwined.

There's more. It is impossible to develop and deploy sophisticated AI without high-performance SCs. No fancy SCs, no fancy AI. This presents the autocracies with a massive strategic risk. With the SC embargo the democracies have their digital boot on China's digital throat. Cold War 2.0, barely a decade old, is already at an inflection point. There is a critical election in Taiwan in January 2024. Will the outcome of that political race cause China to move against the island before China's digital deficit in SCs gets inevitably worse? Or does China agree to become like Japan, a second large Asian power that understands the benefits of a rules-based international order? Such a deal could include China convincing Russia to pull out of Ukraine (including Crimea) and China dropping its own claims to Taiwan, and in return for which the US embargo on SCs to China would be terminated. The year 2022 was important for Cold War 2.0, with the potential for 2024, a US election year, to be even more eventful.

Chapter 7: The Contest for Quantum Computing Supremacy

As powerful as today's computers are, in five to ten years they will be replaced by a different kind of computer, one that is millions of times more powerful. Quantum computers (although they are still very rudimentary) are already showing their superiority. Particularly for the really big computational challenges of our era—to model the entire world's economy and all of its energy consumption activities to help combat climate change, or to model the entire Ukrainian battlefield to help Volodymyr Zelenskyy's army combat the Russians—quantum computers will be better than "classical" ones, even today's supercomputers.

For China, quantum computers hold another significant attraction—they needn't run on semiconductor chips. Thus, if a big bargain between the autocracies and the democracies cannot be achieved (see two paragraphs above), and China continues to operate under the conditions of a high-performance SC famine because of the US embargo on SCs and SC-making equipment, then there could be a path for China to replace its stunted classical computers with new, unimpeded quantum computers. This could become one of the most intriguing subplots of Cold War 2.0.

Chapter 8: The Contest for Biotechnology Supremacy

Biotechnology has undergone rapid and multifaceted innovation over the past twenty years since the human genome was decoded. Drug discovery and medicine are already being transformed because the practitioners of the life sciences have discovered how to modify the moving parts of cells like they program software. A prime example was the development of mRNA vaccines to combat COVID-19, which were effectively designed over a long weekend and were in production several months later. Compare this cadence to the decade it typically took researchers to develop a vaccine previously, thereby saving 10 million lives from the pandemic's ravages. The world stands on the threshold of more such fundamental biotech breakthroughs.

A more complex aspect of the biotech revolution is that scientists will soon be able to gestate human embryos in artificial wombs outside of the female body, in so-called ectogenesis machines, or EGMs. Autocracies with rapidly declining populations will find this technology intriguing—as might middle-class women in democracies hoping to avoid the trials and tribulations of pregnancy and childbirth. Merge this EGM technology with those promising "designer babies," enhanced physical and mental attributes and characteristics (higher IQ, more height), and all of this perhaps coupled with AI and human-embedded SCs, and the potential permutations of new life experiences unlocked by biotechnology really begin to intrigue the imagination. And then there are the truly dark sides of the new biotechnology, such as military scientists being able to produce a bioweapon virus with greater ease, at lesser cost, and in record time. Biotechnology is insinuating itself onto the Cold War 2.0 agenda.

Chapter 9: Other Important Technologies

While the four accelerator technologies (AI, SC, QC, and biotechnology) will drive the core innovation dynamics of Cold War 2.0, a number of other technologies and industries will play important supporting roles, and they are discussed in this chapter. A few, though, could also produce game-changing innovation. If fusion energy ultimately works, it will profoundly transform global energy markets and cause massive shifts of wealth out of today's countries that rely on the export of fossil fuels. Taken together, the businesses designing, developing, and deploying the technologies covered in this chapter and the four previous ones drive a large segment of wealth creation in both the democracies and the autocracies, thereby producing the economic surplus that can then be used to pay for a nation's military. All of these technologies are prone to significant competitive displacement, at least when operating in the relatively open markets of the democracies.

The dual-use dimension of virtually all these technologies is noteworthy. Shipbuilding is a good example; most of the shipyards that build a country's merchant fleet also produce the nation's naval vessels. The industries discussed in this chapter also drive home that although it is easy to think all wealth and innovation creation has gone digital, industrial capacity is still absolutely critical. This is true in the auto industry, as it is in the advanced manufacturing of commercial aircraft and especially their jet engines. At the end of the day, physical and virtual technologies and innovation skill sets need to combine seamlessly in the democracies to produce effective economic and military power if they hope to prevail in Cold War 2.0. And finally, these chapters need to be revisited once the tech decoupling recommendations in chapter 14 are absorbed, because these industries will invariably feel the brunt of the tech decoupling that has already occurred (often at China's behest) as well as what more will follow during the balance of Cold War 2.0.

Chapter 10: Other Powerful Assets

A core theme of this book to this point has been how the two camps facing off in Cold War 2.0 stack up in terms of technology and innovation. Power, though, whether of the economic, military, or soft variety, implicates human and some other powerful assets as well. Especially important for the democracies are alliances, for the simple reason that they have many more meaningful ones than the autocracies. This chapter undertakes both a quantitative assessment (of NATO) and a qualitative one (of the fairly recent AUKUS alliance). The conclusion is compelling—high-quality alliances among the democracies (like NATO and AUKUS) serve as a power multiplier, even if the key linchpin in both is the United States. Equally, autocracies have trouble playing nicely together in their alliance relations. The prospects for the most recent version of China-Russia "friendship without limits" might be pretty limited after all.

Other important assets include certain minerals, particularly those that will be central to the effort of transitioning from fossil fuels to renewable energy sources. In this metric twenty-three minerals are considered in terms of where the current sources are as between the autocracies, the democracies, and the nonaligned countries. This constitutes a weakness for the democracies that will require some serious attention, time, and effort. The good news, though, is that the technological demands for securing this vulnerable flank are rather low, whether in mining or refining. Finally, a review of the rankings of the world's top 100 universities reveals another core strength of the democracies. This is heartening because these institutions do much more than educate—they draw the best and the brightest from around the world, serving as the indispensable honeypots where the next generation of tech leaders get to rub entrepreneurial elbows together. It is then up to the democracies, through enlightened immigration policies, to convince these gifted scholars (and budding world-beaters) to stay on in their respective newfound countries once they graduate, a win-win-win result for all concerned, and one not easily replicated by the autocracies because of their cultural aversion to genuine multiculturalism. This bodes well for the democracies, particularly when viewing Cold War 2.0 as a very long game.

Chapter 11: Cold War 2.0 Flashpoints

Having reviewed the history of Cold War 1, and the major attributes of economic and military power wielded by the leading protagonists of Cold War 2.0 and their principal allies, it now remains to address where the dynamics of the current cold war will play out. In other words, where will the currency of economic and military power, so carefully assembled by the democracies and the autocracies, be spent? The following discussion has to begin in Ukraine, where the unprovoked, unjustified full-scale invasion by Russia in February 2022 proved (if proof was even required) that the world is indeed in the midst of Cold War 2.0.

The second focal point is Taiwan, which, if Cold War 2.0 goes fully hot on and around the island, would also be a major—*the* major—geopolitical event in the 21st century, overshadowing even the current Russo-Ukrainian War given that the United States (and possibly other democracies) would send military forces into this war, not just supply a democracy with weapons, as is the case in Ukraine. Ukraine and Taiwan are big, meaty strategic subjects to digest, and take up the bulk of this chapter. It would be a major deficiency, though, if some light wasn't also brought to bear on the relations of the democracies and the autocracies with the Global South, which was an important theater of hot and cold operations in Cold War 1, and invariably will be so again, but with a renewed set of dynamics and drivers revolving in large measure around technology and innovation.

Chapter 12: Managing Cold War 2.0

This chapter discusses the tools that are available—and that should be available—to the democracies to manage the challenges of Cold War 2.0. The discussion begins with some reform proposals for the United Nations and the collective security alliances of the democracies, because the current institutional frameworks that the democracies have to rely on could be usefully bolstered with additional mechanisms. The UN is almost eighty years old. It needs an important overhaul, otherwise it will lose its relevance altogether, at least for geopolitical security matters. NATO, on the other hand, is a good news story, but one that during the course of Cold War 2.0 could be made great if it can undertake global expansion in a sensible manner.

Then the analysis shifts to sanctions, which are a useful mechanism for sure, but are also due for a rethink in some of the ways they are applied and enforced. The world is a more complex place than even thirty years ago, when sanctions played a meaningful role in ending apartheid in South Africa. Creative anti-evasion solutions are particularly required when the items being denied to the autocracies are technology based. Cyberattacks also require a different response, including shutting down the Internet for some meaningful period for the entire country where a brazen hacker group is protected by an autocratic government—that will catch their attention. Then there are some tricky "people issues." These are important because, as noted earlier in this book, ultimately technology and innovation come down to the people who design, develop, and deploy technology. Making all these issues tougher for the democracies in Cold War 2.0 is the hard, cold fact that China is simply a far more formidable adversary than Russia ever was in Cold War 1.

Chapter 13: Strengthening Democracies

The ability to project geopolitical hard and soft power around the world begins at home. Democracies should take some very muscular action to protect themselves and extend their power and influence in a number of ways that play to their strengths in technology and innovation. These measures, however, require that the democracies be strong enough themselves to be able to take and sustain these actions. Put in the vernacular, the democracies cannot run the long Cold War 2.0 marathon, and certainly not against the Chinese, unless they are in good physical, mental, and emotional shape.

The democracies need to spend more money on defense, but at the same time governments must resist corporate interests who unreasonably argue an "AI gap" or "biotech gap" just to get more government money. In order to effectively fend off the autocracies in Cold War 2.0, the democracies need to help their citizens become more digitally resilient; this was useful for a social media–saturated world, but it is now absolutely imperative for an AI-infused world. Moreover, AI should be regulated, but with a light touch that doesn't dampen the tempo and volume of research and development or build a digital moat around today's leading AI behemoths. This will be one of the most consequential legislative interventions in the economy in the history of the United States; Congress and the White House, with the help of the courts, should be prepared to course-correct a few times before they get it right. And not to end on an ominous note, but the democracies need to better protect themselves internally from the autocrat apologists and autocrat appeasers—and the would-be autocrats—all mingling among their own citizens. Given the assessment of the state of global technology innovation undertaken in this book, it is highly unlikely that the autocracies can win Cold War 2.0 on their own, but their chances improve markedly if it becomes an inside job.

Chapter 14: A World Technologically Decoupled

It remains, as a final task, to sketch out how a world buffeted by Cold War 2.0 should function satisfactorily from the perspective of the democracies. In essence, the democracies would decouple some of their technology from the autocracies, but largely only for the four accelerator technologies: artificial intelligence, high-performance semiconductor chips, quantum computing, and biotechnology. The total volume of trade impacted would be about 25 to 35 percent of the current mix of trade between the democracies and China, though there would be some broader strategic, political, and even cultural geopolitical and security implications, especially for the autocracies.

The reason for the tech decoupling is simple—the democracies should not give the autocracies the rope then used by the autocracies to hang the democracies. Moreover, this suspicion that the autocrats want to "hang the democracies" is reasonably held so long as the autocracies refuse to live in a global community animated by their adherence to a rules-based international order. The second rationale for tech decoupling is so that the democracies do not contribute to the technology that the autocrats use to hang their own citizens. The world's most insidious digital system of human surveillance, control, and oppression should not include AI software written in Silicon Valley or semiconductor chips designed in the US and fabricated in Taiwan. How does Cold War 2.0 end? One of three ways. China decides to emulate Japan, South Korea, and Taiwan; becomes a responsible global citizen and a domestic democracy; and gives up its designs on Taiwan. Or China attacks Taiwan and the democracies win that war. Or the current technology/innovation bifurcated world continues indefinitely, with the democracies enjoying an ever-superior standard of living relative to the increasingly isolated and technologically stunted autocracies, and then when Putin and Xi leave power, their successors effect economic *and* political regime change in order to catch up to the democracies.

This book is dedicated to the preservation, celebration, and promotion of democracy, and to the countless millions of people worldwide whose daily actions, however modest, strengthen the sinews of democracy.

—George S. Takach
Toronto

1

TECHNOLOGY AND NATIONAL POWER

I n 1927 Mao Zedong, China's first communist autocratic dictator, said "Political power grows out of the barrel of a gun."[1] He knew what he was talking about. Twenty-two years later his Chinese Communist Party (CCP) won China's civil war and Mao became the supreme leader of the world's most populous country. His current autocratic successor, Xi Jinping, would probably update Mao's aphorism to "civilian and military power is generated by the semiconductor chip," in response to the embargo certain democracies have placed on the export of semiconductor chips (SCs) to China. A few years ago, Vladimir Putin (Russia's current autocrat) said whoever masters artificial intelligence (AI) will rule the world.[2] Mao and Putin were correct, and Xi would be right to emphasize microelectronics, because today and for the duration of Cold War 2.0, technology innovation is and will be the primary source of national economic, military, and soft power.

To fully grasp what Mao, Xi, and Putin were getting at, and thereby to come to grips with the civilian and military global geopolitical power dynamics at play in Cold War 2.0, it is imperative to understand the mechanics of innovation, industrial capacity, hyper-innovation, digital innovation, and the important role played by "competitive displacement." Some consideration, though, must also be given to the cost of, and value derived from, military innovation, lest an ever-growing defense budget end up devouring the whole of government, like a huge black hole. Finally, Japan's experience with economic and military power over the past 150 years, derived largely from technology innovation, is instructive. Could it usefully serve as a model for China?

CIVILIAN TECHNOLOGY INNOVATION; COMPETITIVE DISPLACEMENT

The Sony Discman, later renamed the CD Walkman, debuted forty years ago. It was revolutionary. It could play a compact disc while the user was walking outside, with the Walkman slung over the shoulder. It skipped a bit (which was annoying) if the user walked too fast, or jogged, but that was a small price to pay for music mobility. In 2001 (twenty-two years after the audiocassette-playing Walkman first appeared), there appeared the Apple iPod. It was one of those wonderful moments in modern tech history when an innovation scratches an itch perfectly. The iPod was small. It was fully digital. And it conveyed a magical power on the user—they could make up, and mix up, their own music playlists. Miraculously, it didn't skip, even when it was taken jogging or skiing. About 450 million people fell hopelessly in love with the iPod, and its dazzling migration of recorded music from a mechanical format to the digital.

Not surprisingly, soon after its initial commercial release the iPod *competitively displaced* the CD Walkman. This happens in economies with open markets, especially in democracies, when a new and better invention completely replaces an incumbent device, machine, process, or technology. Apple, the creator of the iPod, has a special knack for competitively displacing other products. Canadians were quite miffed when the Apple iPhone, around 2011, displaced the made-in-Canada BlackBerry mobile phone. Eventually, though, even Canadians got over it—superior technology has a way of generating infidelity toward one's national tech icons.

The iPhone even made the iPod redundant, given that the iPhone came with a music app. Love of the iPod got transferred to the iPhone.

Competitive displacement operating in an open market produces incredible wealth. Apple is the most valuable tech company on earth, with a market capitalization hovering in the range of $2.5–$3 trillion,[3] and a brand that oozes leadership, cachet, and tech smarts. Not surprisingly, the open market has produced competitors to the iPhone (more evidence of *attempted* competitive displacement), especially South Korea's Samsung Galaxy. These two smartphones, and some less expensive ones from Chinese suppliers Xiaomi, Oppo, and Vivo, have also triggered a tsunami of wealth creation by their billions of users. Every tile on the homepage of a smartphone represents another business that has been competitively displaced (who buys paper maps anymore?), but each such e-business has also created thousands of new jobs, and hundreds of yet more opportunities (without the smartphone there would be no Uber, no DiDi in Asia, and so on). The smartphone has made Apple and Samsung shareholders a lot of money, but they have also brought enormous opportunity and wealth to their users as well.

Consider the self-employed sesame seed farmer in Sudan (the world's leading country for sesame seed production). Before the smartphone, when she harvested her sesame seeds, she would take her crop into town on her bicycle and sell it on terms dictated by the monopoly wholesale buyer. It's not hard to figure out who got the better end of that trade. Today, the farmer uses her smartphone to check the prices paid by wholesalers for sesame seeds in three other towns. The smartphone has given her alternatives and opportunities. Competition, produced by her smartphone, is working for her. The extra income generated by her smartphone has allowed her to upgrade her pedal bike—her only form of transport—to an e-bike. She's planning on planting more sesame plants and hiring her first employee.

The core building block of the smartphone is its high-end semiconductor chips. These SCs choreograph the magic dance of the applications that delight the user of the smartphone. The SC does likewise with literally every electronic device today, including the automobile, the espresso maker, the microwave oven, and the dishwasher. It is not an exaggeration that national economic power increasingly derives from the circuitry of the SC. Moreover, the SC is also the key to unlocking the full potential of artificial intelligence (AI), including the Siri assistant on the iPhone. Suffice it to say at this point that a country's modern national economy depends on digital technology built on top of SCs. States that are unwilling or unable to embrace the requirements of an innovating high-technology culture will be left in the economic dust of the analog world.

It is important to understand the broader impact Apple and other tech companies like it have on its relevant economic environment. Apple's products, by driving productivity-enhancing competitive displacement, generate untold amounts of additional economic activity. Most important, innovation-obsessed companies like Apple, in addition to achieving high levels of consumer satisfaction, generate (again through competitive displacement) an enormous amount of *new* economic activity. In democracies where there are open markets and robust competitive displacement, there is material economic growth, and the distribution of that growth is not a zero-sum game—there can be more wealth for virtually everyone simultaneously (so long as competitive displacement is allowed to run its course). To use the vernacular, not only is the pie getting constantly bigger, but everyone's particular slice of the pie is growing as well. Certainly some participants in the economy earn more income, and accumulate more wealth, than others, but generally there is more inequality in autocracies, especially China, than in democracies (especially countries like Canada, Germany, and Sweden, but even the United States), including because most democracies have better access to education for their lower classes than autocracies.[4]

For purposes of understanding competitive displacement and its critical role in Cold War 2.0, the key lesson is that the open market operating in a democracy drives tech-induced, compounding economic power. In 1960, the size of the United States economy was $0.5 trillion; in 2022 it was $25.46 trillion,[5] reflecting growth of 4,560 percent, even though population growth over that period was only 86 percent. The same happened in other countries around the world, but especially in those where technology innovation was unleashed by an open market. The size of the global economy in 1970 was $3.4 trillion; in 2022 it was $100.22 trillion.[6] Not all the net new growth is attributable to innovation, but an awful lot of it is. This core economic reality is central to so many aspects of Cold War 2.0, including the simple proposition that a nation's military muscle is largely funded by its civilian economic strength. It is because the United States has an economy of $25 trillion that it can afford a military budget of $880 billion, which dwarfs all other countries. And the US has an economy of $25 trillion because it has an open market in which technology innovation, compounded by competitive displacement, drives inexorable economic growth.

MILITARY TECHNOLOGY INNOVATION

Constant technological innovation of the kind that drives competitive displacement in the civilian sphere also propels forward steady improvement in military power. In the opening scene of Stanley Kubrick's iconic 1968 film *2001: A Space Odyssey*, some chimps learn the benefits of technology innovation, using the femur bone from a dead water buffalo to beat the life out of a chimp from another group vying for domination of a watering hole.[7] Kubrick's point? Game-changing technology makes the innovator invincible in arenas where violent confrontations get played out. Put in a more modern vernacular—don't bring a knife to a gunfight.

There is no direct evidence that chimps were smart enough to pick up and use as clubs the femur bones of water buffalo. Human burial sites, though, are full of mass graves in locations where ancient people clearly fought battles with spears, swords, and knives. Their bones have the scars and cuts to prove the violent cause of death, and the weapons used to inflict the wounds are themselves buried in the same mass graves. Periodically, a group of humans would invent and perfect through improvement a fundamentally new technology that produced stunning results on the battlefield (the new device was, as it were, the military iPod of its day). The new weapon system allowed its inventor to competitively displace others in the contest for leadership of a region or even a continent if the new innovation was earth-shattering enough.

In the early part of the 13th century, the Mongols conquered China (and eventually much of Russia, most of Eastern Europe, and everything in between), by using a novel weapon system, an archer perched on a smallish horse.[8] The Mongol horse was fast, nimble, and perfect for allowing the archer to shoot with his bow while in full gallop (utilizing yet another new innovation, the stirrup). The victims of this form of warfare tried to respond in kind, but their own lumbering equines raised in Europe simply couldn't match the speed and dexterity of the animals the Mongols had carefully bred for generations on the steppes of Asia. This is an early example of bio-engineering driving competitive displacement and paying huge dividends on the battlefield.

In a similar vein, in 1415 the English were able to defeat the French at the consequential Battle of Agincourt largely because the English had invented a "longbow," and its use at this battle devastated the French army. The "regular" bow and arrow, invented some 60,000 years earlier, was itself a huge improvement over the spear and sword, because kinetic energy could be temporarily stored and channeled through the bow, and directed into the flight of the arrow, delivering it much farther and with greater force than a thrown spear. With a bow and arrow a serious amount of war fighting and enemy killing could be effected at some distance. The longbow then increased the distance yet again, such that the English archers at Agincourt were killing French archers well before the French archers could even get in their range and do any harm to the British.[9] The British longbow was the HIMARS rocket launcher of its day, it competitively displaced the French bow and arrow and allowed the English to win the battle and ultimately to take over Normandy.

MILITARY-INDUSTRIAL CAPACITY

With the advent of the Industrial Revolution, there is a very tight fusing together of civilian technological progress with the military. What also becomes important is industrial capacity. It is one thing to invent and improve a technologically sophisticated device, machine, or process; it is another thing altogether to be able to produce it quickly on a large scale. To answer this challenge, even before the industrial age, Venice in the 1100s built its "Arsenale" in a sprawling facility of 110 acres, the largest fabrication facility in the world before the Industrial Revolution. Here, Europe's then leading maritime power produced its standard-setting war-fighting ships. After expanding the facility in 1320, the Arsenale also built large merchant vessels (at the astounding rate of one per day, courtesy of employing 16,000 workers and hyper-standardized production processes). To this day, many shipbuilders construct civilian and naval vessels side by side in their enormous dry docks. In addition, as the Industrial Revolution hit its peak in the mid- to late 1800s there was also a material increase in "dual-use" technologies, such as the railroad, where the same technology made its mark simultaneously in the civilian and military domains.

A good example of the importance of industrial capacity in warfare from the 1800s was when Britain and France sent forces to the Black Sea to dislodge Russia from the Crimean peninsula. British and French troops laid siege to Sevastopol for eleven months, to oust the Russian Black Sea fleet from this important port and military base. The Russians ultimately lost this war because they lacked sufficient railroad connectivity to the region with which to resupply their beleaguered troops (the British and French also had superior warships and better rifles). Overall, the Crimean War from 1853 to 1856 was a disaster for the Russians because their military and civilian technologies were inferior to those of the French and British. As noted in the introduction, history never repeats itself exactly, but it does rhyme from time to time, in this case in Crimea. A similar lesson was learned by the Confederate states a decade later during the American Civil War between 1861 and 1865. While initially the South fought effectively against the Army of the North, eventually the more advanced civilian and military technologies invented, manufactured on a large scale, and effectively deployed by the North through superior logistics networks allowed President Abraham Lincoln to achieve his war aims of keeping the United States intact.

The consequences of being able to translate civilian technological progress (including effective industrial capacity) into military supremacy can be seen starkly in the "long 19th century." In the late 1790s, China, India, and Europe each had about one-third of the world's industrial base, in terms of factories, foundries, looms, and the like. In 1900 the split was Japan 2 percent, Russia 8 percent, and Western Europe 70 percent, with the United States the leading individual country at 20 percent. This enormous shift in economic heft then translated into geopolitical military power in the following manner: by 1913 about 80 percent of the landmass of the Earth belonged to the European powers, with the British alone holding 23 percent (and even the US getting into the act of empire when it took over the Philippines and Cuba in 1898). India and China, who both failed to adopt the latest technology from the democracies, ended up being utterly humiliated in the second half of the 1800s. This is a status and outcome they are both working hard to avoid in Cold War 2.0.

The importance of industrial military capacity, now much dependent upon high-tech processes itself, can be seen in the current Russo-Ukrainian War. Again, it is not enough to invent, or enhance, a modern weapon system or its various components; units of it also have to be produced on a large scale. In the war in Ukraine, at the peak of the Battle of Bakhmut, the Ukrainian army was firing about 6,000 artillery shells a day (not HIMARS-type rocket missiles, but "regular" unguided howitzer shells). These shells are sourced from several NATO member countries. The United States, though, Ukraine's largest supplier of artillery, currently has only one factory capable of producing these shells. It makes about 460 a day. This number is not nearly enough to allow Ukraine to keep using the number of shells it would like to. Other NATO countries are making up the shortfall, but by early 2023 it was clear that net production of new additional shells would have to be ramped up if Ukraine was to continue its fight with effective artillery support. Cold War 2.0 planners can never forget that manufacturing physical items still matters a great deal, even if the most intriguing trends in both civilian and military innovation are on the digital front.

There is another very important dimension to military-industrial capacity. It is not enough to have built up stockpiles of military kit in peacetime. The key to a robust industrial capacity is to be able to replace systems, like jet fighters, tanks, missiles, or now drones, that are lost in combat. In peacetime ministers of defense, and often even generals, forget this crucial dimension of military-industrial capacity. It's not a case only of what number of tanks a military starts with, but how quickly losses—both the tank and fully trained tank crews—can be replaced. This is another lesson (re-)learned from the Russo-Ukrainian War. Hopefully war planners in Taiwan are absorbing this wisdom from what they are seeing in Europe's largest war since World War II.

The previous point in turn raises a very critical consideration about training, especially of new human crews. As weapons like the HIMARS are depleted on the battlefield of a major war, not only must new units of the weapon system be built in record time, but individuals need to be trained very quickly so the new HIMARS units (or tanks, or F-16s, let alone F-35s) can be promoted promptly to the conflict zone. Again, digital technology, with significant AI elements, running on high-performance SCs (and eventually on QCs) will be central to cutting down current training times. It is a testament to their military savviness and base knowledge that Ukrainian HIMARS crews were trained in only three months, but even this pace, eventually, with the help of technology, needs to get down to three weeks. The toughest nut to crack will be pilots, on hyper-complex machines such as the F-16.

Once the weapon or other military asset is made, there is also the question of logistics, the requirement to get the right item to the right place at the right time. As powerful as the Mongols were in their heyday, their leader Kublai Khan was unable to successfully attack Japan because the assault ships he used were river boats unsuitable for crossing the ocean waters between China (by then conquered and occupied by the Mongols) and Japan. His ships didn't have a deep enough keel, and they had to return to port. Japan was saved, and left unconquered by the Mongols, because of a logistics deficiency on the part of the would-be attacking force. Presumably the current regime in China is reviewing this history carefully in preparing for their planned invasion of the island nation of Taiwan. It is interesting that the US military is addressing the massive challenge of logistics by leaning heavily on civilian transport companies like FedEx and United Parcel Service (UPS) to help move soldiers and matériel, especially in major conflict scenarios where large volumes need to be transported urgently. To do this well, both the civilian companies and the US military need to share ongoing access to the same logistics computer systems. This is another compelling example of the need to have seamless civilian-military fusion. Cold War 2.0 will be won by the side that can bring a technologically expert "whole-of-society" effort to the conflict.

It's important to understand one additional nuance in the technology permeating military power currently. Offensive weapons systems prompt the creation of defensive weapons systems. With apologies to Isaac Newton, to each offensive military technology advancement there is an equal and opposite defensive military technology reaction. During ancient and medieval times castles with high walls, built at the top of high hills, were a classic example of defense responding to offense. The massive walls of Constantinople (present-day Istanbul), built in the 300s, successfully kept invaders at bay for over 1,000 years. In Malta today there are still standing some of the most extensive walled defenses in the world, dating from the 1500s, especially in Mdina and most of all in the capital, Valletta. Since World War II such walls have rarely been built for defense because aircraft and missiles can simply fly over them. Instead, currently air defense systems are being turned out in large numbers. The most advanced of these in the world, the US Patriot ground-based and Aegis naval-based ADS are a testament to defense technologies responding in kind to offensive ones. This is all part of the "action/offense-reaction/defense" cadence of modern arms races.

This offense/defense rhythm matters, and more on the military side than the civilian. While the dynamic of competitive displacement is largely technologically the same in the civilian and military domains, the consequences of failure in each sphere can be quite different. When Sony was competitively displaced in the personal music device space by Apple's iPod, Sony still had lots of other businesses to fall back on, and to this day their gaming console is by far the leader in the marketplace. Losing the Walkman battle to Apple's iPod was not the end of Sony. In military terms, if the Patriot and Aegis ADS technologies don't prevail in a future Battle of the Taiwan Strait, the Taiwan democracy loses its freedom to the autocratic Chinese. The stakes for competitive displacement are simply higher in the military domain. The consequence of losing the competitive displacement contest in the civilian domain is financial; losing it in the military domain is often existential. The democracies forget this key message of Cold War 2.0 at their peril.

To recap: inventing new military technologies that give significant competitive advantage to the more innovative nation is a key means for increasing hard power relative to peer nations that don't have equivalent technology. What history teaches, though, is that often it is not the initial invention that counts, but rather the subsequent modification, enhancement, and improvement of the machine, device, or process. This is particularly true for civilian inventions that are subsequently modified for use in military applications.

INNOVATION = INVENTION + IMPROVEMENT

Innovation consists of two activities, the initial *invention* of a device, and then the subsequent *improvement* of it. Surprisingly, improvement often proves to be more valuable than invention, in both the civilian and military domains. Most people who have only a vague sense of the Industrial Revolution will think that James Watt invented the steam engine, but that's wrong. It was Thomas Newcomen who (in 1712) actually *invented* it, but what he came up with didn't work that well. James Watt *perfected* it (in 1765), so that it could be used to power factories, and eventually trains, ships, tractors, and the other monumental machines of the Industrial Revolution. Invention is important, but improvement usually more so.

This principle will be important in Cold War 2.0 as the democracies and the autocracies constantly leapfrog one another's technology. Recall that before Google search, there were Lycos, AltaVista, and about a dozen other serious search engines. Clearly improvement also plays a central role in competitive displacement in today's technologically oriented economy. It's been like this for some 150 years. Thomas Edison is generally thought to have "invented" the light bulb, and to this day a light bulb turning on is the very symbol of invention. In fact, though, Edison took an existing light bulb concept, and then tried 600 different metals and substances as filaments before he painstakingly improved his way to the right one.

In the military realm, gunpowder is the classic example of the importance of improvement. In the 800s the Chinese came up with the idea of mixing together saltpeter, sulfur, and charcoal to form a very combustible substance, but initially they used it by throwing the actual flaming mass at an enemy. This was a somewhat scary war-fighting tactic, but not very effective on a battlefield. The Byzantines improved the delivery of the fire in the 1200s by hurling it from a tube, but still it was a fairly exotic weapon, and not quite mainstream. The Chinese were on to something when they experimented with some early cannons in their armories, but they were very rudimentary, and still not very effective.

Gunpowder came into its own as serious ordnance, and eventually *the* defining weapon of its age (by the 1500s), when the West Europeans greatly improved upon the gunpowder munitions used at the time by the Chinese and the Byzantines. The Europeans exploded a small amount of gunpowder in the breech of a rifle or cannon. This controlled explosion then launched the real point of the exercise, by forcing a bullet out of the barrel of a gun or pistol, or launching a cannonball out of a cannon. These projectiles then did heavy damage to the enemy. Using gunpowder to launch a metal projectile against an enemy was a revolutionary moment in military affairs, and it changed the dynamic of national power forever.

The following comparison makes clear the importance of the innovatively repurposed gunpowder. A typical bow would generate about 80 joules of energy in an arrow in flight, while an early musket could produce in its small metal ball (shot out of its barrel) 1,500 joules of energy. A mature musket (a predecessor of the rifle) could get the joule count up to 3,000. This is why metal suits of armor could protect against arrows, but not shots coming from muskets, let alone modern rifles. It is not until the bulletproof vest of the 1890s that there is even some rudimentary defense against rifles and pistols, and really effective protection against bullets has to wait until the 1970s and the invention of Kevlar.

The fundamentally different way in which Europeans perfected the use of gunpowder allowed them to conquer by force of arms the non-European world. It also allowed the Christian naval fleet assembled by Pope Pius V to defeat the Ottoman fleet at the Battle of Lepanto in 1571. This *improvement* around gunpowder also ushered in the great age of West European exploration. On a more sobering note, it also fueled incessant wars between the European nations for 450 years, causing untold numbers of deaths and mass maiming. No one said that military competitive displacement would be a picnic.

LEARNING INNOVATION AND DEMOCRACY—THE CASE OF ASIA

Innovation, and especially its improvement, can be learned. Consider the respective geopolitical reactions of the Chinese and Japanese when in the mid-1800s modern warships from Europe and the United States sailed into their harbors and rivers demanding that the reclusive Asian states open up their countries to trade. These entreaties were successful because they were backed up by gunpowder-fueled cannon and rifles the likes of which the Chinese and the Japanese had never seen. Indeed, so powerful were the British that the Chinese were forced to accept opium in payment for their goods. The British cultivated the opium (from the poppy plant) in India, and eventually this nefarious British export to China caused some

90 million Chinese (30 percent of the population) to become addicted to heroin. The Chinese would not fully recover from these Western indignities until, more than 100 years later, Deng Xiaoping kicked off the amazing economic growth story of modern China. Even today, though, the current Chinese leader, Xi Jinping, talks of China's "age of humiliation," referring to what the British did to China in the 1800s. Ironically, China today is exacting a degree of revenge on democracies by currently supplying the two largest drug cartels in Mexico with the precursor chemicals for making illicit fentanyl, which they smuggle into the United States. These illegal drugs then cause about 100,000 American people a year to die from fentanyl overdoses. Sometimes the rhyming of history can be pretty loud.

In the 1800s, though, the Chinese response to West European predation was weak, hesitant, and supine. The Japanese, on the other hand, responded immediately and with vigor. Determined to do something meaningful about their lack of modern technology soon after the American humiliation, between 1871 and 1873 the Japanese government sent emissaries around the world to learn about the latest and best techniques for innovating, manufacturing, and deploying modern technology. They ultimately adopted an educational program based on the one used in France, they instituted an industrial production system cloned from the British and the Americans, and they created a military that mimicked the German model. In the tech world, there are clear advantages to what is called "first mover advantage," but equally there are benefits to being the "second comer." In the history of technology innovation, the Japanese became the second comer par excellence.

Japan's Meiji regime's efforts to adopt new technologies and techniques, and to apply them to military ends, proved to be a huge success in their goal to build an autocratic empire. In 1905, in an absolutely shocking development at the time, the Japanese military started and won a war with Russia. This effort included, among other maneuvers, a sneak attack on the Russian navy based in Port Arthur (it had been leased to the Russians by the Chinese) in order to kick off the war. Again, history never repeats itself exactly, but the Japanese sneak attack on Pearl Harbor some thirty-five years later certainly rhymes with this event. As in the Crimean War some fifty years before, Russia would learn through this defeat at the hands of the Japanese that technology (both specific innovations, as well as their manufacture and logistical deployment) is the key determinant of national power. Of course, a modern war-fighting doctrine, healthy morale among the troops, a strong officer corps, and other factors are necessary as well, but without the deadly technology the other ingredients would be insufficient. In effect, relative to Cold War 2.0, a country's current military power can be assessed by looking at the stockpile of its currently state-of-the-art weapons, but its power in twenty years' time is best predicted today by how well its brightest current high school students are learning new concepts in math, physics, biology, and chemistry.

Using European and American industrial technologies, Japan became the regional hegemon power in Asia after the Russo-Japanese war, and it was only Japan's defeat in World War II that finally cleaved off their colonial lands. Soon after World War II the Japanese resumed their economic industrious-ness, but this time (with much coaching from the Americans) they made a deep commitment to democracy as their political system. By the 1960s they were an economic powerhouse. In 1964 Tokyo hosted the Olympic Games and showcased to the world a modern, peaceful nation firmly embedded in the global community of democracies. By the 1970s Japan was even seem-ingly threatening American economic dominance; Japanese cars were com-petitively displacing American ones, Japanese televisions were competitively displacing American ones, and so on across many different industrial and consumer goods. In effect, the Japanese had learned that unlike what they did before World War II, they didn't need to fight their way into foreign markets with guns blazing. For many decades they had a standing army of only 100,000 soldiers, while today's figure hovers around 275,000, due largely to the tense situation in Asia caused by Cold War 2.0. The Japanese have learned that to secure economic prosperity it is sufficient to produce well-made products, given that the rules-based international order (especially its trading rules and regulations) allowed them to sell these goods all around the world.

South Korea and Taiwan, on a lesser scale, replicated Japan's success. South Korea in particular suffered tremendous trauma and destruction during its time as a colony of Japan (1910 to 1945) and during the Korean War (1950 to 1953). As a result, South Korea's rise up the industrial league tables starting in the late 1950s and continuing to the present is nothing short of spectacular. In the context of Cold War 2.0, the massive success of South Korea, with its democracy and relatively open market economy, can be contrasted with the abysmal living conditions of North Korea (and repeated famines) resulting from the "hermit kingdom" clinging to a dual autocratic system of politics and economics. Interestingly, the superior performance of West Germany over East Germany between 1945 and 1989 proves the same point; in double, side-by-side growth real-world experiments, the democracy far surpasses the autocracy on every metric imaginable.

For their part, Taiwan's muscular entry into the production of semiconductor chips in the 1980s—and their competitive displacement of American SCs by the 1990s—was gutsy and brilliant in the extreme. (South Korea also entered the SC production market at this point, choosing to focus on memory SCs.) Then, to have both South Korea and Taiwan, like Japan, commit to democracy since the 1980s is a wonderful testament to the patience, maturity, and judgment of their leaders and their citizens over the past five decades. All three countries resolutely refused to believe the propaganda coming out of Beijing and Pyongyang (North Korea) that Asian people were predisposed to autocracy and not at all suited to democracy. Japan, South Korea, and Taiwan have bought into the rules-based international order, and they and their people have benefited greatly as a result.

China would do well to learn lessons from these three Asian exemplars of economic competitive displacement and political democracy as Cold War 2.0 unfolds. China is currently following the path taken by Japan in the 1885–1945 era, when Japan devoted all its effort to becoming the imperial hegemon of Asia by force of arms. China's behavior over the last twenty years—snuffing out personal liberty in Hong Kong, conducting a massive buildup of the PLA (its armed forces and nuclear weapon stockpile), cravenly building islands and military bases across the South China

Sea, oppressing its people (especially the Uighurs) through sophisticated surveillance and control technologies, and tightening Xi Jinping's autocratic hold on politics—rhymes dangerously with Japan's pre–World War II behavior. Rather than emulate this version of Japan, which ended in disaster (for Japan, the region, and, ironically, China as well), China should instead consider the path blazed by Japan after World War II, where China would truly commit to the rules-based international order and become a responsible, valued, and prosperous leading member of the international community. Put another way, the supreme irony of Asian geopolitics today is that China wants to absorb Taiwan to be able to make Taiwan more like China, but in fact what should happen is that China should become more like Taiwan. That's a tall order, but wonders never cease. There is also that ancient Chinese proverb, typically meant as a warning, but in this case useful as an admonition to China: "You become what you oppose."

HYPER-INNOVATION

Starting in the late 1800s, the industrialized countries of Western Europe and North America, and increasingly including Japan as well, experienced hyper progress in science and technology innovation. Breakthroughs in multiple scientific disciplines and technology domains were achieved with accelerating frequency. In medicine, in 1888 Canadian born and educated William Osler moved to Baltimore to lead the Johns Hopkins Hospital. In 1892 he wrote *The Principles and Practice of Medicine*, the last book intended to cover the entire spectrum of modern medicine. The explosion in medical knowledge and technique that followed simply couldn't be contained in a single volume thereafter, as the age of specialization in medicine was beginning. (Today, for example, at the University Health Network in downtown Toronto, one of the top five medical centers in the world,[10] just the surgery department has fourteen subspecialties!)

Around the same time, the chemical industry (particularly in Germany) made leaps and bounds in the thirty years leading up to World

War I (between 1914 to 1918). The result was significant advances in the
biological sciences, such as the invention of nitrogen-based fertilizer. At
the same time, though, the Germans and the allies used chemical warfare
agents, such as mustard gas, in the battlefields of northern France and
Belgium during World War I, illustrating again the potentially nefarious
"dual-use" nature that lurks within virtually all technological innovation.
Tens of thousands of soldiers in the Great War were killed, poisoned, or
made blind as a result of gas attacks.

Around this time the steel industry got a huge boost from the invention of the new Bessemer steel-making process. Skeletons of steel beams
drove buildings ever taller, reaching twenty-five stories in some American
cities, especially in Chicago and New York, by the outbreak of World
War I. The invention of the elevator by American Elisha Otis facilitated
the verticalization of urban life. In yet another example of dual-use technology, the new type of steel used for the frames of tall buildings was also
used to build submarines, which were planned as a revolutionary threat to,
and deadly competitive displacer of, navies and merchant fleets comprised
only of surface ships. War fighting on land became more mobile with the
invention of the tank. World War I tanks were derived from the civilian
automobile invented in the late 1800s but were outfitted with steel armor.
To complete the new, innovative, dual-use deadly trio, the Wright Brothers
in 1903 invented the airplane. They flew a flimsy glider equipped with a
small engine only thirty meters and just a couple of meters off the ground.
A dozen years later, the much-improved airplane would be making reconnaissance missions over the battlefield and sometimes even dropping small
bombs on enemy soldiers.

As noted earlier, when it comes to innovation, improvement will almost
always outshine invention. The three tentative war machine inventions of
World War I, through a constant and successful program of improvement,
eventually became full-scale, industrial strength monsters of destruction
by World War II (between 1939 and 1945). The submarine, which was a
fairly rudimentary device in World War I, became a sleek, powerful menace
some twenty-five years later. German U-boats sank a total of 2,825 allied

merchant and 175 allied naval vessels, and almost brought England to its knees in the early stage of the war, when Britain stood virtually alone against the Nazis. British prime minister Winston Churchill would comment that of all the inventions of the war, the one he really feared was the submarine.

As for the airplane, the small handmade bombs thrown from World War I biplanes made of wood, fabric, and wires were superseded by gargantuan four-engine bombers made of aluminum and glass, purpose-built to deliver a huge tonnage of high explosive bombs on each flight over enemy territory. Breathtaking technology innovation brought total war, as bombers dropped their deadly ordnance on civilians in cities. Of the 70 million dead in World War II, about 50 million were civilians. As for the tank, it became the bedrock weapon system for all land armies, and it was key for delivering early German victories in Poland and France. German tanks almost managed to defeat their Russian counterparts on the steppes of Russia, but that became an objective too far. It helped enormously that Stalin cannily made sure Russian tank factories were all located east of the Ural Mountains, so that they could continue to build tanks while the main fighting with the Germans was going on west of the Urals—once again highlighting the crucial importance of military-industrial capacity.

The development histories of the submarine, the airplane, and the tank during the last 125 years drive home the importance of *improvement* in the innovation equation. These three weapons systems are still core to militaries around the world. They will continue to be critical weapons systems for the coming decades of Cold War 2.0. They will undergo, though, massive further modifications during those years, in particular incorporating more and more AI and high-end SCs into their mechanical systems. They will also use QCs to assist with complex targeting calculations. In Cold War 2.0 lots of new digital wine will be poured into old bottles when it comes to weapons development.

During World War II, scientists, engineers, and technologists pursued the most difficult science project undertaken by mankind to that point in history, namely the design, development, and deployment of the atomic bomb. In the 1930s theoretical physicists calculated that certain types of atoms could be manipulated in a way so as to release great amounts of energy, but bridging the gap between scientific theory and applied engineering was no simple feat. Nevertheless, overcoming great technological adversity under intense time pressure, in the New Mexico desert at Los Alamos, American scientists (ably assisted by colleagues from Britain and Canada) spent over $2.2 billion (a whopping $37 billion in today's dollars) on making the first atomic bomb. At its peak, the project employed thousands of people. In 1945, the Americans dropped two atomic bombs on Japanese cities in order to avoid even more numerous American (and Japanese) casualty figures had the US instead pursued amphibious assaults on the remaining Japanese islands.

Releasing the power of the atom is the epitome of the dual-use innovation. Within a few years after the war the Americans built the world's first civilian nuclear power plant, followed by Britain, Canada, France, and a few others. Nuclear isotopes also came to be used in medicine, particularly in cancer therapy. In a similar vein, the massive bomber planes of World War II gave birth to a commercial aircraft industry after the war, first powered by propeller engines, but improved to use jet engines by the 1960s. A huge new industry was created once the hundreds of new airports and air cargo facilities were factored into the economic equation. This is one of the many new industries that has contributed to the massive global economic growth over the past eighty years, referred to earlier in this chapter.

Meanwhile, further up in the atmosphere the Russians were the first to launch a small satellite, called *Sputnik*, in 1957. The democracies were stunned, as autocratic communist regimes weren't supposed to do innovation very well. Generally, that was true, and continues to be true today, but it turns out that an autocratic regime could pour huge sums of money into a focused technological effort, and eventually large quantity takes on a quality of its own. There was more shock and awe when the Soviet Russians were the first to send a human (Yuri Gagarin) into orbit in 1961. The Americans countered by creating NASA and launching an ambitious program to put a man on the moon by 1970. At its peak, the US space program was costing annually an amount equal to 4 percent of the entire US GDP. During that period the US was also fighting a major (and very expensive) war in Vietnam. Nevertheless, America's juggernaut economy was sufficiently buoyant throughout the 1960s that the world's leading democracy could afford (just barely) these two massive expenditures, right up until the Apollo mission put men on the moon in 1969 and for several years following. Ironically, it was Soviet Russia that ran out of money and decided to abandon its plan to put humans on the moon. Later, their entire autocratic economy fell apart, causing a political collapse as well.

INNOVATIVE DIGITAL WEAPONS

The Apollo moon mission made extensive use of computers. Indeed, no other innovation exemplified American technological supremacy in the 1960s and for decades afterward (and to this day) than the computer industry. Early ancestors of the computer were built during World War II to crack the encrypted code used by the Germans to scramble their long-distance secret army messages. These first computers used vacuum tubes, not that different from the ones in the first radios in the 1920s and television sets in the 1930s. By the late 1950s/early 1960s, though, a new technology was invented in the research labs of several American companies (primarily Bell Labs, Shockley Semiconductor, and Fairchild Semiconductor) using a solid-state semiconductor material that performed better than a vacuum tube, used much less power, and took up a fraction of the space. In 1961, the digital computer based on the semiconductor chip was born in America. It had only four transistors. Today, some sixty years later (in the span of a single lifetime), the most powerful SC is much smaller (the size of a fingernail) and has about 50 billion transistors. Hyper-innovation indeed!

The computer, its various components (especially the SC), and software have insinuated their way into virtually every modern device on earth that uses electronics. Computers are another exemplar of dual-use technology, to the point where modern weapons systems, like submarines, missiles, fighter aircraft, surface naval vessels, tanks, and drones, are really just computers that deliver an explosive warhead. Military smart bombs use the same GPS system as civilian smartphones. The computer-based "fly-by-wire" controls on a helicopter used in the army look and perform an awful lot like the digital control system used in a helicopter operated by a mining company in the remote outback somewhere. The world has reached "Cold War 2.0 singularity," namely that civilian and military innovation are essentially one and the same.

The steady computerization of the military and their weapons systems has a number of important ramifications. Just as in the civilian tech sector, there are now constant updates required for the software in weapons systems. Smartphones are updated once every 12–16 months, and so it is with smart bombs, missiles, radar, Patriot, Aegis, etc. This adds material costs to the procurement and sustainment of modern, digitally enhanced weapons systems. It also impacts ongoing training requirements. If a user cannot figure out the latest features on their smartphone, there is no harm done. If a HIMARS crew doesn't learn thoroughly its latest software release, they could put themselves and their mission in jeopardy. Training on digital military systems is not optional. Indeed, during Cold War 2.0 lifelong technical learning for human users has come to the military before it has fully taken hold in the civilian economy.

Computerization of weapons also leads to increased lethality. This trend is not new. Several hundred thousand years ago the first weapons wielded by humans were simple clubs. Then, as humans developed metallurgy, axes and knives were invented, as were bronze (and later iron) swords. The axe is another thoroughly dual-use weapon, equally effective for cutting down a tree limb as cutting off a person's limb. These weapons required "hand-to-hand" combat, though, so the radius of human harm was greatly limited. As noted above, the bow and arrow represented a step level escalation in lethality. While thrusting weapons relied solely on the muscles of the human wielding the club, axe, knife, or sword, the archer also harnessed the kinetic energy created in a flexed bow or stored through the windup of a crossbow. Gunpowder-based weapons increased lethality by yet another order of magnitude, by taking advantage of chemistry—and nuclear weapons by harnessing physics.

Digital weapons add to lethality by achieving greater precision. Artillery of the 1500s had a range of several hundred meters and cannonballs rarely actually hit the intended target, so lots of volleys had to be fired. By World War I, the general range of artillery was 8–14 kilometers, but the targeting was still largely driven by happenstance and gravity. Today's HIMARS and similar systems are an altogether different proposition. These weapons can deliver their payload over a distance of 50–80 miles, with the warhead landing within several feet of the intended target, thanks to clever digitally-based targeting and guidance features that use GPS systems, the same service that runs "maps" on a smartphone. Then there are numerous guided missiles (such as "cruise missiles"), first widely used in the Gulf War of 1991, where they constituted only 20 percent of the munitions used by the allied forces but inflicted 75 percent of the damage. They are more lethal, but at the same time they can better avoid civilian casualties. These are the new paradoxes generated by innovative digital weapons in Cold War 2.0.

THE FINANCIALS OF INNOVATION

The full impact of the English longbow wasn't merely its superior functionality. It's indirect benefit, part of the secret sauce of competitive displacement from the "supply side," was that an archer with a longbow was much cheaper to put on the battlefield than a medieval knight, the previous dominant weapon system. A knight was very expensive to outfit, and there were only a limited number of them, given the strict rules of noble inheritance at the time. Archers, on the other hand, were a fraction of the cost of a knight to equip, billet, and board. The English king (like Henry V at Agincourt) who switched out knights in favor of longbow archers could decide to retain many more of them, or simply keep the savings, depending on how they viewed the enemy. In effect, the financial parameters of military power are important and always have been. Kings at first, and then prime ministers and presidents in our own day, worry seriously about the cost of battlefield technology because they cannot ignore budget deficits and government debt. This will never change, regardless of how much surplus wealth the civilian economy is able to produce through the Cold War 2.0 period.

This is actually a weakness of democracies relative to autocracies, especially as the intensity of Cold War 2.0 ramps up in places like Ukraine and Taiwan. The cost of a country's military can be quite controversial, particularly in democracies where the budgeting process is open and subject to debate and approval by elected representatives. There was a time in the 1800s when defense-related expenditures represented 90 percent, or even more, of a government's budget. This is somewhat misleading because governments in the early 1800s didn't spend anything on (nonexistent) social programs. Therefore, a king, president, or prime minister who went to the legislature for an increase in government funds (effected through a raise in taxes) generally did so in order to wage war somewhere.

Since World War II, with the steady decline in the number of wars around the world and the massive increase in popular demands on governments in democracies to fund social programs (like healthcare, education, and unemployment benefits), spending on defense in virtually all democracies has declined dramatically as a percentage of the entire public budget. Since Putin's invasion of Ukraine in 2014, there has been plenty of pressure on the democracies to spend more on defense. Since Putin's full-scale invasion of Ukraine in 2022 the pressure to spend on defense is intense indeed. Still, the social priorities for spending haven't gone away. Huge deficit financing to pay for all the social *and* the defense demands is usually the answer, meaning that some unlucky future generation will have to pay the full bill when it comes due.

Autocracies are less buffeted by this particular budgetary dynamic than the democracies. The autocrat is able to direct the funds of the national budget somewhat at will, while a leader in a democracy cannot do this. The autocracy, though, suffers from the scourge of corruption that has a deleterious effect similar to chronic underfunding of the military. When Russian armies invaded Ukraine in February 2022, many tanks, armored personnel carriers, and other vehicles (such as supply trucks) broke down because they had been poorly maintained in the years and months leading up to the invasion. Tires on trucks, for instance, simply fell apart because they were much too old and worn out, and should have been replaced months if not years before. They weren't replaced or maintained properly because corrupt senior military officers skimmed off the money for themselves that should have gone to truck tire maintenance. At least when a military in a democracy is denied funding the money goes to another government department (to educate children or to heal the sick) and not into the illegal bank accounts of army officers. This weakness caused by corruption in the autocracies will pay dividends to the democracies throughout Cold War 2.0.

On the other hand, the democracies (and the autocracies) suffer from another financial burden—simply the incredibly high cost of modern high-tech kit. Precision-guided munitions are very effective, but their cost is also very significant. A single cruise missile will run in the range of $2 million. Then there is the really expensive military weapon system. A single F-35 fifth-generation fighter—just one of them—costs $85 million. That's just to buy it. To run and maintain it, the entire all-in cost for fifteen years is about another $130 million. And that's for just one plane. One. Surely the government has to start asking if an F-35 really is ten times better than a very sophisticated $20 million drone? Is the drone the modern equivalent of a longbow, and the F-35 the medieval knight? Moreover, can reusable drones firing Hellfire missiles (costing "only" $150,000 each) replace cruise missiles ($2 million a piece) in most operations requiring firepower? Bottom line: Should commanders in the field be thinking about cost when they are taking fire in the middle of the fog, pressure, and high-stakes risk of war?

Another question that has to be asked regularly is: Where can savings in the military budget come from? A few years ago, when the United States contemplated upgrading its "triad" system of nuclear defense, the US government ultimately decided that US nuclear deterrence still required a three-legged stool: air force bombers carrying nuclear-tipped cruise missiles, the navy's submarines carrying nuclear ballistic missiles, and nuclear missiles on army truck launchers roaming around the Midwest US to avoid being targeted by enemy first-strike missiles. Renewing the entire triad is going to cost a whopping $1.5 trillion over the next thirty years. Had the US dropped one leg of the triad, they could have saved roughly a third of that cost, so about $500 billion. That would make a lot of sense, and wouldn't appreciably increase the risk to military preparedness, but no service is willing to step up and say that it would take the reduction of responsibility (and funding). It is spending and strategic mistakes such as these that put the US defense budget (and the overall American federal government budget) in jeopardy. Cold War 2.0 is playing out in a time when the US, and most other democracies, are experiencing unprecedented levels of public borrowing. The democracies must be smart about military expenditures. The alternative is a devastating crash against a fiscal wall when financial markets finally start to refuse to buy American treasury bonds. When that day comes the autocrats will have won Cold War 2.0.

CONSTRAINTS ON MODERN WEAPONS

One answer to the concern about the high cost of weapons today can be answered, at least partly, by the general aphorism "you get what you pay for." From this perspective, one major benefit of digitally targeted munitions is that they cause far less civilian and other collateral damage, or at least they can be used with this goal in mind. This is key for leaders of democracies, particularly when their militaries are involved in operations that will generate all variety of images and videos that will be posted on social media. In these circumstances, because leaders of the democracy will have to face voters in the upcoming election, limiting the lethality of weapons solely to the armed forces of the opponent is critical.

Sadly, autocrats typically want to achieve quite the opposite. In Ukraine, commencing in October 2022, the Russian military directed hundreds of missile and drone attacks specifically against civilian infrastructure (such as power plants and other utilities) and civilians themselves (such as targeting an urban marketplace or a residential apartment block) to try to break the spirit of the Ukrainian people, so that they would apply pressure on the leadership of their democracy to sue for peace on terms favorable to the Russian invaders. In so doing, the Russians committed hundreds of war crimes as targeting civilians in this way is clearly prohibited by several Geneva Conventions. This heinous strategy of the Russian autocrat Putin was not an oversight. In democracies the commission of a specific war crime is typically a bug in their military culture (and something to be investigated and dealt with responsibly by legal process). In stark contrast, for an autocracy the commission of war crimes is a central feature of their system of war fighting. Relative to Russia's unjustified war in Ukraine (itself a war crime), Putin has passed a law in Russia giving carte blanche advance immunity from Russian prosecution to any soldier that commits a war crime in Ukraine, so long as it was done to further the goals of the Russian army. This is a trenchant example of the vast moral and legal chasm between the autocracies and the democracies, and why a Cold War 2.0 exists at all.

Digital features in modern weapons systems have also increased the tempo of military activity, particularly in respect of defensive operations. Enemy missiles, drones, and modern fighter-bomber aircraft can fly at very high speeds (with hypersonic missiles at five times the speed of sound, about 6,200 kilometers an hour) and can be over urban or strategic targets in a matter of minutes after entering the opponent's airspace. In order to defeat these attacks, the defender must quickly gather all the relevant sensor information about what is coming at it and exactly where and at what speed, and then countermeasures must be launched virtually immediately, either by scrambling fighters or launching antiaircraft missiles to intercept the incoming enemy ones. Individual humans cannot carry out this function well, or not at all, if there are more than two or three missiles coming at them, as they have difficulty processing all the relevant information in the short time allotted (see the scenario at the beginning of the introduction). As with so many civilian technologies in modern life, current military technology moves at a pace much faster than humans; when it comes to air defense, humans will participate less and less in it as Cold War 2.0 progresses.

Not surprisingly, therefore, in antiair and antimissile defense, computers, software, and especially AI have been pressed into use to help with collecting the relevant information, processing it, and then, critically, launching the countermeasures/intercept missiles—and often automatically because there is simply insufficient time for humans to insert themselves into the workflow required to respond to the enemy threat. This heralds a new age of digital warfare, one that raises a number of important questions for both democracies and autocracies alike. Most of these questions center around what degree of human oversight should be retained over these digital systems. Hyper-innovation in military affairs will present thorny ethical and moral conundrums in Cold War 2.0.

In some respects, this is not an entirely new dilemma. For about 120 years humans have developed weapons that a large number of countries, both democratic and autocratic, have agreed are so murderous that they must be banned, or at least very tightly constrained. In World War I, both sides used chemical weapons on the battlefield by lobbing canisters of chlorine and mustard gases into the opponent's trenches, and even across no-man's land between the opposing forces. The resulting horrendous deaths caused revulsion among even the toughest generals, and in 1925, thirty-eight countries (today 146 countries) agreed to ban the first use of such chemical weapons in warfare (but countries could develop them and use them to retaliate against another country that used them first).

In 1972, signatory countries agreed to add biological agents to the list of banned substances under the treaty, and in 1993 further restrictions on chemical and biological weapons were added.[11] An important impetus for this set of international conventions was the practical issue that these chemical and biological agents, at the time, could not be effectively used without the gas or biological agents coming back onto the troops of the country that launched them, due to unpredictable wind patterns. Today this impediment has been solved with substances like anthrax, where the country using the chemical agent could inoculate its own troops against it, thereby opening up more opportunities for its use. This sort of dangerous dilemma will become more common in Cold War 2.0 as humans conclude (sometimes erroneously) that they have sufficiently mastered the relevant technology.

The other shortcoming with chemical and biological weapons conventions has been the reluctance of countries, mainly the autocrats but some democracies as well, to allow the United Nations to conduct effective inspections of sites to verify that the rules are being followed. Without a supervisory system that all parties agree to adhere to, confidence—and success—in the overall effort to control these gruesome substances will be low. Here surely the technologies of the 21st century can help solve such problems, including with the deployment of visual and other sensors in the relevant labs and factories, and AI to help track all inputs being consumed by the global military-industrial complex.

CIVILIAN-MILITARY INNOVATION FUSION

Nations have reached the point, in the third decade of the 21st century, where economic preeminence and military expertise are both extremely reliant on the digital innovation capabilities of each specific country. Computer engineers, data scientists, software programmers, and their colleagues in the digital supply chains are designing, developing, and deploying the modern systems that bring added digital value to all workflows in the economy. Then their digital cousins perform the same work at the defense contractor companies and within the armed forces in an effort to build weapons systems designed to deter any aggressors, or if deterrence fails, to be able to soundly defeat them. One immediate concern raised by this reality is that the democracies will have severe shortages of these skill sets with both civilian and military employers drawing from the same talent pool in Cold War 2.0. (A cursory survey of job postings on LinkedIn clearly exhibits the high demand for these skill sets in both the civilian and military domains.) One advantage, though, that the democracies will enjoy in this talent war will be that students graduating from universities in various nonaligned countries will be more inclined to emigrate to democracies than autocracies, which will help alleviate somewhat tight labor markets in democracies for skills much in demand in a Cold War 2.0 world.

The complete fusion of the civilian and the military when it comes to modern technology is well illustrated by the stunning result achieved by Ukraine in eighteen months, facing the seemingly insurmountable odds presented by Russia's full-scale invasion of that country in February 2022. Suffice it to say that Russia had an army eight times larger than Ukraine's, and Russia's defense spending is ten times that of Ukraine. When Russia launched its multiple army groups across the Ukrainian border on February 24, 2022, literally no one gave Ukraine any chance of holding out for more than a couple of weeks. The United States immediately offered transport to Ukrainian president Zelenskyy so he could be flown to safety somewhere in Europe, where presumably he could try to rally an insurgency from some remote location. Zelenskyy refused "the ride," asking for weapons instead.

At every turn in the violent conflict, the Ukrainians have proven more technologically capable than the Russian invaders. Their improvised use of modified drones to achieve multiple objectives on the battlefield are now the stuff of legend. It's no coincidence that prior to the full-scale war some 300,000 Ukrainians worked in civilian information technology businesses, often servicing foreign tech clients in Europe or North America. In 2021 Ukraine's 5,000 tech companies exported some $6.8 billion in IT services, comprising 37 percent of its total exports. The value of this significant talent base has become manifest in the war against the Russians. The Ukrainians were able to take the modern weapons donated to them by forty-five democracies, promptly learn their high-tech features, and in very little time begin to push back the Russian enemy with them. Six months into the full-scale war, Ukraine was throwing back the Russians in two important sectors of the fighting, with the Ukrainians taking back thousands of acres of land that just months before was Russian occupied territory. From the vantage point of 2023 it is too early to tell how this war will end, but so far it can be concluded that Ukraine has been a cauldron of military innovation.

The Russo-Ukrainian War will have a wider resonance for Cold War 2.0 as well. Asia, and particularly China, is watching the European conflict closely, especially vis-à-vis Taiwan, and learning the lesson that if Taiwan hunkers down and presents a credible "hedgehog defense," China will have to pay an enormous cost if they wish to take Taiwan by force. Equally, though, the democracies are learning, much to the horror of their citizens, that ruthless autocrats are amenable to paying enormous costs for military conquest, especially when the currency they pay in is young men from rural districts, ethnic minorities, and prison populations. At the same time, Taiwan's hundreds of thousands of tech workers are also, nervously, absorbing important lessons about innovation, technology, and national power from the war in Ukraine. It will be interesting to see if young Taiwanese have increased their job searches in the US and Europe since the advent of the full-scale Russian invasion of Ukraine.

The foregoing analysis about technology and national economic and military power teaches a few prime lessons for the democracies relative to Cold War 2.0. Keep markets open and let competitive displacement work its magic. Regulation of particularly sensitive or dangerous innovation is fine, just not too early so that the regulation doesn't stifle innovation or overly benefit the larger companies in the technology domain. Another important, perhaps critical, insight: autocracies have great difficulty allowing competitive displacement to operate in the economies and technology domains of their countries because the autocrat and his enablers are too deeply invested in the incumbent monopolies and oligopolies that run the economy. As a result, technological innovation will never be as robust and vigorous in the autocracies as in the democracies. This gives huge advantage to the democracies in contesting the autocracies in Cold War 2.0, so long as the democracies don't waste this upper hand.

Principal advice to the democracies: don't fritter away the technological advantage you have courtesy of competitive displacement by allowing the autocrats among the democracies to come to power. Put another way, the autocracies will never be sufficiently technologically capable to be able to shoot down the democracies, so the democracies should avoid shooting themselves in the foot.

The other advice to the democracies: don't give the autocracies the weapons they can use to shoot down the democracies. Put in the vernacular: don't give the autocracies the rope they then use to hang the democracies. Therefore, the democracies must implement an effective program to stop the flow of advanced technologies to the autocracies, as this will stunt their economic prospects fairly materially, reducing their growth by 9 percent over ten years.[12] Given the degree of civilian-military fusion, this will also handicap the efforts of the autocracies in modernizing their weapons systems, and therefore make China, in particular, less confident about being able to prevail in an attack on Taiwan. The sanctions program around high-end SCs launched by the Biden administration in October 2022 therefore makes a lot of sense, but it is only a start. This should be followed by similar initiatives in other technology domains, including in AI, QCs, and biotechnology. And it is not enough simply to hope that the rest of the world will comply with these sanctions. The democracies must become much more muscular in enforcing these sanctions regimes.

2

COLD WAR 1: AUTOCRACY, DEMOCRACY, AND TECHNOLOGY

Cold War 1 was the defining geopolitical preoccupation of the world for the better part of forty years (1945 to 1989). It implicated the vast, globe-spanning ambitions of two divergent ideologies. It was fueled by two very different approaches to the design, development, and deployment of novel industrial, consumer, and military technologies. It spawned space technology and human space travel. It witnessed a divided world struggling to manage the kryptonite of its day—thousands of nuclear weapons. It came close to witnessing the carnage of an unimaginable nuclear war. Then, as the leading autocracy in the bipolar tango struggled to maintain technological pace with the leading democracy, many other inherent weaknesses of the autocracies emerged and ultimately took their toll. Finally, when the cement wall and Iron Curtain separating the two camps were dismantled by the bare hands of frustrated and hopeful citizens, the East Europeans were freed and the Germanies were reunited (but not the Koreas), all with hardly a burst of violence.

There are many differences between Cold War 2.0 and its predecessor. Nevertheless, there are certainly lessons to be learned from Cold War 1 that can help today's leaders navigate the treacherous waters of Cold War 2.0. A common reality of the two conflicts is that both involved democracies pitted against autocracies. This is important. Most international wars spring from domestic factors. Moreover, an autocrat who refuses to abide by the rule of law at home will never adhere to treaties abroad; it is utterly naive—and dangerous—for the leader of a democracy to think otherwise. At the same time, some leaders in democracies pine to be autocrats. And because they find it difficult to vent their autocratic fantasies domestically, they try to pull off the autocratic playbook in some of their foreign affairs. Hence the usefulness of comparing these two conceptions of life and politics at the very outset.

DEMOCRACY

Winston Churchill, Britain's prime minister during World War II, is reported to have said that a democracy is where the people own the government, and an autocracy is where the government owns the people. In essence, in a democracy the people get to decide who will form their government. This decision is exercised through fair, free, and credible elections, where multiple candidates (usually organized into diverse political parties) can stand for office (and no one can prohibit them from doing so), and an impartial organization supervises the election process to ensure it runs fairly in accordance with strict but neutral rules.

Winning an election gives the new government the legitimacy it requires to govern until the next election, typically to be held every four years. A key ground rule for elections in democracies is that if the political party in power loses the election, it will hand over power peacefully to the party that won the election, on the understanding that the winner will allow the losing party to continue to exist during the next four years, at which point it can contest the next election.

Democratic elections require that people be able to exercise key political rights, including the freedoms of speech and assembly (which includes having multiple political parties). If a candidate (especially one not in power) cannot talk to voters, directly or through the media, then the election is rigged, unfair, and not credible. Democracies protect these and other inherent political and legal rights regardless of which political party wins any particular election. Moreover, personal rights extend beyond the right to vote. They are central to the meaning of "democracy." Personal rights include being treated equally under the law, not being discriminated against, and should someone be arrested for a crime, being deemed innocent until and unless found guilty before an independent judge and a jury of peers.

Democracy requires a free press. Most people have neither the time nor the expertise to scrutinize what happens in government, a courtroom, a corporate board room, or any other place where power is exercised in society. Journalists must follow these proceedings as the impartial information proxy of the people. Armed with this information, people can debate the events of the day, form views as to whom they will vote for in the next election, and hold elected officials to account. The free press is also required to report on the ability (or inability) of people to exercise their rights. Particularly in our complex world, it is inconceivable that democracy could survive for a week without independent journalism.

Democracy requires the "rule of law." This means that laws are only made by the duly elected representatives of the people. It also means that no one in the country, not even the representatives elected to government or the president or prime minister, are immune from these laws—the law must apply to everyone and in the same way. Powerful, rich, or famous people are not treated better, or worse, under the law. Everyone is treated the same. No one in a democracy can behave with impunity; everyone must be subject to the laws passed by the democratically elected legislature.

Democracy and the rule of law require independent judges to interpret the laws and to apply them fairly and consistently. Similarly, the country's military, police, and state security services must be independent of the elected government, and subject as well to the rule of law: for instance, the police cannot search a suspect's house without a search warrant approved by an independent judge.

As for the economy, democracy requires an open market, albeit subject to reasonable regulation. "Open" means there are no material legal or political barriers to entry. "Regulation" means adherence to laws, such as those limiting pollution, safeguarding workers' rights, or providing oversight of risky financial businesses[1]—especially in the wake of the implosion of so many cryptocurrency-related businesses. And finally, the economic system, coupled with the rule of law, must allow for "competitive displacement."

A democracy requires *all* of the above elements. There are political systems missing some or other key piece (one of the three legs of the stool of democracy), but then these are not democracies. They are typically some form of autocracy, but they are not a democracy, and therefore shouldn't be called a democracy. The phrases "illiberal democracy," "minimalist democracy," "sovereign democracy," and "managed democracy" make no sense; the system they describe is an autocracy, and should be called an autocracy. On the other hand, a system that uses the phrase "flawed democracies" can be helpful.[2]

Democracy is rare. Since agriculture and cities began some 10,000 years ago, up until World War II, there were only a handful of democracies. It has been better for democracy over the last eighty years, but still today only about half the countries in the world are democracies. Many democracies slide into autocracy. These are usually "inside jobs" where a former leader who once believed in democracy, or at least was willing to behave himself, finally lifts his mask and plunges his country into autocracy.

AUTOCRACY

Autocracies differ markedly from democracies. Autocracy is the rule by a single individual, the autocrat. Autocrats achieve and maintain power with the help of "enablers" (typically including the most senior people in the army, police force, and security services), a few key politicians who throw their lot in with the autocrat, the top members of organized crime syndicates, powerful businesspeople, and some religious figures and cultural icons. These enablers are well paid by the autocrat to keep the autocrat in power. These enablers then pay off, or suppress, whomever they have to in order to preserve the power of the autocrat (and themselves, of course). This structured scaffolding of hierarchical power relations, payments, and suppression is required because the autocrat lacks the consensual legitimacy bestowed by fair, free, and credible elections—one of the three secret sauces of democracy. In the absence of a legitimating vote, the autocrat uses bribes and violence to secure and remain in power.

Autocracies don't hold elections, or if one is held (for show, as part of a propaganda campaign), it is meaningless because it is neither fair, free, nor credible. The autocrat and his (almost all autocrats are men) enablers are expert at rigging elections with false ballots, or they have the police (paid to be enablers of the autocrat) arrest the strongest opposition candidate(s) before the election campaign on false charges, such as fictional tax evasion—just enough to disqualify them from running for office. Sometimes the autocrat arranges for the murder of his opponent. This dissuades other good people from standing for election.

Autocrats govern without constraints, except for the rare one imposed by a powerful enabler. Autocrats typically destroy any non-enabler or any institution that attempts to serve as a check or balance against him. Autocrats rule with impunity, which means they can do as they please, subject to having to make good on certain promises made to enablers. At the same time, smart autocrats do realize that the people, if sufficiently hungry, will rise up and demand food, and then possibly freedom, and then more. To avoid these uprisings, some savvy autocrats share a little more of the country's wealth with the citizens, by increasing pension payments and the like. Autocrats who play the long game don't overly mind this, because they know they'll still have years and years in which to steal and embezzle from the public coffers of the state.

Succession in an autocracy can be a real problem, because there is no organized way to hand power from the incumbent autocrat to his chosen successor. It is very common for many people to be killed in the battle surrounding autocratic succession. Autocracy is not for the faint of heart.

Autocracies do not operate under the rule of law. There is instead the "rule of the autocrat." What the autocrat unilaterally decides has the force of law. In an autocracy there is the rule *by* law. Autocrats are expert at issuing—on their own and without anyone else's input—new laws reflecting their will, but there is no rule *of* law in the sense of the autocrat and his enablers being subject to independent judges.

The autocrat who doesn't abide by the rule of law domestically doesn't respect international law either. Autocrats tend to start wars much more often than leaders of democracies. Equally, when they are in a war, they do not respect the rules of war. They view international treaties as being for suckers; they'll sign them for show, but they adhere to them only sporadically and only for so long as it is in their interest to do so. Autocrats respect only brute force brought or marshaled against them. They have no sense of shame, but neither are they stupid, and they understand when they are outnumbered or outgunned.

There are no personal rights in an autocracy; there is no "private space" where someone is left alone to their own interests, their own lives. A citizen (even an enabler) cannot speak against the leader in public, let alone organize a protest or some other form of group assembly. Instead of an open economic market, in an autocracy all businesspeople need to follow the directions of the supreme leader. Even persons from outside the autocracy who operate a business inside the autocracy find themselves being muzzled.[3] Everyone in the autocracy either falls in line with the wishes of the autocrat, or they suffer significantly; often they are exiled out of the country, typically never to return. Even a once-powerful enabler can suffer this fate if the autocrat turns on them. Autocrats don't have long-term friends or allies, only expedient, short-term interests.

Judges in an autocracy don't exist to interpret the law fairly and impartially. Rather, the judge (who is in the pocket of the autocrat) determines the case in the manner dictated by the autocrat. To the extent the judge has any discretion, it can be purchased for a price—corruption runs rampant in the judicial system of autocracies. The same goes for the police, the army, and the state security services; they don't have any independence but rather do the bidding of the autocrat, as his personal hit squad and enforcement group. The autocrat buys off the senior leadership of the military, police, and state security services, along with the other enablers. Corruption is rampant as the autocrat typically allows his enablers to conduct illegal and unregulated side businesses of all types—in return for a cut of the action, of course.

Autocrats do not abide criticism, for the simple reason they don't have to. There is rarely any freedom of the press or speech, let alone assembly, in an autocracy. Autocrats despise the truth and anyone personally or professionally dedicated to finding out or disseminating the truth. An autocracy survives and thrives in a cesspool of lies, deception, censorship, and disinformation. Not surprisingly, independent journalists are enemy number one for the autocrat.[4] Life in an autocracy is therefore very risky for journalists who exercise the highest standards of their profession, allowing their stories to be driven by facts. Journalists who have contacts with foreigners are closely monitored by the state security police, and often arrested on fabricated espionage charges.[5] Foreign journalists often suffer the same fate at the hands of the autocrat.[6] Autocrats often have journalists murdered. In 2022, sixty-seven journalists around the world were killed, mainly in autocracies, simply for doing their job.[7] Autocrats also despise comedians who do political humor.[8] The degree to which a society is open and democracy-based can be gleaned from humor on offer at the local comedy club. In autocracies no jokes about the autocrat or the military are made in public places.

Autocrats are particularly horrified by public demonstrations against them. They read history and understand that very few autocrats over the last 250 years have died of natural causes in their old age while asleep in bed. Rather, over the last two and a half centuries disgruntled citizens have on many occasions hanged autocrats (sometimes with piano wire), or caused their heads to be otherwise severed from their bodies, typically when the country's great mass of ordinary people have been oppressed by the autocrat to the breaking point. Or he dies in a coup orchestrated by an enabler who wishes to be the new autocrat. The newcomer autocrat becomes so by bribing the head of the army, police, or security services with more money than the incumbent autocrat.

The autocrat understands the risk of a violent end to his career, and he works hard to avoid it. His best-case scenario is to park several billion embezzled dollars in an offshore bank account, and to buy a large estate on a small, secluded island in the territory of another autocrat. The fleeing autocrat will escape to this tranquil place when he hears the shouts of angry citizens, or the clicking heels of the boots of the soldiers of the next autocrat, coming for him.

AUTOCRACY WITH RUSSIAN CHARACTERISTICS

Cold War 1 started around 1945, but it is important to understand how Lenin and Stalin ruled Russia in the previous twenty-five years in order to really grasp how Cold War 1 worked from the Russian perspective. Vladimir Ilyich Lenin was the first communist autocrat leader of Russia. He came to power in late 1917. Russia entered World War I in 1914; by 1916 the war against Germany was going very poorly for Russia. The Russian autocrat-king at the time was Tsar Nicholas II. (*Tsar* means *king* in Russian; a Russification of the word *caesar*, referring to autocrat emperors of ancient Rome.) Nicholas II moved to the battlefront to try to boost morale among the Russian soldiers, but by early 1917 many were mutinying. A liberal politician, Alexander Kerensky, convinced Nicholas II to abdicate in February of 1917. The tsar and his family were put up at a country estate outside of Moscow, while Kerensky convened a constituent assembly to elect a government committed to democracy.

Lenin was a Communist. He followed the teachings of German-born philosopher Karl Marx, who called for workers to revolt against the capitalists who owned the factories. Marx's political philosophy predicted that under communism the workers would eventually own all the means of production, including factories and farms. Lenin was a shrewd political organizer, and he had the Russian Communists run hard in the elections for Kerensky's Constituent Assembly. Nevertheless, Lenin's Communists garnered only 24 percent of the seats, and as such Lenin was not going to be able to implement his Marxist communist manifesto through the ballot box as he originally planned. Good autocrat that he was, however, Lenin orchestrated a coup in the fall of 1917, in which the Communists took over the government of Russia by military force, and the Constituent Assembly was dissolved—autocrats have no need for such institutions of democracy. Today, Putin keeps the Duma around to give a patina of democracy to his ruthless autocratic governing style, but the scales fall from the eyes when the Duma regularly votes unanimously in favor of some legislation proposed by Putin.

To solidify his position, Lenin created the Cheka, the powerful and frightful state security police dedicated to keeping the Russian Communist Party (RCP) in power by force of arms. The Cheka looked and acted a lot like the tsar's previous state security police (the Okhrana), which is not that surprising as Tsar Nicholas II was a supreme autocrat, as were his Romanov dynasty predecessors since 1613. The Cheka, in the 1920s and 1930s (it changed its name several times, becoming the NKVD in 1924), instituted a "terror" by continually rounding up real and fictional enemies of the state, and either executing them or sending them to labor or concentration camps. There, prisoners, after a few years hard labor, typically perished from overwork and insufficient food. Again, these autocratic RCP tactics didn't change much from the tsar's equivalent system, just as today. Putin's FSB is a worthy successor to the Cheka, NKVD, and KGB in terms of its use of intimidation, baseless arrest, and thuggery.

Lenin had one of his most trusted colleagues, Leon Trotsky, create a new military force, the Red Army, that was wholly loyal to the new autocratic regime. Lenin also had another key compatriot, Joseph Jughashvili, more commonly known by his "nom de guerre" Stalin, which means *steel* in Russian. They traveled around the Russian Empire and make all the ethnic republics (conquered by the Russian tsars over the previous 400 years) into communist "soviets" that were still clearly under the direct control of Moscow. This was a critical exercise. In the wake of World War I, the Austro-Hungarian land empire had collapsed, giving rise to a number of new nation-states in the heart of Europe, such as Czechoslovakia. The Ottoman Empire collapsed at the same time, allowing several new states in the Balkans to emerge, such as Croatia and Serbia. The German Empire's foreign colonies were spun out into new, stand-alone countries. The great wave of 20th century decolonization was underway—everywhere except in Russia. Contrary to one of the fundamental trends of the 20th century, namely decolonization, Lenin and Stalin were very careful to ensure that the Russian land empire continued as before, albeit under new management. Putin's actions since coming to power in 2012 can in large part be understood as continuing this imperial agenda.

In the 1920s and 1930s Lenin and Stalin restructured Russian society and its economy in line with communist autocratic principles. Communist Russia became a one-party state. The only political party that was allowed was the Russian Communist Party. It is critical to appreciate that a political party in the democracies is vastly different than the RCP, or today's Chinese Communist Party (CCP). The RCP before the collapse of Soviet Russia in 1991, and the CCP since 1949 (and going strong to this day) is the most important institution in its country by far. In a democracy a political party is a convenient way to bring together like-minded political supporters for the purpose of contesting an election. Between elections the party virtually lies dormant, focusing largely on raising funds for the next election. By contrast, in communist autocracies the party is the vanguard of the Revolution, and the Revolution never ends, it is continually ongoing; hence the communist party is constantly engaged in every minute aspect of the lives of all citizens. Plus, it runs the government. The communist autocratic party is a cross between an army at war and a cult following of the leader. It is everything. Although no longer a communist, today's supreme Russian autocrat Putin cultivates a similar image and position in Russian society.

In Soviet Russia, after the 1917 communist takeover, the RCP nationalized all the factories and land, including farms. RCP bureaucrats in

Moscow implemented autocratic economics. The RCP would henceforth alone determine what and how much factories and farms would produce. The state received all products and crops, which the RCP then redistributed across the country as the RCP saw fit, at prices determined by the RCP. The RCP also dictated who would live in which apartments, and in which cities. All economic and political decisions were made by the RCP, and within the RCP Lenin (and after his death in 1924, Stalin) had the first and last word.

People who stood in the way of the RCP, or today the CCP in China, simply get mowed down. Lenin and Stalin were on a mission, and they didn't let anyone stand in their way. Millions of peasants in Russia (and later in China as well) didn't want to work for collective farms; they were summarily murdered or left to starve when their crops were forcibly taken away by the state. In Ukraine, an "autonomous Soviet republic" within the Russian Soviet Union, this rural social reengineering included the "Holodomor," where millions of Ukrainians perished in a man-made famine. Lenin and Stalin justified these deaths, and millions of others, as the necessary cost to be paid to transform Russia into a communist workers' paradise. The only political leader more deadly than a regular autocrat is one who believes he is implementing a compelling universal system of values and social organization. Chairman Mao, China's first communist autocrat leader from 1949 to 1976, implemented a similar universal social system, and caused the premature deaths of approximately 30 million people as a result. Of course the nirvana of a workers' paradise never did come to pass in either Russia or China, but that misses the point—the autocrats intended to do it, and that end, in the minds of Lenin, Stalin, and Mao, justified their horrible means. History is rhyming again when this utter disregard for human life is compared to Putin sending tens of thousands of young untrained conscripts to their reckless deaths in the full-scale invasion of Ukraine in 2022–2023.

It gets worse. One of the problems with autocrats is that after a lengthy time in office (because there are no term limits in autocracies) they become paranoid. They believe that a large number of people inside (and outside) the country are actively trying to kill them—which is not an entirely erroneous thought, because killing an autocrat is the only way to unseat one from power. When Stalin had these paranoid fears in the late 1930s he had the NKVD (the state security police) kill about 20,000 members of the officer corps in the Russian army, as Stalin believed they were all plotting coups against him. The losses were heaviest at the very senior levels: 11 of 13 army commanders, 57 of 85 corps commanders, and 110 of 195 division commanders. Tens of thousands of other important contributors to Soviet Russian society, from scientists and engineers to cultural figures, were murdered in these "purges" in the late 1930s. The "lucky" ones were merely sent to prison labor camps in Siberia, from which many never returned, as they were fed insufficient calories to survive the brutal conditions.[9] Trotsky, once Stalin's most trusted comrade in arms, fled Russia into exile. He was hunted down by the NKVD in Mexico and murdered with an ice axe. The fatal blow saw the adze of the axe penetrate 7 cm into his brain. The NKVD agent who murdered Trotsky served twenty years in a Mexican prison. When he was released he returned to Soviet Russia, where the autocrat of the day, Leonid Brezhnev, and the head of the KGB presented him with three medals "for the special deed."

Another core defect with autocracy is that the autocrat's "solo" decision-making produces very poor decisions. For example, in the 1930s Stalin watched with concern as Hitler, Europe's other megalomaniac autocratic leader, swallowed up one central European territory after another: first the Saarland in 1935, then the Sudetenland (in Czechoslovakia) and Austria in 1938. Stalin worried that Hitler would eventually come after Russia, and so Stalin was greatly relieved when Hitler offered Stalin a peace deal contained in an agreement called the Molotov-Ribbentrop Pact. In this arrangement the two autocrats agreed not to attack each other. Instead, they both agreed to attack Poland and carve it up completely between the two of them, which they promptly did a month later (in September 1939). Stalin thought this was a masterful joint autocratic solution to satiate Germany's stated expansion plans to the East (and Russia got a big chunk of land out of Poland as well), but his advisors warned this was just Hitler buying time and tying down Russia while Germany attacked and captured all of Western Europe. Stalin disagreed and countered that he knew how to handle Hitler. Stalin was wrong, and was deeply shocked and gravely disappointed when Hitler, on June 22, 1941, unleashed on Russia the largest invasion army ever assembled before or since—a total of 3.6 million soldiers, 3,000 tanks, 2,500 aircraft. [10]

Stalin the ruthless autocrat grossly underestimated Hitler. Presumably Stalin also greatly regretted murdering so many of his army's top officers just a few years before. How many fewer Russians would have died fighting the Germans (and fewer Russian civilians killed by the Germans) had the Russian troops had the benefit of the thousands of seasoned military (and other) leaders that Stalin had executed in the late 1930s? Autocracy simply doesn't produce high-quality decisions. This is a major lesson to be drawn from Cold War 1, and in respect of Cold War 2.0, Putin's full-scale invasion of Ukraine is a similar colossal decision-making blunder.

COLD WAR 1

Largely because of the horrendous losses suffered by Russia at the hands of the Germans in World War II, Stalin insisted, in his negotiation with American president Franklin Delano Roosevelt (FDR) and British prime minister Winston Churchill on the security structure of postwar Europe, that nine countries in Eastern Europe be added to the Russian Empire. They were Estonia, Latvia, and Lithuania (fully incorporated into Russia proper), plus Bulgaria, Czechoslovakia, East Germany, Hungary, Poland, and Romania—collectively, the "East Bloc"—as client states. FDR wasn't happy about the loss of Eastern Europe to the Russian Communists as "buffer states" against a someday possibly resurgent Germany, but he couldn't afford to confront Stalin because FDR thought he might need the Russians to help the Americans fight the Japanese.

Stalin originally hoped that communist governments friendly to Russia would be elected in all of the nine countries comprising the East Bloc in the first elections after the war ended. In fact, in each country—in *all* nine countries—the communists were soundly defeated at the polls. No country chose to voluntarily live under a communist autocratic political and economic system. Having been thwarted at the ballot box, Stalin ordered his state security police to install by force communist governments in the East Bloc countries that were loyal to Moscow. [11] By 1948 the job was complete, including by a brazen coup in Prague, where the state security police threw Jan Masaryk, the foreign minister of Czechoslovakia, out a fourth-floor bathroom window to his death because he would not collaborate with the autocrats. History keeps rhyming. Stalin installed one-party autocratic governments in each East Bloc country after failing to succeed at the ballot box—just as Lenin had orchestrated a violent autocratic coup in Moscow thirty years before when he failed at the ballot box. It is no wonder autocrats abhor democracy—they never do well when the people have a say in choosing their government.

What then began for the nine East Bloc countries was forty-five years of communist autocracy, where there were no free, fair, or credible elections; citizens had no personal freedoms such as freedom of speech or assembly; there was no rule of law; judges were not independent; there was no freedom of the press; the communist autocrats destroyed any vestige of civil society (such as private charities, or clubs like Boy Scouts and Girl Scouts, each having been replaced by state-run communist youth leagues); and the autocrats instituted fully the Russian system of economic autocracy where bureaucrats in the central government ran every aspect of the production of goods and services. As Churchill proclaimed at the time, an "Iron Curtain" had been drawn across Eastern Europe by the Soviet Russians. [12]

Meanwhile, democracy continued in the UK, with Churchill being voted out of office in July 1945, a truly astounding result given that he was *the* war hero prime minister who rallied the country to persevere during the darkest days of the 1940 blitz, when England stood alone against the autocratic Nazi menace, France having been defeated a few weeks before. This is, however, precisely the essence of democracy. The British people knew the war was about to end, they were exhausted of it, and they wanted a different leader to take them into the postwar world. This is the genius, the magic, and the allure of democracy. Stalin must have smiled ruefully when he heard Churchill did not win reelection, particularly as Stalin did not have to worry about such niceties as elections so long as he kept secret police chief Lavrentiy Beria busy killing Stalin's real and imaginary enemies in Russia, and later in the East Bloc as well.

A few years later, democracy delivered another surprise, this time in the United States, when in November 1948 Harry Truman was elected president. The heavy favorite to win was the Republican governor of New York, Thomas Dewey. There is a famous photo of Truman holding up the front page of the *Chicago Daily Tribune* with the banner headline DEWEY DEFEATS TRUMAN. This Truman victory, and Churchill's loss in 1945, are emblematic of what can happen in a democracy when the people truly get to decide. In an autocracy the people merely get to endure. (Incidentally, Churchill was reelected in 1951, and served again as the country's prime minister until 1955, another interesting twist for British democracy.)

An early test in Cold War 1 of the willingness and ability of the democracies to stand up against the autocrat in Moscow began in June 1948 in Berlin. This city was in Russian-administered East Germany, but the three other occupying powers (the United States, the UK, and France) also administered sectors of Berlin, in addition to overseeing respective regions in what was then West Germany. Stalin resented the presence of the democracies in Berlin, and he tried forcing them to leave by closing the route that the democracies were previously using to travel between West Berlin and West Germany across East Germany. Stalin anticipated that this "Berlin Blockade" would "starve" the democracies out of West Berlin.

Stalin's plan did not work. Truman launched a massive armada of US Air Force planes to supply vast amounts of provisions to West Berliners. Each day up to 1,400 US planes landed at Berlin's Tempelhof Airport with food and other provisions. Stalin was very angry, but he was sure the Americans would give up quickly from exhaustion. The US did not quit. Finally, on May 12, 1949, it was Stalin who threw in the towel by terminating the siege. Thereafter, until the fall of the Berlin Wall in 1989, the democracies were able to supply West Berlin using the overland route, and eventually they even used a railway that linked Berlin to West Germany. The democracies stood firm and stared down the autocratic Russian bully. This is a fine lesson for Cold War 2.0.

Given how Russia had installed communist autocratic governments in the East Bloc countries, and how Stalin tried to eject the democracies from West Berlin, the Western European countries worried that Russia would invade them next. The new United Nations Charter enshrined the principle of national sovereignty and inviolable borders, but the problem with the UN system was that Russia could veto any military effort by the UN to act against Russian aggression. This is exactly what happened in Cold War 2.0 when, on February 24, 2022, Russia (an autocracy) commenced its full-scale military invasion of Ukraine (a democracy), and the next day Russia blocked any action by the United Nations Security Council to exercise its veto. Therefore, the desire of Western European countries in the late 1940s to guard against further communist expansion into their own territories would require them to undertake "self-help" defensive measures.

In March 1948 five Western European countries (Belgium, France, Luxembourg, the Netherlands, and the United Kingdom) formed a mutual defense alliance called the Treaty of Brussels. (The French and British had actually started the ball rolling with their mutual defense treaty signed in 1947, the Treaty of Dunkirk.) Such "collective defense" is permitted under the UN system. The core principle in the Treaty of Brussels was that an attack against one country would be considered an attack against all of them; their collective defense posture was intended to deter any military aggression against them by Russia.

Realizing that strength in numbers was desirable in collective defense arrangements, other democracies were invited to join the Treaty of Brussels. The result was the North Atlantic Treaty Organization (NATO), created in April 1949. Ironically, Stalin's intention to weaken Western Europe through the Berlin Blockade instead strengthened Western Europe by inspiring the creation of NATO, just as Putin's invasion of Ukraine in 2022 in order to weaken NATO actually had the opposite effect by prompting Finland to join NATO. Back in 1949, NATO comprised the five Treaty of Brussels countries, plus the United States and Canada, and also European countries Denmark, Iceland, Italy, Norway, Portugal, and, joining in 1955, West Germany. NATO continues to thrive to this day—some seventy-five years later, now with thirty-one member states—as the most successful collective defense arrangement in history. Its Article 5 provides that an attack against any NATO member is considered an attack against all NATO countries. In practical terms, it is often said NATO has succeeded in "Keeping the United States in, the Russians out, and the Germans down."

In parallel with NATO collective military security, the democracies moved quickly to rebuild the economies and civil societies of countries in Western Europe, as leaders believed communism could succeed in taking over a democracy if it had high unemployment or low living standards. The Americans launched the Marshall Fund, which provided loans and grants to sixteen West European countries. The Marshall Fund disbursed about $13 billion—around $150 billion in today's money—mainly on rebuilding infrastructure like power plants, transport, and steel production, but some funds were also spent on technical assistance to improve productivity in manufacturing plants. Western Europeans themselves promoted economic rehabilitation by forming the European Economic Community in 1957, which survives to this day as the European Union (EU). Currently the EU comprises twenty-seven countries, all democracies (though some with serious flaws) that have agreed to tightly integrate their economies, including in respect of the movement of goods, people, and capital. These measures have made the region more prosperous, which in turn makes it more peaceful and secure from outside invasion.

The various efforts to rebuild an entire Europe of democracies worked. Today, the EU is a thriving community of 450 million people. In particular, the rehabilitation of the war-torn autocratic Nazi Germany, both economically and then as a solid bastion of democracy, has been nothing short of spectacular. When West Germany hosted the Olympic Games in 1972 and the soccer World Cup two years later, East Germans, the rest of the East Bloc, and Russians all looked on with envy at the magnificent sports facilities in Munich and the other cities that had been rebuilt from the rubble of World War II. Today, with the world's fourth-largest economy, and regular peaceful transfers of power between different political parties through fair, free, and credible elections, reunited Germany is a marvelous economic and political success story, similar to that of Asian democracies Japan, South Korea, and Taiwan.

A second major early test of the democracies in Cold War 1 was a hot war started on June 25, 1950, when 223,000 troops of the autocratic communist government of North Korea invaded South Korea over the 38th Parallel, running across the Korean Peninsula. After World War II, Korea was divided in a fashion similar to East and West Germany, and the Russians installed a puppet regime in the North, under the new communist autocratic leader Kim Il-Sung. Kim had studied in Moscow during World War II, where he was being prepared to take over all of Korea. Kim's attack on South Korea was approved by Moscow and Beijing, as China had become an autocratic communist state in 1949 under Mao Zedong. It started the Korean War, which in terms of the fighting lasted until 1953, but the two countries still haven't signed an official peace treaty. The initial shock of the invasion worked, and communist troops from North Korea captured Seoul, the capital city of the South Korea, in a matter of days.

In response to North Korea's unjustified aggression, the United Nations Security Council quickly authorized a military force to fight back against Kim's army. (Russia did not veto the action because it was temporarily boycotting the UN.) After three years of very bloody fighting—more bombs were dropped in the Korean War than in all of World War II—the UN forces, under the command of General Douglas MacArthur, fought the North Koreans back to the 38th Parallel. The US commanded the multinational force because it supplied 1.78 million troops, with about 1.5 million coming from South Korea, 100,000 from Britain, and 25,000 from Canada, and smaller numbers still from another eighteen countries. At one point the UN force pushed the North Korean army right up to the Chinese border, and were about to claim the entire peninsula for the South Korean government when China launched an attack of 700,000 troops (a total of

2 million Chinese soldiers would see action over the course of the war) to save Kim's communist government. South Korea never forgot the role the US played in preserving their country. During the Vietnam War, South Korea sent a total of 350,000 troops to support the Americans in trying to keep the communist North Vietnamese from capturing South Vietnam. (The Americans supplied 550,000 troops.)

Russia's willingness to use military force in proxy hot wars against the democracies (and states wanting to become democracies) continued even after Stalin's death in 1953. Stalin's successor, Nikita Khrushchev, initially signaled a possible thaw in Russia's autocratic ways when he gave a six-hour speech to the 20th RCP Congress in March 1956 describing in detail Stalin's many crimes, including the bloody purges of the 1930s and his catastrophic military decisions. Sensing possible room for maneuver, a few local leaders in the East Bloc countries began to test the bounds of Russian authority. In June 1956 there were short-lived riots in Poland.

In October 1956, Hungary's Imre Nagy proposed limited reforms (including multiple candidates for elections), and some distance from Russia in economic policy. University students in Budapest, Hungary's capital, supported Nagy, but wanted to go further. They started to protest Russia's military occupation of Hungary. Events escalated into a violent uprising, with workers joining in cities and towns all over Hungary. Initially, it appeared the Russians might pull out of their vassal state, but on November 4, 1956, Russian tanks and infantry entered Hungary and brutally put down the demonstrators. A war of independence ensued, and 25,000 Hungarian freedom fighters were killed by Russian troops. More than 250,000 Hungarian refugees (from a population of 9.8 million) fled to democracies.[13] Nagy and a dozen of his coleaders were tried for treason; he and five others were executed, and the rest received ten-year prison terms. The brief flicker of the flame of democracy along the Danube River was snuffed out. Post-Stalin, Cold War 1 was still a treacherous, dangerous time for would-be builders of democracy behind the Iron Curtain.

Russia's ambassador to Hungary during this period was Yuri Andropov. He was very hawkish on crushing the Hungarian freedom movement. He played a decisive role in ensuring a bloody Russian crackdown. Subsequently, Andropov was elevated to the head of the KGB (the state security police), and later still (November 1982) he was appointed the paramount leader of Soviet Russia. (He served only fifteen months before he died of kidney failure.) In terms of his legacy, Andropov was Putin's role model, and later in life Putin's mentor. There is a clear parallel between Putin's violent crushing of nationalist movements in Chechnya, Georgia, and Ukraine in the 21st century and Andropov's hard-line treatment of Hungary in 1956.

In Prague in 1968 a similar script played out, when Czech communist leader Alexander Dubcek called for reforms of that country's autocratic economic and political systems. Once again, the Russians sent in their tanks, but this time the Czechs didn't even try to fight, knowing the cause would be hopeless—they had seen the significant blood spilled in vain in Budapest ten years earlier.

In both the Hungarian Revolution of 1956 and the "Prague Spring" of 1968, the East Bloc countries hoped that the West, and at least the Americans, would give some support to their liberation movements, but troops from democracies never materialized. Not even military equipment was shipped to the freedom fighters. Still, televised images were beamed into East Bloc households showing how well middle-class people lived in the democracies. East Bloc residents saw open markets in the democracies producing, and their average citizens enjoying, abundant quantities of high-quality consumer goods. It was crystal clear that autocratic, top-down central planning, Russian and East Bloc style, was not providing sufficient necessities of life, let alone the middle-class comforts that the democracies were showering on their citizens.

The economic statistics supported the images. Underpinned by American leadership, from 1950 to 1990 the economies of the democracies grew at roughly 3.5 percent per year. The autocracies, by contrast, grew at roughly the same rate between 1950 and 1975 (but mainly by investment in heavy industry), but then declined in the following ten years to 2.1 percent annually, and finally between 1985 and the early 1990s annual economic growth in Soviet Russia collapsed to 1.3 percent. Moreover, much more of the economic growth in Russia was allocated to the production of industrial goods and spent on military expenditures than in the democracies. This would exacerbate the chasm between the standards of living of consumers in the two camps. Recall that at an annual 3.5 percent growth rate, wealth doubles every twenty years, while at 2 percent economic growth wealth doubles only every thirty-six years.

By the 1970s the economic race of Cold War 1 was being handily won by the democracies. This could have gone on indefinitely had the East Bloc not been right beside Western Europe, as East Germany, after all, shared a 1,381-kilometer border with West Germany. With such physical, cultural, and visible proximity, the discrepancy between the two camps became untenable. The parallel with Cold War 2.0 is striking, except the item of envy in the 2010s was not only economic wealth but also democracy itself. Putin concluded that he could not long keep his country shrouded in a closed autocracy when neighboring Ukraine blossomed into an open democracy oriented westward toward the European Union.

CORRUPTION AS A FEATURE, NOT A BUG, OF AUTOCRACY

A further important difference between the two systems was that the amount of corruption in the autocracies far exceeded that in the democracies. While no political system is completely immune from it, in democracies corruption is a bug in the system and an affront to the rule of law, and law enforcement will pursue when the corruption is discovered. By contrast, in autocracies corruption is a central feature of the system and derives directly from the fact that a single, supreme leader runs the country with complete impunity. A couple of firsthand accounts of corruption in an autocracy during Cold War 1 involving the author will help illuminate the phenomenon.

In 1984 I had to obtain a visa to travel to autocratic, communist Hungary. The clerk at the Hungarian embassy in Paris explained their office would require forty-eight hours to process my visa. I responded that this timing didn't work for me as I had a train to catch the next morning. "Ah," the clerk exclaimed, "then you will want the *expedited* visa processing service. We can process your visa right now, but the fee would be double the regular price." I handed over the additional money. To my amazement, she tucked it into her purse—right in front of my eyes! (She had already put the "regular" fee into the official cash register.) She then called to her colleague to stick the visa paper into my passport, which she then stamped. The visa processing exercise took them two minutes, as they didn't do any background checks or anything else. Frankly, the entire visa charade existed to squeeze some money out of foreign visitors; the expedited service was a corrupt practice that lined the pockets of petty bureaucrats. A democracy might also have an "expedited processing fee" for some service, but the additional money would also go to the government.

At the end of the same trip, I had a few forints (the Hungarian currency) left in my pocket. The stern-looking border guard asked me whether I had any forints, and reminded me that taking forints out of Hungary was a criminal offense. I sheepishly rifled through my pockets and knapsack and found a few scrawny forint banknotes, amounting to about $10 in value. I pulled them out and showed them to the guard. I thought she would get angry with me. Instead, to my surprise, she pulled out a suitcase from under her counter and opened it to reveal a wide assortment of Hungarian souvenirs, like crocheted tablecloths and napkins. "Lucky for you," she cheerily intoned (her demeanor having changed now that she was in sales mode), "I happen to have some handicrafts you can spend your last forints on," which of course I dutifully did, all the while feeling queasy about the large pistol on her gun belt.

While these examples were fairly minor in nature, more serious incidences of corruption can have very serious impacts on the system that allows it, let alone fosters it. When Russia commenced its full-scale invasion of Ukraine in February 2022, the column of Russian tanks and supply vehicles heading for Kyiv ground to a halt a few kilometers inside the Ukrainian border. One reason for the holdup was the fierce resistance put up by incredibly brave Ukrainian soldiers using shoulder-launched anti-tank missiles to wreak havoc on Russia's mechanized brigades. Also at play, though, was that the tires on many Russian trucks gave out. It turns out the Russian vehicles had not been properly maintained. Russian military officers responsible for procuring maintenance services simply pocketed the maintenance funds themselves.

There is far more corruption in autocracies than democracies. Transparency International,[14] which tracks corruption around the world, ranks Russia and China among the most corrupt. For example, President Putin's official annual salary is about $122,000, yet since taking office in 2000 he has accumulated a personal fortune estimated to be between $70 and $200 billion.[15] Among his assets are two gigantic mansions, one on the Black Sea coast and a newer, custom-built 75,000-square-foot dacha (the master bedroom is 2,800 square feet) in the forests outside Moscow, where his mistress, Alina Kabaeva, and their two children reside. Russian democracy activist Alexei Navalny has bravely brought this corruption to the attention of the Russian people—and the rest of the world—and now Navalny will likely literally rot in a Russian prison for more than thirty years on trumped-up charges brought by Putin.[16]

Then there is the endemic, systemic corruption whereby the autocrat and his enablers always do much better economically than the rest of the citizens. Throughout Cold War 1 there was immense disparity in consumption of consumer goods between the RCP elite and the mass of other Russians. Consumer goods were always in short supply for average Russian citizens—other than RCP elites. In Soviet Russia's system of economic autocracy, most state spending went on heavy industry and the military-industrial complex (MIC), which designed and manufactured weapons and especially rockets and nuclear warheads. There was little money allocated to the everyday household goods that were increasingly taken for granted by growing middle classes in democracies, such as modern houses and apartments, cars, household appliances, and (in democracies) the all-important winter vacation taken in a warm southern country.

By contrast, Russian citizens, even those in the big cities of Moscow and St. Petersburg, generally didn't own a car and lived in tiny apartments.

(Putin, in the 1960s, grew up in a flat where they shared the bathroom with another family, and he chased rats in the building's stairwell.) They also wore tired clothes. I remember buying a pair of shoes in Budapest in the late 1970s. There was nothing on the shelves of a regular shoe store except the single style of dark gray, clunky communist footwear. The store manager saw I was an unimpressed tourist. He motioned me to the back room, where he showed me a gorgeous pair of shoes made in Italy of supple leather. I paid a king's ransom for them relative to the cost of the shoes made in Hungary, but they were worth it. Regular Hungarians, without foreign currency, had to buy the depressing shoes found in the front of the store; foreign tourists with hard currency and members of the Hungarian political elite—friends and contacts of the autocrat and other enablers—got to shop in the back room where the superior stock was located.

Most infuriatingly, regular people in the East Bloc and Russia had to stand in line to buy even basic groceries. Most of the time the common grocery stores had shortages of even basic foodstuffs, like meat, milk, and eggs. I remember visiting Moscow in the early 1980s and walking through a regular grocery store. The only item in abundance was candy. Otherwise, the shelves were sparse or altogether bare. In the meat section there was actually nothing on the refrigerated shelves. Then there was a commotion because the staff was putting out some hams. People swarmed about grasping one or two while they could. I looked more closely at the hams. In North America they would be solid meat with a ribbon or two of fat. These Russian hams were the opposite, entirely white fat with a speckle of dark meat. I was astounded, and I felt bad for the average Russian.

I felt even worse for them the next day when I visited one of the stores for the RCP elite. A guard at the door kept out regular Russian citizens, but the store had windows onto the street so average Russians could see what the RCP members were buying. What they saw was close to a grocery store in a democracy, with lots of food and modern household items sourced from Western Europe. Here was the classic example of endemic, systemic corruption, because the average Russian could not shop there; entry was restricted to members of the Russian elite or tourists with "hard" currency, as I was.

To me, this astoundingly unequal duality in economic opportunity—the autocrat and the enablers enjoying the gravy of the country, everyone else scraping for crumbs—was one of the strongest indictments of autocratic systems. I wondered: How did the Russian masses allow this kind of consumer apartheid to go on? My question was answered in 1989–1991 when the Soviet Russian system of economic autocracy fell apart, and their autocratic political system collapsed along with it, bringing Cold War 1 to an end—although the political autocracy and various elements of the autocratic economy were resuscitated under Putin in 2000.

HIGH TECH WITH RUSSIAN AUTOCRATIC CHARACTERISTICS

Russia has lagged behind the democracies in technology and innovation for more than 300 years. Russian tsar Peter II learned on his 1717 trip to Western Europe just how backward Russia was, and in 1724 established the Russian Academy of Sciences, modeled on the German equivalent. Tsar Peter and his descendants, especially Tsarina Catherine II, also brought German professors to St. Petersburg to teach Russian university students the latest trends in science. For the past 300 years, Russian scientists have done a passable job in keeping abreast of the latest in science. Where Russia faltered, though, was in translating science into commercial technology that could be used by businesses or, in the last one hundred years, by consumers. The principal reason for this shortcoming was the hierarchical, top-down autocratic political structure endemic in Russia.

Stalin understood the importance of science and technology, but he did not trust scientists. He had hundreds of scientists murdered during the "terror" and purges of the 1930s. Many scientists escaped Russia even earlier when they saw the communist writing on the wall. One high-profile emigrant was Igor Sikorsky, a world-class aeronautical engineer who left Russia in 1918 within months of Lenin seizing autocratic power. He invented a working helicopter while still in Russia, but the commercial exploitation of his innovation all happened in the United States. To this day, the giant military contractor Lockheed Martin operates a large rotary wing division (making military and civilian helicopters) under the Sikorsky brand. (A predecessor to Lockheed Martin purchased Sikorsky's company decades earlier.)

The core problem with Russian autocracy relative to the development of science and technology innovation is that the autocrat—whether tsar or leader of the Communist Party or, since 2000, Putin—holds stifling and overbearing personal power. During and after World War II, Stalin disliked computers and their precursor, cybernetics. As a result, computer science was essentially banned during Stalin's lifetime. Stalin thought computers were a plot created by capitalists. He had more time for nuclear weapons, but in the early years of World War II he emphasized conventional technology that would be embedded in tanks and airplanes as he needed those desperately to repel the German army. He allowed several Russian scientists to tinker with nuclear science, but he didn't really grasp the importance of it and so the field lay fallow. The United States, by contrast, invested heavily in building a nuclear bomb during World War II, as outlined in the previous chapter. For their part, the Russian physicists learned the theory behind the atomic bomb, but they were denied the means (the labs, the staff, etc.) to create the technology of nuclear weapons.

This all changed very dramatically when the US dropped two nuclear bombs on Japan in 1945. Stalin then understood the importance of nuclear weapons. Russia, though, was woefully behind the democracies in nuclear research, especially the technology required to make a nuclear bomb. Stalin's response was taken from the autocrat's playbook—he ordered his state security police to purloin from the Americans their secrets so that the Russians could catch up to the US. In short, Stalin's approach was if you can't make it, steal it. This has been the motto for Russian (and Chinese) R&D for decades. Tellingly, because he promoted theft rather than research, Stalin put his trusted lieutenant—head of Russia's much feared state security police—Lavrenty Beria in charge of the world's most important technology espionage project, in addition to Beria's "day job" of murdering people identified by Stalin.

Beria was very successful in stealing plans for the US atomic bomb and its complex associated technology. He created a spy ring within the United States, Britain, and Canada that was able to steal copies of all facets of the design and technology innovation behind the US nuclear bombs. Armed with this industrial espionage gold rush, Russia tested its first atomic weapon in August 1949. It was an exact replica of the US bomb. The Russians, with spies like Klaus Fuchs, also stole plans for America's hydrogen bombs. The Russians tested their first hydrogen bomb in 1953, only one year after the Americans unveiled theirs. The Russians profited immensely from their parasitic model of intellectual property theft.

Stalin built an entire separate city, Arzamas-16, dedicated to housing the scientists and technologists building atomic weapons. These people and their families, and other scientific and engineering talents in forty-one other such closed cities (for example, Zelenograd, dedicated to micro-electronics), were treated very well in terms of access to consumer goods, and even products sourced from democracies. They were a pampered lot, living as members of an exclusive club. These cities were literally closed off to the rest of Russia, let alone the world. Entry was closely controlled by the KGB. The average Russian couldn't just walk around these special cities and have a coffee, let alone decide they wanted to live there. For a communist regime supposedly creating a classless society, these forty-two closed science and military-industrial complex (MIC) cities were a rebuke to such lofty intentions.

Of these closed cities, thirty-three were built to service the military domain, which included the space sector. Collectively the people, research institutes, and companies in these thirty-three cities comprised the MIC of Soviet Russia. Russia's MIC compromised some 2 million direct employees, working in about 300 R&D establishments and another 3,000 manufacturing facilities. As with the nuclear community described above, the members of the MIC clan were well cared for, even while much of the rest of the Russian citizenry was hard-pressed to find fresh vegetables or shoes that fit at the local shops in their neighborhoods. The MIC had some success, as when Russia was the first country to launch a satellite (called

Sputnik) into space orbit. A few years later they beat the Americans again by launching Yuri Gagarin into earth's orbit. In the 1950s Russians were proficient in space technology because it was based on their rocket science, which they required as delivery vehicles for their nuclear bombs. During the first two decades of Cold War 1, the Russians devoted huge research budgets to nuclear weapons, the missiles that delivered them, and then the missiles that took satellites and crews into space.

At the same time, though, researchers working in other areas of science and technology were downgraded, and sometimes starved for research funding altogether. In these nonmilitary areas, the lead scientist would have to establish a rapport with the supreme autocrat, as failure to do so would doom the research project, if not the researcher's entire discipline. In Cold War 1 the autocrat and his political party (the RCP) were the vanguard of society, and they alone decided the direction of Russia, including what scientific fields of endeavor the country would explore and exploit—but also which ones would *not* be pursued. In its most trenchant formulation, a single scientist with the right connections to the supreme leader and the RCP could decide the fate of an entire research domain within Russia.

Consider the role and impact of Trofim Lysenko. He was a biologist, active in the Russian scientific research community starting in about 1938. When in the early 1950s the British biologists James Watson and Francis Crick made their breakthrough discovery of the DNA double helix, and "Western microbiology" began its quest to decode the human genome, Lysenko adamantly refused to go along, as he had concluded that genetics was not useful for understanding biology. That alone should not be a catastrophe, as individual researchers will often have disagreements about specific scientific matters. In this case, though, Lysenko had the ear of Stalin, and later Khrushchev (Stalin's successor between 1954 and 1964), such that the entire Soviet Russian government forbade anyone from conducting research in genetics. This ban began in 1948 and was lifted only when Lysenko died in 1976. The result was a stunning back-wardness in biological research that exacerbated the number of deaths from famine in Russia and in China as Beijing also adopted Lysenko's erroneous theories. His malign influence survived his death for about twenty years, given that when he died there were no young biologists ready to move up into senior ranks of the profession. Even to this day holes in the scientific and research skills in Russian biotechnology can be attributed to the "Lysenko drought."

Learning from the Lysenko example, rocket scientist Vladimir Chelomey tried to get into the good graces of Khrushchev by giving jobs to Khrushchev family members. This plan went well until Khrushchev was abruptly ousted from power by Brezhnev in 1964, and then Chelomey's design was promptly dropped. In an autocracy, the scientist who lives by corruption typically dies by corruption. This is yet another structural flaw in the autocratic system.

Perhaps the most acute deficiency of the Soviet autocratic system of science and technology in Cold War 1 was the general dearth of domestically produced computers (including semiconductor chips) in Russia.[17] There were a number of Soviet Russian scientists who saw the enormous value and potential in computers, and some brilliant theoretical researchers in the basic mathematical and physical subdisciplines necessary for building state-of-the-art computers. Still, when these early pioneers of the computational sciences tried to translate their expertise into manufacturing actual computers of Russian design, the RCP appointees in the various centers of power (including in feuding government ministries) vetoed such plans, or fought among themselves at the political level as to which ministry was to take the lead, and what the five-year economic plan (the core tool for implementing the autocratic economy) ought to say about computers, and so on.

The KGB and the Interior Ministry were particularly nervous that individual Russian citizens might obtain computers for use in their own homes. Given the eventual role of smartphones and other computer devices in helping to organize and support the so-called color revolutions for democracy in Russia (and in other autocratic countries) decades later, these fears in the 1960s would prove prescient. Most important, though, during

Cold War 1 Russia lacked an economic system where individual technology entrepreneurs could work with a scientist to bring a novel innovation to market through advanced manufacturing and marketing techniques. Russian autocracy did not allow a Russian version of Steve Jobs or Bill Gates to work their entrepreneurial magic. The Russian government essentially decided in the early 1970s that they would not invest in creating a domestic computer industry, especially on the hardware side, and that thereafter they would for the most part have to buy or steal computing devices (including SC designs) from the democracies and buy (or steal/pirate) software from the democracies as well. What little computer production was done in Soviet Russia was slavishly derivative from products sourced from the democracies. The Russian *Agat,* for example, was a clone of the Apple II. In effect, Russia decided to sit out the computer revolution in Cold War 1. Given the enormous role of computing in the modern economy and society in the last quarter of the 20th century, this was a huge mistake on the part of the Russian government.

By contrast, California's Silicon Valley took off like a rocket in the 1970s, feverishly driving the world's computer revolution. Soon after the Americans landed a crew on the moon (in July 1969), the Russians abandoned their own quest to do likewise, partly because they didn't have a computer strong enough to support this task. Moreover, it wasn't simply that Russia was behind the United States in the field of computing; it was that computing science was barely a field of study (let alone one of entrepreneurship) in Soviet Russia. I remember visiting one of my cousins in Hungary in the mid-1980s who worked in tech. He said their R&D amounted to smuggling into Hungary two- or three-generations-old American computers and trying to reverse engineer them. He told me he knew this was a pathetic business model. Incidentally, a young Vladimir Putin, fresh out of KGB training in the early 1980s, was sent to Dresden in East Germany to help oversee, among other things, the smuggling of high-tech products into East Germany (from Western Europe), for onward shipment to Russia. Putin was schooled early on in the black arts of stealing technology from the democracies.

In the late 1970s and early 1980s it became clear to leaders in both Soviet Russia and the democracies that computer technologies were becoming central to modern weapons systems. In particular, semiconductor chips were becoming the core technology of guided weapons, such as cruise missiles. As Russia didn't have state-of-the-art SCs, Russia's munitions in this area were becoming clunky, and falling far behind in performance compared to those produced by the United States. Mikhail Gorbachev—who became Russia's supreme leader in 1985, and lasted to 1990—carefully considered the capacity of Russia for keeping up with the US on the technological front, and he concluded (as had many others both inside and outside the Russian government), that in its then current form, Soviet Russia simply couldn't keep up with the Americans. (And by then also the Japanese and, in certain domains, the West Europeans as well.) Already some 30 percent of Russia's federal budget was going to pay for military items. Gorbachev concluded that to increase this by another significant amount to try to stay abreast of US technology was not realistic. The writing of the Soviet Union's demise was on the wall of the Kremlin.

In the mid-1980s, Gorbachev's response to Russia's dire economic situation was to open up Russia politically and economically, in the hope that new entrepreneurial savvy and energy would overtake Russia's ailing state-controlled enterprises—in effect, to try to inject Silicon Valley dynamism into lethargic technology and manufacturing firms. *Glasnost* and *perestroika*, Gorbachev's signature policies, were too little and too late. Economically speaking Russia was bleeding badly, and drastic measures were called for. The first earth-shattering step was that Russia jettisoned the captive countries in the East Bloc that were costing Russia huge sums in subsidies. Literally from one day to the next the Berlin Wall was dismantled, and the Iron Curtain simply ceased to exist. This led to the unraveling of the Soviet Empire in 1989, when all nine countries of the East Bloc left the Russian orbit. Moscow pulled out all 500,000 Russian troops from those countries by the end of 1989, with the exception of East Germany, where withdrawal followed over the next twenty-four months.

After the East Bloc imploded, ethnic nations within Russia itself, like Ukraine, saw an opportunity to push for their own independence. In a series of referendums in 1991, many constituent republics of Soviet Russia (like Ukraine and Moldova) became stand-alone countries. Due to an inability to deliver technological progress and economic prosperity to its citizens, the world's largest land empire collapsed between 1989 and 1991, all without material bloodshed or violence. It was the most remarkable geopolitical event of the 20th century. Cold War 1 had come to an end. The democracies had prevailed over Soviet Russia.

3

THE EMERGENCE OF CHINA

Except for China's critical intervention in the Korean War, when in 1950 its 700,000 troops swooped in to save the regime of North Korean autocrat Kim Il-Sung, China's role in Cold War 1 was fairly peripheral. Moreover, in the middle of Cold War 1, China and Russia had a major falling-out, and in 1969 the two communist autocracies even fought a border skirmish, with several hundred dead and wounded. Under Mao, China was reluctant to play a meaningful role on the world stage. After Mao's death, China began to seriously engage with the world. Under Xi Jinping, bolstered by an unwavering commitment to technology development and deployment, China set out to change the world to its liking.

China, not Russia, is the key autocratic protagonist in Cold War 2.0. Russia is a serious player in Cold War 2.0, given that Russia punches above its weight—largely because it is willing to punch so often. China's enormous population and economy, and its capacity to fund technology development, makes it the prime preoccupation of the democracies in Cold War 2.0. Once the Russo-Ukrainian War is over Russia will be relegated to China's junior partner. It is therefore important to understand the stratospheric rise of China's national economic and military power over the past forty-five years. This has allowed China to foster a great deal of technology design, development, and deployment—and theft where indigenous tech creation has proven particularly challenging. China's model of promoting technology, and translating technology into economic and military power, is not without its (sometimes serious) shortcomings. Cold War 2.0 will be a marathon, not a sprint.

INNOVATION IN CHINESE HISTORY

Until fairly recently, China had a strict habit of keeping to itself on the international stage. This is partly a function of China being a vast country. Simply keeping the various regions of China more or less united was an all-consuming task for any emperor, and certainly not one that left a lot of time and resources for other offshore, imperially oriented endeavors. A good example of not being distracted by the outside world can be seen about 700 years ago with the voyages of Admiral Zheng He.

In 1405, in an unusual move for China, Emperor Zhu Di sent a fleet of ships to explore trading with some other parts of the world. The emperor gave this task to Admiral Zheng He, who in turn had five large vessels built. The hulls of each of his enormous ships could easily have held four Portuguese ships the size of those used by Christopher Columbus to explore the Western Hemisphere. Zheng He sailed these giant vessels up and down the coast of East Africa, then around present-day India, and eventually into the islands that make up today's Philippines. The goods he traded for, though, did not impress the Chinese emperor. In the end the Chinese emperor forbade any more foreign exploration, and China resumed turning inward.

Note the autocratic dimension to this momentous decision 700 years ago. One man, the emperor, decided the fate of Chinese geopolitics. One top-down decision. Zheng He had nowhere else to go in China for a sponsor of additional voyages of discovery; it was a unitary state. Once the emperor decided against the admiral, that was it—case closed. Compare this to Columbus, who was Italian. Columbus first went to Lisbon to get backing for his idea of reaching the East Indies by going west. The Portuguese king declined, as he was all about getting to the Spice Islands by going east, around Africa. In Western Europe, though, Columbus had options. There was competition, and competitive displacement was busy at work. Turned down by the Portuguese, he got a thumbs-up from the Spanish king and queen. The rest, as they say, is history.

Contemplating counterfactuals can be a hit-or-miss exercise. Still, it is intriguing to imagine how history would have unfolded had Admiral Zheng He explored the western United States and claimed the American continent for China. Instead, of course, we know that the European states did not tire from exploring new places or inventing new technologies, and as a result they got very good at both, while the Chinese stayed solely focused on their internal challenges.

The insularity exhibited by China in shutting down Admiral Zheng He lasted for 700 years, virtually right up to the time of Mao's death in 1976. Indeed, in the 1800s the diplomatic representatives of several European countries, including Great Britain, asked the Chinese emperor for permission to trade goods with the vast country. As with his predecessor's attitude to Admiral Zheng He's voyages, the Qing emperor wanted nothing to do with the foreigners; he just wanted China left alone. The Europeans, and especially the British, didn't take no for an answer and effectively just barged in the front door, ignoring a sputtering emperor who felt greatly insulted for having been overruled.

When it was similarly belittled by Europeans in the 1800s Japan changed its worldview by adopting a series of Western practices, including technology, such as modern industrial-era machine guns. China, though, wanted nothing to do with the Europeans, and it certainly didn't want to emulate them or their societies in any way. As a result, by the late 1800s Japan had become a very serious economic and military power while China languished, suffering yet further insults as when they lost a war to the Japanese in 1895 and had to cede the island of Taiwan to them for the next forty-five years. In the 1910s (after defeating the Russians in an 1905 war) Japan occupied Chinese Manchuria, and the Japanese colonized the entire Korean peninsula. By embracing Western science and technology, Japan became the regional hegemon in Asia; by refusing Western science and technology China suffered immeasurably. This lesson is not lost on the current autocratic emperor of China.

Ironically, China did have a tradition of scientific and technological expertise going back several thousand years. Creative Chinese invented such important technologies as silk production, paper, block printing, tea cultivation, the seed drill, farming crops in rows, bronze and iron smelting, porcelain, the rocket, the toothbrush, the mechanical clock, and somewhat later, gunpowder. Chapter 1 discussed briefly the history of gunpowder, and the development of guns and artillery that relied on gunpowder. Still, although gunpowder was invented in China, subsequent improvements to its use, developed in Europe and the United States, were superior to those done in China.

A similar pattern emerges in respect to porcelain. This beautiful genre of art (and function) was invented in China, thanks partly to China having an incredibly pliable (but strong once dry) clay that could be fashioned into very delicate motifs. These became collectors' items in Europe, and the Chinese were rewarded handsomely for these pieces. Then, in typical Western entrepreneurial fashion, several continental European princes (who adored Chinese porcelain) worked hard with technical people, artisans, and businesspeople to create centers of porcelain production in Europe that soon came to rival the original porcelain products from China, and in terms of marketing and global distribution surpassed them. Competitive displacement in commercial matters was the goal even then.

Moreover, illustrative of the European competitive dynamic, when the British concluded they lacked the right clay to produce high-grade porcelain, pottery makers around Stoke-on-Trent settled on making more basic items from a less refined material called "earthenware." The most successful among them, Joshua Wedgwood, used novel marketing and distribution techniques to create a large, international market for middle-of-the-road "china," creating an entirely new industry along the way.

A further example of the historic contrast between China and the West can be seen in the invention and development of printing. In China, block printing first appeared in the 800s. The new process increased the volume of manuscripts, but not by that much, because the emperor wanted to keep a tight lid on who could read. In addition to printing books, block printing was also used for creating images, posters, and documents that the emperor distributed throughout the empire in order to establish his authority in all parts of his realm.

By contrast, the movable type printing process *improvements* developed by Johannes Gutenberg in Germany in 1440 set off a veritable explosion of literacy, as the merchant class, and soon thereafter the middle class, and then even farmers, clamored to read their own copies of written works ranging from the Bible to scientific texts, and to propaganda pamphlets authored by the likes of Thomas Paine, whose *Common Sense* sold 2 million copies in Britain's American colonies and had a significant influence on the outcome of the American Revolution. Gutenberg's genius lay not in the printing press itself—that was invented in China. Rather, he had developed a novel form of "replica-casting" that created very clean and precise letters. He also processed his paper specially to make it very flat, and then he developed a type of ink that made his books strikingly "clean."

The base Chinese invention of block printing was important, but Gutenberg's *improvements* to it made all the difference, especially as they greatly reduced the price of printed books and other materials coming off the European and North American presses. For the first time books came within the reach of common folk. In addition, an ever more dynamic civil society was able to exploit Gutenberg's "perfect prints" to the fullest. Autocratic institutions like the Catholic Church tried in vain to stem the flow of high-quality, inexpensive printed materials that it labeled "heretical," but the flood was too great to hold back. The information dikes were bursting. It was like trying to stop social media today.

Gutenberg's package of printing improvements were also "accelerators." They greatly amplified other trends in addition to boosting its own growth.

The scientific revolution exploded in the wake of hundreds of relatively inexpensive scientific and technical books and manuals hitting the market. These works contained illustrations that were precise and compelling. These were materials people wanted to read. Medicine, engineering, architecture, botany, and other science and technology subjects came alive. China had started a printing revolution, but it reached its apogee in Western Europe and North America.

Skyrocketing levels of literacy in Europe also created a new industry for eyeglasses, as people didn't really need good eyesight until they started reading. The technicians who ground these lenses then figured out how to make microscopes with them, and a little later, telescopes, in both cases permitting people to study what they couldn't previously see with their unaided eyes. Massive scientific and technological progress soon followed, especially in Western Europe and North America where the literacy revolution was in full flower. The Catholic Church took yet another hit when Nicolaus Copernicus and Galileo Galilei, using telescopes, proved that Earth orbited around the sun, and not vice versa as the church had preached. All this, and much more, flowed from the Gutenberg printing improvements released into a fairly open political and economic environment. Gutenberg's improvements were soon known to printers in China as well, but they simply didn't get the same traction there given the different structure of civil society in that country.

Today's China, and certainly Xi Jinping, understand that the current equivalent of the printing press, a particularly powerful "accelerator" technology, would be artificial intelligence, semiconductor chips, quantum computing, and biotechnology. Contemporary China will certainly not ignore these new accelerator technologies, as Beijing realizes their use will be critical to China building and sustaining economic and military power. This is, however, a fairly recent understanding around the role of technology. During Mao's time, and for some 150 years prior, China still didn't want to engage in the world of modern industrial processes and machines.

THE GEOPOLITICS OF INNOVATION

China has a long (about 5,000 years) and generally violent history. War has scarred the Chinese landmass almost continuously since the rise of the Han Chinese 4,800 years ago. About 2,400 years ago the violence was so endemic that a stretch of 300 years is known as the period of "Warring States." Some time later Sun Tzu, one of the leading ancient scholars of war, wrote *The Art of War*, inspired by the events and dynamics of the Warring States period. Sun Tzu's book is still required reading in military colleges around the world, though the book is as much about how an autocrat should wield power to maintain political control. This makes for useful reading today, especially for Chinese and Russian autocrats like Xi Jinping and Vladimir Putin, respectively.

The 1800s were also a violent time in China, and also a humiliating one for the Chinese. The ability of the British and other Europeans to force China to trade with them was probably the low point. As well, in the Taiping Rebellion (1850 to 1864), a charismatic religious leader, who had converted to Christianity from Confucianism, led a mass peasant revolt in which some 30 million died. In the later Opium Wars, the British forced the Chinese to buy opium so that the British would have something to trade in consideration for the attractive goods they sourced from China. An estimated 90 million Chinese became addicted to the nefarious narcotic. In 1897 Germany seized its Shandong concession from the Qing dynasty, another terrible blow to the pride of the Chinese people. In 1895, China lost a war with Japan, and as part of the resulting humiliating peace deal China ceded the island of Formosa (today Taiwan) to Japan, which Tokyo ruled until Japan had to relinquish it and other imperial possessions when it lost the Second World War.

All these incidents from the 1800s are still taught today in Chinese schools as the "Century of Humiliation," emphasizing that foreign powers, especially Europeans, have harmed China egregiously. China's misfortunes continued into the 1900s. In the wake of World War I, the Chinese had to put up with yet further humiliation when the previously German concession of the Shandong peninsula was transferred to the Japanese rather than being returned to China, all as part of the Paris Peace Conference in 1919. (That included the city of Qingdao, where the world famous Tsingtao beer has been made since 1903 in a factory originally built by the beer-loving Germans, then called the Germania Brewery.) Thousands protested this result back in China.[1] One of those protesters was a young activist named Mao Zedong, who a few years later would join the fledgling Chinese Communist Party in Shanghai.

The CCP at the time had a grand total of six members. An old Chinese proverb states that "Every journey of a thousand miles begins with one step." Mao took this wisdom to heart, and he also knew about power, how it is acquired, how it is wielded, and how it can come to be lost. It was around this time that Mao proclaimed: "Political power grows out of the barrel of a gun." Mao's motivation, shared by many Chinese at the time, was that if the democracies were unable to help them in their struggle against the Japanese (as exemplified by the slap in the face delivered at the Paris Peace Conference over the Shandong concession), then perhaps the communist model that was consolidating power in Russia might serve as a better beacon for China's development.

In the 1930s the Japanese conquered yet more territory in China. The technological superiority of Japanese weapons and military organization simply overwhelmed the Chinese army. Japan became the regional hegemon in Asia. The Japanese not only subdued the large Chinese province of Manchuria, but they also colonized the entire Korean peninsula. During World War II the Japanese imperial army, navy, and air force extended Japan's regional sphere of influence to include direct occupation of the following countries: Burma, Hong Kong, Malaya, Indonesia, Thailand, Singapore, and the Philippines.

When Japan was defeated in 1945, prompted by the Americans dropping two atomic bombs on them, the CCP resumed its struggle against the old government, especially in the countryside. By 1947 the Soviet Russian communist government was sending ever more weapons to the CCP. Eventually the CCP prevailed in their civil war against the Nationalist government. In 1949 the CCP took over the entire country, except for the small island of Formosa (today's Taiwan) off the east coast. On Taiwan (including some even smaller peripheral islands like Kinmen and Penghu), the Nationalist government, along with 2 million of its supporters, set up what they thought was a temporary base. Often in history "temporary" turns out to be a very long time, and the island nation of Taiwan (officially the Republic of China or ROC) is still separate politically from mainland China (officially the People's Republic of China or PRC).

Mao did not launch an attack on the largest island, Formosa, but he did attack Kinmen. Just as Russian autocrats (whether tsars, Communists, or now Putin) are big supporters of Russian Empire, in the 1950s China took over Tibet by the threat of force. The Dalai Lama fled his homeland in 1959 and has lived in exile in India ever since. China calls its takeover of Tibet the "Peaceful Liberation of Tibet," while the Central Tibetan Administration calls the same event the "Chinese Invasion of Tibet." To this day, Tibet is ruled by Beijing. In a somewhat similar fashion, China took over the East Turkestan Republic in the face of relatively little resistance. Today, this territory is the Chinese province of Xinjiang, where Beijing uses modern digital and biological technologies to conduct by far the most repressive surveillance and social control system on earth against the "minority" population of 13 million Uighurs. They are a minority in China, but a majority in Xinjiang. In the wake of World War II and during Cold War 1, the democracies that still had empires (the British, the French, the Dutch, and the Belgians), underwent decolonization, but the two largest autocracies in the world, Russia and China, resisted this trend and in fact extended their land empires.

CHINA WITH COMMUNIST CHARACTERISTICS

The CCP's victory in 1949 in the Chinese Civil War was an important milestone in the early years of Cold War 1. During Mao's ironfisted, autocratic leadership of the CCP, communist doctrine emphasized the development of heavy industry and the collectivization of agriculture. The former worked reasonably well, but the latter was a disaster. China in 1949 was still a country made up largely of rural peasant farmers. They appreciated their independence, and they didn't have much, but what they had was theirs. They were also quite productive prior to the coming of communism, and they were able to sell their surplus to the local market for money that was used to buy basic necessities for the home. It was a meager existence, but it was familiar and preferable for tens of millions of peasants.

With encouragement from Moscow, Mao decided to collectivize Chinese agriculture, to make it conform to the communist doctrine of Marx and Lenin. It was an uphill battle. Some 45 million peasant farmers were killed in the effort to collectivize all the agricultural land in China. It was a massive internal bloodbath. Still, Mao never wavered. He approached the massacre with autocratic equanimity, arguing that to make a communist omelette you had to break a few (or in this case many) eggs. Put another way much favored by autocrats, including Lenin and Stalin, the ends justified the means. Mao's bloody experience with China's peasants mirrors very closely Stalin's earlier effort to rid Soviet Russia of its millions of *kulaks*, who were relatively well-off peasants. A consistent theme in Cold War 1, and then later in Cold War 2.0, is that supremely powerful autocrats do not like to be denied.

Science and technology were not a meaningful priority for Mao after 1949, though he did support several strategic centers of innovation, typically where there were military industries. Again, the parallels between China and Russia during Cold War 1 are striking. Moreover, Chinese science and technology during Mao's time were significantly supported by the Russians, at least up until the Sino-Soviet split in the 1960s, when scientific exchanges between them ceased. China tested its first atomic bomb in 1964 (with their design closely based on the Russian version at the time), followed by a hydrogen bomb in 1967.

Generally, under Mao the process of science and technology development in China followed the Russian model during Cold War 1, where the objectives for scientific research were set "top-down" by CCP bureaucrats rather than by scientists themselves, let alone business entrepreneurs. As a result, many of the same deficiencies found in the Soviet Russian model of technological innovation can be found in China in the Mao era as well.

Moreover, science and technological innovation in China suffered greatly in the decade between 1966 and 1976. Mao, in the best autocratic tradition, having decided that the citizenry was losing something of its communist revolutionary fervor, unleashed the "Cultural Revolution."[2] This was a massive attempt to wipe out what the CCP called "bourgeois practices." Millions of urban workers—including scientists and university professors—were sent to work on farms. Universities were shut down. More grimly, about 2 million innocent civilians were murdered in the name of achieving doctrinal purity in Communist Party practices.[3] The similarity with Stalin's purges in the 1930s is uncanny; an autocratic enema aimed at achieving renewed societal vigor through bloodthirsty cleansing of the enemies of the state, real or imagined. In addition to the 2 million who were put to death, additional tens of millions were scarred by experiences suffered during the Cultural Revolution, including Xi, whose father had been sent to an internment camp for a number of months. During the Cultural Revolution many of the best technical minds in the country were prevented from thinking big thoughts or from practicing their craft altogether. Thousands among this community emigrated to democracies, to the detriment of China's later development.

When Mao died in 1976, some relief came to China, just as Stalin's death allowed the Russian Communist Party to turn a new leaf to a less vicious form of communism. This is fairly standard practice for autocracy, given that the supreme leader usually doesn't leave until he dies, or is murdered in a struggle for succession—this is one of the major deficiencies of autocracy. In any event, other than winning the civil war in 1949, Mao's legacy was not impressive. In 1976 China was an economic and technological backwater. China had relatively few people engaged in scientific or technological activities. At the time its manufacturing advantage was based solely on the low wages paid to its workers. I remember as a young child in the 1960s that my cheap toys—and most of my toys were cheap

as my immigrant single mom had a modest income—were all stamped
with MADE IN JAPAN. In the late 1980s, when I bought simple toys for my
daughter, they were stamped MADE IN CHINA; by then MADE IN JAPAN
was affixed to the higher-value electronically based toys. In the mid-1980s
China had reached the point where Japan had been two decades before.
Still, with Mao's passing, change was in the air.

CHINESE ECONOMIC GROWTH WITH DENG CHARACTERISTICS

After Mao's death, certain economic rules changed in China, at first slowly,
but after a few years much more quickly. The transformation was driven by
Mao's successor, Deng Xiaoping. His essential reform was to allow market
forces back into the economy. They started at first modestly, by permitting
farmers to sell most of their produce in local markets, rather than having
to deliver the bulk of their foodstuffs to state-run wholesale buyers. This
single change to the economy unleashed enormous commercial activity,
not only in the agricultural sector, but in many adjacent domains. After
a few years, Deng also permitted equivalent economic flexibility in light
manufacturing. Eventually, under Deng's leadership, 40 percent of the
economy would be in private hands—calculated by market capitalization,
though today some 60 percent of GDP is produced by companies in the
private sector. It is important, however, relative to Cold War 2.0, that in
the high-tech sector virtually all economic export-related activity is undertaken by private sector companies.[4]

Spectacular results have flowed from loosening the previous communist
autocratic economic rules. Economic growth rates in China were between
9 percent and 14 percent throughout the 1990s and into the first decade
of the 21st century, keeping in mind that a growth rate at the 7 percent
level doubles wealth in the economy in only ten years! Over the past forty
years, some 700 million Chinese were elevated out of poverty courtesy of
the jobs they had secured in the construction, manufacturing, and more
recently service sectors of the newly liberated economy. Since figures have

been kept of economic statistics, nothing close to the Chinese growth miracle has been seen on such a mammoth scale. It's one thing to achieve high growth rates in a Singapore of 5.5 million people, quite another to do so in a country with a population of 1.4 billion.

China's light manufacturing sector was focused on export growth in low-tech goods—think of all the "Made in China" items found at Walmart—where the modest wages of the bulk of China's workforce (at that time) was a competitive advantage. In less than a generation China became the manufacturing workshop of the world. Many global industrial companies felt compelled to integrate China into their manufacturing and distribution supply chains. By 1998 China's trade surplus was running at around 4.26 percent of GDP. In April 2023 China had foreign currency reserves of $3.1 trillion. Figures this large have never been witnessed before, anywhere in the world, though the closest were the economic growth trajectories of the other "Asian Tigers," namely Japan, South Korea, and Taiwan.

There are many other mind-bending metrics in and around the Chinese economic miracle. In terms of demographics, 12 cities in China have more than 9 million people (one, Shanghai, over 20 million); another 29 cities have between 3 and 9 million people; another 18 between 2 and 3 million; and 98 cities between 1 and 2 million. These figures are important for Cold War 2.0 because local municipalities provide important financing for technology companies. Essentially, the tech companies are "bribed" to set up operations in their region in return for a number of municipal tax, loan, and other financial benefits.

In terms of generating material consumer wealth through industrialization, over the last forty years China's growth figures are also over the top. There are now about 319 million automobiles in China; in 1980 there were still essentially none, and car dealerships only opened in 1985. The same sort of growth has occurred in a range of other domains, including household appliances and consumer tech gadgets. China has assiduously avoided the Soviet Russian mistake during Cold War 1 of limiting industrialization to producing only industrial and military goods; Beijing has ensured that the fruits of China's industrial might are shared with Chinese consumers.

Relative to Cold War 2.0, China has a very specific geopolitical agenda for a large portion of its newfound wealth. China has built a large army, the People's Liberation Army or PLA. The PLA has a navy of 348 ships (last tallied in 2021), 52 more than the United States. The US, though, still leads in total naval tonnage and has thirteen aircraft carriers, while the Chinese have only two. In an age of precision-guided strike missiles it is an open question, though, whether an aircraft carrier is a net asset or liability, even if it uses the high-tech Aegis antimissile defense. The answer will rest on how well the artificial intelligence within the ship's antimissile system works under real war conditions.

With 2 million active personnel China has the largest army in the world (the US has 1.4 million). China has 4,600 tanks (the US 2,500); its air force has 2,500 fighter aircraft, but is still dwarfed by the US (at 5,200). Still, China is catching up steadily. China also has an important and growing arsenal of nuclear weapons, and the capability to deliver nuclear warheads to any target anywhere in the world. China also has a large space program, presumably much of it aimed at military applications, though some of it ostensibly devoted to pure scientific research and space exploration. If China succeeds in space, it will derive from that a major soft power benefit all its own. As a twelve-year-old kid, I was never more impressed by the United States than when on live television I saw Neil Armstrong land on the moon in July 1969.

The quality of some of China's military assets may not be up to US standards, but the growth in the quantity has been stunning; and quantity, above a certain level, has a quality all its own. When assessing the relative strengths of the autocracies and the democracies, though, it is necessary to add, for the US, the equivalent figures from the NATO countries and Japan, South Korea, Australia, Taiwan, and the Philippines in Asia. On its side of the ledger, China might be able to rely on Russia to some extent, but strictly speaking China and Russia do not have a mutual defense agreement. Neither do Taiwan and the United States, but on several occasions President Joe Biden has made clear the US will defend Taiwan if China attacks it. Alliances (or the lack thereof) matter for the chief protagonists of Cold War 2.0. Therefore, it is noteworthy that the US stands at the epicenter of a dense web of alliances among the world's leading democracies, while China and Russia basically have only each other.

In assessing the respective strengths of the autocracies and democracies in Cold War 2.0, it also needs to be remembered that China's military is largely untested in real combat conditions. The last time it fought a war of any size, with Vietnam in 1979, China got its nose bloodied. It remains to be seen how effective these large numbers of Chinese military assets will prove to be in a serious kinetic conflict. To the surprise of most military analysts, the performance of Russia's military in Ukraine since the February 2022 invasion has been well below expectations. Will China's military underwhelm as well if it attacked Taiwan—mindful that an amphibious assault is much more difficult than a land-based invasion?

From the perspective of Cold War 2.0, it is critically important to remember that the majority of the wealth generated by China to pay for its military has been made possible because tens of millions of consumers in the democracies over the past few decades have appreciated buying relatively inexpensive "Made in China" goods at Walmart (United States and Canada), Carrefour (France), Woolworths (Australia), Lidl (Germany), and Tesco (UK), not to mention in thousands of "dollar stores" in these countries. What would happen to the Chinese economy if, upon a Chinese attack on Taiwan, trade embargoes implemented by the democracies put an end to at least a majority of this trade? Would the vaunted Chinese economic miracle come to a screeching halt? Would the massive unemployment shake the foundations of the Chinese social model, putting the CCP at great risk from the resulting social instability? Presumably these questions weigh heavily on Xi Jinping as he contemplates his plans for Taiwan, and his critical decision as to when (and whether?) to unleash the PLA on his small island neighbor.

It is also true that the core difference between the present and previous Cold War is the degree to which the democracies rely on the Chinese economy. The reverse, though, is also true—China is very dependent on the export markets China has developed in the democracies. Will this economic reliance by China on the democracies cause China to think twice before invading Taiwan? Or will national pride, hubris, and one autocrat's potential miscalculations all conspire to override economics and cause Xi to take that fateful plunge into the abyss?

MODERN CHINESE TECHNOLOGY INNOVATION

As the Chinese economy started to take off after Mao's death, the CCP began to encourage the development of technological projects and enterprises. Deng Xiaoping, the paramount leader of the CCP after Mao, understood how far China had to progress in order catch up to the democracies in the domains of science and technology. He curated the March 1978 National Science Conference, where he told 6,000 assembled scientists that achieving a high-speed economy urgently required high-speed development of science and technology.

While Deng loosened the screws of economic autocracy, he kept political autocracy firmly in place. As a result, the funding of scientific research and development remained a top-down exercise with most of the money coming from government. In 1986 China adopted the 863 Program, a government investment fund for high-tech companies.[5] Initially the government spent $200 billion (which was about 5 percent of the central government's entire budget) on IT initiatives, 75 percent of which went to telecom ventures. In later years, material amounts of financial assistance went from the government into these additional domains: energy, automation, lasers, space, new materials, and biotechnology. Essentially, the grand project to modernize China became inextricably intertwined with the government attempting to fund a world-class culture of high-technology throughout the economy.

Since the launch of the 863 Program, China has introduced a number of other industrial policy initiatives aimed at improving its rate of growth in technology innovation, including: The National Medium- and Long-Term Program for Science and Technology Development; the Strategic Emerging

Industries Initiative; the Internet Plus Initiative; the Made in China 2025 Program; and the Artificial Intelligence Plan. Some of these have been more successful than others. Chapter 6 discusses the Big Fund Investment Program introduced by Beijing to help the Chinese semiconductor industry, although its track record, frankly, is not very impressive.

China's first generation of tech companies date from the 1980s. The importance of Huawei, established in 1987, cannot be overemphasized. Huawei became the tech darling of the CCP, and later, even more important, a core tech champion. Huawei initially scrambled for market share in the telecommunications equipment space. Its early gear was considered inferior by international standards. Global players in the democracies tried to dismiss Huawei in their competitive bids. Then Huawei's products got better, sometimes through a steady program of copying the intellectual property of other suppliers. Huawei also priced its products very aggressively. It soon started displacing foreign suppliers in China. Then Huawei moved on to winning projects in the Global South. Eventually it started competing meaningfully on bids in European markets. In 2012 it became the world's largest telecom equipment supplier by sales, with top-line revenues in that year of $35.1 billion. Later in that decade came the boycotts of its products in the democracies and devastating sanctions from the United States.

Huawei is but one of many significant players in China's tech industry. Two years before Huawei's birth, ZTE commenced life as a telephone handset maker. Today, ZTE has sales of $17 billion, which are primarily earned from wireless telecom operators in the Global South. ZTE has had numerous run-ins with regulators in the democracies, and today its products are banned in the United States. Telecom equipment companies like Huawei and ZTE play critical roles in designing, developing, and deploying what can be termed the "oppression technology stack"—the suite of hardware, software, and network products and services central to facilitating China's autocratic surveillance-based control over its citizens, particularly in Xinjiang Province. This citizen surveillance and control system, perfected in China, has now been sold by Huawei, ZTE, and other

Chinese tech companies to seventy other authoritarian countries around the world. ZTE and Huawei are important in the discussion of "tech decoupling" between the democracies and the autocracies, which needs to be a key agenda item for the democracies in Cold War 2.0.

In the late 1990s a second wave of Chinese technology companies came onto the market, initially servicing only China but then expanding their reach into other regions. TenCent was launched in 1998, and Alibaba a year later. These companies, together with later entrants Didi, Baidu, and Ant Group, rode the Internet wave to great heights. First they imitated Amazon and eBay (established 1994 and 1995, respectively), but by the middle of the next decade they overtook the American Internet giants in terms of certain consumer Internet-based services and business models. For instance, they were the first Internet companies to bring e-payments to the mass market.

Over the last twenty years, there has been significant growth in other tech companies in China. There is Chinese domestic tech capacity in artificial intelligence, semiconductor chips, quantum computing, and biotechnology. While companies in the democracies generally invented the core technologies and products in these domains of innovation, meaningful Chinese counterparts now exist in all of them.

Today, Xi's public statements make clear his profound commitment to innovation as a cornerstone of Chinese economic and military power. In his statement to the plenum of the 20th Party Congress in October 2022, Xi said: "We must regard science and technology as our primary productive force, talent as our primary resource, and innovation as our primary driver of growth." He also stated that China needed to be tech self-sufficient in its supply chains. Presumably Xi was alluding to the export controls that the United States had placed a short time before on semiconductor chips and the manufacturing equipment for semiconductor chips that flow into China not only from the US but also from third countries. In effect, Xi was confirming that the significant global tech decoupling between the democracies and the autocracies was underway. This will be a central theme of Cold War 2.0.

CHINA'S ONGOING CHALLENGES

It would be a mistake to conclude that the Chinese economic miracle has been an unqualified success. China has some serious challenges. Any honest, rational observer of China must be able to hold two contrasting viewpoints simultaneously. Apparently, the ability to maintain such a bifurcated assessment (on any issue, not just China) is a clear indicator of great wisdom.[6] Therefore, in order to be wise about China and Cold War 2.0, the following weaknesses of the country also need to be weighed when assessing China's overall role in and impact on Cold War 2.0:

- *Recent economic performance.* The Chinese economy grew by a "mere" 3 percent in 2022. While this would be an acceptable result in just about any other economy, especially a democracy (given the OECD average had been in the 2.5 percent range in the years before COVID), 3 percent for China is a disappointment, especially considering China's official annual growth target for 2023 of 5 percent[7] and that Chinese annual growth had averaged 6–8 percent in the 2010s. Clearly COVID-19 took its toll, as did the economic slowdown from the rest of the world during the pandemic. Some of the sting is countered by Chinese predictions for another 5–6 percent growth rate for calendar 2024, and perhaps even better for 2025, though these forecasts seem overly optimistic.

- *Structural economic challenges.* Beyond the current dip in economic activity, there is a structural issue that is already serious but may become absolutely dire, with even a chance of turning existential. The backbone of personal wealth of most Chinese citizens is built on real estate. The bad news is that Chinese real estate is heading into some very shaky times. The massive number of municipally based real estate projects, which saw literally thousands of multilevel high-rises built over the past ten years, could be coming to an end. This exercise had the feel of a multilevel marketing scheme—or scam? It is always worrisome to consider what happens to the last person holding the real estate condo or apartment when the music stops. As the crisis at the Evergrande Group has already shown, the final episode of the Chinese real estate sector drama, whenever it occurs, will not have a happy ending.[8] There is similar concern with many of the banks in China, all of which are owned by the state. The only question is, when the largest financial bailout in human history comes, what will Beijing be able to save, and what, if anything, will it allow to go down the drain? And how many millions of investors will be materially—or even significantly—affected by the resulting chaos?

- *Government-business relations.* Since October 2020, Beijing has cracked down on Chinese technology companies in a number of ways. This anti-tech program was triggered when Jack Ma, the Elon Musk of China, gave a speech critical of a Chinese financial regulator, prompting the immediate disappearance of Ma, who was not seen again in China for two years. (He was reportedly teaching in Japan.) More recently, the leading Chinese investment banker in the technology company space (Bao Fan) went missing. This sort of "prolonged disappearance" from China's commercial scene doesn't help China's credibility in the domestic or international business community. This tactic mirrors China's abduction of two Canadian citizens, Michael Spavor and Michael Kovrig, off the streets of Shanghai in 2018 in retaliation for Canada arresting a Chinese national, Meng Wanzhou, a senior executive of Huawei, as a result of a legal extradition request from the United States. While she waited for the court process to unfold in Vancouver, she lived in a mansion in a swanky district of Canada, while the two Canadians languished in jail cells in China.

- *Population decline.* For the first time, in 2022 the overall population of China declined. Chinese women are having fewer babies, and the medium- and long-term consequences for China could be profound. Without significant immigration to bolster the active workforce, population decline on the level now forecast (dropping from 1.4 billion to 800 million in by 2100)[9] will have fundamental impacts on the Chinese economy and society more broadly. Can China survive such a demographic time bomb without resort to some fairly controversial techniques, such as ectogenesis (essentially, a major program of population increase using artificial uterus technology)?

- *Climate change.* In 2022 China approved the building of about 100 coal-fired electricity plants, a 50 percent increase over 2021. Enough said.

- *Pandemic preparedness.* COVID continues to take lives prematurely all over the world, but the highest numbers of COVID deaths are in China, especially among people over sixty-five, because 35 percent of persons in China in this age group are not fully vaccinated. Many Chinese don't trust the Chinese COVID vaccine(s), and neither does the World Health Organization, because China has yet to deliver to the WHO the relevant clinical studies results related to them. This credibility gap will cause deaths; the only question is how many. Moreover, China is too proud to accept the offer to buy mRNA vaccines from the democracies. This single decision by paramount leader Xi will likely cause several hundred thousand Chinese to lose their lives over the course of a year.

- *Few alliances.* Other than Russia, China has few deep alliances with countries. It has trade relations with virtually all countries in the world, and then with a smaller set of countries it has built important multiyear commercial relationships. These include loans and infrastructure construction deals it has concluded with 150+ countries under the Belt and Road Initiative. These are not, however, very deep relationships, and wouldn't allow sustained military engagement in support of one another. The democracies, for the time being, have many more enduring security alliances, typically anchored by the United States in some fashion.

- *Deficit in several challenging technologies.* Since Mao's death China has made great strides in its economic development and in pursuing technological innovation. Still, China has not caught up to the United States on this front, and if the leading democracies are taken together, then China's deficit in this domain is quite pronounced. In particular, there are a number of critical technologies where China is very significantly behind the democracies, including high-performance semiconductor chips and semiconductor chip manufacturing equipment, some types of artificial intelligence, fusion energy, commercial aircraft, aircraft jet engines, and robotics. Moreover, there are no specific technologies in which China has an insurmountable lead over the democracies. China has some minerals that are in short supply currently in other countries, and China especially has some exclusive refining capacity for such minerals, but with some time, effort, and financial investment the democracies could become self-sufficient in these assets, while the effort that China will have to expend on replicating industries in the technologies noted above (where China is currently significantly behind the democracies), will take much longer, and in some cases success is not assured China because of the extremely high technical barriers to entry.

These are only the major challenges facing China. There are many lesser issues as well. The bottom line is that the Chinese are not ten feet tall, and when they get up in the morning they put their pants on one leg at a time, just as people do in the democracies. Moreover, if the relative weakness of the Chinese persists in the technology domain, their economic and military power will decline, or at least it will reach a plateau and not progress further while the strength of the democracies continues to grow, given their stronger skills in developing technology and then harnessing that technology to build economic and military power.

4

STORM CLOUDS
AND NEAR WARS

Wars (hot and cold) never simply start. Just as Cold War 1 really began in 1917, but then broke out fully in 1945, the early warning signs of Cold War 2.0 appeared many years before Russia's 2014 annexation of Crimea and China's aggression in the South China Sea around the same time. Putin actually began his descent into autocracy right after he was elected president in 2000. Post-Mao China actually started to bare its autocratic fangs when numerous Beijing leadership hard-liners overruled many fewer reformers and ordered the army to murder several hundred unarmed student political protesters in Tiananmen Square in 1989. A keen observer of these events would have realized in an instant that international cold war behavior was going to follow closely on the heels of these internal stains of autocracy.

In 2012 Xi Jinping further confirmed China's break with the democracies when he declared that China has no interest in pursuing democracy practices, extolling instead the Chinese one-party system led by the glorious Chinese Communist Party. Xi also proceeded to implement the most draconian citizen surveillance/oppression technology on earth, and began to export it to seventy countries. Xi spent huge sums on the largest military buildup program in history, while chronically underfunding the Chinese healthcare system. He also waged economic coercion against half a dozen democracies. Intellectual property theft, such a critical plank in the Cold War 1 playbook, came back in vogue for China and Russia; they both updated their electronic skill sets so they can launch large numbers of cyber-attacks against the democracies. The action turned physical when in 2014 Russia annexed Crimea and sent irregular soldiers into Ukraine's Donbas region. China used a range of armed ships to make a play for ownership of 90 percent of the South China Sea, thumbing its nose with impunity at the sputtering democracies. Cold War 2.0 had begun.

AUTOCRACY WITH MODERN CHINESE CHARACTERISTICS

The year 1989 was the critical pivot point between Cold War 1 and the eventual Cold War 2.0. In 1985, Mikhail Gorbachev became supreme leader of Russia's Communist Party (RCP) and effectively the autocrat of Russia. His record ultimately proved to be very different from his predecessors, largely because he instituted two groundbreaking reforms. Most importantly, Gorbachev's policy of *glasnost* opened up political freedoms, including in respect to speech, assembly, and eventually, in 1989, Russia's first relatively fair and free elections to Soviet Russia's first elected legislative assembly, called the Duma. Gorbachev's second reform was *perestroika*, which was a policy that began to restructure the economy. It was not full-on privatization, but definitely the start of a move away from the top-down command and control system of economic planning where government decides what the economy would produce and what the prices for everything would be. By 1989 the momentum caused by glasnost and perestroika had grassroots movements in the East Bloc countries, especially Poland, planning their own multiparty elections, which for forty years had been outlawed in the Soviet Empire.

In China at this time these same winds of change and reform were blowing. By 1989 China had a decade of experience with a version of perestroika, Chinese-style, as Deng gradually opened up the Chinese economy. In China, however, there had not been any official policy equivalent to glasnost. Nonetheless, there were a number of student leaders—and even some senior members of the Chinese Communist Party—starting to talk openly about the need for some political reforms. In the spring of 1989 about 8,000 students were camped out in Tiananmen Square in the heart of Beijing, peacefully calling for some political freedoms. This was an unprecedented development in China. Many of the students in Tiananmen Square pointed to the political liberalizing trends in Russia and the East Bloc, and asked for the same rights in China. The world waited in anticipation for Deng's response.

On June 3, 1989, Deng gave a loud and unequivocal answer. He ordered army tanks and armored personnel carriers into Tiananmen Square to clear out the protesters. The army used violence on a grand scale.[1] Conservative estimates put the number of dead protesters at 800 and the wounded at 10,000. By this military operation against his own people, Deng made Beijing's position very clear regarding Gorbachev's reform efforts—yes to market liberalization (perestroika), but a firm no to political freedom (glasnost). Even market liberalization, though, has become in China a "top-down" exercise directed at all times by the CCP. The CCP is firmly in control of the general direction in which private companies can develop, thereby making sure that entrepreneurs never stray from the "correct path" as articulated by the CCP.

After the Tiananmen Square massacre most democracies refused to give up on the objective that over time, if only China were integrated more fully into the global trading system of the democracies, its political rough edges would smooth out and would one day become politically liberal like the democracies. Fueled by this hope, the democracies permitted China to join the World Trade Organization in 2001, even though many practices in its domestic economy disqualified it (i.e., a number of domains in China were closed for foreign investment). Apologists for China in the democracies argued that by extending the olive branch to China, the democracies would be handsomely repaid by China eventually changing its most problematic political and economic practices. They argued that "peace would follow economic integration," a theory long proposed by leading political thinkers in the democracies. More cynical businesspeople argued that regardless of the state of personal civil rights in China, there were billions of dollars to be made in trading and otherwise doing business with the country.

In the first decade after China joined the WTO there did sprout some "green shoots" of a thaw in Beijing. Measured criticism of the regime was being permitted. The infamous censors eased up somewhat on books, magazines, and other written materials. Chinese human rights campaigners even saw small signs of progress. These early efforts at a glasnost lite, though, came to an abrupt halt in 2012, when Xi Jinping became the paramount leader of China. Xi terminated the political loosening, and in fact under his stern gaze China turned ever more autocratic. For example, he undermined term limits for his position and has essentially solidified his status as "leader-for-life."

Deng abhorred Mao's excesses like the Cultural Revolution. Deng wanted to ensure that never again could the leader of the country become as powerful as Mao. Deng instituted two checks and balances on the role of paramount leader (the head of the CCP). First, Deng made the Politburo Standing Committee into an important deliberative organ with meaningful influence on the supreme leader. The Politburo was composed of the paramount leader and six others, one of whom was the premier, who would lead the government bureaucracy, and thereby act as a particularly important counterweight to the CCP chief. The premier, for example, was typically tasked with managing the day-to-day affairs of the economy. If the leader of the CCP proposed something seemingly rash for the economy, presumably the premier could rein it in before damage was done. To be clear, this was not an American-style division of labor between the legislative and the executive, but it was worth having in an autocracy.

Deng's second reform was also through the Politburo, where he instituted a system of "term limits" on the rule of the paramount leader, limiting him to two consecutive terms of five years each. At the start of his second five-year term, the supreme leader would identify his successor from among the other members of the Politburo, so that in five years' time the supreme leader would step down (having served a total of ten years) and this new supreme leader would be confirmed. Five years later, the second supreme leader's successor would be identified, so that at the end of the second leader's ten-year reign his successor would take over, and so on. This system of term limits worked during the leadership spans of each of Jiang Zemin (who actually served thirteen years), and Hu Jintao (who served exactly ten years). Deng was brilliant to construct such a system of peaceful transfer of power because he knew that not having one would create a serious weakness to the overall system. It was expected that Xi, as Hu's successor, would continue with the same system.

Instead, Xi smashed this system of term limits to pieces. Xi came to power in November 2012. Five years later, at the then nineteenth CCP party congress (where the new Politburo is unveiled to the country), Xi did not appoint a designated successor to himself. Many people were shocked, but by then he had engineered a sufficient grip on the CCP that he could get away with this bold move. There was no surprise, then, that at the 20th Five Year Congress, in October 2022, Xi renewed his tenure for another five-year term. Moreover, he once again refused to designate a successor in October 2022, meaning that he will likely extend his personal leadership in the top spot for at least a fourth five-year period (i.e., 2027 to 2032). In addition, the new Politburo that Xi unveiled in October 2022 contained six new members that had only one feature in common—they were all staunch Xi loyalists from having worked for him in junior roles previously. In effect, Xi has accomplished precisely what Deng hoped to avoid. The current supreme leader of China, just like Mao, has ensconced himself for life on the autocrat's throne surrounded by Politburo sycophants.

As for the direction Xi would take China, a document published by the CCP in 2013 makes clear that under Xi's leadership the following will be the ideological orientation of China:

- Western constitutional democracy's separation of powers, multiparty political system, and judicial independence are simply "bourgeois" concepts that have no place in China, where "socialism with Chinese characteristics" will govern, as interpreted by the CCP.

- Western values, such as human rights and personal liberties, are to be avoided in China, where instead Socialist values will prevail, as interpreted by the CCP.
- The concept of "civil society" is to be avoided, and instead the CCP will be the forum for citizen activities.
- Economic liberalization is to be avoided, as the state (managed by the CCP) should override the private sector.
- There is no place for an independent press in China, as this would lead to the "ideological infiltration" of China, and instead the CCP manages all media and publications, including managing the Internet.[2]

With his newfound power and infused with this CCP-centered ideology, since 2012 Xi has implemented a number of programs that have cemented his autocratic control over Chinese society. He has designed, developed, and deployed the world's most comprehensive system of digital and biological surveillance of citizens.[3] The system was perfected in Xinjiang Province, where facial recognition cameras (among other devices) loom over sidewalks at regular intervals and capture images of all citizens, neighborhood checkpoints take DNA samples of all residents, all phone calls are monitored in real time by gargantuan supercomputer centers, and "people of interest" (whose names are generated by the digital surveillance system) are regularly stopped on the street for questioning by police. Another version of this system involves a "social score" mechanism, where regular citizens all over China are given a starting number of points. They lose points if the surveillance system records them acting in an antisocial manner (such as spitting on the pavement), but they can also gain points if they do good deeds (helping an elderly person across the street). If they drop below a certain score, they are given a talking-to by the local authorities.

There is another variation on this system of intrusive hyper-surveillance for use in schools. With cameras in each classroom, students' faces are tracked in real time to see if they are focusing on the subject matter being taught, or if they are daydreaming. Particular attention is paid when civics is taught, such as "Xi Jinping Thought," the immortal teachings of the paramount leader. If the system finds a student is insufficiently engaged in the school environment, or not listening intently enough to CCP propaganda, then an in-person talking-to will follow, typically with the student's parents also in attendance. George Orwell is rolling in his grave.

These astoundingly intrusive, some would say suffocating, social control systems had been predicted. Orwell wrote of such a dystopia in his classic book *1984*. He used Soviet Russia as the inspiration for this book, but it took modern digital and biotech technologies, deployed today by China's autocratic political system, which does not recognize personal human rights, to make it a reality. The "oppression technology stack" draws on artificial intelligence, high-performance semiconductor chips, cloud computing, supercomputers, telecommunications, Internet platforms, satellites, biotechnology, and soon quantum computers as well. That an autocratic government has combined this tech into a monstrous panopticon is one of the core drivers of dispute in Cold War 2.0, though the democracies have to be vigilant that their own governments and private sector companies don't veer off into a similar world, especially driven by commercial imperatives. [4]

Another program of oppression in China involves the Xi government's complete control of the information space. Beijing has instituted a "Great Firewall of China," by which the government blocks the entry into China of a number of social media and related services that emanate from the democracies. Google and Facebook, for example, cannot be accessed by the typical Chinese citizen; their smartphone or personal computer won't be able to breach the technological firewall that Xi has built in China. This is one of the first "technological decouplings" between the autocracies and the democracies, and it is noteworthy that it was first instituted by the autocrat in Beijing. This book certainly looks at some programs where the democracies are pressing the technology-decoupling agenda, but to be clear-eyed about Cold War 2.0, so is China. The fundamental difference, of course, is that the democracies are implementing the policy of technology decoupling to help protect their democracies and to enhance the freedoms of Chinese citizens, while the Chinese are doing it to further remove personal freedoms from its citizens. As well, the scope for this digital oppression technology is not merely China, as Chinese tech companies have sold variations of this digital oppression system to sixty autocrats all over the world. This is another axis along the rift of international technology decoupling. To be clear, the democracies use surveillance technologies as well, but not nearly to the same extent, and, most important, they do so under rules intended to respect and promote human rights—though strengthening these norms in the democracies can always use improvement, and the enforcement of these rules when they are violated is a continual work in progress.

China also devotes massive resources to censoring information within China. It is estimated that the Chinese state employs about 100,000 people as Internet censors.[5] This is a large number of people entirely devoted to checking email and text messages, blog posts, and other forms of content, simply to see if their words mention politics, or in any way are critical of the supreme leader and the hundreds of other topics that engage the censors in their task of oppression management. Equally, these extensive censorship practices have been woven into the rules governing AI applications. This is why if you ask a Chinese AI-driven search engine a question about politics, it will fail to answer—it simply returns a blank screen. This type of political restriction makes it harder to develop AI in China than in the democracies, though AI programs in the US will also filter out certain questions (i.e., "How do I make a bomb from simple parts?"), but not nearly as many as in China.

There are other ways that Xi's regime, for autocratic political purposes, has made life more difficult for companies and entrepreneurs in China's technology sector. The most successful tech entrepreneur in China, Jack Ma, spoke out at a conference in October 2020 about how Chinese financial regulation wasn't keeping up with trends in Chinese fintech. A few days later Mr. Ma disappeared, and he wasn't seen again for two years, although he surfaced again in China in the spring of 2023 after reportedly "teaching" in Japan. During this same period many other tech companies were told by the CCP to curb certain behaviors, and to toe the party line on "common prosperity" and other CCP goals. Xi was sending a clear message that no company or industry group or other entity or organization in China could or should challenge the supremacy of the CCP or Xi's own personal leadership position. In addition, Xi reinvigorated the practice that every company must have a CCP "cell" that is coequal with the CEO and senior management of the company, and that major decisions of the management group have to be vetted by the CCP cell. Again, the point is to ensure that no entity in civil society can act on its own; all legitimacy in China flows from the CCP. This is modern autocracy with Chinese characteristics.

In light of these oppressive practices against its own citizens, for forty years the democracies have tried to use the influence of their economic relationship with China to get Beijing to liberalize its political system, and in particular to grant more freedom to its citizens. After four decades of trying, it is now fairly clear that the strategy of using economic integration to achieve these political ends has failed. Commercial engagement has not led to an inexorable meeting of the minds on the political front. Moreover, irony of ironies, today it is actually China that leverages the close degree of economic integration between itself and numerous democracies—to China's distinct advantage. Below is a list of cases where China has used economic coercion against a democracy:

- *Australia:* The government in Canberra suggested that an inquiry should look into the origins of the COVID-19 epidemic in Wuhan. China retaliated by banning imports of fourteen commodities from Australia, including beef, wine, and barley, but not iron ore, for which China depends on Australia.
- *Lithuania:* China blocked imports from Lithuania because this small Baltic country established diplomatic relations with Taiwan.
- *Japan:* China halted exports of rare earth minerals because of a dispute over contested islands.

- *Norway:* China halted imports of salmon because a Nobel Peace Prize was awarded to a Chinese human rights activist.
- *South Korea:* Chinese media called for a consumer boycott of goods from South Korea because South Korea bought a missile defense system from the US.
- *Canada:* The government in Ottawa carried out an extradition request from the US government, following proper legal procedure; China retaliated by kidnapping two Canadians from the streets of Shanghai in broad daylight and holding them for over 500 days. China also "lost" test results related to imports of canola from Canada, and blocked further shipments of the commodity for thirty-six months.
- *US/NBA:* China cut sponsors and streaming of National Basketball Association games after an NBA player sent a tweet supporting freedom protesters in Hong Kong.

Again, when some commentators urge the democracies not to begin taking actions that would decouple the democracies from China, it is important to remember these cases, where it was China, not the impacted democracy, that began the practice of decoupling. In Cold War 2.0 there are many situations where pots are calling kettles black.

AUTOCRACY WITH MODERN RUSSIAN CHARACTERISTICS

Six months after the massacre in Tiananmen Square, Russia had its first parliamentary elections, which were relatively fair and free. The following year, in 1990, Russians went to the polls and elected Boris Yeltsin their new president. It seemed like glasnost was paying off, and democracy was finally coming to Russia. Still, the autocratic vultures started circling during the same decade. In 1991, in reaction to the departure of the East Bloc countries and the implosion of the Soviet Union itself (fifteen autonomous republics, including Ukraine, finally truly became autonomous), some disgruntled ex-communists with the assistance of leaders of the KGB, Russia's state security police, staged a coup attempt. To his credit, Yeltsin stood firm and the coup plotters soon capitulated and were arrested. Nevertheless, a sense of unease about democracy had entered the collective psyche of the country with the world's largest landmass and most nuclear weapons.

Fueling the discomfort with democracy was a Russian economy in free-fall. Try as he might, Yeltsin was unable to make the fiendishly difficult shift from the autocratic/command economy to open market economy fast enough. And when, toward the end of the decade, the switch had been made, it turned out that about eighty so-called oligarchs had bought the shares or assets of the largest industrial companies in Russia for bargain-basement prices. In short, Russia's period of democracy, the 1990s, left most Russians with a very bad taste in their mouths. Democracy would never recover.

When in 1999 Yeltsin decided to leave politics, largely for health reasons, for some reason that has still not been explained very well, he endorsed Vladimir Putin as his successor. The most plausible explanation is that Putin, who was head of the FSB (the state security police), was a "pair of safe hands," who would run a steady ship, and likely wouldn't come after Yeltsin for any transgressions committed during his time in the Kremlin. In any event, Putin was elected president of Russia on March 26, 2000, in a fairly free and fair election (but already with clear signs of state television favoring Putin). Putin received 53 percent of the vote, and the next two candidates received 29 percent and 5 percent, respectively.

Putin wasted no time bringing autocracy back to Russia after he was elected president. During the election campaign Putin was satirized by NTV in an ongoing political commentary show called *Puppets*. It was biting satire, not dissimilar to what a viewer would see on America's *Saturday Night Live*, or especially Britain's *Spitting Image*—a British comedy show that used puppets to caricature politicians, royals, and celebrities that was the inspiration for *Puppets*. In mature democracies politicians know that political satire comes with the territory; in the US some politicians are even good enough sports to appear as guests on *Saturday Night Live*. It's all part of the dialogue between the citizens and their elected representatives in a stable, sensible democracy.

Putin's reaction to the Russian *Puppets* show that lampooned him was very different, and it ominously foreshadowed his general approach to democracy. Literally two days after the election, Putin had the FSB state security police (where he had just been the boss before being elected president) raid the offices of NTV. The FSB confiscated NTV's computers, allegedly as evidence of some wrongdoing. A few weeks later trumped-up criminal charges were brought against Vladimir Gusinsky, the owner of NTV. Eventually, Gusinsky was persuaded to leave Russia, and to this day he lives in exile. This incident heralded the return of autocracy to Russia. The experiment with democracy, between 1985 and 1999, did not survive the departure of Gorbachev and Yeltsin from the political scene. Putin's tenure in democracy lasted all of forty-eight hours.

In the 2004 election, Putin's autocratic tactics started to pay large dividends, especially courtesy of his complete control of state television, which is how most people in Russia received their news. In that election Putin received 72 percent of the vote, and his nearest rival got 14 percent. To give Putin his due, he was also very astute to increase pensions 30 percent in the few years immediately after taking office in 2000. While he and his oligarch cronies were ransacking Russia financially, he was willing to share some of that enormous wealth with average people. As an autocrat for life, he knew he had a long tenure before him, and so he chose not to embezzle every last ruble right away; he knew he would do better financially if he spread his embezzlement out over many years. Longtime investor in Russia William Browder (and staunch critic of Putin) pegged his net worth at $200 billion in 2017,[6] an astounding number considering his official state salary as president was only $130,000 a year.

In 2008 Putin orchestrated a classic autocratic sleight of hand. Term limit laws prevented him from running for president a third consecutive time, so he handpicked Dmitry Medvedev to run for president. Medvedev received 71 percent of the vote for the position of president (again, courtesy of very unequal media coverage by state-owned television outlets) and he immediately appointed Putin prime minister. In 2012, Putin was back as a candidate for president, and he won 63 percent of the vote. The Organization for Security and Co-operation in Europe, the independent group that monitored the election, found that there was no real competition in the election, and Putin's victory was assured from the beginning of the process (which included, as always, grossly unfair coverage in state-owned media, as well as material voting fraud on election day).

Putin got 78 percent of the vote in the 2018 election (extended to six years from four through another Putin move to autocracy). The most viable anti-Putin candidate, Alexei Navalny, was not allowed to stand for election. Also, several political parties in the Duma that could run candidates without having to collect signatures did not do so, instead announcing they would support Putin. The European Union found that fraud riddled the election; estimates of millions of illegal ballots were documented, including on webcams.

Some apologists for Putin in the democracies have argued that this Russian type of election under Putin is simply a variation of democracy, which they have variously dubbed as "sovereign democracy," "managed democracy," or even, as one commentator in the US has called it, "illiberal democracy." These hybrid terms make no sense and are dangerous, given that words matter in Cold War 2.0. A democracy cannot be qualified with these adjectives. A country is, politically speaking, either a democracy or it is not a democracy, and Putin's Russia is not. What Putin has done is destroy any meaningful alternative locus of political power in Russia beyond himself.[7] He runs the show completely. He has built a personality cult around himself. He increasingly venerates Stalin, one of the top three bloodiest autocrats from the 20th century. If you need to label Putin's perversion of democracy in Russia, you can refer to it as "autocratic capitalism," but it should not be called any kind of democracy.

Beyond his disdain for free, fair, and credible elections, Putin has utter contempt for human rights and freedom of the press. The high-water mark for Putin's absolute impunity within Russia on this score was the murder of journalist Anna Politkovskaya in the lobby of her apartment building in 2006. Some years later Boris Nemtsov was also assassinated for investigating corruption in the Putin regime. Putin also encouraged the Duma, Russia's semi-elected body of representatives, to implement anti-LGBT legislation. Putin regularly arrests, and poisons with nerve agents, opponents of the regime, including in April 2022 a forty-one-year-old father of three, opposition politician Alexei Navalny. He was treated in Germany for the poisoning, and when he returned to Russia he was literally taken from the airport straight to prison, where he now languishes in a tiny cell having received a thirty-year sentence for fictitious crimes.

After invading Ukraine, Putin passed yet more laws driving Russia into a dark, totalitarian version of autocracy. Putin has made it illegal to call the full-scale war that he started in Ukraine a "war"; instead, by law, it is a "special military operation" (again, Orwell is rolling in his grave). Hundreds have been imprisoned for speaking against the war, even if only to a family member in a restaurant. Vladimir Kara-Murza, a member of the Duma who is a long-standing critic of the Putin regime, received a twenty-five-year prison sentence for speaking out publicly against the war in Ukraine.[8] Putin's other favorite tactic is to label opponents "agents of foreign states." Russian citizens with this moniker often have to find a new life in exile outside of Russia, thereby seemingly justifying the Putin label in the first place—it's another classic autocratic trick. It is not a surprise that in 2017 Freedom House gave Russia a global score of 20 out of 100; in 2022 this score had fallen to a miserable 16 out of 100. Other countries ranked around Russia include Angola, Chad, China, Burundi, Cuba, Gambia, Iran, the UAE, and Vietnam. This is as low and authoritarian as Russia has fallen under Putin. For context, here are the scores of some other countries in 2017: Sweden, Finland, and Norway each rank 100; Canada and the Netherlands, 99; Denmark, 97; Japan, 96; Germany, 95; Chile, 94, and Costa Rica, 91—each of them democracies.

As Putin turned increasingly autocratic he went about reassembling the old Soviet Russian Empire. When countries like Britain and France lost their empires after World War II, they found other roles in the world (Britain as America's junior partner, and France as a co-builder with

Germany of a united Europe). Russia, by contrast, has never reconciled itself to the Berlin Wall being torn down in 1989, the unification of the two Germanys soon thereafter, and the collapse of the Soviet Union two years later. In a fit of autocratic (and very dangerous) nostalgia, Putin wants to rebuild the Russian Empire. In doing so he has been very muscular in breaching the rules-based international order, including the paramount rule (as enshrined in the charter of the United Nations) that no state shall violate the territorial sovereignty of another state. And after he invades a country, he has his soldiers inflict incredible human suffering on civilians, committing a range of war crimes, and even more grave crimes against humanity. In Ukraine he has been committing ethnic cleansing, including genocide. In 1999, Russia invaded Chechnya. Putin ordered his superior forces to absolutely level the capital, Grozny; even he choked up when he toured the devastated city soon after the sadistic Russian bombing. In a similar vein, in 2008 Russia invaded Georgia. Later there would be major Russian military operations in Libya and Syria, where he kept the bloody autocrat of Damascus, Bashar al-Assad, in power. (Assad has killed an estimated 500,000 of his own citizens.) Putin's Russia, while a huge landmass, only has 147 million people, and an economy the size of South Korea. Yet Russia punches above its weight in military matters because, frankly, Putin enjoys punching so much, and he does not concern himself with the large loss of life his military actions foist on civilians.

In 2014 Russia invaded and annexed Crimea (previously part of Ukraine) and dropped "semi-flagged" Russian military personnel into the two eastern provinces of Ukraine (the Donbas) to spur the secession of the Donbas from Ukraine. In 2014 Ukraine was not a member of NATO, and so NATO did not respond militarily to assist Ukraine in fighting Russian troops directly. Nevertheless, NATO countries did send trainers into Ukraine between 2014 and 2022 to help Ukraine build its own capacity to fend off the Russians aggressors. A number of NATO countries also supplied Ukraine with weapons and munitions commencing in 2014, supply arrangements that continue to this day. Eight years later Russia launched a full-scale invasion of Ukraine. Cold War 2.0, though, began with the

Russian annexation of Crimea in 2014. This was also the final nail in the coffin of democracy in Russia. Russia can have either a democracy or an empire—it cannot have both, and certainly now with Putin's pursuit of empire through the full-scale invasion of Ukraine, Russia certainly can have no democracy (at least while Putin reigns in the Kremlin).

INTELLECTUAL PROPERTY THEFT AND CYBERATTACKS

Chapter 2 discussed how Russia stole copious amounts of intellectual property from the United States, initially to build Russia's atomic bomb. The practice continued for several other weapons systems, and then relative to civilian projects such as large commercial aircraft, jet engines, and computer software (lots and lots of computer software). In the case of the British Nene jet engine, the Russians were allowed to use it only in commercial aircraft, but they promptly put it into military jets as well, which caused considerable difficulty for the US, the UK, and their allies in the Korean War. This habit was then picked up by the Chinese autocrats as well. Add to computer software cultural products such as music, videos, and films. One practice that greatly troubled businessmen in the democracies was the requirement that in order to be given access to Chinese markets, the foreign business had to license its technology to a Chinese partner on very favorable terms. Both under cover of these licenses, and otherwise, there was the growing problem of Chinese companies stealing these technological assets from the democracies.

Faced with these serious challenges to doing business with the Chinese, in the 1990s the business community in the democracies, and their political allies, presented to China the huge incentive discussed above—membership in the World Trade Organization if China curtailed its most egregious commercial practices, such as intellectual property theft. Within a decade of China's entry into the WTO, however, it became clear that China had no intention of directing its companies to stop stealing intellectual property from the democracies. Product designs, software, and cultural products such as music recordings and films all were being "ripped off" (to use the vernacular) by Chinese entities without any financial compensation. A great deal of technology that China was using to become more competitive on the global market in fact originated in university and company technology labs in the democracies. This problem has never gone away, and persists to this day. Moreover, when the Internet was adopted by business the world over, Chinese and Russian hackers (condoned, encouraged, and sheltered by the Chinese and Russian governments), became expert in stealing intellectual property from the democracies by using online methods.

Soon after the commercial Internet blossomed in the 2000s, computer hacking by Chinese and especially Russian actors expanded beyond IP theft into several other nefarious practices. These all came to constitute major flashpoints in the relationship between the democracies and the autocracies. It is axiomatic that for a war to be "cold," there cannot be direct kinetic military conflict between the two leading contrary protagonists. A cold war turns hot when bombs are dropped, missiles are fired, people begin to be killed, and buildings and other hard assets start to blow up in the physical world. In the current digital era, though, there are operations that, while not exactly hot, aren't quite cold either. These can be called "near war" or "hybrid" actions, and the Chinese and the Russians quickly became experts at them as soon as computers, and later the Internet, experienced widespread growth around the world.

Particularly as the Internet developed into a ubiquitous form of global electronic communication, China and Russia employed the Internet to "hack" websites operated by democracies. At first this activity was merely annoying, but it quickly escalated into dangerous behavior as the hackers—sponsored and paid by the Chinese and Russian governments— grew more expert, bolder, and more successful in terms of what they could accomplish inside the computers they hacked that were in the possession of governments, businesses, research universities, and other institutions in the democracies. Sometimes the hackers' objective was to steal money, trade secrets, or personal data, but over time their techniques expanded to include inflicting damage that actually caused direct, physical consequences.

Consider the now infamous 2021 DarkSide ransomware cyberattack against Colonial Pipeline, a company that operates the longest oil pipeline in the US—5,500 miles from Texas to New York. Over 12,000 gas stations rely on Colonial for their wholesale gas. DarkSide is a Russia-based Internet hacking group that the Russian government permits to operate in Russia so long as it targets only non-Russian victims. On May 7, 2021, hackers from DarkSide penetrated the computers of Colonial Pipeline and inserted malware software into its systems. Colonial had to shut down its computers for six days, which then brought pipeline operations to a sudden halt. This in turn caused shortages at hundreds of gas stations in the days that followed, which had ripple effects for consumers who could not drive to work or take alternative transportation. The price of gas also spiked in the states impacted by the outage. The incident only ended when Colonial Pipeline paid a $4.4 million ransom (of which the FBI was able to recover $2.3 million).[9]

Another form of hacking involves Russian and Chinese interference in the election and related processes of democracies. The 2019 *Report on the Investigation into Russian Interference in the 2016 Presidential Election* (Mueller report), for example, outlines in great detail the "sweeping and systematic" interference by the Internet Research Agency (IRA), a Russian organization backed by Yevgeny Prigozhin, in the 2016 US presidential elections.[10] Prigozhin, who at the time was very close to Russian president Vladimir Putin, was a criminal who served nine years in jail for assault, and then he became Putin's personal caterer. Later Prigozhin became the principal behind the Wagner Group, a mercenary army fighting on behalf of the Russian government in Ukraine and in many other nations, especially in the Global South, before he led an insurrection against Moscow in June 2023. These social media influence activities, analyzed in the Mueller report, were undertaken by Prigozhin's group of IRA hackers and Internet trolls, starting in 2014 and included the following: their Facebook and Instagram accounts reached about 126 million Americans; roughly

3,800 Twitter accounts reached about 1.4 million Americans; and some of these Twitter accounts achieved tens of thousands of followers, including some US politicians who retweeted IRA material.

The core objectives of this social media campaign by the Russian IRA was to influence users of American social media services such as Twitter and Facebook in ways that would "provoke and amplify political and social discord in the United States."[11] For example, Prigozhin's IRA would open US-based social media accounts, and then pose as Black Lives Matter protesters, Tea Party activists, or anti-immigration groups, posting controversial statements that would generate political division and social conflict. They also posted biting criticism of Hillary Clinton, all with a view to influencing the outcome of the 2016 presidential election. (Putin was worried about Clinton getting elected, as she was on record as ready to take a much tougher stand against Putin and Russia's various nefarious activities against the democracies than the Republican candidate, Donald Trump.)

In addition to the social media interference campaigns run by the Russian "Internet trolls" (expert operatives hired and paid by the Russian government who post incendiary material on the Internet for financial gain), the Main Intelligence Directorate of the general staff of the Russian Army (the GRU) also hacked their way into the computers of the Democratic National Committee—the organizing body of one of the two major American political parties—stole hundreds of thousands of documents, and released a subset of these materials into the public domain, all with a view to damaging the campaign of the 2016 Democratic nominee for president, Hillary Clinton. While the social media interference campaign and the hacking of documents, constitute criminal offenses in the United States, going after the criminals in Russia presents some very difficult hurdles. In December 2016, the US government imposed sanctions on Russia in response to Moscow having interfered with the election held the month before. Of course this was too little, too late to prevent the harm caused by these social media campaigns and computer hacking attacks.

THE PROPOSED AUTOCRATIC WORLD ORDER

China and Russia complain daily that they neither like nor accept the "rules-based international order." This should come as no surprise, because just as autocrats fail to see the value in the "rule of law" domestically in their own countries, so they have no patience for similar rules applying to the international relations between states. This begs the important question—if not a rules-based order for global affairs, then what?

China has answered this question very tellingly in its approach to the dispute engulfing the South China Sea (SCS). The SCS is a massive body of water that lies off the coast of China (as its name suggests), but also the coasts of a number of other countries, including Taiwan, the Philippines, Malaysia, Indonesia, and Vietnam. (For example, the Philippines calls the portion of the SCS that lies off its coast the "West Philippines Sea." Often in international relations the view held by a government official depends on where he or she sits.) The SCS is an important body of water. About $4 trillion of international trade is carried by ships traversing the SCS each year. China, the world's largest oil importing country, received about 80 percent of its oil by tankers coming to China over the SCS. There is also likely a great deal of fossil fuels and minerals on and under the seabed in various areas of the SCS.

There is a major dispute among the countries with coasts along the SCS as to how to draw its maritime boundaries (i.e., each country's 12-mile territorial sea boundary as well as each country's 200-mile exclusive economic zone). The conflict exists because the states bordering the SCS (other than China) want the various boundary and other claims settled in accordance with the United Nations Convention on the Law of the Sea (UNCLOS). By contrast, China wants to settle the dispute by having the other states simply accept its so-called nine-dash line boundary in the SCS. This nine-dash line gives China the vast majority—about 90 percent—of the SCS (see map of contesting delimitations in the images section, where the nine-dash line is drawn in red).

To drive home its position, and given that especially in international affairs it is often that "possession is nine-tenths of the law," around 2014

China began building docks and permanent buildings on a number of the SCS island atolls. On one such small location, aptly named Mischief Reef, the Chinese built an island large enough to accommodate a runway for military aircraft and an area to station missile defense weapons. In effect, China has been changing the "facts on the ground" (or more precisely, making ground-based facts in the water) in order to bolster its maximalist territorial claims to the SCS. In a similar vein, China gave rifles and other small arms to Chinese fishermen who work in the SCS, ordering them to harass the fishermen of other countries that they encounter there, even though China has no internationally accepted right to the territorial waters where it promotes such harassment.

China's nine-dash line has been rejected by most members of the international community, especially the other littoral countries bordering the SCS. It is considered such a massive overreach of jurisdiction that these other countries deemed some action to be essential. To counter China's position, the Philippines (one of the countries that has a great deal to lose from the massively expansionist position on the SCS taken by China) brought a legal case (under international law) against China in the Permanent Court of Arbitration in the Hague, in the Netherlands in 2013. The Philippines was backed up by several other countries, who all prepared and submitted supporting briefs to the court. On July 12, 2016, the court released its lengthy (479-page) judgment.[12] While the court did not draw the actual maritime boundaries that would be consistent with UNCLOS principles and previous court decisions, it did find that the UNCLOS principles should determine the rights of the countries and that the Chinese nine-dash line is illegal as it exceeds the delimitation provided by the UNCLOS rules. In short, the court decided that China cannot draw boundaries wherever China wishes; rather, China must follow the rules of international law. (By the way, China helped negotiate, and then agreed to, the UNCLOS rules back in the 1980s.) Those in the world community who are adherents of the rule of law (in this case international law) unanimously agreed with the decision of the court that China's nine-dash line was an egregious affront to the world's rules-based international order.

China, for its part, immediately denounced the decision of the court, and did not even participate in the hearings there, although it was invited to do so. Essentially, China's nine-dash line, and its contempt for international law in resolving this major dispute, shows the disdain in which Beijing holds the "rules-based international order." Xi Jinping has decided that China's territorial sovereignty and marine rights in the SCS will not be determined by legal rules as required by the court's decision. In effect, Beijing has laid down an important marker: if the international legal system holds back China from achieving its own objectives, then China is dead set against that system of norms used by the rest of the world to order their international relations.

This case illustrates perfectly, and clearly, what China wants when it says it requires a new conception of international affairs where the system of rules promulgated by institutions like the United Nations no longer apply to China (or Russia, or other major powers). This is the essence of the dispute at the heart of Cold War 2.0. For so long as China (and Russia in its equally "might is right" approach to Ukraine) continue to act with impunity on the global stage, Cold War 2.0 will be a struggle where the democracies push back against such dangerous behavior by the autocracies.

Put most starkly, China has told the world in no uncertain terms that it believes in a global model of geopolitics where "might is right" and where smaller states must defer to China simply because China is bigger, more populous, and more powerful. The nine-dash line is a perfect example of China's approach to international affairs. China is by far the largest country bordering the SCS, therefore China's nine-dash line must be accepted by the smaller states. This is an astounding approach to global diplomacy in the 21st century; indeed, China's position is that there actually is no need for diplomacy, because whatever the large autocracy says, goes. Smaller states, well, they'll just have to grin and bear it.

The world has seen this movie before, because prior to the end of World War II "might is right" was the prevailing approach to international relations. As early as 2,500 years ago, Thucydides, one of the founders of modern history writing (one of the first to say that beyond describing the facts, a historian also had to understand and explain the motivations of the protagonists of historical events), described a scene in ancient Greece where the Athenians meted out punishment to Megara, another Greek city-state that had crossed Athens. The Athenian army ransacked Megara, killed all the men, and took all the women and children into captivity. It was exceptionally harsh treatment, given that Megara's transgression was not that grave, but Athens wanted to set an example for other members of the Delian League, the alliance system of about 300 Greek city-states run by Athens. Thucydides described in some detail the brutal behavior of the Athenians, the massive bloodshed, and then writes the famous line: "The strong do what they can and the weak suffer what they must."[13] This is a perceptive description of the autocratic mentality, even though it was wielded in this case by Athens, at the time a democracy.

Thucydides sets out the central challenge posed by Cold War 2.0: How should the democracies respond to a pair of large autocracies who refuse to behave in accordance with the rules-based international order? The answer is partially lodged in Thucydides's text, when he quotes (just before the sentence excerpted above) the Athenians admitting that the strong lording it over the weak in any way they wish *doesn't* apply to states of the same strength. Rather, where you have states of "equal power," instead of always fighting they will often discuss and settle issues peacefully based on what is "legally right," rather than solely on military might. This insight should be one of the central principles animating democracies today. The best way for them to confront the Chinese and Russian autocracies is to ensure that the democracies band together and approach the autocrats as a collective alliance of democracies.

5

THE CONTEST FOR ARTIFICIAL INTELLIGENCE SUPREMACY

Artificial intelligence (AI), a software-based capability already being harnessed by businesses, governments, and militaries all around the world, is poised over the next decade to become the most important, valuable, and dangerous technology ever innovated by humans. AI will profoundly impact—and be impacted by—Cold War 2.0. The worst fears of the current cold war, and some of the world's most life-changing hopes, rest with this relatively new technology. There will be constraints put on AI by governments, but these will look very different depending on whether they are levied by the democracies or the autocracies. This will be a critical fault line in Cold War 2.0.

AI is an "accelerator technology," in that it not only progresses rapidly itself, but it serves as an accelerant turbocharging all other technology innovation as well. The other principal technologies discussed in the next three chapters, namely semiconductor chips, quantum computing, and biotechnology, are also accelerators, with each of them (and especially AI) releasing powerful waves of competitive displacement through the economy and national security structures. Whichever camp—the autocracies or the democracies—can best capture the added value of these accelerators will prevail over the other in Cold War 2.0.

ACCELERATOR TECHNOLOGIES

Chapter 1 argued that technology and innovation will play a central role in determining whether the democracies or the autocracies win Cold War 2.0. Four accelerator technologies will be critical to this determination: artificial intelligence, semiconductor chips, quantum computing, and biotechnology. Each of these is an accelerator technology for three reasons: (1) each is profoundly transformative, standing alone; (2) each will accelerate developments and progress in each of the others, and in a range of other important technologies; and (3) each reminds humans of the limitless potential of new technology and innovation. Each will also drive competitive displacement in the civilian and military domains. Whichever camp (i.e., the democracies or the autocracies) masters these accelerator technologies before the other, and then sustains that lead through perpetual innovation, will achieve a more robust economy and a more powerful military. Cold War 2.0 will have a winner and loser as a result of technology, just as was the case with Cold War 1.

History has known a number of accelerator technologies, but actually not that many, considering that literally thousands of technologies have come and gone over the millennia. Some other accelerator technologies include fire (not so much "invented" as tamed), agriculture, writing, Gutenberg's printing press (with the clean face movable type), the steam engine, and the Internet. These are good examples, but perhaps the most accelerating technology of the past 200 years is the telegraph. Prior to its invention in the 1840s, information could only be transmitted from one person to another as fast as the sender's paper-based document could be carried by a horse, wagon, or ship. The information did not travel faster than the substrate on which the information was expressed.

Consider that prior to the telegraph important news that unfolded in London could only be shared with someone in New York about fourteen days later, the time it generally took for an ocean steamer to cross the Atlantic. Then in 1858 the first telegraph cable was laid under the vast ocean. Thereafter, telegraph messages took only minutes to get from London to New York (and vice versa). What an accelerator technology! Commercial, political, and scientific news could be shared across the Atlantic virtually in real time. This single invention profoundly changed the way people looked upon the earth—how small the globe began to feel. The telegraph changed how people did business internationally, how people fought wars, how businesspeople organized companies and commercial ventures, and how people could travel (and still stay in touch with their business associates and family members back home), to name just a few ramifications. The Internet was certainly important when it was unveiled forty years ago, but the telegraph (sometimes referred to as the Victorian Internet) more so because the feeling of collapsing distance in the world offered by the Internet was actually first felt some 150 years before when the initial cross-Atlantic telegrams were sent. Similar "firsts" are being experienced by millions of users of ChatGPT when they have the new AI system write them an essay, poem, or story on demand.

Accelerator technologies are invariably "dual-use," in that they can be deployed in both the civilian and military domains. The control panel of a modern clothes washer is run by an SC. Literally the same SC can be repurposed to facilitate the guidance system on a military drone—the drone itself is the quintessential dual-use technology. This dual use of SCs has been witnessed recently on the battlefield in Ukraine. Russia is running out of new SCs. As a backstop, it is taking SCs out of clothes washers, and plugging them into drones. They are not perfect, but good enough. It is hard to think of anything more "dual-use" than that!

Given the dual-use nature of accelerator technologies, and certain of the other important technologies, it is to be expected that militaries in major powers around the world will work diligently to ensure that the academic community that researches these technologies, and the civilian and military-industrial companies that design, develop, and deploy them, are at all times healthy and producing state-of-the-art versions of products encompassing them. This is why governments, ministries of defense, and the militaries themselves fund innovation and purchase prototypes in these domains.

The precise cadence of the release of products containing the most advanced versions of the accelerator technologies is always difficult to estimate. Forecasting the exact future with respect to all technologies, let alone those that are accelerators that will lead to profound competitive displacement, is an exercise that usually ends in embarrassment. There have been some fascinating predictions of technology that have proven ludicrously wrong. Here is a sample of some from the last 150 years that were really off the mark:

- 1876: *"The Americans have need of the telephone, but we do not. We have plenty of messenger boys."*—William Preece, British Post Office
- 1876: *"This 'telephone' has too many shortcomings to be seriously considered as a means of communication."* —William Orton, president of Western Union (explaining why he passed on buying the telephone patents)
- 1889: *"Fooling around with alternating current (AC) is just a waste of time. Nobody will use it, ever."* —Thomas Edison, who was a proponent of direct current electricity
- 1903: *"The horse is here to stay but the automobile is only a novelty—a fad."* —president of the Michigan Savings Bank advising Henry Ford's lawyer, Horace Rackham, not to invest in the Ford Motor Company
- 1946: *"Television won't be able to hold on to any market it captures after the first six months. People will soon get tired of staring at a plywood box every night."* —Darryl Zanuck, 20th Century Fox (film studio)
- 1961: *"There is practically no chance communications space satellites will be used to provide better telephone, telegraph, television or radio service inside the United States."* —T. A. M. Craven, federal communications commissioner
- 1966: *"Remote shopping, while entirely feasible, will flop."* —Time magazine

- 1977: *"There is no reason anyone would want a computer in their home."* —Ken Olsen, founder of Digital Equipment Corporation, which made computers only for businesses
- 1995: *"I predict the Internet will soon go spectacularly supernova and in 1996 catastrophically collapse."* —Robert Metcalfe, founder of 3Com and inventor of the Ethernet
- 1995: *"Even if there were a trustworthy way to send money over the Internet—which there isn't—the network is missing a most essential ingredient of capitalism: salespeople."* —Clifford Stoll, astronomer
- 2004: *"Two years from now, spam will be solved."* —Bill Gates
- 2006: *"Everyone's always asking me when Apple will come out with a cell phone. My answer is 'Probably never'."* —David Pogue, technology journalist, *The New York Times*

Moreover, militaries are also often greatly off the mark when assessing the future use of a nascent technology. Robert Fulton, the American inventor of the steamship, approached for financing none other than Napoleon Bonaparte with the idea of a steam-powered naval vessel, and Napoleon rebuffed him for what the celebrated military genius believed was a nonsensical idea. Similarly, the US Army Air Corps took a look at the embryonic rockets being built by Robert Goddard in 1936 and concluded they would have no military application, not even as targets for aerial gunners, let alone as offensive weapons.

People, even experts, are unable to predict the precise pace of change in technology innovation because everyone typically underestimates the long-term impact of a technology, though innovators often grossly overestimate its short-term impact. Fully autonomous, self-driving cars should be crowding streets in most cities in huge numbers by now, if the estimates from fifteen years ago had come true. On the other hand, once self-driving technology becomes viable and accepted, most vehicles will be driven autonomously most of the time, given the huge economic and time savings it will generate. At that point the autonomous vehicle will competitively displace the traditional car with a human driver.

Another surprising feature of accelerator technologies is that certain aspects of them invariably end up being regulated by government, for the simple reason that their power and performance makes them somewhat dangerous. AI, for instance, presents serious risk factors, in both civilian and military use. Semiconductor chips seem less risky on their face, except when they are implemented in a dangerous setting (i.e., a nuclear power plant control room, the cockpit of a commercial airliner, etc.) and they don't work as they should. If the use of quantum computers is limited to only the richer countries of the world, they could exacerbate an already dangerous computer divide (perhaps "chasm"?) between the democracies and the Global South. And if biotechnology is not regulated carefully, some human life-ending virus might be released—and the general performance of the world recently with COVID-19, which was quite a mild virus in the scheme of things, does not bode well that the world could handle a really deadly one. It remains to be seen whether the democracies and the autocracies, in the course of their Cold War 2.0 entanglements, are able to address risks such as these posed by the accelerator technologies.

ARTIFICIAL INTELLIGENCE

Artificial intelligence will be central to all the protagonists involved in Cold War 2.0, for the simple reason that it will become a core technology—perhaps *the* core technology—of the 21st century. In addition, as an accelerator technology, AI is having and will continue to have enormous impact on a range of other innovation. For instance, in terms of biotechnology, AI is impressively speeding up new drug research, by finding molecule combinations that humans would never dream of on their own. (What's fascinating about some of the chemical compounds proposed by AI is that scientists don't actually know why they work, but they do.)[1]

Computers have already had a massive impact on literally every aspect of society. AI will amplify exponentially that influence. In the high-technology horse race that is driving Cold War 2.0, AI is certainly the stallion to keep an eye on. As a result, governments in both the autocracies and the democracies will have to learn how to ensure adequate production and deployment of AI assets, and they will certainly try to regulate and control—including in some cases block—the flow of AI assets from one Cold War 2.0 camp to the other.

It is useful to consider where AI fits into the history of innovation. For tens of thousands of years, humans limited their tool-making to devices that extended their own muscular strength. A rock scraper allowed humans to clean the fat off an animal's hide more effectively than when people used only bare hands. A knife delivered a more effective blow when humans were hunting than if they simply punched an animal with bare fists. A shovel could dig at three or four times the pace of using fingers alone. With a lever and a pulley system, much more weight could be lifted than with bare arms. With wheels humans could transport loads that would break a bare back.

The great advance in innovation in the Industrial Revolution was the invention and improvement of self-powered machines that were hundreds of times superior to manual tools. The automobile and truck could move much faster than human legs, and even faster than the horse. The railroad, in some places sometimes called the "iron horse," replaced the equine for long-haul routes. The steam engine could pump water without interruption, and even without wind, which was a limiting factor in the windmills that had been invented hundreds of years before. Still, none of these industrial-age technologies were intended to extend, let alone substitute for, human senses (especially sight and hearing) or human brain-derived cognitive capabilities.

That all changed with the invention of the computer, in and around the time of World War II. The first serious computer, the IBM ENIAC, was invented in the United States during World War II to perform the gargantuan mathematical calculations required to build the first atomic bomb. The British, under the leadership of Alan Turing, also during that war invented a type of computer to assist British code breakers to decipher encoded Nazi messages. Both computers played important roles in helping the allies win World War II. AI will have the same impact for Cold War 2.0.

The generation of computers from the 1940s until about thirty years ago (with the advent of the first AI systems) assisted humans with calculations; indeed, these computers quickly surpassed the human ability to add, subtract, multiply, and divide, because they were able to perform these and many other such mathematical functions millions of times faster than humans. These computers in a sense weren't always smarter than humans (although they seemed to be), rather they just performed very basic processes at blazing speed.

Then came the big breakthrough, in Toronto, some forty years ago. The methodology used to develop most of today's AI programs was unleashed when University of Toronto professor Geoffrey Hinton, with some graduate students, published a seminal paper on how to teach computers to "conduct deep learning."[2] Essentially, using some complex mathematics, AI software could be taught, through "machine learning," how to digest large amounts of data, and then learn from the data certain lessons: what a "cat" looks like; how to translate English words, sentences, and paragraphs into French; and how to determine Thursday night if a restaurant will have enough lettuce to get through the weekend rush, or whether it should order some more on Friday morning.

The result was that starting in the 1990s, certain computers that were loaded with AI software and trained on large sets of data started to excel at performing functions that previously only humans could do. These AI computers started beating humans at games, such as chess and the Asian strategy game called Go. Then a truly amazing thing happened. The second-generation chess computer didn't need to be "taught" by having it memorize thousands of chess games played by the old masters; rather, this chess-playing computer was merely taught the rules of the game, and, presto, it still won games against really good human chess players.

Other forms of civilian AI began to pour out of AI labs, and they insinuated themselves into many critical workflows in most advanced societies. In banking they constituted the systems that detected credit card fraud by being able to conclude whether a credit card had been stolen based on the cardholder's recent shopping history. In medicine, AI systems appeared that could help a human pathologist decide whether an X-ray from a patient showed a tumor that was cancerous or benign. Apple put an AI-driven Siri assistant into its smartphone, while Amazon put a similar functionality into its Alexa speaker. There was also a marvelous real-time language translator on the smartphone that let the user exchange sentences with the baggage clerks at the foreign airport in an easy and efficient manner that no paper-based foreign phrase book ever could. The age of AI was upon us.

Most recently, several new AI programs have come to market that have really caught the attention of computer users all over the world. OpenAI has released several versions of chatbots (such as ChatGPT) that are uncanny in their ability to respond to requests to generate prose of a certain length (as short or as long as the user would like) about any subject. The same company's DALL-E AI allows users to request, verbally, a certain image ("please, draw a bear eating a French crepe full of honey"), and presto, moments later the AI-generated illustration appears. Beyond the functionality of these latest AI applications is the phenomenon of just how quickly they are improving. ChatGPT 3.5 scored in the 10th percentile when completing an LSAT exam (the exam used by law schools to measure general aptitude relevant for the law), but ChatGPT 4, released just six months later, took the same test and scored in the 90th percentile. This is competitive displacement on steroids.

One interesting dimension about OpenAI is that it has received billions of dollars of investment from Microsoft, much of it in the form of brute computing power from Microsoft's vast system of cloud computing centers. This was required because it takes a very significant amount of computer power to train an AI program (built on a large language model) on huge datasets, which Microsoft also has in abundance, given its ability to scour the Internet through its Bing and related online services. In turn, the building blocks for Microsoft's vast "computer farms" are tens of thousands of expensive, AI-oriented semiconductor chips inside those computers, sourced from companies like Nvidia.

Returning to what AI does (rather than how it does it), use cases for AI in the civilian domain have proliferated massively over the past decade. A gambler with a gambling problem can ask the local casino to prevent him from entering the casino. No problem. They have a facial recognition system they use at the front entrance. It "learns" the particular gambler's face, and so long as that gambler enters the casino without a beard or balaclava covering their face, the computer will detect them upon entry, and alert human security to stop them from going into the establishment. Or, your company has just a launched a new movie, and they want to know what moviegoers are saying about it on social media. No problem. There is AI software now that performs "sentiment analysis," by crawling social media looking for mentions of your film. When it finds such a Facebook or Twitter post, the AI software reads the relevant sentences, and with some further nifty mathematical algorithms, can report back by summarizing in a few short paragraphs how hundreds of thousands of movie watchers feel about your new film. These are but two examples—the actual number of AI applications in the civilian world is growing exponentially. AI is well on its way to becoming the defining innovation of the 21st century, and it will play a central role in Cold War 2.0.

AI WITH CHINESE CHARACTERISTICS

As recently as a few years ago, there was a lot of hype that China was becoming the leader in AI. In particular, a Chinese venture capital investor who had worked at Google, Kai-Fu Lee, had returned to China and began to invest in a number of AI start-ups. Lee then wrote a book about why China would beat America in the AI race. [3] He argued that most important, researchers and AI companies in China had access to much more data than in the United States because there were so many more Internet users in China (and China had looser rules around the use of third-party data). It looked like China would finally have a technology where it would be able to leap ahead of the United States.

What is missing in Lee's book is a discussion of the leading application of AI technology in China, namely as a critical component in surveillance systems used to monitor, and frankly oppress, large swaths of the population. For example, facial recognition, a core form of AI, coupled with biometric systems also turbocharged by AI technology are used to track constantly the location and actions of millions of Chinese citizens. Similar systems are used for running the "social score" system in China, where everyone's public behavior is tracked and measured against government-imposed norms, and consequences result if a citizen's actions are considered antisocial in some manner. The faces of young children in school are also monitored during certain classes to determine if they are suitably engaged in the subject matter, such as lectures on "Xi Jinping Thought." If the facial recognition system determines they are daydreaming, then a stern talk with the child, and typically the parents, follows. And this is just early days for AI-driven surveillance technology in China.

Notwithstanding the proliferation of AI surveillance systems in China, it is now clear that Lee's prediction that China would lead the AI technology race is not working out. Instead, with the release in March 2023 of ChatGPT 4, discussed above, it is apparent that the Americans are clearly out front of the Chinese (and the rest of the world) when it comes to AI. This was made painfully clear to the Chinese when, a few weeks after the release of ChatGPT 4, Baidu (the equivalent of Google search engine in China) gave a hugely anticipated demo of Ernie Bot, Baidu's response to ChatGPT. It wasn't an awful demo, as some have reported, but it was certainly not the major breakthrough or even tactical victory that Lee would have hoped for.[4] First of all, Baidu's CEO, Robin Li, didn't give a live demo; rather, the various features and requests that Li walked through were all prerecorded videos. That doesn't show a lot of confidence in his own product.

One of the fundamental problems of Ernie Bot, like other Chinese AI programs, is that there is content that a user cannot query because of Chinese censorship rules. For instance, a user cannot ask about the actions of the Beijing government in massacring hundreds of protesters in Tiananmen Square in 1989. In effect, all politically harmful or even sensitive material is banned from the Chinese chatbot. Going forward, the oversight provided by censors will prove to be more and more difficult to manage for Chinese AI developers because they will have to solve for ever stricter rules on expression. Moreover, a user will never really be able to learn what, exactly, the censorship rules have blocked out of the system.

The underwhelming response to Baidu's release of its competitor to ChatGPT is reminiscent of what happened upon the release of a large language model AI by the Chinese Institute of Computing Technology in mid-2022; essentially, reaction from the Chinese marketplace was very lukewarm, and no reports have surfaced of any third party picking it up and integrating it into their system. As for other Chinese Internet giants, who presumably would be rushing out ChatGPT-type functionalities, such as Alibaba and TenCent, have yet to do so. Taking all these elements together, it is fair to conclude that the Chinese are quite a ways behind the Americans when it comes to deployment of AI. Once again, the main problem seems to be that China has put a lot of AI eggs into a single basket—namely Robin Lee's Baidu—and when that team didn't come forward on time with the requisite functionality, a large cloud started to hang over the entire AI domain in China.

In the United States, and certainly when all the democracies are considered in the aggregate, there are typically three, sometimes six, and often even more teams in the race. That is in case one or two disappoint with their technology, the cadence of their innovation, or the fundamental acceptance of their products in the marketplace. Moreover, it is the competition between these players in the same domain that helps fuel their drive to success; in effect, the economic system of the democracies reinforces that there is a race, and that the bulk of the spoils will go to the winner as dictated by the dynamics of competitive displacement. This is precisely what is currently happening in the AI domain in America, with the result that superior AI technology is coming out of multiple labs and companies. For example, fairly soon after the release of ChatGPT by OpenAI/Microsoft, Google released Bard, its equivalent product. It's considered not as advanced as ChatGPT, and Bard's less impressive showing caused Google to shake up its AI business units. In effect, competitive displacement in all its raw power is playing out in real time. Which is incredibly important, because supremacy in AI will drive oversized economic benefits, and an important advantage in national security as well.

MILITARY ARTIFICIAL INTELLIGENCE

It is naive to think that a technology as powerful as AI would not be quickly scooped up by the military and be put to use in their world. AI is a fundamentally dual-use technology, and chapter 1 highlighted that dual-use inventions invariably do well in both the civilian and military domains. Indeed, AI is already firmly embedded in all manner of operations that are key to military success on the battlefield. Here is a general rundown of how and where AI is used by armed forces:

Intelligence, Surveillance, and Reconnaissance (or ISR, as it's referred to in the military). Computer vision is an important subspecialty of AI. Computers powered by AI ISR capability are much better than humans at reviewing huge volumes of photos, videos, and other images and detecting various objects in them, be they certain people, weapons systems, buildings, high-value targets, or anything else with military value. Equally, ISR systems can scan millions of text, voice, email, and other conversations in real time to distill the few nuggets of value that might make the difference in understanding an enemy's battle plan. It's not that people cannot do these things, but that mere humans cannot do them at the scale, and in the compressed time frame, as properly configured AI computers.

War-Fighting Systems. In a busy, sometimes frenetic battle space that includes infantry on the ground, air force assets above ground, and naval vessels just offshore, there might be 200 to 300 discrete data items to try to keep track of. Eventually the objective would be to keep track of each soldier as well, increasing the number of critical data items to 2,000 to 3,000. A commanding officer will be hard-pressed to take in all the information flowing into headquarters from thousands of sensors deployed in or surveying the battle space, especially when in the heat of battle time is of the essence. An AI system becomes critical because it alone is able to collect all this data, process it, organize it into manageable streams or chunks, and serve it up for the commander so that prompt decisions can be made based on it. Increasingly, though, the AI system will also be making an ever-larger number of decisions on its own, like collecting and processing the data points, but then also giving soldiers and platoon commanders orders. Again, the harried, time-starved commanding officer simply cannot do so in the time allotted.

Air Defense/Missile Defense Systems. Consider the previous scenario, but now the enemy has launched several hundred cruise, hypersonic, and ballistic missiles, as well as hundreds of drones, some in swarm formations. This scenario is described in some detail in the beginning of the introduction to this book relative to a hypothetical attack by China on Taiwan. Again, one person or even a team of officers sitting in a C4 center on the ground, in an aircraft, or on a naval vessel are unable to effectively deal with the incoming onslaught of data-rich information. An antimissile defense system, like the American Aegis (for naval vessels) or Patriot (for ground-based combat) equipped with an AI control system can detect the incoming fires, track them, determine their targets and time to targets, and then display operational options for the commander, or the system can be tasked autonomously to itself launch countermeasures—including interception missiles—if time is just that tight. This ability to operate comprehensive and timely air defense is one of the signature military uses of AI.

Cybersecurity. The enemy has launched massive hacking and malware attacks on a democracy's critical banking, electrical, and government infrastructure assets, likely as a prelude to a kinetic attack. A total of about 1,500 key sites are being targeted. Prior to implementing AI technology, such a wide-ranging cyber strike would simply overwhelm the individual IT departments of these organizations. With AI-driven cyber defense systems, the nature of the specific cyber weapons can be determined in short order, and appropriate defensive software code can be deployed online in no time at all. Again, the role for humans is much diminished in the actual process of getting solutions out to the targeted sites; human controllers are largely on mission to ensure that the AI is working and doing its job.

Training/Simulation. It is very difficult to train military personnel, and the necessary civilian team members as well, for the kinds of scenarios noted in the three examples above in what would have been called "live-fire" exercises. Instead, what will be critical is to have computers equipped with AI systems simulate such attacks, so that personnel can be trained on how to oversee operational AI systems that are engaged to respond to attacks. AI-based training systems will also be used in all other areas of the military where operational and munitions functions are being learned. It is simply too expensive to train soldiers on real systems, especially with live-fire ordnance. Accordingly, a key indirect determinant on the battlefield will be how well one side's AI-based training simulator worked relative to the other side's equivalent system.

War Gaming. Considering strategic, and even tactical, options beforehand in order to prepare armed forces for scenarios they might face in the near future has been done for decades. Now, though, by using AI to help with the gaming parameters and option analysis, much more meaningful mock-ups can be run, and far better lessons can be learned from the exercises. Moreover, these AI-powered war-gaming systems will also be running in real time during the battle. They will be updated constantly with new data from the battlefield, and their human operators will coax out of them real-time recommendations for modifying battle plans and terms of engagement. There will be, in a real sense, an "AI digital twin" to what is going on in the real world, so that commanders have another source of advice for crafting strategy and for executing on tactics.

Logistics. However high-tech war fighting may become, at the end of the day it is still critical to get the right military assets to the right place in the world (or the right place on the battlefield) at the right time. For a major armed conflict this can be a daunting exercise. What an AI logistics system can do is track munitions depletion in real time, for example, so that as an artillery shell is fired, a new one is automatically being assembled thousands of miles away and prepared for shipment to the battlefield. Again, as with much of military AI, the system is built from a commercial application that performs essentially the same function for a large retail chain (the minute a shirt is purchased from one of their stores, the factory organizes sending a replacement shirt to the same store the next day, etc.). Moreover, after a few days of battle, the AI system would be able to predict future munitions depletion rates such that new supplies were ordered well in advance so that there would never be shortages on the front line.

Maintenance. The United States Air Force has an AI software product from C3.ai that is used to predict when a plane, or one of its key components, will require maintenance. This might not sound important, but something else learned from the Ukraine War was that about 20 percent of the equipment provided by democracies to Ukraine was actually not fit to be sent into battle. (The Russian army's equipment suffers from lack of maintenance through corruption, as maintenance money is scooped up by crooked officers.) The armies in the democracies don't have this problem, but providing their equipment the proper amount of maintenance is still a challenge, a task AI can certainly help with.

The war in Ukraine is teaching certain lessons about the use of AI in a military environment.[5] AI, as used by reconnaissance drones as well as ISR satellites and C4 planes, is making it very difficult for soldiers (let alone command posts or supply depots) to hide anywhere on the battlefield. And then AI-guided precision weapons, like HIMARS, are making it much easier to destroy command posts, supply depots, and the like that are found on the battlefield by the various AI-connected radars and other sensors. Accordingly, munitions like artillery shells must be well dispersed, and artillery batteries must be mobile. This also means that mass artillery firing in major wars are becoming a luxury of the past, and therefore artillery must itself become as smart as its rocket and missile cousins. Indeed, China is testing AI-controlled artillery to deliver more bang for the buck (literally and figuratively). [6]

Interestingly, while not widely appreciated, artillery was in fact critical in the early phases of the war in Ukraine; in addition to the importance of Javelin and other anti-tank weapons noted above, two Ukrainian artillery batteries were key in stopping the Russian column advancing on Kyiv in the first few weeks of the war. Firing thousands of artillery shells a day, though, simply becomes untenable in the mid- to long-term (as discovered by the Ukrainian army), and basic industrial capacity constraints will contribute to the drive to adopt smart artillery practices, including to exempt civilians from being inadvertently hit by dumb artillery shells. Indeed, it is an open question whether one day it will be a war crime for a military to use non-smart artillery when the smart variety is available, even if it costs more per round.

CIVILIAN AI CAPACITY

Most AI breakthroughs have been coming from universities with exceptional STEM experts in the various fields relevant to AI, including psychology, computer science, mathematics, linguistics, and cognitive science. These innovations are then operationalized by tech companies large and small. Then some of these AI systems are absorbed by the large defense contractors (who now have thousands of software programmers working for them in research and development) and cloned for the military. It is, therefore, a "whole of tech community" exercise to have state-of-the-art AI functionality and performance powering weapons systems that can deter, or defeat, enemy forces. Accordingly, to get a sense of the respective strength in AI of the militaries of the autocrats and the democracies, a review of various civilian metrics is helpful, as follows.

In terms of the leading AI development teams in the world, it would be logical for them to be within the large cloud computing firms, or closely affiliated with them, as the cloud companies have the massive datasets and gargantuan computer power required to train the large language and image models necessary for state-of-the-art AI. Alibaba is the Amazon of China, but is currently being broken up into six groups, reportedly at the behest of the Chinese CCP/government. Its Cloud Intelligence Group will continue its AI efforts, but again, the CCP crackdown on big tech in China has not helped Alibaba. The few big "horizontal" players are noted below, and are all headquartered in America and China, while some of the AI "vertical" expert companies—for example, focusing on AI in the energy or health sectors, etc.—are based outside of the US and China, but mainly in other democracies like Canada and the UK. Also telling, though, is the sheer volume of the American funding of AI by private capital, which towers over all other countries:

TABLE 1—HORIZONTAL AI COMPANIES

United States	Sales	Market Cap
Apple	$394 billion	$2.91 trillion
Google	$279	$1.56
Microsoft	$198	$2.51
Facebook	$116	$0.71
AWS	$80	$1.29 (Amazon, entire)
IBM	$60	$0.12
Oracle	$42	$0.33
Salesforce	$26	$0.20
China	**Sales**	**Market Cap**
Alibaba	$129 billion	$0.229 trillion
TenCent	$82	$0.429
Baidu	$18	$0.043

TABLE 2—VERTICAL AI COMPANIES

National share of vertical AI companies: [7]

US	40 percent
UK	7 percent
India	6 percent
China	5 percent
Canada	4 percent
Other	mainly democracies

TABLE 3—EARLY-STAGE AI COMPANIES

National share of funding of early-stage AI companies (to the end of 2022): [8]

US	$88 billion
China	$42 billion
UK	$8.9 billion
Israel	$4.3 billion
Canada	$3.8 billion
Japan	$2.9 billion
Germany	$2.3 billion
France	$2.1 billion
Singapore	$1.5 billion
India	$1.2 billion

It is also noteworthy that neither Russia nor other autocracies (besides China) have AI companies of any note.

MILITARY AI CAPACITY

The large military prime defense contractors play the central role in implementing AI into modern weapons systems. The list is dominated by five American defense contractors: Lockheed Martin, RTX (formerly Raytheon), Boeing, Northrup Grumman, and General Dynamics. Their role is central for two reasons. First, it is not enough simply to write the AI software code once, but rather it must be constantly maintained and upgraded, and expert software-capable engineering talent is required for this onerous role. Second, these large defense contractors play the crucial role of integrating the software of smaller third-party contractors into specific weapons systems. For example, Lockheed Martin is developing a digital battle-management system in a joint venture with Nvidia. In such a relationship, Nvidia brings deep technical expertise in graphics and AI technologies, but Lockheed Martin brings the invaluable experience of knowing how all the protocols and interfaces work to properly connect the new system to the multiple sensors (from aircraft, radars, satellites, naval vessels, ground units, etc.) and other data development systems that all need to be seamlessly integrated into a single, high-performance system.

It is not surprising, therefore, that out of a total workforce of 115,000 employees at Lockheed Martin, there are 60,000 engineers and scientists, of which about 12,000 are software engineers and data scientists, many of whom specialize in AI. At RTX, the figures are even more software-oriented: 195,000 staff in total, with about 60,000 engineers, and 75 percent of these are software engineers, therefore about 45,000 software specialists, which again includes a large number of AI experts. In terms of AI specifically, here is a sampling of a recent job posting at the top four US defense contractors that highlight the AI-related skill sets that are being recruited for currently.

Lockheed Martin: In June 2023 it had 220 openings for software-related jobs in the US; it was also recruiting on LinkedIn for a chief scientist, artificial intelligence and machine learning, which made a particular callout for a project on "Neuro-Symbolic Reasoning applied to sense making in autonomy and battle management." It was recruiting for an AI/machine learning software engineer to work on the Trident II D5 fleet ballistic missile, and others to work on Sensor Fusion/AI algorithm design and system integration; the Cognitive and Advanced Strategic Solutions (CASS) team within Lockheed Martin Space; on AI/ML in computer vision; on AI in the

Unmanned Aircraft Systems (drones) product line; one of the world's first quantum computers; a machine-aided vision program with the Sensors and Spectrum Warfare team; AI/ML in large-scale radar products.

RTX (formerly Raytheon): Job opening for staff to work on dependable AI-enabled intelligent systems; application of machine learning to optimization problems; drive adoption of AI at Collins Aerospace; integrate AI into the technology stack at Collins Aerospace.

Northrup Grumman: AI engineering manager to join the Artificial Intelligence and Analytics Department of NG Mission Systems, to probe large quantities of sensor data with signal processing and advanced data analytics to exploit complex phenomenology, using AI and machine learning; radar exploitation and signal processing in the AI and Analytics department, developing algorithms for a novel radar capability.

Boeing: Software manager to lead a team working with AI and machine learning on aerospace, satellite, and autonomous programs, including advanced training and simulation, autonomy, cyber security, electro-optical/infrared sensing, disruptive computing; data scientist to test novel machine learning approaches to analyzing unstructured data, for Boeing Intelligence and Analytics division; AI/ML software engineers to work on next generation of AI-enabled autonomous aircraft.

CONSTRAINTS ON ARTIFICIAL INTELLIGENCE

AI systems are proving to be so powerful that in both the military and civilian domains there have been demands for constraints to be put on them. In respect to military AI systems, a number of commentators have argued for restrictions to be placed on so-called killer drones.[9] These are drones that would be equipped with facial recognition AI, and they would be programmed to hunt down a particular enemy individual who is targeted for execution. The drone, once it finds this individual, would fire some form of weapon to kill the person, all without further human intervention by the military unit ultimately responsible for the drone. In a similar vein, there has also been commentary proposing a broader prohibition on all autonomous lethal weapons; again, like killer drones, these would be military assets that would release their munitions simply based on what the AI system detected as an appropriate target, without any human intervention in the ultimate firing decision.

Two important points need to be made about these proposals. First, the democracies should not implement any such rules of constraint unilaterally; that is, without the autocracies agreeing to similar constraints on their AI weapons systems. As with any weapon system, conventional, digital, nuclear, or otherwise, unilateral disarmament is a bad idea. And where mutual constraints are agreed to, there should be very rigorous compliance, inspection, and neutral oversight systems agreed to as well. The second point on constraints is that great care should be exercised about them when it comes to AI systems that are exclusively defensive in nature. Defensive weapons systems, whether exhibiting AI capabilities or not, are generally very useful for supporting the peace, while offensive systems are the more problematic from the perspective of maintaining the peace. Therefore, the democracies should be very slow, and extremely careful, to agree to putting constraints on wholly defensive AI-based weapons systems, like the Patriot and Aegis ADSs highlighted in the beginning of the introduction.

In the civilian realm there have also been a number of initiatives in recent years calling for constraints on AI systems. Singapore was first out of the gate with its Model for AI Governance Framework in 2019. In 2022 three members of Congress introduced an Algorithmic Accountability Act. Other democracies are considering similar legal regimes, such as Canada's Bill C-27. The European Parliament has made the most progress, and is close to finalizing an Artificial Intelligence Act that it would send to the European Commission for consideration. None of these initiatives have yet produced a working legal regime governing AI.

It is worth noting two overarching thoughts about these types of potential constraints on AI. First, they need to be structured and implemented in a way that doesn't impede research and development. Thus, if a democracy goes down this path, the regulatory effort should be focused exclusively on commercial distribution of the AI product to the public or into the stream of commerce. The second point is that ideally such domestic constraints are limited to those measures that the autocracies agree to as well, so that there would be a level playing field in the sale of these systems into one another's markets; but even if an autocracy agrees to pass a law equivalent to the one passed in a democracy, the important question remains: How is that law enforced in the autocracy when it doesn't have a general system of the rule of law, with the required independent judges and the like? This might lead to the conclusion that the most likely alternative, when it comes to constraints on civilian AI systems, would simply be to disallow entry into the democracies of AI systems designed, developed, and manufactured in the autocracies. This would be consistent with the general approach of adding AI systems to the list of matters that are dealt with through the overall tech decoupling of the democracies and autocracies.

Second, in March 2023 a group of 1,000 researchers and entrepreneurs in the tech space in the democracies signed a letter (crafted by the Future of Life Institute) [10] calling for a six-month moratorium on all development work on AI systems like Chat GPT, because they were worried these kinds of AI have risks that need to be assessed and addressed before further work is done on them. Frankly, in a manner consistent with the comments above, such a hiatus would not be a good idea. From the perspective of Cold War 2.0, the autocracies certainly won't be halting their R&D into AI systems for any stretch of time. Plus, it is not realistic to think all AI researchers will voluntarily give up their jobs, and paychecks, for six months and what, go sit on a beach for half a year?

The pause called for by the Future of Life Institute is clearly not a sensible way forward. It turns out that even Elon Musk, perhaps the highest-profile signer of the Future of Life letter, seems to be proceeding with AI efforts.[11] Rather, the legislatures of the relevant democracies should have appropriate science and technology subcommittees hold hearings into AI, and specifically the risks posed by it, but even then the urge to regulate AI should be pursued with restraint, given that there is simply insufficient evidence of harm at this point that would warrant a heavy-handed approach to lawmaking. There might be one day, but that day has yet to come. In the meantime, in order to ensure that they prevail against the autocracies in Cold War 2.0, the democracies should not handicap themselves relative to the autocracies by shutting down AI research unilaterally.

More recently Sam Altman, the CEO of OpenAI (the developer of ChatGPT), appeared before the US Congress and said he would welcome regulation of AI. Again, a cautionary note is in order when a leader of a specific industry calls for regulation of that very industry. Government regulation, if too heavy-handed, can quickly become a barrier to entry, especially to smaller or newer entrants into the domain. A company like OpenAI, courtesy of its partnership with Microsoft, can afford just about any regulatory burden imposed by even a well-meaning Congress. That same regulation, though, could easy stifle the next new AI start-up with a revolutionary idea, technology, or business model. Or worse, the regulation has the effect of exiling the thwarted founders of such a start-up to another country, particularly if it is an autocracy, presumably offering a lot of money for the company's migration. Whenever regulation is proposed over a fairly specific industry domain, the question must always be asked: Will this measure serve to protect the public interest fairly, or will the measure fail its essential purpose because it will shut down the process of competitive displacement? If it's likely to do the latter, the regulation is too overbearing and needs to be refashioned or at least pruned materially. Particularly in the Cold War 2.0 world of global rivalry, the democracies cannot afford to hamper competitive displacement in their market for software development, which is the secret sauce of so much of their success.

There is one other potential constraint on AI software worth mentioning briefly. In October 2022, the Biden administration placed hard-hitting controls on the export to China of high-performance semiconductor chips made in America, or made with equipment made in America. Washington has been considering similar restrictions on the export to China of AI, as well a prohibition on Americans (including individuals, companies, banks, and investment funds of all types) investing in Chinese AI companies and research entities. Given the thoroughly dual-use nature of AI, the White House is having some difficulty defining with some precision what type of AI such restrictions will apply to.

Clearly any such restrictions cannot apply to all AI, as that would capture thousands of different variations of AI and machine learning software, and there is the prospect of yet thousands more such programs coming to market in the next few years. There is a scenario where, in ten to fifteen years, virtually all software has at least *some* AI embedded into it. Therefore, simply defining the newly restricted category as "AI and machine learning" is much too broad. One approach, instead, is to define the prohibited software by function, which might include any AI actually designed to work in a military setting, or delivered to or used by an arm of the military or a research institute affiliated with the PLA, or where the exporter initially delivered the AI software to a civilian entity but knew, or ought to have known (given the surrounding circumstances) that its customer was going to transfer the AI software to a military entity in China. Frankly, the uncertainty attached to any such system will likely mean that few entities will risk exporting American AI software to China for any purpose. This would mean that there would be, in effect, a technology decoupling between the democracies and the autocracies in respect to AI software.

6

THE CONTEST FOR SEMICONDUCTOR CHIP SUPREMACY

Two events in 2022 changed profoundly the course of Cold War 2.0. The first was Russia's full-scale military invasion of Ukraine. The second was the embargo on high-performance semiconductor chips placed by the United States on China. Most people understand viscerally the gravity of the hot war in Ukraine. The deep ramifications of the cold war denial of SCs, and especially equipment to make SCs, against China are somewhat more subtle, but just as critical. SCs are the lifeblood of the modern economy and military. Without them there are no functioning electronics. Without high-performance SCs there are no smartphones and no precision-guided weapons, like missiles. Turns out the two most important events of 2022 were crucially intertwined.

There's more. It is impossible to develop and deploy sophisticated AI without high-performance SCs. No fancy SCs, no fancy AI. This presents the autocracies with a massive strategic risk. With the SC embargo the democracies have their digital boot on China's digital throat. Cold War 2.0, barely a decade old, is already at an inflection point. There is a critical election in Taiwan in January 2024. The outcome of that political race could cause China to move against the island before China's digital deficit in SCs gets inevitably worse. Or perhaps China agrees to become like Japan, a second large Asian power that understands the benefits of a rules-based international order. Such a deal could include China convincing Russia to pull out of Ukraine (including Crimea), and China dropping its own claims to Taiwan, and in return the US embargo on SCs to China would be terminated. The year 2022 was an important one for Cold War 2.0; 2024, a US election year, might be even more eventful.

THE SEMICONDUCTOR CHIP REVOLUTION

The last twenty years of growth in the SC industry reflect the significant role they now play in our society. Between 2000 and 2022, annual sales of SCs worldwide increased from $139 billion to $573 billion, a growth rate of 313 percent (roughly 13 percent per year over the last twenty years), while the number of SCs shipped per year increased by 290 percent.[1] This growth has been driven by the proliferation of new devices that require SCs. For example, forty years ago cars were still largely solely mechanical devices, but today 20 percent of all SCs end up in automobiles. (TSMC, the world's leading SC manufacturer, tries to keep all its factories in Taiwan, but it is building several new facilities, including a factory in Germany, to produce SCs specifically for the car market.) Taking all product markets together, in 2021 about 1.15 trillion SCs were made globally.

In the previous chapter AI was discussed as an "accelerator technology." SCs are accelerators as well, because they have unleashed enormous waves of innovation in many other domains. Research into high-energy physics would not be where it is today without high-performance SCs. The same goes for leading-edge drug discovery, bioinformatics, personalized medicine, nuclear weapons development, or large-area weather forecasting, just to name a few domains of endeavor dependent on high-end SCs. Moreover, the computer, in all its various forms and sizes, has insinuated itself into virtually every nook and cranny of society, triggering massive innovation and efficiency gains at all levels of human endeavor, an achievement made possible only by the SC. Although each SC is tiny, the SC industry is a very big thing.

To grasp the geopolitical ramifications of SCs for Cold War 2.0 it is necessary to understand, at least generally, how SCs are made. In turn, it's useful to recall how SCs came about; some engineering history is useful here. Computers store data and software as electrical signals and charge. The IBM ENIAC computer of the 1940s (the world's first "real" computer), contained hundreds of cathode ray (vacuum) tubes. Each tube controlled the flow of electrical charge, which the computer's central processing unit employed to carry out its fast computations. It made sense to use cathode ray tubes in early computers, because they could be found in radios and televisions, and so their physics and engineering were well understood and their cost was reasonable.

Still, everyone who made computers in the 1950s knew that cathode ray tubes had fundamental limitations. It's actually very similar to the dilemma with battery technology today. Lithium-ion batteries have brought the world quite a distance in the great energy shift from fossil fuels to renewable sources of electricity, but at the same time scientists and politicians understand that the current battery technology will not be sufficient to get to net zero. The world needs a very significant technology breakthrough in batteries; in effect, the energy storage industry is still waiting for its SC to be invented.

In computers the huge breakthrough came when two engineers at Bell Labs, a private research arm of a US telecommunications equipment manufacturer, innovated the concept of engraving a pattern of copper into a small substrate of sand, or silicon, to form a tiny circuit. The two American inventors of the first SC called the device a "semiconductor" because of the way the copper and the silicon worked to let some electrical signals through but block others. Subsequent improvements produced a more stable technology for the SC that could accommodate hundreds (and ultimately hundreds of millions, and today billions) of tiny circuits.

A single circuit, when it was on, registered as the number 1, and when it was off it was 0 (zero). The computer, in effect, could only speak in the language of 1s and 0s, while our general mathematical language contains ten symbols: 0, 1, 2, 3, 4, 5, 6, 7, 8, and 9. With these ten symbols any number, however long, can be represented. So how can the SC work as effectively (and indeed even better) with only two symbols, namely 0 and 1? The answer, partly, is speed, incredible, unbelievable rates of speed.

The first SCs sixty years ago weren't all that fast, and in fact weren't a lot faster than cathode ray tubes, but SCs (even the earliest ones) were much smaller. Computers, because of their SCs, have gotten a lot faster over time. The ENIAC computer circa the 1940s took up an entire mid-sized room and could do about 5,000 additions per second. By 2008, the first iPhone could do about 200 million additions per second. Today's iPhone does even much better than that. An Apple iPhone 13 Pro series contains a single chip with the following separate parts to it: two high-performance processors, four high-efficiency processors, a five-processor graphics SC, and a 16-processor neural engine that performs 16 trillion operations per second—and all of this avalanche of processing power is contained in a single smartphone! *Small* is the operative word when it comes to SCs.

SCs have always been small, but their real magical quality is how they have kept getting ever smaller every few years. Moreover, stunningly, with each generation of miniaturization the SCs also became more powerful by squeezing many more transistors onto the SC. Gordon Moore, one of the founders of Intel, a leading American SC maker, even predicted in 1965 that every two years (or so) the computing power of SCs will double because the size of the transistor continued to shrink. This became coined as "Moore's Law," and up to about 2015 the SC industry made good on Moore's prediction. As if this wasn't already pretty amazing, their cost, relative to their computing power, has dropped dramatically as well. If a car had undergone the same price-performance improvement ratio over the past seventy years, today's gas-fueled vehicles would get millions—and probably billions—of miles on a gallon of gas.

It is difficult for the human brain to actually grasp just how miniature the guts of SCs have become. For instance, the different levels of SC performance are measured in "nanometer processes." The lower the nanometer number associated with the particular SC, the more powerful it is, because that SC has yet more billions of transistors squished onto a tiny surface of silicon. A 7 nm SC (made using a 7-nanometer process) can get between 95 and 115 million transistors per square millimeter. A 5 nm SC can squeeze 125 to 300 million transistors onto the same space. Therefore, today, a 3 nm SC is about 60 percent more powerful than a 5 nm SC.

In one sense, the difference between 5 nm and 48 nm seems fairly academic to the average layperson. The unaided human eye cannot even begin to register these tiny measurements, and the human brain cannot absorb their dimensions either. SC designers and makers, though, have the tools with which to make these minuscule differences meaningful, and so they are important in the SC world. More to the point, the difference between a 48 nm SC and a 5 nm SC (and between a 5 nm and a 3 nm SC) is quite pronounced when it comes to processing certain software and data in the real world. Given the discussion of critical AI in the previous chapter, it is noteworthy, for instance, that AI running on a 48 nm SC will not do nearly as good a job training on large data sets, especially those relating to images, as a 5 nm SC. In short, a company wanting to do state-of-the-art AI today needs a 5 nm SC, and in a few years' time, the same company will want a 3 nm SC, and so on. The ramifications of this reality for companies in the AI space will become apparent when discussing below America's sanctions on China for certain high-performance SCs.

There are several kinds of SCs, with the two major categories being processor SCs and memory SCs. The processor ones are, as the name suggests, those that do most of the computer's heavy lifting; they contain the logic algorithms of the SC, and they actually carry out the secret-sauce functions of the SC. Often traditionally called a CPU, for central processing unit, those SCs that do training of the computer on large data sets for AI are now called GPUs, for *graphical* processing units, especially if they are expert at capturing and learning from images and videos; computers doing

AI functions will also contain a neural processing unit, distinct from the CPU and the GPU. The performance of these processor or logic SCs are measured in nanometer processes, as noted immediately above, such as a 3 nm SC that is more powerful than a 5 nm SC.

Memory SCs specialize in storing data. Their performance is measured differently from that of processor SCs, because memory SCs are generally trying to expand their memory capacity on the same sized chip space, and they do so by adding many layers on top of each other. Today, the best-performing memory SCs are at the 128-layer level, but some SC makers are working on coming out with a 176-layer memory SC in a few years, which will improve performance significantly.

MAKING SEMICONDUCTOR CHIPS

Making an SC is a complex, laborious, and expensive process. It is not for the faint of heart, or the impecunious. First, the SC is designed by making a "blueprint" of how the millions of tiny circuits on a minuscule piece of silicon wafer should be arranged. This can only be done using very complex and very expensive SC design software from one of only three software companies in the world specializing in making this unique electronic design automation (EDA) software. There are also some companies that own "templates" useful for making some elements of these designs. These templates can speed up the design process significantly if they are used as part of the base of the new SC's design. A British company, ARM, has the leading template for smartphone computer processor SCs, while Intel has a leading template for anyone wanting to make an SC for x86 type computer servers.

Once the design for the SC is complete, it is sent to an SC fabricator, or "fab," where the actual SC will be made. The fab etches the design onto a wafer of silicon, creating the minuscule circuits. The machines used for the etching processes are some of the most complex in the world. The fab operator doesn't make these machines, but knows how to operate them in conditions where the light, heat, and other conditions are very carefully calibrated for quality control. Operating all the complex equipment in the fab, and producing world-class SCs is very, very difficult. Even major SC manufacturers can get the etching process wrong, and then ruin the performance of the resulting SCs. [2]

It used to be that only large manufacturers like Intel designed SCs, and then they designed general SCs that everyone else would use more or less for the same purposes. Those days are long gone. Today Intel still designs SCs, but so do two other categories of SC designers. First are SC companies that do nothing but design SCs, and then sell them widely to other companies once the SC is fabricated by someone other than the SC designer. AMD and Nvidia are the two leading such SC design firms in the world for processor SCs. The other SC designers are tech companies who want to design SCs for their own use exclusively. Apple is a good example. It has very particular demands of the SCs it uses, for example for its smartphones, so that it designs its own SCs, which it then has manufactured for it exclusively. Amazon is also starting to design its own SCs. The designers of SCs, like AMD, Nvidia, Apple, or Amazon, use the EDA software from one of three EDA suppliers: Synopsys, Cadence, or Siemens EDA (formerly Mentor).

The SC designers, like Nvidia or Apple, do not have the factory able to actually make the SC they have designed. For this stage of the process, the designer goes to a "fab" operator, like TSMC, and TSMC makes the SC at its fab but to the strict requirements of the designer. The fab operator needs to undertake about 1,000 process steps to get the silicon wafer ready for etching. This could require about fifty types of very specialized equipment (called SME, or semiconductor manufacturing equipment).

As part of the SC manufacturing process in the fab, for the most advanced process nodes (such as 5 and 3 nm), the fab operator will take the "blueprint" design (created with the EDA software), and load it into a huge machine that is at the heart of the SC fabrication process for the most powerful SCs in the world. The machine, made by ASML in the Netherlands, is about the size of a large truck. This machine can "read" the SC design in the blueprint, and then etch that design onto a piece of silicon wafer using a tiny beam of light. It sounds simple described in these general terms, but this single process is perhaps the most complicated industrial activity known to humankind. There is only one such etching machine (made by ASML) in the entire world that can manufacture SCs in the 7, 5, and 3 nm process nodes, and it uses a method called Extreme Ultraviolet Lithography (EUL).

The scientists and engineers at ASML in the Netherlands—and the many engineers and customers in the rest of Europe, America, Taiwan, Japan, and South Korea who assisted—who built the EUL etching machine took twenty years to wrestle with the related basic science, and then the very finicky engineering, to get the machine to work.[3] As the innovation process around the EUL machine took thirteen years longer than anticipated, ASML had to rely very heavily on its optical light supplier (Zeiss in Germany), as well as the three lead customers, namely TSMC in Taiwan, Samsung in South Korea, and Intel in the US, each of which ended up taking an equity stake in ASML. Ultimately, though, all this international collaboration paid off. For several years the price of a single EUL machine was $100 million, but the latest version, which contains even more state-of-the-art innovation, sells for $500 million.

Once the ASML machine etches the required pattern for the billions of circuits onto the SC, various chemical processes deposit just the right amount of semiconducting material in the appropriate places on the SC. Subsequently, individual SCs have to be cut out of the wafer, and then each SC can be cleaned up, tested, and sold. (If you are AMD or Nvidia; if you are Apple, you will keep all your custom SCs coming out of the fab for inserting into your own devices, like iPhones.) As noted above, making an SC is a complex process.

THE GLOBAL SEMICONDUCTOR CHIP INDUSTRY

The market and supply chains for SCs are fairly complicated and quite global. An SC might be designed in the US using American EDA software, but also some intellectual property from ARM in the UK, and then the SC is made in Taiwan at a TSMC plant, but then packaged and finished in a facility in China. Throughout this process, the supply chain would touch various specialists. South Korea's Samsung specializes in making memory SCs that reside in all sorts of computers; they store the data relevant to the various processes being asked of the SC. In the United States, there is the former world leader, Intel, who used to make the dominant SC in the marketplace, namely the processor chip for the personal computer.

In the United States, Intel is still the largest SC manufacturer, but there are other players as well, including Micron, which makes memory chips for the most part. Then there are a number of other designers of chips in the US. Most American SC designers have their SCs made by a fab owned and operated by Intel or Micron, except for their highest-performance SCs, which need to be made at one of TSMC's fabs in Taiwan (though soon also at a TSMC facility in the US), because the world's most advanced fabs are on that small island, 160 kilometers across from a quite hostile China. What's wrong with this picture, especially if the ultimate customer for the particular SC is the United States military?

In China, SMIC (Semiconductor Manufacturing International Corp) operates fabs that can make SCs in the 25 to 14 nm range. There are a few smaller companies that can make less powerful SCs in the 48 to 25 nm range. Yangtze Memory Technologies Corp. (YMTC) makes memory SCs, including at the 128-layer performance level. All these fabs, though, use the ASML etching machine, or less powerful etchers from one of two Japanese companies, Nikon and Canon. In short, China is not self-sufficient when it comes to the SC supply chain. In 2022 China imported about $400 billion worth of SCs, many from the fabs in Taiwan. As for the less powerful SCs made by fabs in China, they currently rely almost completely on SC manufacturing equipment from Japan, the United States, and the Netherlands. It is estimated that Chinese companies produce less than 10 percent of the SC manufacturing equipment being used in fabs in China.

The M&A market is critical to the leading suppliers of SME's and others in the SC supply chain ecosystem. Some recent major acquisitions have been AMD acquiring Xilinx, and Intel acquiring Tower Semiconductor. At the same time, though, Nvidia's acquisition of ARM was blocked by regulators in early 2022, but other than that, most deals involving buyers and sellers in democracies have been allowed to proceed. On the other hand, Chinese firms will have an increasingly tough time buying companies in the democracies, just as Tsinghua Unigroup's acquisition of Micron Technologies was blocked by the US government in 2015, Fujian Grand Chip's acquisition of SME Aixtron was blocked by the German government in 2016, and a Chinese company's proposal to buy the Newport Wafer Fab in 2022 was blocked by the UK government.

Here is a list of the key players in the global SC industry, indicating where they are active in the vertical supply chain of the industry, and their sales and market capitalization. Also noted is the country's market share of the particular portion of the SC industry. Note that for purposes of this list, Taiwan is assumed to be in the camp of the democracies.

TOP FOUR ELECTRONIC DESIGN AUTOMATION (EDA) SOFTWARE COMPANIES

Democracies		
United States, 70 percent market share	Revenues	Market Cap
Synopsys	$5.2 billion	$65 billion
Cadence	$3.6	$62
Mentor (now Siemens EDA, Germany)	$3.1 (Siemens $79 B)	$138 (Siemens)
Autocracies		
China, 10 percent	Revenues	Market Cap
Empyrean Technology Co.	$0.115	$9.4

TOP 10 INTELLECTUAL PROPERTY SUPPLIERS (DESIGN IP)

Democracies		
United States, 28.3 percent market share	Revenues	Market Cap
Synopsys	$1.314 billion	$65 billion
Cadence	$0.357	$63.4
Ceva	$0.134	$0.58
Rambus	$0.087	$6.59
United Kingdom, 46.5 percent	Revenues	Market Cap
ARM	$2.74 billion	est. $60 billion
Alphawave	$0.175	$1.16

Taiwan, 1.6 percent	Revenues	Market Cap
eMemory Technology	$0.105	$5.38
Autocracies		
China, 2 percent	**Revenues**	**Market Cap**
VeriSilicon (with some investment backing by Intel and Samsung)	$0.133	$4.9

SEMICONDUCTOR CHIP DESIGN

Democracies		
United States, 64 percent market share	**Revenues**	**Market Cap**
Nvidia	$26.9	$1.04 trillion
AMD (Advanced Micro Devices)	$23.6	$184 billion
Qualcomm	$44.2	$127 billion
Apple (SCs for own use)	$394.3 (total)	$3.01 trillion
Amazon (SCs for own use)	$514 (total)	$1.32 trillion
Microsoft (SCs for own use, esp. AI)	$198.2 (total)	$2.54 trillion
Meta (SCs for own use, esp. AI)	$116.6 (total)	$753 billion
Google (SCs for its own use)	$279.8 (total)	$1.53 trillion
IBM (SCs for its own use and R&D)	$60.5 (total)	$120 billion
Taiwan, 18 percent	**Revenues**	**Market Cap**
MediaTek	$18.7	$35.3
Realtek	$3.6	$6.9
Autocracies		
China, 15 percent	**Revenues**	**Market Cap**
HiSilicon (owned by Huawei)	[private]	[private]
Unisoc (owned by Tsinghua Unigroup)	[private]	[private]

SILICON WAFERS

Democracies, 90 percent of the global market		
Japan	**Revenues**	**Market Cap**
Shin-Etsu Chemical	$17.2	$65.7
SUMCO Corp.	$3.1	$4.9
South Korea	**Revenues**	**Market Cap**
SK Siltron css (part of SK, a very large South Korean conglomerate)	$103	$5.9

Taiwan	Revenues	Market Cap
GlobalWafers	$2.2	$6.8
Autocracies		
China	Revenues	Market Cap
Hua Hong Semiconductor	$2.4	$4.3

SEMICONDUCTOR MANUFACTURING EQUIPMENT

Democracies		
United States	Revenues	Market Cap
Applied Materials (90 percent of market for deposition and doping equipment)	$26.6	$120
KLA	$10.6	$64
Lam Research (etching machines)	$18.8	$84
Japan	Revenues	Market Cap
Tokyo Electron (90 percent of photoresist market)	$16.5	$69
Canon	$30.3	$26
Nikon	$4.4	$4.5
Netherlands	Revenues	Market Cap
ASML (100 percent of EUL [Extreme-Ultraviolet] lithography/etching equipment for SCs below 7 nm)	$25.5	$282.3
Autocracies		
China, 8 percent of local requirements and 2 percent of global supply	Revenues	Market Cap
SMEE (Shanghai Micro Electronics Equipment) (only at 90 nm process)	[private]	[private]

SC MANUFACTURING (FAB OPERATOR)

Democracies		
United States	Revenues	Market Cap
Intel	$56.4 billion	$136.6 billion
Micron	$23.0	$67.9
GlobalFoundries	$8.1	$34.9
Taiwan	Revenues	Market Cap
TSMC	$74.5	$526.4
United Microelectronics	$9.0	$19.2

South Korea	Revenues	Market Cap
Samsung	$65.6 ($233 entire)	$367
SK Hynix	$36.2	$63.3

SC MANUFACTURER

Autocracies		
China	Revenues	Market Cap
SMIC (Semiconductor Manufacturing Int'l Corp)	$6.8 billion	$28.6
YMTC (owned by Tsinghua Unigroup)	[private]	[private]
GigaDevice	$1.12	$10.1

ASSEMBLY, PACKAGING AND TESTING

Taiwan	Revenues	Market Cap
ASE Technology Holding	$12.5	$16.4
China	Revenues	Market Cap
JCET Group Co. Ltd.	$4.6	$7.9
NAURA Technology Group	$2.0	$15.5

SEMICONDUCTOR CHIP SANCTIONS

In September 2022, Jake Sullivan, the national security advisor to President Joe Biden, gave a very important speech regarding the SC industry.[4] He outlined what steps the United States was planning to take to deny Chinese companies, and thereby the Chinese military, access to the most powerful SCs. Sullivan indicated this had to be done for two reasons. First, China has a policy of civilian-military fusion, such that any SCs imported or developed by Chinese companies would invariably be made available to the People's Liberation Army (the PLA), China's armed forces. Second, China has instituted an oppressive system of citizen surveillance and oppression unmatched anywhere in the world, and this structure, which denies basic human rights to average Chinese citizens, is built upon technologies that have included components sourced from the democracies. Accordingly, Sullivan indicated that the US government would be taking steps to block high-performance SCs, and the equipment to make them, from finding their way into China.

For some time, China had requested TSMC build and operate in China a semiconductor fab for SCs in the 7 to 5 nm range, but the Americans have told TSMC and the Taiwanese government not to do so. More generally, following the Sullivan speech, on October 7, 2022, the Biden administration announced an embargo on American companies selling SCs to China that are 14 nm or more powerful (so, nothing in the 14 to 3 nm range for current SCs). Therefore, companies like Nvidia, AMD, and Intel cannot sell any more of their most advanced SCs to China, or to anyone that they know will pass along the SCs to Chinese companies or entities.

These sorts of restrictions have been in place for certain SCs for some time. In 2018, the Trump administration blocked the sale of American-made SCs to certain companies in China, essentially those involved in making devices for the Chinese military and those making devices used to conduct surveillance on Chinese citizens or the Uighur minority in Xinjiang. One company that was embargoed was Huawei, the giant Chinese telecom equipment maker and leading supplier in the world of telecom equipment for networks, with sales worldwide in 2017 of $92.5 billion. When this US embargo came into force, Huawei had to cancel billions of dollars of orders for equipment that used American SCs. Huawei's sales plunged by 25 percent in 2018 and 2019. Huawei could find substitutes for some of the embargoed American SCs, but not all of them.

What's new about the Biden administration's embargo announced in October 2022 is that they prohibit the sale of not only high-end SCs, but also the equipment used to make those SCs. A number of US companies have lost material sales to Chinese companies as a result, and have suffered losses in the range of hundreds of millions of dollars in the six months following the announcement of the embargo. From the industry chart above, it is clear that there are a number of important SME makers outside of the United States. Therefore, an important question was whether the Japanese and the Dutch would go along with the embargo in respect to SC-making equipment they would otherwise sell (very profitably) to China. The answer so far is yes, and again the Chinese are none too happy about their high-end SC manufacturing base being crippled in this way. It is likely China will be able to continue making SCs in the 45 nm and older nm processes range, but will be stymied for some (and perhaps many) years in making higher-end SCs. Most critically, if China cannot buy ASML's EUL lithography etching machine, it may take China about twenty years (or more?) to build a replacement for this marvel of high-tech manufacturing.

The effect of the SC and SC-making equipment embargo on China and Russia implemented by the US and some other democracies will be significant. Not only will China and Russia not be able to procure high-end SCs for some years—likely between fifteen and twenty years—from the democracies, but this embargo will stunt the growth of the AI industry in China and Russia because increasingly the leading AI programs need very powerful computers to run on. If those computers don't have AI-specific SCs (such as the AMD V100, or Nvidia A100), then this will block China's plan to become a world leader in AI by 2026. In effect, the democracies likely have about ten years of breathing room before the Chinese push to create a homegrown substitute SC etching machine bears fruit, but even then, replacing ASML's EUL machine might well take double that time.

For a number of months China did not retaliate generally against the Biden administration and American companies in respect of the US equipment embargo, but in June 2023 Beijing announced that state-owned utility companies, especially in the telecoms domain, were henceforth prohibited from using SCs sourced from the American company Micron Technology because they had security shortcomings. This is widely seen as a tit-for-tat response to the US embargo on SCs (and SC-making equipment) implemented in October 2022. It is likely that additional retaliatory actions by the Chinese will be forthcoming. In the meantime, China will likely make an even greater push to build its own indigenous supply chain of Chinese businesses and technologies that can make higher-end SCs than is the case today. If China fails in this effort, it will fall behind seriously in AI development, as well as the production of military-related AI products and other weapons or industrial products that require the most powerful

SCs. Given the massive importance of AI to China (and to the US and every other country on earth), an outcome where high-end computing power—including in the AI domain—was denied China would pose a very serious problem for China.

The challenges posed to China by having to work with a long-term technology deficiency will likely become even more acute should the Biden administration enact further technology-related controls on China. Given the relative success of the export controls on high-performance SCs, the additional measures being discussed in Washington include restrictions on US investment in Chinese AI, QC, and biotechnology companies; blocking the export to China of all SCs that are intended to process AI applications; and prohibiting Chinese AI companies from accessing computers through cloud arrangements with American suppliers.

Beijing might retaliate against these (and even just the existing) measures by limiting the export from China to the US of certain critical minerals that China has a virtual monopoly on at this point, such as dysprosium and terbium. The question for Xi will be: Does he want to start a full-scale trade war with the United States? It began when the Trump administration launched its own restrictions on SC sales to Chinese entities that ended in a draw. Would Xi do as well now, particularly since the Biden White House is livid that China is assisting Russia as much as it is in respect of the war in Ukraine? China has stepped in to buy Russian oil and gas when the Europeans ceased buying these vital exports from Russia, as the Europeans applied sanctions against Russia over its unprovoked attack on Ukraine. As well, China's exports to Russia are up about 34 percent since Russia began the war in Ukraine—this is the figure that particularly riles the White House, as it includes the sales of reconnaissance drones from China to Russia.

For his part, President Biden is also worried that China might invade Taiwan. If that were to happen, TSMC's most advanced SC fabs would certainly be adversely affected by the military conflict, if not completely or partially destroyed. If fighting cut off the supply of high-end SCs to the United States, that could be devastating for the economies of the democracies. For this reason, the Biden administration is pursuing two important initiatives in SC industrial policy.

SEMICONDUCTOR CHIP INDUSTRIAL POLICY

In terms of reliance on foreign SC manufacturing expertise, the US government is unhappy with America's heavy dependence on TSMC to make 90 percent of the high-end SCs that US companies require. Accordingly, the Biden administration has negotiated with TSMC to build two fabs in the United States over the next few years. (Fabs take a long time to build, and they cost about $15–20 billion to construct, including installing all the SC manufacturing equipment noted above.) One fab is intended to make SCs in the 7 to 5 nm range for the US military and its prime defense contractors. The other fab will make SCs in the range of 5 to 3 nm, as advanced as the SCs that TSMC currently makes in Taiwan. TSMC has also agreed to put up a fab in Japan to make SCs in the 7 to 5 nm range. TSMC will also establish a fab in Europe. If all these fabs get built in the next number of years, they will go a long way to usefully diversifying the risk of a Chinese military move against Taiwan.

In a similar vein, in the summer of 2022 the US president proposed, and the American Congress approved, the Chips Act, which, among other things, makes available about $52 billion in subsidies and tax breaks to American and foreign SC makers (like TSMC) that build new fabs in the United States that are able to produce the highest-end SCs. Intel and Micron (both American companies) and TSMC (from Taiwan) have taken advantage of this US government program, and each have announced they will build fabs in the US in the next couple of years. Many other companies have expressed interest in participating in the Chips Act program.

Between this industrial policy requiring TSMC to build new fabs in the United States, providing financial incentives to US-based and non-Chinese foreign SC manufacturers, and the American embargo on sales to China of high-end SCs and SC-making equipment, Cold War 2.0 is certainly underway in the SC sector of the global economy. The Biden administration's goal is nothing less than the commercial crippling of the Chinese high-end SC industry sector. Presumably at some point in the near future the Chinese will respond with their own actions against the US and the other democracies implicated in policies that could prove devastating to China's previously ambitious plans for developing their SC and AI sectors. (Because they are key accelerator technologies, they would also have a deleterious impact on virtually all other innovation in China.) As noted above, the Chinese have taken a relatively small retaliatory step against the US company Micron, but it is unlikely this will be the end of China's pushback.

China will invariably partly respond to the actions of the Americans by looking to build up China's own SC manufacturing equipment supply chain. Chinese SC fabricators SMIC and YMTC could likely operate factories that produce 7 nm and 3 nm SCs, so long as they had SC manufacturing equipment that replaced the ASML, Japanese, and American equipment needed to do so. What is the likelihood of Chinese companies succeeding in producing that equipment and the thousands of components that go into these hyper-complex machines? Not very good, based on recent history.

In 2014, the Chinese government in Beijing created an investment fund specifically aimed at creating greater capability in the SC manufacturing domain. It is called the China Integrated Circuit Industry Investment Fund, but is known more colloquially as "Big Fund I." The fund raised just under $22 billion. The way the fund worked is that bureaucrats in Beijing would select the recipient of financial support from Big Fund I, and then that company would approach a local government in China to negotiate tax breaks or other matching funds from the municipality in consideration for agreeing to site a new fab or other factory in the municipality. Only when deals were done with both levels of government would the Chinese company invite other investors from the private sector into the new venture.

There were two big problems with this mechanism for conducting industrial policy. First, by having the government lead the investment initiative, it was government bureaucrats who decided which Chinese companies received the money and how much. Not surprisingly, the bureaucrats went with the safe option and gave most of the money to well-established companies like SMIC and YMTC, in order for them to build more of what they were already doing. Each of these companies used the Big Fund I money to build more fab capacity (SMIC for processor SCs and YMTC for memory SCs), but that isn't what China needed out of a SC industrial policy. In 2014 what was desperately missing in the Chinese supply chain for SCs was a viable Chinese player that can make world-class SC etching/lithography equipment, and that was hardly an afterthought in the first round of Big Fund I investments. In short, China crucially needed a "Made in China" ASML, but that was exactly what the bureaucrats responsible for Big Fund I failed to try to seed with their money, largely because they simply didn't know how to go about such a daunting task. China also needed a world-class player in the EDA space, so that SC developers could have adequate tools with which to design the highest-performance SCs. Again, Big Fund I missed this market segment as well.

The second, related problem, is that at the end of the day, there was (and continues to be) insufficient input from private sector investors as to which companies the Big Fund I money should be invested in. Chapter 2 discussed how dysfunctional the Russian central planning, top-down approach to industrial strategy was in Cold War 1, and how it especially stunted the Russian technology sector, both for the computer industry and biotechnology sector. China repeated the same type of mistakes when it completely missed the opportunity to build a SC manufacturing equipment industry in China.

The result is a very serious disaster for China in the SC domain (and for the design, development, and deployment of AI software), now that the US is restricting the flow of high-end SCs and equipment necessary to make them. For many years Big Fund I was reluctant to fund the development of Chinese vendors of EDA software; now, the Chinese deficit in EDA software is proving to be a very serious hole in China's domestic SC supply chain.[5] Moreover, consider the daunting wall that China has to get over to make viable EDA tools. The leading Chinese player in EDA is Empyrean. It has tiny sales relative to the American giants of the EDA space. Empyrean has no meaningful sales outside of China, and less than 10 percent of the Chinese market. It has about 150 people working in R&D. Compare that to Cadence, the American global market leader, which has about 5,000 engineers working on EDA R&D. As well, Synopsys supplements its technical capacity through an aggressive program of acquiring talent; in the last 30+ years it has acquired some 80+ companies.[6] In the field of EDA software China does not have a player that can substitute, even remotely, for the American leaders in the market.

It gets worse for China. In the several months following the October 2022 announcement of the new US SC sanctions program, the Chinese government assessed how the investments made from Big Fund I have helped build an indigenous Chinese SC manufacturing equipment industry. When the bureaucrats in Beijing concluded (correctly) that Big Fund I did very little, if anything, to foster technology that could replace high-end equipment from the democracies, instead of calling Big Fund I a failure and trying something new, they did two things. First, in August 2022 they blamed the failure of Big Fund I on corruption by the three leaders of Big Fund I and one of the leaders of the SC industry in China, a tech entrepreneur who ran Tsinghua Unigroup, one of the stalwarts of China's SC industry. These four people have been arrested and detained for corruption.[7] The outcome of this proceeding is still unknown, but the arrests alone prompt a second observation.

The government in Beijing is trying yet again with another Big Fund (called "Big Fund II"). This one is aimed more squarely at building manufacturing capacity in the SC manufacturing equipment space. It's too early to tell how this one will work out, but if Beijing uses the same model as Big Fund I, there is very little hope of it succeeding. Moreover, who from China's private sector will be keen to take on the project of building the Chinese competitors to Cadence, Synopsys, and ASML, when the last fellow from the private sector who got involved in Big Fund I is now languishing in jail? Not many, or at least not many of quality, which is precisely the type of executive China needs for this ambitious project. The essential point, though, is that top-down politically managed funding of tech ventures, as practiced by autocracies, simply doesn't work. It will be interesting to see how many more billions of dollars worth of public investment China wastes before it learns this simple lesson.

It should be noted that the failure of the Chinese model of investment strategy/funding for very sophisticated technology projects is not restricted to the SC sector. China has also been unable to design, develop, and manufacture jet engines for commercial aircraft. In May 2023 China announced with great fanfare that its project to bring to market a commercial aircraft that could compete with Boeing and Airbus had finally come to fruition, with the first successful flight of the new Comac C919 narrow-body short-haul jet. The bad news, though, for China at any rate, is that the engines for this plane are supplied by an American/French joint venture company. Moreover, the plane's avionics (the complex software that is used to actually fly the plane and operate many of its features) is also sourced from the democracies. Once again, Chinese technology innovation is showing how far behind it is relative to the democracies. As well, if a Chinese invasion of Taiwan triggered an across-the-board sanctions policy from the democracies, the C919 would cease to fly.

A final point about SC industrial strategy is timing. It took the incumbent, ASML, about twenty years to crack the code for EUL etching. Assume it takes China only ten years, given that they have a number of ASML machines that they can reverse engineer. By the time China completes this exercise and is producing 5 nm or 3 nm SCs at SMIC, ASML will be well into the next generation of etching machine, and will be doing 1 nm and more powerful, so China's inferior position relative to the democracies will not be alleviated. This is why China is putting so much energy into quantum computing, to which we now turn.

Could all of the above factors—the American SC and SC manufacturing equipment embargo, further US technology embargoes, and China's weakness in making technology at the highest levels—lead to a grand bargain between the United States and China? Here's what it might look like. China convinces Russia to pull out of Ukraine including

Crimea; China allows Taiwan to become fully and legally independent; and China agrees to become a normal member of the international community and adhere to the rules-based international order—i.e., China drops its maximalist claims to the South China Sea and agrees to abide by the UNCLOS, and also agrees to enter into a nuclear arms limitation treaty. And in return the United States lifts all technology embargoes against China. Might such a grand bargain be the capstone of the second term of a Biden presidency?

7

THE CONTEST FOR QUANTUM COMPUTING SUPREMACY

As powerful as today's computers are, in five to ten years they will be replaced by a different kind of computer, one that is millions of times more powerful. Quantum computers (although they are still very rudimentary) are already showing their superiority, particularly for the really big computational challenges of our era, such as: modeling the entire world's economy and all of its energy consumption activities to help combat climate change or modeling the entire Ukrainian battlefield to help Zelenskyy's army combat the Russians. Quantum computers will be better than "classical" ones, even today's supercomputers.

For China, quantum computers hold another significant attraction—they needn't run on semiconductor chips. Thus, if China continues to operate under the conditions of a high-performance SC famine due to the US embargo of SCs and equipment that makes them, then there could be a path for China to replace its stunted classical computers with new, unimpeded quantum computers. This could become one of the most intriguing subplots of Cold War 2.0.

THE ADVANTAGES OF QUANTUM COMPUTING

The world's fastest classical computers, "supercomputers," are being challenged by even faster ones of an entirely different design, called quantum computers (QCs). To understand QCs it helps to appreciate classical supercomputers, which can complete calculations at amazing speeds because they consist of thousands of central processing units (the core logic processors of computers) strung together, like pearls on the biggest necklace imaginable. Then, using very sophisticated management and networking software that orchestrates all the different cores to work together, the entire supercomputer can perform tasks requiring brute computing power that mere stand-alone computers cannot achieve.

An example of a classical supercomputer system is the global network of 170 powerful computers strung together by the European Organization for Nuclear Research (or CERN by its French initials). CERN operates the world's largest high-energy physics particle accelerator, which fires atoms around a 20-kilometer magnetic underground track, gets the particles into the fastest state capable by humans, and then smashes the atoms into each other in a special chamber. There, thousands of sensors track the emissions of millions of tiny particles. It was here that CERN discovered a new particle, called a Higgs boson. When these experiments are run, the huge volumes of data generated in the chamber are divvied up and sent to its network of 170 partners, so each partner's computer can do a portion of the computing required; collectively, these 170 computers could be considered a massive supercomputer. The volume of data produced by the CERN accelerator is gargantuan because particles collide in their facility about 1 billion times a second, producing about 1 petabyte of collision data every second. Even with CERN's many networked computers working on the data, it is still an overwhelming project, and the results are teased out of the collective processing only slowly.

Sugon is another example of a classical supercomputer. It sits in a highly guarded compound in Xinjiang. A province in Western China, Xinjiang is home to about 12 million Uighurs, an Islamic minority who speak a dialect of Turkish. The Chinese government has created a system of surveillance of the Uighur minority that includes facial recognition cameras placed every ten meters on major streets. What the massive computers in Sugon do is analyze simultaneously 1,000 video feeds from these cameras and orchestrate them together with data harvested from: phone calls being made at thousands of Wi-Fi hotspots, cellphone information, live phone conversations over telecom networks, a multitude of e-commerce transactions, and real-time facial recognition tracking. All of this data is integrated with information on each and every Uighur, including displays of religious piety; how many mobile phones they own (one is fine, but no phone, or two phones, might be evidence of some form of anti-state attitude); and whether the subject has family outside of China. The point of this elaborate system of surveillance and monitoring is to be able to predict deviant and anti-government behavior, in effect, to stop what the Chinese government considers a crime before it even happens. This system of surveillance and oppression is one of the more disturbing realities of Cold War 2.0.

The classical supercomputers used by CERN and Sugon, while among the most powerful on earth, are actually insufficient for the incredibly ambitious tasks they are being asked to undertake. Current computers, even with their high-performance semiconductor chips, simply cannot achieve the processing power and speed to successfully complete these two tasks—and many others like them, such as taking into account thousands more factors of our climate forecasting systems to produce much more accurate predictions about the weather. The only realistic hope for these massive computing challenges is a relatively new form of data processing, called quantum computing, as embodied in today's embryonic quantum computers (QC).

A quantum computer is much (very much) faster (perhaps 200 million times faster) than a classical computer because while today's computers use bits as their base currency of computing, the QC uses a qubit. A bit is an atomic particle that at any one time is either electrically charged (then it is positive) or not (then it is negative). The qubit, by contrast, can be both positive and negative at the same time! Instead of thinking about bits as either one or other side of a coin (head or tails) when it lands on a table or a floor, think of a qubit as a coin when it's spinning, thereby exhibiting both heads and tails simultaneously. In physics-speak, this is called "superpositioning." There is another key difference between the two systems: bits are separate and distinct, but qubits are both separate but then closely coupled together, what the physicists called "entangled." These are all overly brief and general explanations of the underpinnings of quantum computers, but even seasoned physicists have trouble wrapping their heads around quantum properties. The key point is that quantum physics is very different than classical physics, and the result is a QC that is much (very much) faster than a classical computer.

How much faster is a QC? In 2019, Google announced that its Sycamore qubit SC carried out a processing task in 200 seconds that would have taken a classical computer 10,000 years to complete. In 2021, China's leading quantum physicist, Pan Jianwei, working with the Zuchongzhi 2.1 QC, a 56 qubit QC, reported being able to complete an incredibly complex calculation in 1.5 hours that would have taken a classical computer eight years. Moreover, leaving aside speed, in some applications a QC can simply do calculations and solve problems that a classical computer cannot, or not as accurately.[1]

For China, especially, there is a further very significant advantage in QCs: several of the proposed quantum hardware architectures don't use traditional SCs, of the sort discussed in the previous chapter. Accordingly, while the use of traditional SCs will present China with a real strategic and tactical problem in the coming years and decades because of the embargo the key SC producing democracies have placed on the devices vis-à-vis China and other autocracies, the QC presents a very important possible solution to this computing conundrum for the Chinese leadership. In effect, in a few years time the impact of the SC sanctions might diminish dramatically for China if it can get the same, if not better, performance from a QC than it could from a 7, 5, or even 3 nm process SC. It would be a momentous development in computing, and in Cold War 2.0 if today's SC eventually became a legacy ancestor to the QC.[2]

It is, however, too early to predict anything in this regard because there are still a number of potential quantum architectures competing with one another for overall acceptance as the new quantum standard. IBM and Google are going down the path of "superconducting," while Honeywell and IonQ are pursuing the approach of "trapped ions." Yet other suppliers, such as PsiQuantum, are trying out a photonics-based technical platform, which is partly of interest because it may be compatible with classical semi-conductor chip technology and fiber optics. This is one reason why Intel is showing interest in this latter approach.

In effect, what all this diversity in scientific and technological innovation illustrates is competitive displacement on steroids. Indeed, the competition and potential substitution is happening on two levels. First, it will be fascinating to observe whether, and to what extent QCs replace classical computers. And if they do, it will be interesting to see which specific QC model wins the QC race.

In terms of their approach to coming up with a QC solution, it is also telling that the US has generated such a multiplicity of players, with a diversity of technological approaches, while China is largely betting on one key scientist, Pan Jianwei, who is then receiving a significant funding stream from the Chinese government to pursue one key technological avenue to achieve quantum computing success, namely photonics. Once again the funding model for new technology in the leading democracy and the leading autocracy stand in stark contrast. The Chinese approach has not produced to date a positive outcome in SC manufacturing equipment; it will be interesting to see whether the government backing one superstar scientist with one approach in the quantum domain with the same state-oriented, top-down model can produce for China a different, more successful outcome in the nascent QC industry.

QUANTUM COMPUTING USE CASES, CIVILIAN AND MILITARY

The computational advantage of QCs has most civilian and military users of classical supercomputers looking very seriously at the promise of this new technology. The following is just a sampling of the use cases that are being considered for QC at the moment: [3]

- *Drug discovery.* Combine a QC with AI, and it will be possible to determine in a matter of days, rather than years, what possible unusual combination of molecules might produce promising new medicines.

- *Simulating new materials.* Just as simulating new molecules will be a great assist for drug development, a QC will allow major advances in simulating a range of scientific assets, including chemical compounds, metals, and other materials. R&D using QC modeling software will accelerate time to market for a wide variety of useful new inputs into supply chains, as well as drive upgrades in products like solar panels, batteries, and a range of other mechanical goods. Indeed, the quantum structure of chemical compounds makes them particularly good candidates for modeling by quantum computing. [4]

- *Route optimization.* ExxonMobil has several hundred tankers carrying oil and natural gas to hundreds of ports and customers. The current scheduling software it uses is not nearly sophisticated enough to factor in thousands of additional variables, like the weather and political risk in various parts of the world, and especially not in real time. ExxonMobil is working with the IBM QC to see if it could produce a better model and real-world results. [5]

- *Weather forecasting.* Much more accurate weather forecasts using QC techniques (including hundreds more real-time variables) would assist QC route optimization (see previous point). It would also provide the general public and specific segments of society—such as farmers, forest fire–fighters, and outdoor recreation venues—with much greater accuracy in weather prediction.

- *Credit card fraud detection.* There is already software that does this, for example software that detects when a credit card has been stolen by tracking suddenly different purchasing patterns using the card. These programs often produce false positives because they cannot take into account sufficient variables, such as when the cardholder is traveling. (This is why many credit cards get declined when the cardholder is out of town, which is of course when the cardholder needs it the most!) A QC-based credit card fraud detection program will be able to include many more variables (hundreds and hundreds more), including many very specific to the individual credit cardholder, with the result that it produces many fewer false positives.

- *Anti–money laundering screening software.* As with credit card fraud detection (see above), current software used by banks and other financial institutions to detect money laundering is useful, but not optimal because it can only handle tracking a limited number of factors. A QC-based anti–money laundering system is far superior. [6]

- *Stock market trading strategy optimization.* Like route optimization, if hundreds more variables could be added to today's proprietary financial trading models, they would be much better at predicting risk and avoiding it, and perhaps financial markets wouldn't be as volatile as a result, or they might make stock markets even more volatile because many of these new QC-oriented trading systems will be customized for each trading company, and therefore there may be more erratic trading from time to time as different traders implement unique trading strategies and tactics. In any event, QC-based systems for brokers and other financial players could accommodate stock trading models with many hundreds of additional variables and data sets.

- *Credit risk management.* Current software for this important function takes relatively few data points into account about the prospective borrower, whether they are an individual looking for a mortgage or a large company requiring a major line of credit. Once again, a model for credit risk assessment built on hundreds, rather than tens, of inputs should create a more powerful, but also fairer, system for credit approvals, especially those that are powered by AI software, seeking to make many credit-granting decisions automatically without human input.

- *Personalized medicine.* The holy grail of medicine, to be able to customize drugs and therapies to each individual patient, rather than slot the patient into the general model of diagnosis and therapy, is difficult to do with the limited data resources available to computers currently. A QC-powered clinical medicine support system, driving off of hundreds more variables and factors, all geared to the patient's own detailed data, and processed in real time while the patient sits in their doctor's office, would constitute a real advance—a revolutionary advance?—in medicine.

- *Medical devices.* Current MRI imaging technology is already based on the manipulation of quantum principles to achieve impressive resolution images of the human brain and other organs. With the latest quantum breakthroughs, the quality of the images will increase exponentially, ushering in a greatly improved clinical and research tool.

- *Post-quantum cryptography.* The US National Institute of Standards and Technology has selected a group of encryption standards that NIST believes cannot be hacked even by quantum computers. Militaries and eventually civilian organizations will have to transition to software and other devices using these new protective algorithms if they want to be hacker-proof in the new QC era.

- *Quantum machine learning.* Chapters 5 and 6 highlighted the close interdependence of AI and high-performance SCs. It is therefore not surprising that researchers are already testing whether and how AI machine learning models and data sets might operate on a QC.[7]

At the same time, of course, militaries are very interested in quantum computing as well. Many of the above-noted civilian use cases resonate in the military world as well. For example, the military is very sensitive to weather conditions,[8] and having a system that is 99 percent accurate rather than only 80 percent accurate would be a huge tactical advantage on the battlefield. In addition, though, there are particular QC use cases that would be limited to the military:

- *War gaming.* The average computerized war game used by top commands rely on several dozen input factors. These important systems would be far more useful if they could be populated by multiple hundreds of factors, and then updated in real time so that virtual war game scenarios could be running as a particular battle was unfolding in the real, physical battle space.
- *Weapons testing.* Currently new nuclear weapons are tested in computer simulations, but QC could multiply both the inputs and the outputs producing much more accurate simulations.
- *Missile defense.* The American Patriot and Israeli Iron Dome (ground-based missile defense) and Aegis (sea-based missile defense) systems are quite good, and detect and bring down enemy missiles and drones with perhaps a roughly 85–95 percent success rate. But anything short of 100 percent is unacceptable. QC promises to improve antimissile defense to 100 percent.
- *Inertial navigation systems.* A quantum sensing device can give a vehicle or watercraft their geographical position without using an external service, like a GPS. This would be invaluable for submarine navigation, but it will also be extremely handy for surface vessels, or anyone else, in case their GPS service is knocked out in combat.
- *Battlefield management.* Quantum computing will allow greatly improved performance of battle management and other command, control, communication, and computer systems in conflict zones. A great number of inputs will be accommodated, and all inputs will be analyzed more quickly, fueling greater precision and speed in decision-making. Quantum-based battle-management systems will overwhelm other digital systems that are powered only by classical computers.

- *Unhackable communications.* A major impetus for China's accelerated program of achieving full quantum communications was the Edward Snowden revelations in 2013 that the US regularly listened in on sensitive Chinese government transmissions.[9] A few years later China began to use the Micius quantum-based communication satellite, which apparently cannot be hacked. Presumably in a few more years no government signals surveillance organization in the democracies will be able to listen in on Chinese messages that are routed through Micius or similar systems using quantum encryption techniques. This will be a real problem for intelligence services in the democracies.

Every computer system, whether traditional or quantum, has its limitations. There are several very material shortcomings with QC systems. Qubits are very finicky, and very unstable. They can easily be knocked out of their peculiar spin, in which case the power and accuracy of the QC drops dramatically. To counter these weaknesses, the qubit chamber, where the qubit super positioning and entanglement happens in current superconducting QC designs, are kept very cold, down to 20 millikelvin. This means there will not be a personal QC smartphone or PC any time soon.

Instead, all QC services will be delivered by the cloud model of computing. Large computer services companies, like Alibaba, Amazon (AWS), Baidu, Google, IBM, Microsoft, Oracle, and TenCent will operate QCs, and a user will access the QC over the Internet, or likely a proprietary network if they are looking for a secure connection. The military will invariably have their own QC running in one of their own data centers, or at a data center hosted by one of the big commercial computer services providers—but with the military having sole access to its computing power (known as a "private cloud"). In this hosted-cloud model, the data center operator will layer on the requisite AI applications as well, providing an entire packaged solution for the customer (civilian or military). The cost will not be cheap. But the services will be very powerful. Whoever gets the model right and can operate these remote services at very high availability will have a distinct advantage in Cold War 2.0.

QUANTUM AND ENCRYPTION

One particular application of the QC is very troublesome. Currently, encryption is the most popular means for ensuring security and privacy on traditional computers and over digital networks. There are many types of encryption products and services, but generally they work the same way. The files that are intended to be protected are encrypted by a mathematical algorithm that uses incredibly large prime numbers. The encrypted file can only be opened by using the "private key" that contains the specific prime number that corresponds with the "public key" that was used to encrypt the file in the first place. Given the nature of very large prime numbers, the public key that is protecting the sensitive information cannot be broken by even the most powerful current computers—the supercomputers discussed above—in a relevant time frame. (It would take even the world's most powerful supercomputer something in the order of several million years to break the encryption code.)

Then, along come QCs. Their entire value proposition is that they can accomplish in a matter of hours what traditional computers would take years to do. While this amount of computing power is very attractive to an organization's chief technology officer, from the perspective of the security profile of the CTO's encrypted systems the threat posed by QCs is actually quite stunning. It means that once QCs are powerful enough, they will be able to take down today's encryption locks, unless countermeasures are innovated and implemented by then.

The information technology industry has been buffeted by predictions of Armageddon before. In the mid- to late 1990s it came out that computers and most software programs weren't programmed to accommodate the date change to the year 2000, the new millennium. They only went as high as 1999, and then the program wouldn't work when the date actually changed to 2000. The QC encryption problem feels a lot like the so-called Y2K scare, but actually much worse. It was relatively easy to fix the Y2K problem in an existing software program, or, worst case, the user organization could buy a new program that did contain 2000 and subsequent dates (and the user had been meaning to upgrade their software anyhow).

The QC challenge to encryption is more serious. One stark difference between Y2K and "Y2Q" is that the world knew precisely how much time it had left to solve the Y2K crisis. (Action-forcing deadlines have always been very useful in remedying technology challenges.) The Y2Q problem, though, doesn't have a date or deadline *per se*, so the crisis might just creep up on the world and then explode with a big bang when some unsavory autocracy, terrorist or criminal group releases its QC-based classical computer encryption killer program. Presumably some alternative security solutions will be coming to the market (ideally soon, as time is of the essence) that will be able to resist QC-originated attacks on them.

Still, even if an initial solution is available to alleviate the risk in this encryption doomsday scenario, how long will this solution be good for? As QC computers get better and better, it is likely that the defense will be overwhelmed by the offense, just as cyberattacks by computer hackers today are causing so much disruption in the current entirely classical computing world. Hackers generally are also favored by the odds of their penetration business model; they have to be successful only once, while the defending organizations have to be successful all the time. The militaries in the leading democracies and autocracies are working diligently on this challenge, both defensively, to protect their own companies and organizations, and offensively, to be able to crack the encryption defenses currently used by the other camp. There is one system, based on quantum key distribution (QKD), that is already being used in China, Japan, South Korea, and Europe, but to date the US military has not adopted it due to what it perceived to be technical limitations.

One more quantum application is worth mentioning, namely "quantum sensing." The concept behind quantum sensing is to use the inherent properties of subatomic particles to determine various aspects of physical position or duration/time. We already use an atomic clock to officially keep time. It works on the basis of measuring the oscillations of certain atoms in precise environmental conditions, most important, temperature. The standard atomic clock, for instance, knows that an electron from a cesium atom vibrates at 9,123,123,123 times per second. Therefore, so long as the perfect conditions are maintained, a "cesium atomic clock" will be accurate forever, overcoming the deficiency of measuring time relative to orbiting bodies like the moon, or Earth's orbit around the sun. Every few thousand years this latter approach would be off by a second or two.

Quantum sensing could be used, for instance, in detecting items underground but without having to dig them up. Or a similar system could "sense" something coming around a mountain pass, which the driver of the vehicle could not see around. These sorts of applications have obvious civilian and military applications. It will be a number of years, however, before these quantum sensing devices are ready for release into the commercial world, as they require quite a few engineering refinements, such as producing quantum devices at hand-held scale. Already, though, the scientists and technologists are working on positioning, navigation, and timing (PNT) applications for military use. One of the first PNT products will likely be a navigational device for submarines that does not require the craft to surface to check its location; an accurate underwater location tracker would revolutionize submarine operations.

THE QUANTUM COMPUTER INDUSTRY

Here are the current public companies, and private companies which have raised around $100 million in outside private financing, working on developing a quantum computer, including showing the specific type of quantum technology being used and the current strength (in qubits) of their most advanced product offering:

TABLE 1—QUANTUM COMPUTER COMPANIES

Democracies	Funding	Tech Approach	No. of qubits
United States			
IBM-Q	public	superconducting	433
Google	public	superconducting	70
Microsoft	public	topological	20
Intel	public	superconducting	49
Amazon (AWS)	public	(pass through QuEra)	79
IonQ	public	trapped ion	32
Rigetti	public	superconducting	79
PsiQuantum	$665 M	photonic	indefinite
Atom Computing	$81	photonic—neutral atoms	100
Quantinuum	$325	trapped ions	32
Other Democracies			
D-Wave—CAN	public	annealing	indefinite
Xanadu—CAN	$265	photonic	216
Fujitsu/Riken—JPN	public	superconducting	64
Pascal—FRA	$139	neutral atom	100
Atos/Bullsequana—FRA	public	quantum simulator	41
IQM—FIN	$255	superconducting	54
Planqc—GER	$32	neutral atom	100
Autocracies			
China			
Jiuzhang 2.0 (Chinese Academy of Sciences—CAS)	government funded	photonic	76
Zuchongzhi 2.1 (CAS)	government funded	superconducting	176
Alibaba/CAS	public	superconducting	11
Baidu	public	superconducting	10
Origin Quantum Computing	$148 M	superconducting	24

A number of qualifications need to be made about the figures on this list. First, the number of qubits is merely one indicator of useful computing power. Other important details are how fault-tolerant the QC is; how long the qubits sustain coherence; whether the particular qubits produced by the device produce a lot of "noise" or only a little; how scalable the device is (one current trend is to network QCs, much as classical supercomputers are built by connecting hundreds of processors); how complex they are; and how complex (or relatively simple) is the entire device. There is then the question of whether the device is in the field actually solving practical problems for real-life users, or still largely performing rather esoteric functions for scientists alone.

A third consideration is the most important. Most of the funding for the Chinese quantum companies has come from the government, or investment funds that are owned by the government, while most of the financial backing of companies in the democracies comes from venture capital, private equity, and other private sources. In the US, for instance, private investment in tech companies is 1,350 percent higher than in China. This distinction about the public and private sources of investment money is critical. The Chinese top-down model of funding new innovation entities largely through public money, especially regional/municipal funds, has not produced very good results.

By contrast, the model in the democracies, where experienced industry players drive investment decisions with their own money very much on the line, produces companies of the highest caliber. What has happened with the SC domain (where the superior position of companies in the democracies is quite pronounced) is repeating itself in the QC space. Even if some specific science related to quantum comes out of a Chinese university lab showing great promise, the subsequent funding decisions made by central and regional government bureaucrats in China simply don't foster the commercial and marketplace savvy needed to make the venture a success.

For example, consider that the lead investor in Origin Quantum Computing, the great hope of quantum computing in China, is a public fund (namely Shenzhen Capital), and several other public funds are big equity investors as well. This profile of investor in turn causes the company to underperform, destroying a lot of actual and potential wealth creation, and then to also "rob" the full potential of the technology from its implementation in the military in the service of national security. Compare, by contrast, the investors in IonQ, which include Google Ventures,

Lockheed Martin (the world's largest defense contractor, also privately owned), Hyundai, Kia Motors, and Fidelity (one of the largest private asset managers in the world). When all is said and done, this single defect in the Chinese innovation system—too much influence of bureaucrats—serves to confer a huge competitive advantage in favor of the democracies that will ultimately cause the democracies to prevail in Cold War 2.0, so long as they don't fritter away this advantage.

8

THE CONTEST FOR
BIOTECHNOLOGY SUPREMACY

B iotechnology has undergone rapid and multifaceted innovation over the past twenty years since the human genome was decoded. Drug discovery and medicine are already being transformed because the practitioners of the life sciences have discovered how to modify the moving parts of cells like they program software. A prime example was the development of mRNA vaccines to combat COVID-19, which were effectively designed over a long weekend and were in production several months later. Compare this cadence to the decade it typically took researchers to develop a vaccine previously, thereby saving 10 million lives from the pandemic's ravages. The world stands on the threshold of more such fundamental biotech breakthroughs.

A more complex aspect of the biotech revolution is that scientists will soon be able to gestate human embryos in artificial wombs outside of the female body, in so-called ectogenesis machines, or EGMs. Autocracies with rapidly declining populations will find this technology intriguing— as might women in democracies hoping to avoid the trials and tribulations of pregnancy and childbirth. Merge this EGM technology with those promising "designer babies," enhanced physical and mental attributes and characteristics (more IQ, more height), and all of this perhaps coupled with AI and human-embedded SCs, and the potential permutations of new life experiences unlocked by biotechnology really begin to intrigue the imagination. And then there are the truly dark sides of the new biotechnology, such as military scientists being able to produce a bioweapon virus with greater ease, at lesser cost, and in record time. Biotechnology is insinuating itself onto the Cold War 2.0 agenda.

BIOTECHNOLOGY THROUGH THE AGES

Humans have been practicing biotechnology innovation since ancient times. When pastoralists in Mesopotamia, Egypt, or the Indus Valley bred a horse with a donkey to produce a mule, they were consciously bringing two sets of chromosomes together to produce a third species. Of course they didn't yet know—and farmers for thousands of years would not know—that that was what they were doing in terms of the cell biology, but at the level of "output" they certainly knew what they wanted to achieve, and they were not surprised at their success. Equally, when a farmer in Europe or Asia crossbred one plant with another, perhaps by forming a graft between them, they knew exactly why they were doing what they did, and they anticipated the resulting plant or cereal. But again, like the horse/donkey/mule breeders, they didn't understand how what they did actually worked inside the plant at the cellular and molecular level. In effect, the technique came well before the science. Thus it was that the medieval brewer of beer knew she needed to add yeast to her brew to make it ferment, but she knew nothing of how the bacteria in the yeast actually worked its magic. And so it was even in the inorganic world of ancient metallurgy. The blacksmith of ancient Greece understood that mixing some tin with copper would give him bronze, but he didn't—and couldn't yet—grasp how chemical bonds worked to fuse different minerals together into new alloys. He knew, though, that bronze was a superior metal to work with, and much stronger for making swords than copper alone.

It hadn't been until fairly recently that the science for pursuits like metallurgy, and even later for biology, caught up to explain the raw innovation. For chemistry, it wasn't until the late 1800s, while for biology it has only been the last eighty years. The big (huge) breakthrough in biology dates from 1953, when Watson and Crick discovered DNA, the code of all life. The next milestone was the decoding of the human genome in December 1999, an effort that took thirteen years of painstaking work. And finally, to complete the trifecta of biological accelerations, was the invention of CRISPR-Cas9, a procedure that allows scientists to actually splice and edit genes, mainly to remove a defective one, thereby saving that person the suffering of having to live with a specific genetically caused handicap. For example, a person with sickle cell anemia can have their beta-globin gene removed, after which their symptoms of pain and exhaustion stop almost immediately.[1]

Biotech products and procedures have had a significant impact on agriculture worldwide. In the early to mid-1970s two books caused widespread fear for the future of the earth: *Limits to Growth*[2] and *The Population Bomb*.[3] The upshot of each was that the globe's population was rising quickly, and there was no way collective food production could keep growing in order to feed all these people. The books predicted that the inevitable result would be starvation on a massive, never-before-seen scale. This forecast of unprecedented human suffering deeply worried people in the poor as well as rich countries of the world.

In the end, however, biotechnology saved the planet's billions of people (indeed the world's population grew from 3.6 billion in 1970 to 7.8 billion today). Hundreds of new agricultural innovations were deployed that created more productive plants with much higher yields. This so-called Green Revolution saved India from mass starvation. For a lot of average people, these events and trends in biotechnology were overshadowed by the seemingly flashier, and very novel, computing sciences. Nevertheless, it was indeed the biosciences, applied to agriculture, that saved the world from a gruesome famine scenario.

It was also around this time (in the 1970s) that scientists began to experiment with inserting certain genetic material into other organic substances, in particular bacteria, to form new living organisms. One such researcher was Ananda Chakrabarty, who emigrated to the United States after completing his doctorate in biosciences in India and facilitated the creation of a hybrid bacterium that could break down oil from oil spills. Chakrabarty obtained a patent for his invention in 1980.[4]

In Cold War 2.0 biotechnology will be pressed into action by both camps for agricultural purposes. In the Russo-Ukrainian War the Russian government has already used foodstuffs as a strategic resource by preventing some exports of Ukraine's wheat and other cereals, especially to the Global South, where Ukraine had many markets for its cereals prior to the war. As temperatures keep rising around the world, and as the number of significant droughts increase globally, it will be necessary for scientists to innovate new crop varieties that can withstand hotter growing conditions while receiving less water. Ideally, agricultural scientists around the world will pool their knowledge and technological expertise in agri-science and new seed development, but the technological decoupling attendant with Cold War 2.0 might block cross-camp collaboration, thereby raising the incidence of food insecurity in many parts of the world.

HUMAN-CENTERED BIOTECHNOLOGY

The biotechnology innovations mentioned to this point all related to the "outside world," either animal or plants. By contrast, when the human genome was sequenced, biotech got really up close and personal to people themselves. Interested onlookers were starting to see massive developments impacting not just flora and fauna, but real, live and in the flesh human beings. One early beachhead was in orthopedic surgery, where worn-out knees and hips were starting to be replaced by gleaming metallic substitute parts. A little later, cardiac surgeons slipped valves from pig hearts into poorly performing human hearts. People became somewhat nervous about trans-species transplantation, but fairly quickly these fears were allayed when transplant patients started living long, purposeful lives. Nothing breeds confidence in biotechnology better than success. Debate was largely curtailed by the publication of pictures of heart transplant recipients playing golf not that long after their open-heart surgeries.

Debate could not be forestalled, however, when in vitro fertilization (IVF) came along in the 1980s. Biomedical researchers figured out a way to put a human egg in a petri dish, add a male sperm, watch the two gametes fuse into an embryo, which was then inserted into the mother's uterus so that the following pregnancy could bring a baby into the world for the previously infertile parents. With IVF, the discussion around biotechnology became really intense really quickly. Not surprisingly, regulatory action followed in order to establish some parameters around this radically new biotech domain, so that physicians could earn the confidence of their patients and prove to the general public they weren't trying to play God. Today, some forty plus years later, "routine" IVF is well accepted, and about 20 percent of couples in economically advanced democracies make use of one kind of IVF procedure or another to conceive a child.

While today bioscience helps mothers with artificial insemination, at the other end of the gestation process, leading medical centers now can keep extremely premature babies alive that were born as early as the 23rd week of pregnancy. (A normal pregnancy usually lasts about forty weeks.) A few years ago, a research group in a Philadelphia children's hospital invented a uterine sac that could keep lamb embryos alive, essentially by getting the lambs nutrients and removing waste material much as a placenta and amniotic sac would in a natural lamb mother.[5] The lead physician of this experiment said explicitly this technology wasn't intended to replace a mother's uterus, but rather was simply a device to assist a very premature fetus, to give it further time to gestate before it had to be born.[6]

Nevertheless, this device *could* be a prototype of what may be called an "ectogenesis machine" for humans. An EGM could be coupled with IVF, and a few other recent breakthroughs, including a device that re-creates an entire female reproductive system,[7] and another that allows for making human embryos without zygotes from humans,[8] to permit the human conception, gestation, and birth process to be done outside any human female body. The EGM could one day facilitate the gestation of a human embryo without a mother's uterus.

Who would use an EGM? In a Cold War 2.0 context, one important candidate would be a major autocratic government whose country's population is in deep and irreversible decline, and where immigration is not acceptable to the either the government or the mass of the citizenry. Two autocracies meet this double criteria: Russia and China. Both countries are experiencing significant population decline, and over the past few years it wasn't simply the COVID-19 pandemic. The single biggest driver of population decline in Russia and China is that female fertility rates have plummeted in both countries (and in thirty-eight other countries around the world) to well below the replacement rate of 2.1 children per mother over her lifetime. In Russia the figure for 2022 was 1.8, and in China for the same year it fell to an even lower 1.2. Russia has been losing population since 1993, dropping from 148 million in that year to 144 in 2022. It is projected by the United Nations to fall to 112 million by 2100. China's population fell for the first time only in 2022. Once a country's population begins to fall due to a declining fertility rate, the decline can accelerate itself just by the law of big numbers. The Shanghai Academy of Sciences forecasts that China's population, currently at 1.4 billion, will fall to 732 million by 2100.[9]

Population declines such as these predicted for Russia and China will invariably be unacceptable to the autocratic leaders of these countries. While there will be some positive outcomes as a result, such as less pressure on the housing market, it will also cause a fall in economic growth, which will likely cause massive social unrest. In both countries the survival of the political regime would be at serious risk. Moreover, there would be far fewer military-age young men and women to populate the ranks of the armed forces, making it yet harder to suppress any domestic uprising.

Both countries have tried to forestall dropping female fertility rates by instituting various social programs encouraging larger families and offering a number of financial incentives for mothers to have and raise children. None of these inducements have worked. This result is consistent with smaller countries, including a number in the democracies. (South Korea's fertility rate in 2022 hit 0.8 percent, the lowest in the world.) Might the two autocratic regimes turn to the EGM for a technological solution to reverse a drastic decline in population?

The EGM could be integrated into Russian or Chinese society fairly readily. Both countries have long-standing, well-established orphanage systems for babies, toddlers, and small children who have lost their parents. These could be expanded to accommodate an exponential rise in EGM children. Then, if insufficient prospective foster parents came forward to take in EGM children by the age of three to five, then the state could expand its school system to include boarding schools in modest but functional quarters for EGM children.

Such an EGM program will of course be highly controversial. This is why they will initially be rolled out in autocracies, where public opinion generally does not have the impact it can have in a democracy. The last similar system of child-making and child-rearing "for the good of the nation" was tried in another autocracy, namely Nazi Germany in the 1930s,[10] although this program did not make use of an artificial uterus, and it was done on a rather modest scale.

Once a program of EGM child-making reaches the point where the technology has been fine-tuned and is working well, it is not inconceivable that certain groups in the democracies might find the device a useful mechanism for avoiding human gestation. Certain religious groups, for example, that feel their numbers dwindling might resort to such an EGM program. Or a woman, or a couple, who would like to have children but feel their work or other commitments (including care for elderly parents) are such that they wish to avoid a nine-month pregnancy, as well as the risk and pain of childbirth,[11] might be quite interested in making use of an EGM program.[12]

Such interest in the democracies for EGM might be further heightened if, in addition to the procedure as outlined above, some or all of the following sub-procedures were available with it: limited sex selection of the child, which would entail, for a second child, being able to choose a gender different from the first child (so that a couple wanting two children could have a boy and a girl—but no other sex selection would be permitted); genetic screening for medical problems; and limited genetic enhancement, such that the EGM child's genes are optimized for general intelligence, empathy, and emotional strength. A technology that may permit a tentative form of human trait enhancement (i.e., IQ, height) is already on the market in the US.[13]

Such procedures permitted by bioengineering will initially be very controversial, and they likely will only be permitted (if permitted at all) after lengthy and detailed discussion and debate within civil society and the governmental bodies of the country, and likely only after significant legal challenges up to and including the highest courts of the land. This was the general trajectory of debate for IVF, and nothing less is expected in the case of EGM. Presumably, though, debate will be more muted, if permitted at all, in the autocracies; rather, the autocratic leadership of the country will decide the matter on its own. In all likelihood, then, EGM will be another fault line between the democracies and the autocracies, as there will likely be two versions of the technology and, more important, different cultures in the laws, norms, and ethics surrounding its use, in a world separated by Cold War 2.0.

BIOTECH WEAPONS

With the world having recently experienced a global pandemic with the swift spread of the COVID-19 virus from China to all corners of the world, and having witnessed the immense harm caused to human life and the economy by this virus, it is no surprise that the specter of bioweapons now hangs more heavily over the world than ever before. Moreover, using human-made biological agents in war fighting is not a new phenomenon. Once more, the concept of dual-use technology is very apropos. In 1913, Fritz Haber invented nitrogen-based fertilizer, one of the biotech wonders of the 20th century, as it probably did the most to improve crop yields in the sixty years between its invention and the development of genetically engineered seed and crops of the 1960s—though nitrogen-based fertilizer is still a huge part of large-scale agriculture. It is the same Fritz Haber, though, who also helped develop chlorine gas as a hideous military weapon. It is estimated that chlorine and other gases killed 91,000 soldiers in World War I.

As a result of the human cruelty and devastation caused by this and several other gases in World War I (including mustard and tear gas) the International Committee of the Red Cross lobbied governments strenuously for banning such substances as weapons of war. The Red Cross's efforts bore fruit, and in 1925 the League of Nations adopted the Geneva Protocol on Poisonous Gases, effectively outlawing the production, distribution, or use of biological weapons. Interestingly, the treaty has no verification or enforcement mechanism; its proponents hoped the stigma of breaching the treaty would be sufficient for states to comply with it. And generally it has been, though there have been some transgressions, including when Syrian president Assad dropped the sarin chemical agent on his own people in Ghouta in 2013. Russian president Putin also breached the treaty when he had two Russian state security agents administer the banned substance Novichok in a park in southern England against a former FSB agent who had defected to the UK. This scandalous attack was reminiscent of the worst such excesses of Cold War 1 perpetrated by Moscow against foreign governments.

These transgressions raise the possibility that especially an autocracy might manufacture a highly lethal virus and use it against an enemy, particularly against a democracy, where proactive defense against such an attack would generally be quite low, if the track records of the democracies vis-à-vis the COVID-19 virus are any indicator. One of the self-limiters on using biological warfare agents in both world wars in the 20th century was that the various gases could easily backfire on the country releasing them; all it took was for the wind direction to change. Today, with a highly contagious and lethal novel virus agent released as a bioweapon, the releasing country would merely have to make an antidote vaccine and administer it to its own troops and citizens. This is a scenario that democracies must take very seriously in Cold War 2.0.

In response to the COVID-19 virus, no fewer than eight biotechnology companies in the democracies quickly came out with an effective vaccine. Competitive displacement was much in evidence. Two of them were designed and developed using novel mRNA technology, and these became the vaccines of choice in the democracies, particularly because one of the other vaccines, made by AstraZeneca (in conjunction with Oxford University), proved to have a slightly higher risk factor for heart complications. Nonetheless, AZ shared its drug trial data openly and promptly, which still helped build confidence in the vaccine. All vaccine makers in the democracies received government financial assistance when they began their search for a vaccine, but these governments did not "pick winners." They let competitive displacement run its course in an open marketplace.

Contrast this competitive process and the AZ posture on data sharing against the two main vaccine makers in Russia and China. In Russia, the Sputnik V vaccine was rushed out, in order to allow the Kremlin to play global vaccine diplomacy with it, but the manufacturer was never able to provide the World Health Organization (WHO) with the vaccine trial data that is a standard requirement in order to obtain WHO approval of the vaccine. As such, without WHO approval, many countries that would otherwise have ordered the Russian vaccine ended up having to procure a vaccine from another supplier. Moreover, the percentage of Russians vaccinated was very low, at about 20 percent. This is not a level that can offer herd immunity. As a result, the impact of COVID-19 on the Russian people, and its impact on the Russian economy, was far greater than it would have been had Russia accepted doses from the two mRNA vaccines from the United States and Europe. Strike one against autocratic vaccine diplomacy.

Almost the same fate befell China's premier vaccine company, which was (and continues to be) unable, or unwilling, to provide WHO with the required data from vaccine trials to show the efficacy and safety of the Chinese vaccine, such that, again, the WHO has yet to approve the Chinese vaccine for international use. Moreover, the trials finally undertaken by other countries show that the Chinese vaccine requires a full three doses of vaccination to achieve the same level of protection as is obtained by only two doses of the mRNA vaccines from the democracies. This makes the Chinese vaccine extremely problematic, including in China, where 90 percent of the population have achieved two vaccinations, but only 50 percent have had a third jab. At the same time, however, the dynamics of Cold War 2.0 make it seemingly politically impossible for Beijing (or Russia) to procure mRNA vaccines from the democracies, even though they are clearly superior to the vaccines produced in China and Russia.

The inability of China to respond to COVID-19 with effective vaccines then led the government in Beijing to spend most of 2022 implementing a very harsh zero COVID-19 policy that saw, among other astounding lockdowns, one for Shanghai (China's commercial capital of 25 million people) that lasted fully two months, and that saw no exceptions. This finally led to serious street protests, which then caused the government to do an about-face and cease lockdowns altogether. This in turn has caused a huge increase in COVID-19 infections in China, but now the government in Beijing is distributing false COVID-19 statistics (in terms of number of hospital admissions and deaths) because it fears embarrassment and, possibly worse, if the truth were told about the government's mismanagement of the entire affair.

There is much that needs to be improved in democracies relative to preparations for the next pandemic—and there will be another pandemic. Nevertheless, even with their flaws, the democracies handled the COVID-19 pandemic better than the two leading autocracies. This has been an important episode in Cold War 2.0, and not the last act that both camps will play on the stage of global health.

Another fault line between the autocracies and the democracies in Cold War 2.0 regarding biotechnology is China's development and deployment of a widespread system of genetic sampling and surveillance of its own people. Chapter 4 discussed the massive digital surveillance and control system implemented by the Chinese government over the past twenty years, initially in Xinjiang Province to oppress the Uighur minority, but then rolled out in various forms elsewhere in China. This system, though, is not limited to digital inputs. It includes Chinese authorities regularly taking DNA samples from Chinese citizens for no reason other than to build a huge database of biological data on the entire population. This can then be used for a variety of surveillance and control operations, particularly when linked to other personal data by AI programs.

Police in the democracies also use DNA data, but ostensibly only for law enforcement activities, and then only under the supervision of an independent judiciary. There is no general requirement of average citizens in democracies having to give DNA samples routinely for government tracking purposes. On the other hand, there have been cases in democracies of private suppliers of genetic testing services abusing the samples they have collected from customers, but thankfully these have been prosecuted under laws that protect against such misuse of data collection. The lesson is that in the democracies great care has to be taken to regulate such services, precisely so they do not become private purveyors of genetic malfeasance. In Cold War 2.0 the democracies have to constantly remind themselves how powerful the new biotechnologies are, and why they have to be used and managed very carefully, precisely so that autocratic practices don't seep into the democracies.

THE GLOBAL BIOTECH INDUSTRY

There are several metrics that can be used to measure the relative standings of the autocracies and democracies in biotechnology league tables. The charts below track the ranking of universities with biology expertise, as well as the size (by market capitalization) of public biotech companies. (This latter metric indicates the relative value of each company measured by the aggregate price of its outstanding shares.) Finally, it is worth noting that while Chinese research medical centers (i.e., major medical centers that also carry out leading-edge research) are not ranked relative to their counterparts in the democracies, conclusions can be drawn from the fact that each year some 500,000 rich Chinese travel to medical centers in democracies for major medical procedures.[14]

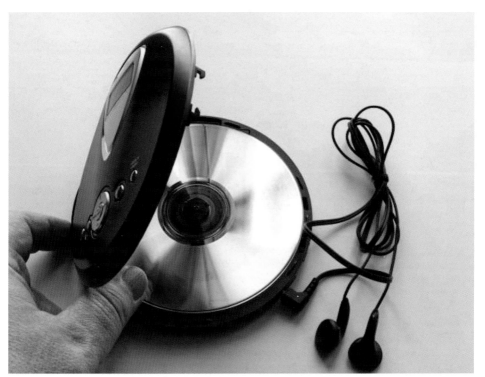

Modern civilian technological innovation and competitive displacement. Above, the Sony Discman music player; below, the much smaller fully digital Apple iPod Shuffle. The iPod, with its superior customer experience, drove the Discman out of the personal music device market. *Both images from iStock.com.*

Medieval military technology innovation and competitive displacement. Above, a knight in expensive chain mail armor; below, a longbow archer. The much cheaper, and more effective, longbow archer allowed the English to defeat French knights in multiple battles. *Top image from openverse.org; bottom image from Wikipedia.*

Modern military technology and partial competitive displacement. Above, a traditional artillery piece that uses regular shells; below, a HIMARS (High Mobility Artillery Rocket System) artillery rocket launcher that uses "smart" precision-guided ordnance. Both are found on the Ukrainian battlefield, but the HIMARS, with its superior technology, offers exceptional competitive advantage. *Both images from Wikipedia.*

Autocratic military non-innovative technology development. Above, the first American atomic bomb; below, the first Russian atomic bomb some years later. The two look much alike because the Russians copied every design feature of the American bomb, all learned by the Russians from classified plans stolen from the Americans through espionage. *Top image from Wikipedia; bottom image from Wikimedia Commons.*

Autocratic civilian non-innovative technology development. Above, the Apple II; below, the Russian Agat computer some years later. The two look a lot alike because the Russians copied the overall look and feel of the Apple II computer, and many of the internal features of the Agat were even closer to the Apple II. *Top image from iStock.com; bottom image from Sergei Frolov.*

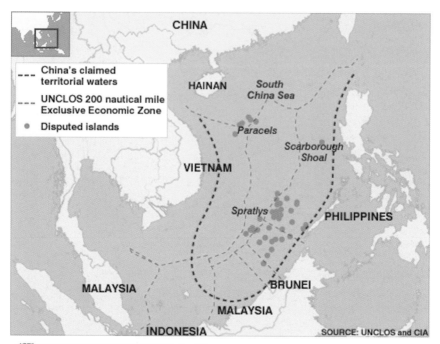

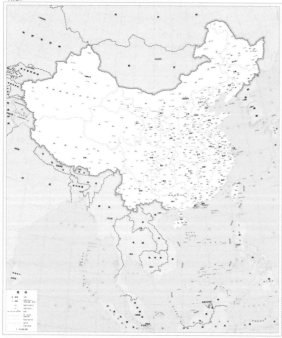

China's aggressive posture in the South China Sea. Above, the blue lines show the boundaries determined by international law (the rules-based international order) while the red dashes show the nine-dash line boundaries claimed by China. Below, the recent Chinese expansion to a ten-dash line now expressly including Taiwan. China is claiming 90 percent of the South China Sea for itself, an astounding claim. *Top map from BBC News; bottom map from the Chinese Ministry of Natural Resources.*

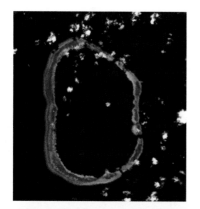

Cold War 2.0 in the South China Sea. Above, Mischief Reef (from a satellite), located in the Philippine Exclusive Economic Zone (but claimed by China within its nine-dash line), as it was before Chinese construction on it; below, Mischief Reef (from an airplane) as a Chinese military base with a 3.1 km military air base runway, concrete aircraft hangars, missile shelters, and large radar installations. *Both images from Wikipedia.*

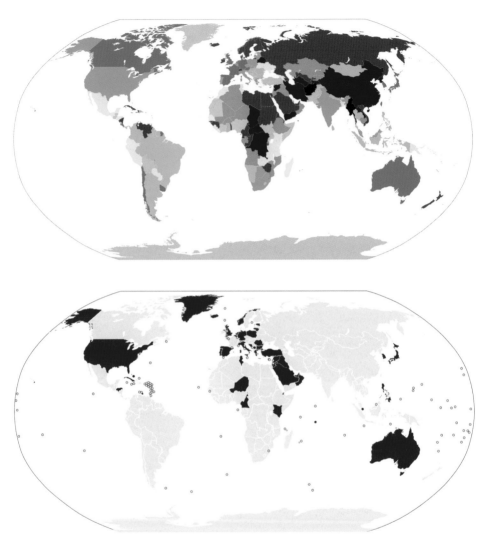

The geography of Cold War 2.0. Above, the Arc of Autocracy from North Korea and China, through Russia, and then down to Iran, through the Middle East and across and down Africa. Below, the indispensable American leadership of the democracies, showing American military bases around the world. In the top image, full democracies are dark green, flawed democracies are lighter green, hybrid regimes are yellow and light orange, and authoritarian regimes are darker orange and darker shades of red. In the bottom image, the US and its allies are in red and the dots are additional US military bases. *Both images from Wikipedia.*

Universities with strength in the biosciences and medicine are critical, as these are the launchpads of innovation in the biotechnology domain; they also groom the researchers who start biotech businesses and/or go to work in larger pharmaceutical companies. Here is the ranking of the top 100 universities in terms of their attributes in biosciences and medicine.[15]

TABLE 1—UNIVERSITIES: BIOSCIENCE/MEDICINE

	Top 20	Next 30	Next 50
Democracies			
United States	12	9	9
United Kingdom	5	4	7
Australia	1	3	3
Canada	1	3	2
Sweden	1	0	3
Germany	0	2	1
Netherlands	0	1	5
Belgium	0	1	1
France	0	1	1
Japan	0	1	1
South Korea	0	1	1
Denmark	0	1	0
Singapore	0	1	0
Switzerland	0	0	3
Finland	0	0	1
Italy	0	0	1
New Zealand	0	0	1
Norway	0	0	1
Spain	0	0	1
Taiwan	0	0	1
Autocracies			
China	0	2	3
Saudi Arabia	0	0	1
Russia	0	0	0
Nonaligned			
Brazil	0	0	1

TABLE 2—PUBLIC BIOTECH COMPANIES

Largest (over $10 billion in market cap) public biotech companies by market cap: [16]

Democracies	
United States	
Johnson & Johnson	$510 B
Eli Lilly	$356
Merck	$289
AbbVie	$285
Pfizer	$224
Bristol Myers Squibb	$146
Amgen	$130
Gilead Sciences	$105
CVS	$93
Regeneron Pharmaceuticals	$87
Vertex Pharmaceuticals	$84
Zoetis	$80
Moderna	$54
Biogen	$41
Seagen	$38
Europe	
Novo Nordisk—Denmark	$372
Roche—Swiss	$249
AstraZeneca—UK	$231
Novartis—Swiss	$209
Sanofi—France	$139
Merck KGaA—Germany	$75
GlaxoSmithKline—UK	$74
Bayer—Germany	$65
Lonza—Swiss	$45
BioNTech—Germany	$39
Japan	
Takeda Pharma	$52
Chugai	$41
Mitsubishi	$35
Takeda	$31

Other Democracies	
CSL—Australia	$100
Autocracies	
China	
Jiangsu Hengrui	$45
WuXi AppTec	$32
BeiGene	$27

Russia has no companies in the top fifty pharma companies, and clearly China is in a different league than the democracies, with only four companies in the top fifty, and they are small by market cap. If ranked by sales, two Chinese companies are in the top fifty (Sinopharm and WuXi).

Special mention, though, should be made of BGI Group (formerly Beijing Genomics Institute), a company begun in 1999 in China focused on sequencing the human genome. It has sales of about $250 million annually, and now sells a line of gene-sequencing machines. It pioneered low-cost gene sequencing and offers the service for about $100. In 2020, and again in 2023, the US government put BGI on its sanctions list for providing genetic analysis services involving Uighur citizens in Xinjiang to further their surveillance and repression by Chinese authorities.

BGI competes against the American company Illumina, which has a market cap of $35 billion and annual sales of $4.5 billion. Illumina offers a full human gene-sequencing service for $200. There has been patent litigation between BGI and Illumina over their gene-sequencing machines. In May 2022, a court in Delaware found Illumina willfully infringed two patents of Complete Genomics (a subsidiary of BGI) and awarded damages of $334 million.

9

OTHER IMPORTANT TECHNOLOGIES

While the four accelerator technologies (AI, SC, QC, and biotech) will drive the core innovation dynamics of Cold War 2.0, a number of other technologies and industries will play important supporting roles. A few, though, could also produce game-changing innovation. For example, if fusion energy ultimately works, it will profoundly transform global energy markets, and cause massive shifts of wealth out of today's countries that rely on the export of fossil fuels. Taken together, the businesses designing, developing, and deploying the technologies drive a large segment of wealth creation in both the democracies and the autocracies, thereby producing the economic surplus that can then be used to pay for a nation's military. With the exception of large-scale nuclear reactors and high-end jet engines, all of these technologies are prone to significant competitive displacement, at least when operating in the relatively open markets of the democracies.

The dual-use dimension of virtually all of these technologies is noteworthy. Shipbuilding is a good example; most of the shipyards that build a country's merchant fleet also produce the nation's naval vessels. The industries discussed in this chapter also drive home the important point that although it is easy to think all wealth and innovation creation has gone digital, industrial capacity is still absolutely critical. This is true in the auto industry as it is in the advanced manufacturing of commercial aircraft and especially their jet engines. At the end of the day, physical and virtual technologies and innovation skill sets need to combine seamlessly in the democracies to produce effective economic and military power if they hope to prevail in Cold War 2.0.

CLOUD COMPUTING

Cloud computing is about twenty years old, but it has earlier analogs in "outsourcing" and even "service bureau" type computing resource models from the late 1980s. Today, massive amounts of computer power are accessed from cloud service providers. In a major development, in 2022, the US military entered into large cloud computing relationships with AWS, Microsoft, Google, and Oracle. Moreover, cloud computing companies are very important in the AI supply chain because they have choice datasets upon which AI programs need to be trained, and they have invested billions of dollars in developing AI software. Some of them are also developing high-performance AI-specific SCs, which is not surprising given the volume of computer servers they operate in their data centers. (AWS has about 1.3 million servers.) It is not a coincidence that many of the names below appear on the AI league table at the end of chapter 5.

Here is a list of the world's principal cloud computing providers, showing their annualized revenue and market share:

TABLE 1—CLOUD COMPUTING PROVIDERS

Democracies	Cloud Revenue	Market Share
AWS (Amazon)	$74 billion	34 percent
Microsoft Cloud	$93	22 percent
Google	$23	9 percent
Oracle	$11	2 percent
Kyndryl (IBM)	$18	2 percent
Autocracies	**Cloud Revenue**	**Market Share**
China		
Alibaba Cloud	$12	6 percent
TenCent Cloud	$4	2 percent

In terms of tech decoupling as an objective and consequence of Cold War 2.0, it is interesting that Alibaba Cloud and TenCent Cloud have the large majority of their data centers in China, with only small footholds in the democracies. Equally, Google Cloud has no data center in China, but has one in Taiwan. The two market leaders, though, AWS and Microsoft, both have a few data centers in China (AWS, 2; Microsoft, 5) and none in Taiwan. In effect, there is already a fairly bifurcated market for cloud computing services as between the United States and China. If the US government brought in a restriction that required US-owned cloud service providers to cease offering AI services to customers in China, presumably such a rule could be observed without too much difficulty for these two market leaders.

SOFTWARE

Software that performs a function for a human user is as necessary for a computer as the SC that drives the computer. A computer, including its SCs, just sits like a boat anchor until the device comes alive with end user software. AI is a category of software. There are dozens of such categories, but generally most software can be lumped into two big buckets. Horizontal software does a fairly general function, and for many different kinds of users. Word processing software is horizontal, because all sorts of companies, organizations, and individuals make use of it. By contrast, software specifically designed to help a golf club manager operate a golf club is vertical software, as it is solely intended for golf clubs—a user couldn't, for example, run a company's financial accounts on it. AI, while a horizontal software, is also an "accelerator," because elements of AI will invariably be woven into virtually every software program eventually, be it horizontal or vertical software.

When considering a society's strengths and weaknesses in the context of Cold War 2.0, software is also important as an indicator of how fluent the society is in programming computers. This same thought can be expressed as: What percentage of the population has capacity in software coding? The people in a modern society are expected to have fairly strong literacy skills: they can read, comprehend what they are reading, write in at least the language of their region, and ideally, they have some rudimentary English if their "native" language is not English, given that English is the international language of business, science, and technology. Equally, people are expected to have fairly well-developed numeracy skills—the math skills required to understand the basics of business, science, and technology—though nowadays a high-end calculator can hide a numeracy deficiency, at least to a point. (It could hide it for many entry level jobs but not necessarily for managers.) The modern society, though, now needs its students to learn two more languages, namely software coding and how to read financial statements, or the language of business. Therefore, a country with a strong cohort of software programmers stands a much better chance of succeeding economically and militarily than one deficient in this skill. The comparative strengths of the democracies and the autocracies in software programming will impact the course of Cold War 2.0.

Here are the twenty-five leading software companies in the world by market capitalization (showing how the stock market values them). For Cold War 2.0 analysis purposes, it is important to note that all are based in the United States, unless otherwise noted.

TABLE 2—PUBLIC SOFTWARE COMPANIES

Company	Market Cap
Apple	$2.5 T (trillion)
Microsoft	$2.08 T
Alphabet (Google)	$1.353 T
Oracle	$238 B (billion)
Salesforce	$190 B
Adobe	$171 B
SAP—Germany	$143 B
Intuit	$120 B
IBM	$112 B
ADP	$88 B
ServiceNow	$87 B
Schneider Electric—France	$86 B

Palo Alto Networks	$57 B
Synopsys	$57 B
Cadence Design Systems	$55 B
Dassault Systèmes—France	$53 B
VMware	$52 B
Fortinet	$49 B
Workday—Ireland	$49 B
Snowflake	$43 B
Autodesk	$43 B
Atlassian—Australia	$39 B
Constellation Software—CAN	$37 B
Mobileye—Israel	$32 B
Wolters Kluwer—NL	$31 B

It is hard not to miss the prominence of the United States on this list of twenty-five. Indeed, of the top 100 public software companies, fully 73 are in the US, and there are no Russian companies in the top 100, and only two from China (Yonyou, at number 53 at $13.3 billion, and Kingsoft at number 86 at $6.4 billion); the rest, all 98, are in democracies: United States, 73; Canada and Israel, 5 each; France, Australia, Japan, China, and United Kingdom, 2 each; Germany, New Zealand, Netherlands, Spain, and Luxembourg, 1 each. With this pedigree of software companies, the top 78 being in North America, it is perhaps no surprise that the top AI companies (AI being a form of software) are also in North America.

SOFTWARE SERVICES

Software services represent the large information technology consulting companies that help other companies implement large technology projects, which can range from customizing the base software supplied by the companies noted immediately above, or writing some entirely new software for a function that does not yet have a base software product. These companies (other than IBM) are all fairly young, having grown up in the wake of the computer revolution. The following shows their latest annual sales and market capitalization. The ones under "democracies" are American unless shown otherwise.

TABLE 3—SOFTWARE SERVICES/CONSULTING COMPANIES

Democracies	Sales	Market Cap
Accenture	$192 billion	$63 billion
IBM	$60	$120
Deloitte	$59	[private]
DXC	$14	$5.7
Atos (France)	$12	$1.7
Capgemini (France)	$23	$32
CGI (Canada)	$10	$24
Autocracies		
There are numerous small computer services consultants headquartered in China, but none of the size and sophistication of the other companies listed in this table. A number of the software service providers listed in this table also provide services to clients in China.		
Nonaligned		
Infosys (India)	$18	$66
Wipro (India)	$11	$25
Cognizant (India)	$19	$33
TCS (India)	$27	$146

INTERNET PLATFORMS

Internet platforms are the companies that bring consumers the many and varied range of e-services over the Internet, including messaging, apps of all kinds, video, text, browser-based search, etc. When reviewing the list of companies below, and especially considering their eye-watering market valuations, it must be remembered that not one of them existed before the general advent of the commercial Internet in the 1990s, and they all began as tiny start-ups. In 1994, Amazon was largely Jeff Bezos, his wife MacKenzie, and a few employees packing boxes to fulfill their first Internet orders. Today Amazon is a tech company extraordinaire that happens to sell goods over the Internet. Its cloud computing services arm, AWS, is by far its most profitable division—it is the leader in Table 1 above.

With respect to Cold War 2.0, it is fascinating the degree to which the market for Internet platforms has already bifurcated by technology decoupling between the democracies and the autocracies, given that the autocracies regularly block access from their citizens to many of the Internet platforms that have grown to prominence in the democracies. The only material social media platform that is shared by the United States and China is TikTok, and currently the US Congress is considering whether TikTok presents Americans with a security risk due to their data being accessible by the Chinese government. If congressional sentiment is that there is a material risk, then ByteDance, the parent company of TikTok, will likely be regulated into selling TikTok to non-Chinese owners, and the back-office operations of TikTok will be forced to move out of China. Frankly, this is fairly close to the treatment already meted out to American platforms when they are blocked from reaching consumers in China.

Set out below are the leading Internet platform players in each of the democracies and autocracies, also showing their market capitalization (or if private, their amount of funding):

TABLE 4—INTERNET PLATFORM COMPANIES

Service	Democracies	Autocracies
e-Commerce	Amazon $1.3 trillion	Alibaba $0.232 trillion
Search	Google $1.5	Baidu $0.050
Messaging	WhatsApp (Meta/Facebook)	WeChat (TenCent)
Social	Meta $0.744	TenCent $0.415
Video (long)	YouTube (Google)	YouKu (Alibaba)
Video (short)	TikTok (ByteDance)	TikTok (ByteDance)
Rideshare	Uber $0.086	Didi $0.014
Accomodation	Airbnb $0.082	Tujia [private $0.755]
Travel	Expedia $0.016	Tujia [private > $1 billion]
Hotels	Booking.com $0.097	Haoqiao [private $0.026]
Payments	PayPal $0.074	Alipay (Alibaba)

It is worth noting that on the democracy list, all of the companies are based in America, except Booking.com, which hails from the Netherlands.

TELECOMMUNICATIONS TECHNOLOGIES

Telecommunications technologies are critically important for the full functioning of modern life. People love to talk to one another by phone, for a whole host of purposes, and increasingly they can do that cheaply at a distance with the marvels of broadband Internet access and mobile/cellular network connections. Telecom networks also form the backbone of the Internet, the most important communication medium today. The suppliers of the network equipment to the telcos, such as Huawei (China), Ericsson (Sweden), Nokia (Finland), and Cisco (US) have become important players in the technology space. Of these four, which collectively are the leading suppliers in the world by market share and revenue, the rise of the Chinese company Huawei has been nothing short of spectacular.

Prior to the 1960s, telephone systems were essentially mechanical devices. The central telephone exchange was a massive jumble of steel and wires, where calls were connected literally by bringing two wires together to complete a circuit. These units were marvels of mechanical engineering. Then, in a decade, everything mechanical about this environment became digital, software-driven, and SC-enabled. Today, SCs containing sophisticated software are central to the design and operation of the telecom networks that underlay the digital communications revolution that has swept over the world since the advent of the Internet. There is no better testament to this than Huawei's role in Cold War 2.0 on behalf of China over the last five years.

Huawei has supplied most of the network backbone equipment within China to mobile communications services companies like China Telecom, the world's largest carrier, with about 390 million subscribers. Huawei's sales outside of China have been growing as well. In many countries it sells turnkey solutions, going beyond basic network equipment to include

sophisticated human surveillance and control systems that especially autocratic regimes can use to closely monitor and track their populations. Huawei
also supplies the Chinese military with critical telecom gear for connecting
all components of the PLA in both logistics as well as operational settings.

These civilian surveillance oppression and military activities in China
and abroad prompted the US government in 2019 to begin a policy of
prohibiting Huawei from selling its products and services to US telecom
carriers. Australia and New Zealand continued this effort, both banning
Huawei in 2018, and then other "Five Eye" partners followed the US's lead
(United Kingdom in 2020, Canada 2022), as well as Japan and Taiwan.
One additional concern expressed by these countries—beyond Huawei
selling to the PLA and facilitating the oppression of people through digital
surveillance—is that Huawei could not ensure that traffic flowing through
its systems would not be shared with the Chinese government. It is a central
tenet of telecommunications law in the democracies that common carriers
(the telecom company) cannot intercept, study, or in any way discern the
nature of the content of the traffic that it carries on its network, except
pursuant to law enforcement demanding such access authorized by a search
warrant approved by an independent judge. It is precisely these rule-of-
law protections that don't exist in the autocracies, including China. Thus,
in the democracies there is a legitimate concern that as the supplier of
telecom equipment, Huawei could siphon off information flowing through
the network and share this highly confidential and commercially sensitive
data with the Chinese government and its agencies. Amplifying all these
concerns is the fact that Huawei is not a public company, and without its
shares being listed on a stock exchange, the public doesn't get to see the
detailed financial, commercial, and other information that public companies
have to disclose once every four months.

The American government, though, didn't stop at merely prohibiting the
use of Huawei equipment by US carriers. The Trump administration, in
2019, instituted an embargo on the sale to Huawei by American suppliers of
SCs and other components. Later (in 2020), this SC embargo was expanded
to include no sale to Huawei of any items, including SCs, that were made

using American origin equipment or software. This effectively stopped the flow to Huawei of critical SCs and other types of kit, causing a dramatic loss of sales by Huawei. In 2019 Huawei had sales of $129 billion, and then because of the American trade restrictions this figure fell to $93 billion in 2022. The success of this sanctions policy then emboldened the American administration to extend the same treatment to other Chinese commercial entities, including ZTE, the other leading player in the Chinese telecom equipment space. This SC sanctions experiment with Huawei and ZTE then led a few years later to the Biden administration implementing, in the fall of 2022, the broader sanctions policy on SCs and related equipment.

The world's leading telecom equipment companies are listed below (with annual sales and market capitalization):

TABLE 5(A)—TELECOMMUNICATIONS TECHNOLOGIES SUPPLIERS

Democracies	Sales	Market Cap
Cisco—US	$52 billion	$207 billion
Nokia—Finland	$26	$23
Ericsson—Sweden	$26	$18
Autocracies	Sales	Market Cap
Huawei—China	$93	[private]
ZTE—China	$18	$26

Also listed below are the leading smartphone suppliers showing respective market shares:

TABLE 5(B)—SMART PHONE SALES—WORLDWIDE—Q4 2022

Company	Market Share
Apple	23 percent
Samsung	19 percent
Xiaomi	11 percent
Oppo	10 percent
Vivo	8 percent
Other	29 percent

TABLE 5(C)— SMART PHONE SALES IN THE UNITED STATES—Q4 2022

Company	Market Share
Apple	57 percent
Samsung	20 percent
Lenovo	6 percent
Google	6 percent
TCL	2 percent
Other	9 percent

TABLE 5(D)— SMART PHONE SALES IN CHINA—Q4 2022

Company	Market Share
Apple	22 percent
Oppo	16 percent
Vivo	18 percent
Honor	15 percent
Xiaomi	12 percent
Other	16 percent

It is interesting to note that with respect to Tables 5(c) and 5(d) above, except for the resilience of the Apple iPhone brand at the high end of the Chinese smartphone market, a virtually complete tech decoupling has occurred between the American and Chinese markets.

SPACE AND SATELLITE TECHNOLOGIES

Space and satellite technologies have grown in importance and prominence since space programs were first pursued by the Russians and the Americans during the height of Cold War 1 in the late 1950s and early 1960s. Militarily the upper atmosphere of Earth, and above that into space, is of course the ultimate "high ground," and therefore has special meaning to generals and their planning staff. It is estimated there are over 7,800 working satellites in this part of space, and thousands more are planned. The miniaturization of electrical and other components facilitated by the SC revolution has allowed satellites to reduce greatly in size, and their numbers to grow exponentially. The other big news in the last decade is that the rocket delivery systems have been completely redesigned to be much smaller, cheaper, and in some cases reusable. The result has been that in the democracies several private companies have entered the field of designing, building, and operating these smaller rockets, which has caused the cost of putting a satellite into orbit around the earth to plummet—the cost has fallen from $65,000 per kilogram of launch weight to $1,500 per kilogram. The leader here is SpaceX, which has been Elon Musk's ultimate corporate vehicle for shaking up the launch sector with a form of competitive displacement on steroids.

On the satellite front, the dramatically new economics of sending smaller satellites into low earth orbit has opened a veritable floodgate of innovation in technology advancement around new ways of sensing the world, and in the business models bringing these new services to civilian and military markets. The following shows only builders of satellites and launch vehicles ("rockets"), and not the operators of various other satellite systems. Again, Elon Musk has broken prior taboos and economic models with his Starlink business, which currently has about 4,000 small satellites in orbit, but plans for ten times that many. There are several others, though, also bringing entirely new innovations and business models to the civilian and government/intelligence/military markets, including Capella, which uses novel synthetic aperture radio wave/radar sensing technology so images can be taken at night and in cloudy weather—not just during sunny days—and then Capella conducts real-time analysis of objects and trends using novel AI systems.

In many respects the contrast between the hyperactivity in the democracies in commercial space activity and the lackluster, top-down government-heavy Chinese approach couldn't be more stark. What new companies there are in China for this burgeoning market are generally offshoots from the two large state-owned legacy space contractors (CASIC—China Aerospace Science and Industry Corporation, and CASC—China Aerospace Science and Technology Corporation). Then, the spun-off company often has state-controlled investors, presumably to keep a close eye on developments; for example, a large investor in ispace, the leader in China in commercial launch, is the Shanghai Pudong Science and Technology Investment Co., which is wholly owned by the Chinese government. Moreover, the rockets being used by ispace are variations on the Chinese military's missiles, sourced from CASIC and CASC.

On the satellite front, instead of relying on the private sector to create a Starlink-type competitor, the Chinese government created yet another state-owned company, China Satellite Networks Limited (CSCN) to bring a system of low earth satellite constellations to fruition. In two years CSCN, working with two legacy state-owned behemoths (China Electronics and Technology Group Corporation, CETC, and China Electronics Corporation, CEC) has made very little progress. As a result, the central government in Beijing sent its corruption investigators into the offices of CSCN to determine if there has been wrongdoing, which is a typical response from Beijing when the top-down, government-heavy system of technology innovation fails. Bottom line, the Chinese autocrats, both for launch vehicles and satellites, simply will not allow competitive displacement to work its magic and their technology innovation is stunted as a result.

Set out below are the major players in the launch and satellite domains, showing either their market capitalization (if they are public companies), or how much funding they have raised (if they are still private companies):

TABLE 6—SPACE LAUNCH AND SATELLITE COMPANIES

Democracies	Funding or Market Cap if Public
SpaceX—US	$9.8 billion
Starlink—US	$0.041
Rocket Lab—US (public)	$2.74
Blue Origin—US	$0.167
Lockheed Martin—US (public)	$0.116
Boeing—US (public)	$0.127
Amazon—US (public)	$1.331 trillion
Viasat—US (public)	$5.2 billion
Planet Labs—US (public)	$0.573
Slingshot Aerospace—US	$0.118

York Space Systems—US	$0.009
BlackSky—US (public)	$0.292
Iridium—US (public)	$7.59
Globalstar—US (public)	$1.88
Axiom Space—US	$0.432
Orbex—US	$0.109
Omnispace—US	$0.140
Northrup Grumman—US (public)	$68.7
Capella Space—US	$0.239
Relativity—US	$1.3
EchoStar—US (public)	$1.55
Pixxel—US	$0.069
Maxar/SSL—CAN/US	$4.00
Kepler—CAN	$0.177
Intelsat	$0.054
Arianespace—FR/EU	$0.111
Eutelsat/OneWeb—FR/UK (public)	$1.62
Airbus—EU (public)	$113
Thales/Leonardo—FR/IT (public)	$31
Ovzon—SWE	$0.065
Virgin Galactic/Orbit—UK (public)	$1.05
Astroscale—JPN	$0.338
Mitsubishi Heavy Ind.—JPN (public)	$15.4
Autocracies	**Funding or Market Cap if Public**
China	
ispace	$0.276
Galactic Energy	$0.193
ExPace	$0.514
One Space	$0.116
Deep Blue Aerospace	$0.027
Space Transportation	$0.060

It is telling that Russian companies don't appear on the above list. Even with respect to the "big science" space missions, Russia's activity level has fallen off. Starting in the 1990s, Russia and the United States together built and operated the International Space Station (ISS). In a seemingly preemptive move following Russia's invasion of Ukraine, the Russian space agency, Roscosmos, indicated in June 2022 that it will be withdrawing from the ISS after 2024. The ISS was born out of discussions between Soviet Russian leader Mikhail Gorbachev and US president Ronald Reagan in 1985, when relations between the United States and Russia began to thaw as Gorbachev pressed his perestroika and glasnost initiatives forward. With the new Cold War 2.0 heating up, and Russia announcing it will pull out of the ISS, the Russians seem to have decided to build their own space station. The Chinese have indicated they will do the same and build their own. (The Chinese were never invited by the Americans to participate in the ISS.) It seems that Cold War 2.0 will not see much great power cooperation in space (not even between the Russians and the Chinese). Indeed, the head of Roscosmos, a number of months after the start of the Russo-Ukrainian War, reminded the Americans that given that Russia was the first to land a probe on Venus, that planet belonged to Russia. This sort of sentiment, even if expressed more in jest, does not augur well for the international cooperation that will be required from the three large space powers, and the many others vying for discovery of the planets, if peace is to continue in the vastness beyond the upper atmosphere.

NUCLEAR INDUSTRIES

Nuclear industries are the purveyors of classic dual-use technology. It is also a very schizophrenic industry, in the sense that it can bring great benefit one minute in the form of a nuclear energy (greenhouse gas–free) electricity-generating power plant, but then the next minute that nuclear power plant can turn incredibly dangerous if there is a major accident and the material used to power the reactor melts down and releases nuclear particles into the atmosphere, putting human and other life at risk. Operating nuclear power plants, including on submarines with small nuclear-powered engines, requires a significant degree of scientific and technological expertise, which tends to be in short supply nowadays. In the AUKUS nuclear-powered submarine deal, the development of nuclear science engineers by Australia will be key.

SCs and software proliferate in nuclear-based products and techniques. The equipment used to manufacture the precision components of a nuclear power plant or a nuclear-powered submarine (whether it carries nuclear weapons or not) is now indelibly controlled by microcircuits. Advanced manufacturing is simply another phrase for "lots of computers controlling how we make things," and the nuclear industry supply chain relies very heavily on precision engineering and advanced manufacturing. As for the nuclear power plant itself, it used to be the domain of the civil and mechanical engineer, and of course those disciplines are still vital. The technology now that permeates the plant's control system, its brain and nerve system, as it were, is all imbued with software and SCs. Nuclear physics still drives the formulae for coaxing power from the atom, but the processes that make that a viable and safe procedure are all overseen and controlled by microelectronics running on software and SCs.

From the perspective of Cold War 2.0, one of the challenges to the democracies is Rosatom, the company in Russia that is owned and controlled by the state. (Putin himself can give it direction under its by-laws.) Rosatom has a very large business designing, building, and operating nuclear power plants, and then supplying customers with fuel supplies and maintenance services. It is very active internationally, currently building nuclear plants in eleven countries.[1] It also has a sizable global business in enriching uranium for use as fuel for nuclear reactors. Currently about 40 percent of the fuel used by US nuclear plants is supplied by Rosatom, and this Russian company is also the third-largest supplier of nuclear fuel to Europe. Since Russia's invasion of Ukraine, there has been a great deal of attention on eliminating the dependence of the democracies on Russian oil and gas, but not nearly enough focus on removing Rosatom from the supply chain for nuclear products and services purchased by customers in the democracies. The democracies must decouple themselves from Russia with respect to nuclear technology and supplies—this is an important priority objective for the democracies in Cold War 2.0.

Ukraine is in a particularly vulnerable posture, as it has fifteen nuclear reactors based on Russian design and technology, a hangover legacy of the Soviet Russian era. Nevertheless, starting right after the Russian annexation of Crimea in 2014, Ukraine began to switch its source for nuclear fuel to Westinghouse, an American company (but owned by Canadian entities). With the full-scale Russian invasion of Ukraine in February 2022, more democracies are heading in this direction (including Czechia, Slovakia, and Bulgaria), but much more could be done on this front. The democracies need to band together and create some large-volume commitments for nuclear fuel supply so that suppliers there can substitute for services and products currently provided to them by Rosatom. A similar strategy was executed by the European Union in March 2023 when it placed a large order for ammunition using a €1 billion financing facility, which member states then paid back as they took actual delivery of ammunition. Acting together, nuclear-power democracies like Canada, France, the Netherlands, and the US have enough capacity to displace Rosatom completely in their nuclear fuel supply chains, but they need to implement collective solutions to do so cost-effectively and with some dispatch. There are some legacy programs that contributed to the current state of affairs, such as the "Megatons to Megawatts" deal in the 1990s, where the US agreed to buy fuel from Russia that was derived from Russian military nuclear warheads that were dismantled after the collapse of the Soviet Union. But new exigencies face the democracies, and these historic practices cannot interfere with the new tech decoupling of the democracies from the autocracies required in response to the Russo-Ukrainian War.

Within NATO itself, Hungary and Bulgaria pose a particular risk as they obtain 37 percent and 43 percent, respectively, of their electricity from Rosatom-built nuclear plants. As is often the case nowadays, Turkey has been unhelpful within the NATO system by signing a huge contract with Rosatom for the design, construction, and operation of a large nuclear power facility, where the nuclear power generation facilities themselves will remain owned by Rosatom during the course of the multidecade contract. The concern is that the Russian government could hold these three countries hostage given their dependence on a Russian company owned and directed by the Kremlin. Russia has a track record of using its energy exports to promote its geopolitical agenda with other countries in similar circumstances, as when it cut off Ukraine from supplies of gas, or when it told the Germans there were maintenance issues with Nord Stream 1 pipeline. The deep commercial relationships required by nuclear power deals also offer opportunities for sabotage, influence peddling, corruption, and espionage, or merely hard-nosed diplomacy. About half the countries that abstained from voting in favor of UN General Assembly resolutions condemning Russia's invasion of Ukraine had material nuclear power arrangements with Rosatom. Sensible Finland has shown the way by canceling a nuclear plant project with Rosatom soon after Russia's invasion of Ukraine. In a similar vein, Poland and Ukraine have selected Westinghouse to build their new nuclear reactors. All three of these actions are good examples of the tech decoupling required by the new Cold War 2.0.

At the same time, it should also be mentioned that Russia's international nuclear power diplomacy can backfire with ugly consequences. In the mid-2010s, Putin tried to force South Africa into a long-term commercial relationship whereby Russia would build eight nuclear reactors for that country at an estimated cost (once all maintenance and fuel services are included) of $76 billion. The procurement was done without South Africa going through the usual competitive bid processes, and SA civil society erupted once details of the deal became public. South Africa's legal system was invoked, and quashed the transaction. SA's president, Jacob Zuma, and the Gupta clan, were severely castigated, but Putin also lost tremendous face, particularly in Africa, for failing to assist SA in following accepted best practices for these types of transactions. Ultimately SA's democratic institutions (including its adherence to checks and balances) saved the day.

The key players in the global nuclear industry are listed below, associated with their "home country," with a rough number of the large-scale nuclear reactors in operation in that country (which gives a general sense of the expertise of the industry players):

TABLE 7—LEGACY LARGE NUCLEAR (FISSION) REACTOR SUPPLIERS

Democracies	No. of reactors
United States (Westinghouse—Canadian ownership; GE Hitachi)	93
France (Framatome)	56
South Korea (GEH; KAERI)	25
Canada (SNC-Lavalin)	19
Japan (GEH) and Germany (GEH/Rosatom) are decommissioning their reactors	
Autocracies	**No. of reactors**
Russia (Rosatom) (excluding foreign sites)	37
China (China National Nuclear Corporation, and China General Nuclear Power Group)	54
Nonaligned	**No. of reactors**
India (Bhaba) (also Rosatom building 6 reactors)	23

An interesting development in the nuclear power space is the number of new entrants that are promoting their fission technology for small-sized reactors, producing up to 300 GW of electricity per year, instead of 1,000 to 3,000 GW for the large, legacy nuclear technology systems. It's too early to tell if these new players will pose a challenge of competitive displacement to the legacy companies/technologies. Here are some of the larger new players, including showing the amount of funds raised by each of them:

TABLE 8—SMALL NUCLEAR (FISSION) REACTOR SUPPLIERS

Democracies	Funding
TerraPower—US	$83 million
NuScale Power—US	$469
BWX—US	$650 [public]
Moltex—UK/Canada	$50

There are also several of the legacy suppliers proposing/building solutions for the "small" reactor market:

Democracies	Funding
Westinghouse (eVinci)—US	N/A
GE/Hitachi—US/Japan	N/A
Rolls-Royce SMR—UK	N/A
Autocracies	**Funding**
CNNC—China	N/A

It will be very interesting to observe how the smaller new entrants in the compact reactor domain fare against the downsized reactor offerings of the bigger companies, and whether competitive displacement will work its magic when the nimble new entrants go up against the established thinking of the industry veterans.

FUSION TECHNOLOGY

Fusion technology is being pursued by a number of companies and governments around the world, given the massive potential of atomic fusion to satisfy the world's energy needs in a manner that has fewer downsides to the environment. Fusion is the process of compressing atoms together, which gives off gargantuan amounts of energy. Fusion is the process that powers the sun, as well as thermonuclear bombs. ("Regular" atomic bombs are driven by fission, where an atom is split, rather than fused with another atom.) The current research program for fusion is proceeding by two general avenues. First, there is a group of nations participating in building the International Thermonuclear Experimental Reactor (ITER), which, when completed, will be a massive Tokamak reactor to conduct fusion experiments. The participants in ITER are the European Union, the United States, Russia, China, India, Japan, and South Korea. The total cost of the project is estimated at about $60 billion, with most funding being satisfied by in-kind contributions of the various sections of the reactor, which is being built in the south of France.

The audacious construction technique employed in creating the ITER facility simply couldn't be contemplated without modern computer-based (that is, software and SC-driven) design, procurement, and construction management techniques. The bulk of each country's contribution is actually not money, but the manufacturing of specific sections of the huge Tokamak reactor. Therefore, its design is first created using a "digital twin" technique, where each component, down to the screws, are replicated electronically in digital wire frame and then fuller renderings. This electronic blueprint is then used by each country to precision-engineer and advance manufacture the pieces of this huge jigsaw puzzle (again, with reams of high-performance SC-driven machines). These pieces are then delivered to the construction site in Cadarache, France, where a multinational engineering team does final quality control, and supervises the construction team in putting the pieces together. It is the largest science experiment ever attempted by humankind. It simply couldn't be contemplated without software running high-performance SCs, humming continually in the background.

In terms of Cold War 2.0, after Russia's invasion of Ukraine in February 2022, there was discussion within the democracies about expelling Russia from the ITER consortium, but this would have proven impractical as Russia had already completed fabrication of several of its major contributions and was working on others which, if not forthcoming, would be difficult for other partners to backfill. Interestingly, though, if the ITER experiment proves to be a success, the EU has already indicated it will carry forward the fusion work through another research consortium that is limited to EU members, presumably in order to better ensure which non-EU entities will be invited to participate. This is more in keeping with other international research consortia that expelled Russia from their organizations after the start of the Russo-Ukrainian War. For example, CERN, the international physics research consortium based in Geneva, indicated in March 2022 that it would not renew its research collaboration agreement with Russia when it expires at the end of 2024, yet further evidence of tech decoupling flowing from Cold War 2.0.

The second avenue along which fusion research is proceeding is a profusion of private companies building smaller demonstration plants, the last step before they build commercial plants capable of producing electricity from fusion processes that would be sold to their respective countries' electricity grids. There are about forty companies in the world with interesting fusion technologies, but here are the six who have each raised over $100 million, and therefore they are the serious players (showing national base, and amount raised to date).[2] What's key about these private companies is that they are funded by venture capital firms and individual venture investors from Silicon Valley, who then bring American early-stage high-tech company disciplines to these moonshots.[3]

TABLE 9—NUCLEAR FUSION COMPANIES

Democracies	Funding
Commonwealth Fusion Systems—US	$2 B
TAE Technologies—US	$1 B
Helion Energy—US	$.577
General Fusion—Canada	$.300
Tokamak—UK	$.250
Zap Energy—US	$.200
First Light Fusion—UK	$.100
Autocracies	**Funding**
ENN Fusion Technology—China	$200 M

What's very telling from this list is that there are seven companies on it from democracies, and only one from the autocracies. This is one of the (not so) secret sauces of the democracies when it comes to their success in technology innovation. They make many more bets, with greater volumes of financial resources, than the autocracies, and so it stands to reason that the democracies will simply produce more scientific and engineering breakthroughs than the autocracies. This then drives a greater rate of competitive displacement in the democracies, and superior economic growth, and finally a greater surplus of wealth that can be allocated to various social objectives, including national security, as required. As noted previously, this phenomenon is a major reason why the democracies will prevail over the autocracies in Cold War 2.0. Moreover, in China and Russia, the entrenched position of the legacy fission nuclear industry will pose a supreme obstacle to the eventual introduction of companies built upon nuclear fusion technologies, because all the major players in the fission domain are state entities in which the current political leadership has huge vested interests.

AUTOMOBILE MANUFACTURERS

Automobile manufacturers today constitute the largest high-tech industry in the world, whether considered by sales, number of employees, or the vast supply chains they have. Between the time of its invention (in the 1880s) to around the 2010s, cars and trucks were purely mechanical devices. Today, there are about 1,500 SCs in each automobile, and this number is rising quickly. When vehicles achieve full autonomy (i.e., driving without a human driver), the number of SCs will double. From a Cold War 2.0 perspective, while civilian automakers don't make military vehicles in peacetime, in World War II it was the vast auto factories of Detroit that ultimately swung the war in favor of the allies, as auto plants were transformed into factories pumping out tanks, trucks, jeeps, ships, and aircraft.

Here are the top automakers in the world, and their annual sales:

TABLE 10—AUTO MAKERS

Company	Annual Sales
Democracies	
Volkswagen—Germany	$296 billion
Toyota—Japan	$279
Stellantis—US/Italy (Chrysler, Fiat)	$176
Mercedes-Benz—Germany	$158
Ford—US	$136
BMW—Germany	$131
Honda—Japan	$129
General Motors—US	$127
Hyundai—South Korea	$102
Nissan—Japan	$75
KIA—South Korea	$61

Renault—France	$54
Tesla—US	$54
Suzuki—Japan	$32
Autocracies	
China	
SAIC—China	$121
FAW—China	$109
Dongfeng—China	$86
BAIC—China	$75
GAC—China	$66
Geely—China (owns Volvo)	$56

With respect to China it should be noted that a new generation of makers of electric vehicles has recently sprung up, including Li Auto, BYD, and Nio Xpeng Motors. It is too early to tell which (if any) of these will do well in the Chinese, let alone other, markets.

SHIPBUILDERS

Shipbuilders at first glance may not seem all that high-tech or strategic, but in fact their operations, and the precision manufacturing and the use of robotics in their shipyards, and the array of high-tech gear that today operates a merchant vessel (and of course dominates the weapons systems on naval vessels), easily qualify them for listing here. Moreover, the importance of the world's shipping industry cannot be ignored. Notwithstanding the critical role of digital high tech in the world today, physical goods still matter hugely, such as natural resources, agricultural products, foodstuffs, and all the things that may be purchased at Walmart and IKEA—and 70 percent of all these sorts of goods traded between countries is carried by ship (only perishable cargos, for the most part, are delivered by aircraft). Therefore, for Cold War 2.0 purposes, it matters who the world's leading shipbuilders are, how tech-savvy they have become, and in which countries they have their shipyards.

Here is a list of key shipbuilders, grouped by country and their respective market share of the global shipbuilding market:

TABLE 11—SHIPBUILDERS

Democracies
Japan: 29 percent
Sumitomo Heavy Industries
Imabari
Mitsubishi Heavy Industries
South Korea: 17 percent
Hyundai Heavy Industries
K Shipbuilding
Samsung Heavy Industries
Daewoo
Other: 3 percent
Damen—The Netherlands
Fincantieri—Italy
Huntington Ingalls—US
Autocracies: 46 percent
China State Shipbuilding Corporation—China

Essentially, large merchant ships and most naval vessels get built in three countries in Asia, namely two democracies (Japan and South Korea) and one autocracy (China). For instance, South Korea builds 90 percent of the world's ships for transporting liquefied natural gas. These vessels became absolutely critical when Russia commenced its invasion of Ukraine, and Europe had to be weaned off Russian natural gas thanks largely to significant shipments to Europe of American natural gas by new LNG tankers. And while high-end SC production, centered in Taiwan, can be replicated in the US by TSMC and Intel in their new plants in America, reproducing a huge shipbuilding capability, with the attendant dry docks and very specialized supply chains, would prove to be of an order of magnitude more difficult. This is another important reason for the democracies, as a Cold War 2.0 imperative, to create a PATO collective security organization in East Asia.

COMMERCIAL AIRCRAFT

Commercial aircraft are among the most complex machines built today. As is the case with many of the other industries discussed in this chapter, airplanes were once exclusively mechanical devices. Today, however, high tech permeates virtually every process from takeoff to landing and everything in between. Each of the larger commercial aircraft, and the military planes of any size, contain software programs that comprise millions of lines of computer code, all stored and manipulated on SCs. As the amount of digital increases, the quality of the software code becomes key, as Boeing found out when software design problems with the 737 MAX caused it billions of dollars of damage—and the deaths of 346 people when two of these planes crashed when the onboard computerized flight system malfunctioned. Boeing also learned that precision engineering and advanced manufacturing is a critical stage of building aircraft, when some structural/joint problems with its 787 Dreamliner caused another large problem for the company recently, delaying the delivery of hundreds of planes.

In terms of Cold War 2.0, the civilian aircraft industry is largely a global duopoly dominated by the democracies. Boeing, the American company, had the industry virtually to itself for several decades after World War II. Then in 1970 the European Union decided it needed a homegrown champion, and a fascinating consortium of expertise and funding from businesses in Britain, France, Germany, and Spain got together to produce Airbus, which today sells more airplanes per year than Boeing. Not surprisingly the Chinese, tired of buying huge fleets of planes from Boeing and Airbus, have merged various domestic businesses together to form COMAC, which is desperately trying to break into the market with both a short-haul middle-aisle plane and a larger two-aisle plane for longer international routes. At the same time, though, in April 2023, when French president Macron was in Beijing trying to get Chinese paramount leader Xi Jinping to engage in a peace process for the Russo-Ukrainian War, he found some time to sign an important contract between France and China that would give China even more scope to manufacture and assemble key components of the Airbus planes to be sold to Chinese airlines.

From a Cold War 2.0 perspective, large aircraft are of course exemplary dual-use devices. It is no surprise that Boeing, Airbus, and COMAC make military planes as well. Shown below are their sales and market cap:

TABLE 12—AIRCRAFT MANUFACTURERS

Democracies	Sales	Market Cap
Boeing—US	$66 billion	$128 billion
Lockheed Martin—US	$66	$116
Airbus—Europe	$61	$113
Northrup Grumman—US	$37	$68
Leonardo—Italy	$15	$6.8
Textron—US	$12	$13
Dassault—France	$7.4	$15
Bombardier—Canada	$6.9	$4.3
Korea Aerospace—SK	$2.0	$4.0
Autocracies	**Sales**	**Market Cap**
Commercial Aircraft Corporation of China (COMOC)—China	[state—secret]	state owned
Aviation Industry Corporation of China (AVIC)—China	$20	state owned
United Aircraft Corporation—Russia	$7.2	$21
Nonaligned	**Sales**	**Market Cap**
Hindustan Aeronautics—India	$3.3	$15.4
Embraer—Brazil	$4.5	$2.7

There are about a dozen major systems that go into a modern jet aircraft, and no single company can make them all. For example, when China's COMAC launched the C919 single-aisle commercial airliner a few years ago, Beijing hailed the event as a breakthrough for China, that they finally had a "made in China" aircraft that they could use in place of the Boeing and Airbus planes they had been buying for decades. Well, from a Cold War 2.0 perspective, while the final assembly of the C919 is indeed done in China, the following critical subsystems come from companies based in the democracies: hydraulics, landing gear, avionics, flight controls, and, most important, the engines. This speaks to the issue about potential sanctions to be levied on China if it were to attack Taiwan in order to force the island nation to become a part of China. Were such sanctions implemented by the democracies, the C919 production line would cease to operate, and fairly soon the existing C919s operated by Chinese airlines would be grounded for want of spare parts and software upgrades. A central question of the 21st century will be whether this sort of economic consideration will hold sway over Xi Jinping, or whether geopolitics will trump economics for the Chinese supreme autocrat.

JET ENGINES

Jet engines, as noted above, are critical for commercial airliners and military aircraft, but interestingly they are not made by the aircraft manufacturers. Rather, they are an industry unto themselves, largely because they are extremely complex and expensive to design, develop, and manufacture. As with the aircraft makers, the leaders in the market are all in the democracies, but the Russians and the Chinese are working hard to catch up, though from a Cold War 2.0 perspective there is a real weakness in this domain in the autocracies. Russia was going to use engines from the democracies (GE and RR) on the new long-haul commercial aircraft that Russia and China were building as a joint venture (the CR929), but then the sanctions levied in response to the Russian invasion of Ukraine in 2022 threw a wrench into that plan. The autocracies now have to develop a new engine, using no components from the democracies. This will be very difficult—perhaps not as hard as developing sub 14 nm SCs, but almost. And see chapter 10 for a discussion of how the CR929 ultimately fell apart because the Russians did not want to share their jet engine know-how with the Chinese for fear of having it stolen by them, as there was plenty of prior evidence where Chinese "partners" reverse engineered Russian engine technology to avoid having to pay royalties on additional Russian components.

China has a further challenge with making high-end jet engines that is similar to its ambition to make high-performance SCs. State-of-the-art machine tools are needed to produce the finely engineered parts for aircraft. China doesn't have the capability to manufacture these very sophisticated machine tools, and so has to import them from the democracies, largely made by German, Japanese, Italian, and South Korean firms. This is very similar to the conundrum China has with self-sufficient production of 5 nm and 3 nm SCs—China simply doesn't have the etching machine from the Netherlands which is a must to be able to make SCs at this very advanced level. These are deficiencies that the Chinese will be hard-pressed to rectify as Cold War 2.0 unfolds over the coming years.

Here are the current sales and market capitalization figures for the aircraft engine manufacturers:

TABLE 13—AIRCRAFT ENGINE MANUFACTURERS

Democracies	Sales	Market Cap
General Electric—US	$69 billion	$120 billion
Pratt & Whitney (Raytheon)—US	$68	$142
Safran—France (and CFM JV with GE)	$17	$66
Rolls-Royce—UK	$16	$16
Autocracies	**Sales**	**Market Cap**
United Aircraft Corporation—Russia	$7.2	$21
Aero Engine Corporation of China (still in development mode)	N/A	N/A

China is investing heavily to develop its own national jet engine capable of powering a commercial airliner (the CJ-1000A and CJ2000 engines). It is also working hard on perfecting jet engines for its air force jet fighters (the WS-15 and WS-20 models of engines). But high-performance jet engines are fiendishly difficult to innovate and engineer. Its not just propulsion engineering that needs to be mastered, but also a myriad of other domains of expertise, such as metallurgy with titanium and dozens of other alloys. Russia has provided China with about 4,000 jet engines for military purposes (airplanes and helicopters) over the past twenty years. For Cold War 2.0 purposes, it is likely that

China will need another ten to fifteen years to build its national civilian and military jet engine–making capability to be able to cease relying on the Russians. In the meantime, the sanctions of the democracies on Russia make the continued flow of Russian engines somewhat problematic. For the foreseeable future, jet engines pose a real Achilles heel to the headlong expansion of the Chinese PLA air force.

The Chinese are not helping themselves by ignoring, and indeed consciously opposing, the principle of competitive displacement as they pursue the development of a world-class jet engine. They have concentrated all their efforts into one company, Aero Engine Corporation of China, to make their civilian jet (the CJ series), and one company (Shenyang Aeroengine Research Institute, an AVIC subsidiary) to make the military jet (the WS series). In effect, neither company has competition—and without competition there is no competitive displacement. Contrast this with the democracies, where there are four meaningful competitors, and competition is enhanced by allowing customers of commercial airliners, for example, to buy a jet family equipped with one of two engine options, so that the jet engine manufacturers are kept on their toes. Interestingly, in 1999 AVIC's jet engine business was split in two, but in 2008 they were remerged together again—apparently the degree of competition did not sit well with the companies; a poor decision if the goal is to produce a state-of-the-art jet engine.

ROBOTICS

Robotics is the last civilian industrial domain highlighted in this chapter because the building of most of the other sophisticated products/goods noted above require a great deal of precision engineering and advanced manufacturing, both of which typically manifest themselves through high-tech industrial robots. Indeed, industrial robots (as opposed to "social" or "delivery" robots, which are not dealt with here) are central to most manufacturing concerns today, including factories ranging from autos, biomedical devices, consumer electronic devices, food processing, and in logistics warehouses—there are about 3.5 million industrial robots installed in factories worldwide. And of course, at the risk of beating a dead horse, it goes without saying that the guts of these robotic devices are the software and SCs in them that control their physical appendages and core functionalities, and their software is increasingly of the AI variety.

Here are the top dozen industrial robotics companies in the world, the number of units shipped, and their annual sales and market capitalization:

TABLE 14—INDUSTRIAL ROBOTICS COMPANIES

Democracies	Sales	Market Cap	Units Shipped
FANUC—JPN	$6.5 billion	$32 billion	750,000
ABB—SWE/SWI	$30.3	$69	500,000
Yaskawa—JPN	$3.7	$11	500,000
Epson—JPN	$1.3	$6 (Seiko)	150,000
Kawasaki—JPN	$1.2	$35	210,000
Denso—JPN	$46	$49	120,000
Kuka—GER	$3.9	$3.4	100,000
Mitsubishi Electric—JPN	$36	$30	70,000
Universal—DK/ US	$0.3	$16 (Teradyne)	50,000
Omron—JPN	$6.3	$12	20,000
Autocracies	**Sales**	**Market Cap**	**Units Shipped**
Siasun—China	$.5	$3.1	[private]

China has the largest number of installed industrial robots (about 270,000), as you might expect from the "workshop of the world." The subsequent six countries, and their numbers, are Japan, 47,000; United States, 35,000; South Korea, 31,000; Germany, 23,000; Italy, 14,000; and Taiwan, 9,600. At the same time, though, China's indigenous industrial robot makers are struggling, even though they receive significant support from the Chinese government. They tend to compete on price (coming in about 30 percent cheaper than the Japanese or German suppliers), but most Chinese factory managers seem to agree with the old truism "You get what you pay for." Still, the CCP is trying hard to win market share from the foreigners, and the Ministry of Industry and Information Technology, along with fourteen other central departments, has a five-year plan for the robotics industry in China. And there are certainly some interesting smaller players with novel technologies, like Dobot and Mech-Mind, but they are mainly in the nonindustrial subdomains of the sector. All of the Chinese manufacturers, though, tend to rely heavily on critical parts made in the democracies, and so from a Cold War 2.0 perspective, a mass trade embargo by the democracies over a China invasion of Taiwan would effectively bring the Chinese industry to a halt.

MILITARY DEFENSE CONTRACTORS

Military defense contractors obviously must also be discussed under "Other Important Technologies" because no conversation about national military power would be complete without giving them a prominent place in the analysis. In many respects the defense industry combines all the elements of the discussion noted previously, in order to produce state-of-the-art weapons systems in a cost-effective manner—no easy task. The products of these "original equipment manufacturers" can be put into the following buckets: munitions (warheads, the explosive part of bombs, etc.); delivery vehicles that transport the munitions to their intended target (planes, tanks, ships, and the missiles launched from the planes, tanks, and ships); communications, command, and control systems (some now add a fourth "C," for *computers*, so C4); systems that collect intelligence, surveillance, and reconnaissance (ISR) and other data necessary for undertaking C4.

Increasingly, these military contractors also serve as very important "system integrators," where they take the individual components pro-duced by smaller entities, often even start-ups in the tech space, and then ensure that these pieces are modified properly to fit within the overall weapons system, are properly interfaced with other related systems and components, and then they take responsibility for ensuring the ongoing maintenance and sustaining of the overall system.

Military defense is a very large business. Countries spent $2.24 trillion on defense purchases in 2022. Here are the top fifteen players, each with sales of over $10 billion, ranked by size of sales, and then the next 70 players aggregated by country:[4]

TABLE 15—MILITARY DEFENSE CONTRACTORS

Company	Annual Sales
Lockheed Martin—US	$60.340 B
RTX (Raytheon)—US	$41.850
Boeing—US	$33.420
Northrup Grumman—US	$29.880
General Dynamics—US	$26.390
BAE—UK	$26.020
NORINCO—China	$21.570
AVIC—China	$20.110
CASC—China	$19.100
CETC—China	$14.990
CASIC—China	$14.520
Leonardo—Italy	$13.870
L3Harris Technologies—US	$13.360
CSSC—China	$11.130
Airbus—France	$10.850
Sales totals for top 15	
Democracies	$294.160
Autocracies	$101.420
The next 15 are based in:	
United States, 6, sales total	$38.180
France, 4, sales total	$25.820
UK, EU, Israel, 1 each, sales total	$14.680
Russia and China, 1 each, sales total	$10.360
And the next 70 (to round out the top 100) are based in:	
United States	28
United Kingdom	6
Germany	4
Japan	4

South Korea	4
Turkey and Israel	2 each
Sweden, Canada, Australia, Poland, Spain, Norway, Italy, France, Singapore, Taiwan, EU, and Ukraine	1 each (12 total)
Russia	5
China	1
And India (nonaligned)	2

FINANCING SOURCES

Financing sources are critical for technology innovation—new products, whether involving AI, SCs, QCs, or biotechnology, or in the other domains noted in this chapter, simply don't get developed unless they are adequately financed. That money can come from public sources, but frankly if too much comes from the government, then the public overseers of those funds will inevitably serve to slow down, compromise, or often downright destroy the innovation, even if the bureaucrats exert the best of intentions. A core argument in this book has been that in an autocracy especially, innovation can be held back, if not entirely thwarted, because of the heavy hand of the autocrat or one of his sycophantic enablers; but frankly, even in democracies, government civil servants, as well intentioned as they are, shouldn't try to pick winners in technology submarkets. They have neither the expertise nor the incentive to do it expertly. Therefore, the amount of private funding, and the added value behind it—such as is brought to the relationship with the start-up or early-stage entrepreneur by experienced venture capital investors who have built, operated, and grown tech companies themselves—is central to the success of a technology innovation ecosystem. No money, no breakthroughs—it's just that simple.

Set out below are statistics showing the relative size of the venture capital investments made in the top ten recipient countries of such financing over the past five years. Venture investment is critical for early-stage technology companies. At the other end of the financing spectrum are the stock exchanges for public companies; set out below are the relative sizes of the stock exchanges in about twenty countries. (These figures include all companies, not just those focused on technology businesses.) In both cases, the premier role of the United States in financing new and established businesses is readily apparent. They also show, however, the important aggregate contribution of the other leading democracies as well; in the last two years, the venture investment in the other five leading democracies (excluding the US) itself exceeded China's venture investing. The same result is seen in Table 17, showing the size of public stock exchanges; again, leaving out the US for a moment, the size of the stock exchanges in the other democracies, in the aggregate, is more than twice that of China. Alliances certainly matter, especially when it comes to Cold War 2.0.

TABLE 16—VENTURE CAPITAL FINANCING

Democracies	2018	2019	2020	2021	2022
US	149B	156B	175B	364B	245B
UK	12	18	17	41	31
France	5	6	6	14	16
South Korea	5	5	5	16	15
Germany	6	9	7	21	12
Canada	5	7	6	16	11
Israel	4	4	5	11	8
Total (Dem)	186	205	221	483	338
Autocracies	2018	2019	2020	2021	2022
China	108	65	61	84	61
Nonaligned	2018	2019	2020	2021	2022
India	13	17	15	43	25
Singapore	6	5	4	8	8

At the other end of the capital markets spectrum, here is the size of the stock exchanges of the top twenty-one countries (calculated by the World Bank in the 2020 period):

TABLE 17—COUNTRIES BY STOCK MARKET CAPITALIZATION

Democracies	Total Market Cap	Percent of GDP	No. of Firms
United States	44.7 trillion	194	4,266
Japan	6.7	122	3,754
United Kingdom	3.2	100	1,858
Canada	2.6	160	3,922
France	2.3	85	457
Germany	2.2	60	438
South Korea	2.1	133	2,318
Taiwan	2.0	267	1,627
Switzerland	2.0	267	236
Australia	1.7	129	1,902
Sweden	1.3	230	832
Netherlands	1.1	132	103
Spain	.7	59	2,711
Total Democracies	72.6	N/A	24,184
Autocracies	**Total Market Cap**	**Percent of GDP**	**No. of Firms**
China	13.2	83	4,154
Saudi Arabia	2.4	347	207
Iran	1.2	635	367
Russia	.7	46	213
Nonaligned	**Total Market Cap**	**Percent of GDP**	**No. of Firms**
Hong Kong	6.1	1,768	2,353
India	3.2	100	5,215
South Africa	1.0	348	264
Brazil	1.0	68	345

10

OTHER POWERFUL ASSETS

A core theme of this book to this point has been how the two camps facing off in Cold War 2.0 stack up in terms of technology and innovation. Power, though, whether of the economic, military, or soft variety, implicates human, and some other powerful assets as well. Especially important for the democracies are alliances, for the simple reason they have many more meaningful ones than the autocracies. This chapter undertakes both a quantitative assessment of NATO, and also a qualitative one—of the fairly recent AUKUS alliance. The conclusion is compelling. High-quality alliances among the democracies (like NATO and AUKUS) serve as a power multiplier, even if the key linchpin in both is the United States. Equally, autocracies have trouble playing nicely together in their alliance relations. The prospects for the most recent version of China-Russia "friendship without limits" might be pretty limited after all.

Other important assets include certain minerals, particularly those that will be central to the effort of transitioning from fossil fuels to renewable energy sources. In this metric twenty-three minerals are considered in terms of where the current sources are as between the autocracies, the democracies, and the nonaligned countries. This constitutes a weakness for the democracies that will require some serious attention, time, and effort. The good news, though, is that the technological demands for securing this vulnerable flank are rather low, whether in prospecting, mining, or refining. Finally, a review of the rankings of the world's top 100 universities reveals another core strength of the democracies. This is heartening because these institutions do much more than educate—they draw the best and the brightest from around the world, serving as the indispensable honeypots where the next generation of tech leaders gets to rub entrepreneurial elbows. It is then up to the democracies, through enlightened immigration policies, to convince these gifted scholars (and budding world-beaters) to stay on in their respective newfound countries once they graduate, a win-win-win result for all concerned, and one not easily replicated by the autocracies because of their cultural aversion to genuine multiculturalism. This bodes well for the democracies, particularly when viewing Cold War 2.0 as a very long game.

ALLIANCES MATTER

Both the current and previous cold wars are often portrayed as a contest solely between the leading democracy, the United States, and its "counterpart" autocracy, be that Russia in Cold War 1, or now China in Cold War 2.0. There is some truth and utility in this frame, but it leaves out a hugely important phenomenon, particularly on the side of the democracies, namely the vast utility of allies. What follows are several charts of the various assets of each camp, showing the makeup of the leading democracies and autocracies, but then also the principal allies of each, showing for each: population,[1] size of the economy,[2] number of active-duty military personnel,[3] whether or not the country has mandatory military service, whether it is a member of NATO or another military alliance with the United States, a member of the European Union, and a member of the Organization for Economic Cooperation and Development (OECD):

TABLE 1—THE LEADING DEMOCRACIES

Country	Pop.	Econ.	Sold.	Mil. Budget	Mil. Service	NATO/ Alliance	EU	OECD
US	340Mi	25Tr	1.4Mi	$800 B	No	Yes	No	Yes
Japan	123	4.9	247Th	54	No	Yes	No	Yes
Germany	83	4.2	183	56	No	Yes	Yes	Yes
UK	67	3.2	153	68	No	Yes	No	Yes
France	64	2.9	203	56	No	Yes	Yes	Yes
Italy	58	2.1	161	32	No	Yes	Yes	Yes
Canada	40	2.0	66	26	No	Yes	No	Yes
South Korea	51	1.8	555	50	Yes	Yes	No	Yes
Australia	26	1.5	60	31	No	Yes	No	Yes
Mexico	129	1.3	216	8.6	Yes	No	No	Yes
Spain	47	1.2	122	19	No	Yes	Yes	Yes
Netherlands	17	1.0	34	13	No	Yes	Yes	Yes
Turkey	85	0.8	355	15	Yes	Yes	No	Yes
Swiss	9	0.8	20	5.7	Yes	Yes	Yes	Yes
Taiwan	24	0.7	169	13	Yes	Yes	No	Yes
Poland	41	0.6	114	13	No	Yes	Yes	Yes
Sweden	10	0.6	20	5.7	Yes	Yes	Yes	Yes
Belgium	11	0.6	6	6.3	No	Yes	Yes	Yes
Ireland	5	0.5	8.5	1.2	No	No	Yes	Yes
Israel	9	0.5	170	24	Yes	No	No	Yes
Denmark	6	0.4	15	5.3	Yes	Yes	Yes	Yes
Singapore	6	0.4	51	11	Yes	No	No	Yes
Norway	5.4	0.4	25	8.2	Yes	Yes	Yes	Yes
Philippines	116	0.4	145	4.0	No	Yes	No	No
Chile	19	0.3	68	6.2	No	No	No	Yes
Finland	5.5	0.3	19	5.9	Yes	Yes	Yes	Yes
Romania	19	0.28	71	5.5	No	Yes	Yes	No
Czech	10	0.28	26	3.9	No	Yes	Yes	Yes
Portugal	10	0.25	27	4.9	No	Yes	Yes	Yes
New Zealand	5	0.25	9.7	3.3	No	Yes	No	Yes
Greece	10	0.21	143	8	Yes	Yes	Yes	Yes
Ukraine	36	0.2	196	5.9	Yes	No	No	No
Hungary	10	0.18	34	2.7	Yes	Yes	Yes	Yes

Slovakia	5.4	0.11	8	1.9	No	Yes	Yes	Yes
Bulgaria	6.8	0.08	37	1.2	No	Yes	Yes	No
Lithuania	2.7	0.06	23	1.2	Yes	Yes	Yes	Yes
Slovenia	2.1	0.06	7	0.7	No	Yes	Yes	Yes
Latvia	1.8	0.04	8.7	0.8	No	Yes	Yes	Yes
Estonia	1.3	0.037	7.2	0.7	Yes	Yes	Yes	Yes

A qualifier is required on the military statistics. The column on "soldiers in active duty" do not include paramilitary organizations, which for some countries, especially autocracies, can be material. For example, Russia leans very heavily on the Wagner Group, which just prior to the invasion of Ukraine had a head count of about 50,000. This group played an oversized role in the first sixteen months of the Russo-Ukrainian War. In other countries, the number of "reservists" is also very important, especially if the country has a mandatory military service regime (where most men between nineteen and generally thirty have to serve between one and three years in the army), as these men then become fairly strong call-ups if there is a need for them.

Clearly the United States is the largest country by all the metrics shown above—population, size of the economy, size of the military, etc. But, while the US economy, taken alone, is $25 trillion, the rest of the democracies on this chart, taken together, amount to $35 trillion. Although the Netherlands has only 17 million people, it is home to ASML, the only company in the world able to make etching machines for the highest-performance semiconductor chips; or consider Taiwan, with only 24 million people, has 90 percent of the factories that make those highest-performing SCs (using the ASML machines in their factories).

The smaller countries can contribute in unique ways as well. Tiny Estonia has probably the most successful educational campaign for making children resilient against disinformation and propaganda emanating from the autocracies (in the case of Estonia, especially Russia). Therefore, notwithstanding Estonia has only 1.3 million people (fewer than live in Helsinki or San Diego), Estonia's educational system has a lot of lessons to convey to the other democracies around the world, if only there was an effective way for Estonia to share that knowledge and experience. The question then becomes how best to ensure that the democracies in fact do work together to amplify their strength, so that 1+1=3; or put another way, the whole of the community of democracies is greater than the sum of their parts. We'll return to this after we review the lineup from the autocracies.

FIRST-RANK AUTOCRACIES

Set out below is similar information for the two "leading autocracies" and their closest partners, including whether the country has compulsory military service and whether it is a member of the Collective Security Treaty Organization (CSTO), which is a loose replica of NATO, or a member of China-led Shanghai Cooperation Organization:

TABLE 2—FIRST RANK AUTOCRACIES

Country	Pop.	Econ.	Sold.	Mil. Budget	Mil. Service	CSTO	SCO
China	1,400 Mi	18 Tr	2.035 Mi	$293 B	Yes	No	Yes
Russia	144	1.78	900 Th	$65	Yes	Yes	Yes
Belarus	9.5	0.06	48	$0.76	Yes	Yes	Yes
Kazakhstan	19	0.225	39	$1.6	Yes	Yes	Yes
Tajikistan	10	0.07	9	$0.081	Yes	Yes	Yes
Kyrgyzstan	7	0.09	10	$0.124	Yes	Yes	Yes
Uzbekistan	35	0.81	48	$1.4	Yes	No	Yes
Turkmenistan	6.5	0.08	36	$0.02	Yes	No	No

Clearly China and Russia are the leading autocracies in Cold War 2.0. For all intents and purposes, they are each other's only serious ally, but even their relationship doesn't amount to a mutual defense treaty. Nevertheless, with the democracies imposing deep sanctions on Russia as a result of its invasion of Ukraine in 2022, China has become a critical trading partner for Russia, with the former buying almost as much oil from Russia (86 million barrels, but at heavily discounted prices) as it bought from Saudi Arabia (87 million barrels) in 2022. As the war continues it appears that

China has not, however, provided Russia with material weapons systems or large stocks of ammunition.

As for the Central Asian countries listed above, while two of them are members of the CSTO, since Russia's poor showing in the war in Ukraine, all the "stans" have tried to distance themselves to some degree from the Russian orbit. At the same time, China has tried to gain influence in the Central Asian countries, including by Chairman Xi holding a session of the SCO in Uzbekistan in September 2022. This is very telling evidence of the rather tenuous relationship of Moscow and Beijing, given that China is actively fishing for closer friends in Central Asian waters, a region previously considered an exclusive Russian domain.

SECOND-RANK AUTOCRACIES

Beyond the two main autocracies of China and Russia, there are a number of smaller autocracies which, while not officially aligned with the two leaders through treaties of mutual defense, often act in concert with them, though their relationship tends to be more transactional than relational.

TABLE 3—SECOND RANK AUTOCRACIES

Country	Pop.	Econ.	Sold.	Mil. Budget
Iran	89 Mi	0.36 Tr	610 Th	$24 B
North Korea	25	0.16	1,200	$4 B
Cuba	11	0.01	50	$0.500
Venezuela	28	0.04	123	$0.745
Syria	23	0.02	169	$2.5
Algeria	45	0.18	139	$9.2 B

NONALIGNED DEMOCRACIES

In addition to the democracies already listed above, there are a number of democracies that have large populations and militaries, but do not have mutual defense arrangements with the United States or NATO. Still, if push came to shove, and they had to take sides in a major confrontation between the democracies and the autocracies, particularly one involving their own territory or deep national interests, presumably they would join the ranks of the democracies, although they may well remain neutral as well.

TABLE 4—NONALIGNED DEMOCRACIES

Country	Pop.	Econ.	Sold.	Mil. Budget
India	1.4 B	3.2 Tr	1.4 Mi	79.6 B
Brazil	216 Mi	1.6	366 Th	19 B
Indonesia	277	1.1	395	8.2 B
Nigeria	222	0.50	143	4.4 B
South Africa	60	0.43	74	3.2 B
Colombia	51	0.34	360	10.5 B

India is in a very interesting situation in terms of Cold War 2.0. On the one hand, it is experiencing a very tense relationship with China, as they share a highly contested border in the Kashmir. As recently as 2021 their respective border guards clashed—no casualties, but lots of hard feelings. At the same time, though, India is heavily reliant on weapons purchased from Russia, now China's foremost partner. India, however, is one of many countries not impressed with the performance of Russian arms in Ukraine, and so it is in a hurry to buy weapons from the democracies. And India is part of the "Quad," which includes Australia, the United States, and Japan, ostensibly to discuss measures to block the excesses of China in the Indo-Pacific region.

India also greatly helps the democracies as a source of very bright talent in the STEM domains, which is crucial for technology innovation. Assume about 2 percent of any population have IQs in the 98th percentile. With a population of 1.4 billion, China will have about 30 million very bright people (and great candidates for formal STEM education at the university level). Applying similar math, the US will generate about 7 million really smart people, and Europe about 10 million. Taken together, the democracies produce about half the number of really bright people as China. But then consider India, also with a population of 1.4 billion, so accounting for another 30 million really smart people. About 775,000 Indian students study abroad each year, mostly in the STEM disciplines. Many of these students—in some countries *most*—will stay and become citizens of the countries where they studied. All told, India crucially helps the democracies fill a huge gap in their raw STEM human resource rivalry with China.

NONALIGNED AUTOCRACIES

The final category of countries worth noting are autocracies that are not firmly under the leadership of either China or Russia, and in that sense are "nonaligned," but at the same time their autocratic tendencies predispose them to relations with the leading autocracies. Still, from time to time they can be persuaded to act in concert with the democracies. It is, at the end of the day, a complex world, and these countries in particular view their relations with other countries on a very case-by-case transactional basis. Set out below are their populations and the size of their economies:

TABLE 5—NONALIGNED AUTOCRACIES

Country	Pop.	Econ.
Egypt	112	0.4
Saudi Arabia	36	0.8
Vietnam	98	0.36
Malaysia	36	0.37
Algeria	45	0.16
Bangladesh	172	0.46
Pakistan	239	0.35
Ethiopia	126	0.11
Iraq	5	0.20
Peru	33	0.22
Angola	36	0.12
Morocco	37	0.14
Kenya	55	0.11

NUCLEAR WEAPONS

An additional metric worth noting are those countries that possess nuclear weapons (essentially atomic bombs and hydrogen bombs), as well as the capability to make them and to deliver them by some combination of bomber aircraft or submarines. Here's the list:

TABLE 6— NUMBER OF NUCLEAR WARHEADS

Democracies	No. of nuclear warheads
United States	5,428
United Kingdom	225
France	290
Israel	90
Autocracies	**No. of nuclear warheads**
China	350
Russia	5,977
North Korea	20
Nonaligned	**No. of nuclear warheads**
India	160
Pakistan	165

While nuclear weapons played an outsized role in Cold War 1, there is reason to believe they will have a diminished part in Cold War 2.0. Clearly they serve to deter a nuclear or major conventional military attack on a nuclear power, particularly by another power also holding nuclear weapons. In effect, the doctrine of "mutually assured destruction" is alive and well, and that brings peace to the world at one level of potential engagement—nuclear powers haven't made war on one another since nuclear weapons first appeared on the international scene in 1945. The Russo-Ukrainian War also shows that national leaders are also hesitant to use so-called tactical nuclear weapons on the battlefield. It is not clear what military advantage they provide the user, particularly when weighed against the intense opprobrium their use would generate from the entire international community.

HIGH-QUALITY ALLIANCES MATTER THE MOST

Statistics can explain only so much. After all, going by the plain statistics, most military analysts predicted Russia would walk over Ukraine in a matter of days. Consider the two following very different types of alliances.

The United States and the United Kingdom have been close allies since World War I. Both are in NATO. They conduct very extensive military exercises together, and with other allies. Both share extensive military and other intelligence under the "Five Eyes" information-sharing relationship—the three other "eyes" are Canada, Australia, and New Zealand. The United States has an alliance treaty with Australia, which provides that should Australia be attacked by a foreign power, the US will come to Australia's defense.

In 2021, the US, the UK, and Australia announced their AUKUS initiative aimed at bolstering democratic defenses in the Asia-Pacific, focusing around the development and coordinated deployment of nuclear-powered (but not nuclear-armed) submarines. In March 2023, more details of the AUKUS plan were unveiled. In essence, Australia would invest around $200 billion over the next thirty years, first for helping the UK build the new subs (which would be based on American nuclear power technology), and then Australia would begin building some as well. In the meantime, the US would rent some nuclear subs to Australia, something that is very rarely done.

AUKUS will result in the three countries sharing their deepest military and nuclear technologies, which military contractors in the three countries will work with as if they were a consortium—there will be a tremendous amount of technical, business, and system building intertwining. The three countries also agree to a deep collaboration in artificial intelligence, quantum computing, and hypersonic missiles. The UK and Australia get unprecedented access to American nuclear technology—and related technology in the area of underwater communications, sonar, and unmanned undersea vehicles—while the United States effectively increases the democratic deterrent force in the Asia-Pacific by eight state-of-the-art nuclear-powered submarines. On these subs there will be American, British, and Australian service members, usually on the same boat. In essence it will create a single navy from the three countries.

There will be difficult moments for the AUKUS partners. There will be regular changes of government in all three countries: How will new presidents and prime ministers figure in the future of the program? This will be particularly acute if the three disagree whether a certain event in the Asia-Pacific region warrants the deployment of the subs, or the firing of their missiles or torpedoes against a third-party target. The answer seems to be ingrained in the closeness of the program itself—they will simply have to work out their differences because they have to. They will be assisted, though, in the main theme of Cold War 2.0, namely, an existential threat to the democracies posed by the autocracies, especially China in the case of the Eastern Pacific.

Contrast the AUKUS alliance centered around nuclear-powered submarines with the alliance developed by Russia and China around the building of a state-of-the-art commercial airliner. Between 1945 and 1970, the American Boeing company enjoyed a virtual monopoly in the design and manufacture of commercial planes, both carrying passengers and those devoted to transporting cargo. In 1970 several European governments (initially France and Germany, then later Spain and Britain as well) formed a consortium to build a European competitor to Boeing, and Airbus has been a great success (albeit with loads of financial help from these four governments). The British company Rolls-Royce builds the all-important engines for the Airbus planes; a German company builds the wings; and the planes are assembled in Toulouse, France. Today, the world commercial airline manufacturing business is an effective duopoly (i.e., in 2022, Boeing delivered 480 planes, and Airbus delivered 661 planes).

In 2016, Russia and China formed a consortium to build the CR 929 wide-body plane that could compete against Boeing and Airbus, after both Boeing and Airbus refused to become joint venture partners with the Chinese. Both governments were tired of buying foreign aircraft and saw the significant benefits of having a civilian airline business that would help their respective military aircraft builders. Following the example of the Airbus consortium, Russia's United Aircraft Corporation was to supply the engines, while China's COCOM (Commercial Aircraft Corporation of China), would build the body and do finally assembly of the plane in China.[4] The CR929 plane ("C" standing for China, and "R" standing for Russia) never got off the ground, as the Russian-Chinese consortium was never even able to agree on technology-sharing protocols. One huge barrier was that Russia never could come to agree to let China have full access to the technology that was intended to comprise the engine for the CR929. In turn, the Chinese were very worried about giving the Russians access to the very large Chinese market for wide-body aircraft. What was lacking, fundamentally, was a required degree of trust among the consortium participants, and this one involved only two partners. This failed case study does not bode well for the "friendship without limits" Russia and China announced just before Russia's invasion of Ukraine. The contrast with the AUKUS partnership (between the US, the UK, and Australia) couldn't be starker.

Today there is also a great deal of mistrust between Russia and China. With the implosion of Soviet Russia, for example, the countries of Central Asia (i.e., Kazakhstan, Tajikistan) broke free from Moscow's grip, but now Putin wants them back in a close form of association. At the same time, though, China is wooing the five Central Asian countries, including with many Belt and Road investments. In short, the relationship between Russia and China is complicated, and often entails zero-sum competition. Also, while China imported some extra oil from Russia in 2022 after sanctions from the democracies were slapped on Russia, China has not bought nearly as much as the Russians would want them to buy. Similarly, at the Xi-Putin summit in Moscow in March 2023, Xi did not agree to build a second natural gas pipeline between Russia and China. In essence, Xi doesn't want to become too dependent on Russia for its energy supplies.[5]

Most important, China has not been able to ship high-end semiconductor chips to Russia—which is what Russia really needs to be able to build advanced weapons systems—because China is also under sanctions for SCs. China is also quite peeved that because of shortages caused by the war-related sanctions, Russia is no longer respecting the intellectual property rights of its trading partners, China included. This also causes China to not ship certain technology to Russia. Finally, China has decided it does not want to ship weapons to Russia, because if it does China will be hit by America's secondary sanctions, which prohibits American firms from selling goods to a country that ships munitions to Russia. North Korea and Iran don't worry about these secondary sanctions because they are already under US sanctions, but China is loath to be caught by the same trade-limiting sanctions regime. Bottom line, it turns out that the China-Russia "friendship without limits" actually has lots of limits. Moreover, Russia doesn't have all that many other friends in the international community who can supply them with what the democracies did before the Russo-Ukrainian War. Allies matter and Russia doesn't have many.

STRATEGIC MINERALS

For about 150 years fossil fuels (first coal, then oil and natural gas) were the primary source of energy in the democracies and autocracies, used either directly (to heat homes, for example) or indirectly (to power electricity-generation plants). The democracies and autocracies are now undergoing a fundamental shift to renewable energy sources, and away from fossil fuels, given the detrimental environmental impact of fossil fuels, including the global warming they produce through greenhouse gas emissions when they are burned.

The new renewable energy systems, however, require huge amounts of certain minerals ("strategic minerals") for, among other things, the battery systems that are required for storing and using electricity generated by wind, solar, and other cleaner forms of energy generation. Electric vehicles and portable electronic devices (smartphones, tablets, laptops, etc.) for the most part currently use lithium-ion batteries, which in turn require lithium, graphite, cobalt, and other raw materials. (Rechargeable batteries use 80 percent of lithium and 80 percent of cobalt.) Lithium production increased from 107,000 tons in 2021 to 130,000 tons in 2022, and prices rose dramatically, from $35,000 a ton in January 2022 to $67,000 in November 2022. In the US there are currently four lithium-ion battery factories, and twenty-one under construction. Similarly, the amount of graphite going into batteries since 2018 has grown by 250 percent since 2018.

As part of Cold War 2.0 there is a race between the democracies and the autocracies for finding new deposits of strategic minerals, as well as for mining and refining them. Over time, recycling of these minerals will increase, and at some point, but not in the near- to midterm, demand from mining will fall as recycled materials fulfill most of the demand. The US 2022 infrastructure law allocates $2.8 billion to American mining and refinement of materials used to make EV batteries.

The following chart lists the strategic minerals where democracies do not have greater than 50 percent of combined global extraction, as well as their current actual production from various countries currently, and for the two very most important ones (cobalt and lithium) the estimated percentage of future reserves.[6] There are other minerals that are important, where China has a majority of the worldwide production (i.e., magnesium), but they are not listed below as they are only "important" metals but not "strategic." Still, a second source strategy (other than China) needs to be found for them as well. There are also some minerals, like potash, that are critical as the key ingredient of fertilizer for agriculture, but China and Russia are not a threat due to sufficient production, and growth capacity, in the democracies, in the case of potash from Canada:

TABLE 7—STRATEGIC MINERALS

Aluminum: high-tech alloys, lightweight for aircraft wings/fuselage
Democracies—10 percent (Canada, Australia, Norway, US)
Autocracies—63 percent (China: 58 percent of total, Russia)
Nonaligned—12 percent (India, Bahrain, UAE)
Antimony: hardener in lead for storage batteries
Democracies—4 percent (Australia)
Autocracies—89 percent (China: 54 percent of total, Russia, Tajikistan)
Arsenic in gallium arsenide SCs (especially military), electronics, space research, telecom, solar cells, optics, short-wave infrared tech
Democracies—1.6 percent (Belgium)
Autocracies—41 percent (China: 39 percent of total, Russia)
Nonaligned—57 percent (Peru, Morocco)
Bismuth: additive in pharmaceuticals, SCs
Democracies—7.4 percent (Japan, South Korea)
Autocracies—80 percent (China)
Nonaligned—10 percent (Laos)
Cesium: atomic clocks, aircraft guidance systems, GPS systems, medical treatments, research in chemicals
Currently not mined, except perhaps in China; stockpiles are being depleted.
Chromium: used in stainless steel, and in superalloys—used in gas turbine engines
Democracies—22 percent (Turkey, Finland)
Autocracies—16 percent (Kazakhstan)
Nonaligned—54 percent (South Africa, India)
Cobalt: principally in the US in superalloys for aircraft gas turbine engines, and in China 80 percent is used in rechargeable batteries
Democracies: Total—8.8 percent
Australia: 3.3 percent—18 percent
Canada: 2.5 percent—3 percent
Philippines: 2.6 percent—3.4 percent
US: 0.4 percent—1 percent
Autocracies: Total—8.0 percent
Russia: 4.4 percent—3.2 percent
Cuba: 2.3 percent—6.6 percent
China: 1.3 percent—1 percent
Nonaligned: Total 75.8 percent
Congo: 70 percent—46 percent

Indonesia: 1.2 percent—8 percent
Papua New Guinea: 1.8 percent—0.6 percent
Madagascar: 1.5 percent—1.3 percent
Morocco: 1.3 percent—0.2 percent
Fluorspar: used in processing of aluminum and uranium, and as input into chemicals used in EV battery electrolytes, graphite, and separator materials
Democracies—14 percent (Mexico, Spain, Germany, Canada)
Autocracies—68 percent (China)
Nonaligned—27 percent (South Africa, Mongolia, Vietnam)
Gallium: used in SC wafers (including defense and high-performance computers) and laser diodes and light-emitting diodes (LEDs), solar cells, telecom equipment, optoelectronic devices for aerospace)
Democracies—Canada, France, Japan, and Slovakia produce high-grade gallium, but did not produce low-grade gallium in 2022
Autocracies—99 percent (China: 97 percent of total, Russia)
Nonaligned—(negligible)
Germanium: fiber-optic systems, infrared night-vision systems, solar applications, thermal sensing
China leading producer, and 90 percent of its exports sent to Germany, Hong Kong, Japan, Belgium, the US and Russia.
Graphite: battery and fuel cells, high-temperature lubricants, brushes in electric motors
Democracies—5 percent (South Korea, Canada, Ukraine)
Autocracies—67 percent (China (65 percent of total), Russia)
Nonaligned—29 percent (Mozambique, Madagascar, Brazil)
Hafnium/Zirconium: superalloys; related zirconium in nuclear energy industry
Democracies—35 percent (Australia)
Autocracies—10 percent (China)
Nonaligned—39 percent (South Africa, Mozambique)
Indium: flat-panel displays, especially in liquid-crystal displays in computers, electrical components, SCs
Democracies—40 percent (South Korea, Japan, Canada, France)
Autocracies—58 percent (China)
Nonaligned—(negligible)
Lithium
Democracies: Total—77.4 percent
Australia (47 percent—24 percent)
Chile (30 percent—36 percent)
US (5 percent—est.[7]—4 percent)
Canada (0.4 percent—4 percent)

Autocracies: Total—15 percent
China (15 percent—8 percent)
Nonaligned: Total—7 percent
Argentina (5 percent—10 percent)
Brazil (2 percent—1 percent)
Manganese: critical component of steel, and no substitute
Democracies—19 percent (Australia)
Autocracies—6 percent (China, Kazakhstan)
Nonaligned—73 percent (South Africa, Gabon, Ghana, India, Brazil)
Niobium: critical input in steel, and superalloys in aerospace industry
Democracies—8 percent (Canada)
Autocracies—0.5 percent (Russia)
Nonaligned—90 percent (Brazil)
Platinum/Palladium: Includes iridium, osmium, rhodium, and ruthenium; used in catalytic converters for autos, and in electronics, computers hard drives, hybrid SCs, multilayer ceramic capacitors, laboratory equipment.
Palladium
Democracies—12 percent (Canada, US)
Autocracies—42 percent (Russia)
Nonaligned—44 percent (South Africa, Zimbabwe)
Platinum
Democracies—5 percent (Canada, US)
Autocracies—11 percent (Russia)
Nonaligned—76 percent (South Africa, Zimbabwe)
Rare Earths: Seventeen elements, comprising scandium and yttrium, and the following fifteen lanthanides: lanthanum, cerium, praseodymium, neodymium, promethium, samarium, europium, gadolinium, terbium, dysprosium, holmium, erbium, thulium, ytterbium, and lutetium. They are actually quite abundant, and used in catalytic converters and alloys, but most important in magnets, including in wind power–generating turbines and EV traction motors.
Democracies—20 percent (US, Australia)
Autocracies—71 percent (China, 70 percent of total; Russia)
Nonaligned—9 percent (Burma, Thailand)
Tungsten: heavy-metal alloys in armaments, wear-resistant alloy parts, superalloys for turbine blades
Democracies—2.5 percent (Austria, Spain, Portugal)
Autocracies—87 percent (China, 84 percent of total; Russia)
Nonaligned—9 percent (Vietnam, Bolivia, Rwanda)

Uranium: fuel for nuclear power plants generating electricity, medical radiology/cancer therapy, nuclear weapons
Democracies—19 percent (Canada, Australia)
Autocracies—62 percent (Kazakhstan, 45 percent of total; Uzbekistan, Russia, China)
Nonaligned—18 percent (Namibia, Niger, India)
Vanadium: strengthener in metals, especially for titanium alloys in jet engines and high-speed airframes, and in large-scale energy storage
Democracies (Australia has reserves, but no current production in the democracies)
Autocracies—77 percent (China, 70 percent of total; Russia)
Nonaligned—15 percent (South Africa, Brazil)

There is material industrial strategy assistance forthcoming from governments on strategic minerals. For example, the US government funded twelve lithium projects with $1.6 billion from the 2022 infrastructure law to mine and refine lithium, make battery parts, recycle batteries, and develop new technologies to increase US lithium resources.

QUALITY OF THE
INNOVATION COHORT

Having identified the member countries of the two camps, it is now worth understanding how many university students graduate each year from the research universities in each of these countries in the disciplines that cover, directly or indirectly, the four accelerator innovations, plus some critical other technologies and asset classes. Here is how the democracies and the autocracies stack up.

In terms of the current status of the race between the democracies and the autocracies for supremacy in the field of artificial intelligence (AI), semiconductor chips (SC), and quantum computing (QC) a useful ranking to consider is the world's top 100 universities in computer science and information systems:[8]

TABLE 8– UNIVERSITIES: COMPUTER SCIENCE AND INFORMATION SYSTEMS

Democracies	Top 20	Next 30	Next 50
United States	9	10	9
United Kingdom	4	1	3
Singapore	2	0	0
Switzerland	2	0	0
Canada	1	4	0
France	0	4	1
South Korea	0	2	3
Australia	0	1	5
Germany	0	2	1
Netherlands	0	1	5
Italy	0	1	3
Belgium	0	1	1
Japan	0	1	1
Sweden	0	0	1
Denmark	0	0	1
Finland	0	0	1
Spain	0	0	1
Taiwan	0	0	1
Austria	0	0	1
Mexico	0	0	1
Ireland	0	0	1
Autocracies	**Top 20**	**Next 30**	**Next 50**
China	2	3	6
Saudi Arabia	0	1	0
Russia	0	0	2
Nonaligned	**Top 20**	**Next 30**	**Next 50**
India	0	0	5
Brazil	0	0	1
Malaysia	0	0	1

These university rankings are important for two reasons. It is in these universities where professors typically research and write papers that set an entire field following a certain avenue of technology development—they are the path breakers. For example, in AI, perhaps the most seminal such paper was one by Geoffrey Hinton, at the University of Toronto, in 2012.[9] After this paper came out, the subfield of AI based on neural nets exploded, and today it is the most important method of doing AI. Universities also play a critical role in technology company formation. Most universities have incubator offices that help STEM students start up their own ventures. And it is important to keep in mind that students who don't actually graduate from the official university program can end up just as entrepreneurial as those who do. Here is a partial list of tech success stories who did not actually graduate from their programs: Bill Gates (cofounder of Microsoft), Mark Zuckerberg (founder of Facebook), Sergey Brin and Larry Page (cofounders of Google/Alphabet).

11

COLD WAR 2.0 FLASHPOINTS

Having reviewed the history of Cold War 1, and the major attributes of economic and military power wielded by the leading protagonists of Cold War 2.0 and their principal allies, it now remains to address where the dynamics of the current cold war will play out. In other words, where will the currency of economic and military power, so carefully assembled by the democracies and the autocracies, be spent? The following discussion has to begin in Ukraine, where the unprovoked, unjustified invasion by Russia in February 2022 proved (if proof was even required) that the world is indeed in the midst of Cold War 2.0.

The second focal point is Taiwan, which, if Cold War 2.0 goes fully hot on and around the island, would also be a major—*the* major—geopolitical event in the 21st century, overshadowing even the current Russo-Ukrainian War, given that the United States (and possibly other democracies) would send military forces into this war, not just supply weapons, as is the case in Ukraine. Ukraine and Taiwan are big, meaty strategic subjects to digest, and take up the bulk of this chapter. It would be a major deficiency, though, if some light wasn't also brought to bear on the relations of the democracies and the autocracies with the Global South, which was an important theater of hot and cold operations in Cold War 1, and invariably will be so again, but with a renewed set of dynamics and drivers revolving in large measure around technology and innovation.

THE HOT WAR IN UKRAINE

On February 24, 2022, Russia launched a full-scale military invasion of Ukraine, with Russian army groups crossing the Russian-Ukrainian border in the north, northeast, east, southeast, and south of Ukraine. The one from the north was launched from Belarus, as Kyiv, the capital of Ukraine, is only 150 kilometers from the Belarusian border. Russia's war aim was to capture and decapitate Ukraine's government, and to bring its territories and population into Russia—essentially, to wipe Ukraine off the map as an independent country. The 2022 invasion was a continuation of Russia's partial invasion of Ukraine in 2014, when Moscow both (a) implanted irregular/Russian troops and mercenaries into the Donbas region of Ukraine to foment a movement there to join Russia, and (b) illegally annexed the Crimean peninsula through armed force. (Crimea being a land mass of 27,000 square kilometers, about the size of the state of Massachusetts.)

In 1954 (during Cold War 1) the supreme Soviet government in Moscow transferred Crimea Oblast (province) from the Russian Soviet Republic to the Ukrainian Soviet Republic. The transfer made sense to Moscow as the Crimean peninsula needed to better connect with the contiguous mainland (which was under the administration of the Ukrainian Soviet Republic) for purposes of irrigation, transport connections, and the like. In 1991, when the Soviet Union collapsed, there were referendums in each oblast of Ukraine (including Crimea and the two in the Donbas, namely Luhansk and Donetsk). In each oblast a majority of the people voting supported Ukraine and their oblast, leaving the Soviet Union and Russia, and becoming part of an independent Ukraine. In 1994, Ukraine, Russia, the United States, and the United Kingdom signed the

Budapest Memorandum, whereby Ukraine agreed to give up to Russia the nuclear weapons on Ukrainian territory in exchange for Russia agreeing to recognize and respect the 1991 borders of Ukraine.

When it started its hot war against Ukraine in 2014, Russian president Putin breached Russia's obligations under the Budapest Memorandum (as well the Charter of the United Nations), thereby starting a new hot war against Ukraine and a cold war against a host of other democracies, especially the US, the UK, and the other members of NATO. It was not, though, simply the resumption of Cold War 1, because there are a number of new factors today that didn't exist between 1945 and 1989. The principal difference between then and now is that Russia is not the leader of the autocracies, China is.

That is why, two weeks before Russia's invasion of Ukraine in 2022, Putin flew to Beijing to discuss with Xi Jinping Putin's plan to invade and assimilate Ukraine. Xi was supportive for two major reasons. First, Putin and Xi anticipated (wrongly, as it turned out) that the West's reaction to the invasion would be a shambles, largely because they thought the United States and Europe would disagree on how to respond to the invasion. Xi and Putin also believed that there would be massive divisions even within Europe—for example, the former East Bloc countries, led by Poland, would want to help Ukraine as much as possible, while Germany, which at the time was heavily dependent on Russian gas for its energy needs, would be reluctant to assist Ukraine at the risk of upsetting the Russians. Overall, then, Xi and Putin figured invading Ukraine would weaken the West, which was an important objective for both of them.

Xi's second reason for supporting Putin is that Xi has something akin to his own Ukraine, namely China's stated intention to "repatriate" Taiwan into China. Therefore, Xi believed that Putin's quick capture and annexation of the whole of Ukraine would be a good precedent militarily and diplomatically for China's takeover of Taiwan. Driven by these types of considerations, on February 4, 2022, a mere two weeks before Russia's full-scale invasion of Ukraine, Xi and Putin stood side by side in Beijing and issued an eye-popping 5,364-word statement, signed by both countries, in which they pledged to work together in a host of areas, including joint military exercises. The statement concluded that, "The friendship of Russia and China knew no limits."

The signing of this document in Beijing by Xi and Putin confirms that in Cold War 2 China is the senior autocracy and Russia is the junior partner. This is a complete flip from Cold War 1. In 1950, before North Korean autocrat Kim Il-Sung invaded South Korea, and later before Chinese autocrat Mao Zedong sent 700,000 Chinese troops to save President Kim's untenable position, both autocrats got permission from the autocrat Stalin in Moscow. Equally, Russia did not ask China's permission in 1956 before sending Russian tanks into Budapest to put down the Hungarian independence uprising, nor did Russia seek China's permission in 1968 when it sent tanks into Czechoslovakia to snuff out the Prague Spring. The world's two leading autocratic powers—Russia and China—have switched places, and this will have important ramifications for Cold War 2.0 (and for Russia's execution of hot wars like those in Ukraine).

Still, one critical factor experiencing continuity between the two cold wars is the central role played by technology in the creation and deployment of national military and economic power. Although there is still no end in sight for the war in Ukraine, some conclusions can be made about the immense importance of state-of-the-art high-tech weaponry, particularly to the Ukrainians, and hence the nomenclature for the current rivalry as Cold War 2.0 is entirely appropriate. A few examples of the role of the new technology on the Ukrainian battlefield include the following.

In the early days of the full-scale war, hundreds of Russian armored vehicles raced toward Kyiv, the Ukrainian capital. Observers were reminded of the Nazi autocrat Hitler's *Blitzkrieg* ("Lightning War") in World War II, when highly mobile tank units crashed into northern France and subdued a huge French army (and a sizeable British expeditionary force) in a matter of weeks, to the immense shock of the democracies. In February 2022 no Western military analyst or think tank gave the Ukrainian government any chance of survival. The United States apparently offered to airlift Ukrainian President Volodymyr Zelenskyy out of Kyiv and to a safe exile somewhere in a democracy. Zelenskyy, in a phrase that will rank among the great war pronouncements of history, reportedly replied: "The fight is here; I need ammunition, not a ride."

In those first few days and weeks of the war, the weapons that saved Ukraine were high-tech, portable, precision-guided anti-tank missiles, primarily the American Stinger and Javelin and the British NLAW. Wielded by incredibly brave Ukrainian soldiers, these missiles could be fired from a range of about 2,500 meters, but because of their software-enabled guidance system they were deadly accurate. The previous generation of anti-tank missiles were not smart, and hence they had to be fired from much closer range. With the new computer technology in the current anti-tank missiles, a soldier merely had to fire them sufficiently in the direction of the target. After launch they would home in on the tank in the course of their flight.

The Javelin, for example, is made jointly by Raytheon (now RTX) and Lockheed Martin, the two leading US defense contractors. Due to intense computer miniaturization over the past few decades (courtesy of high-performance semiconductor chips), the entire unit weighs only fifty pounds, allowing it to be carried and handled by a single soldier. They are not cheap, costing around $80,000 apiece, which means that training soldiers on them has required the development of a simulator, which generates images of real terrain and a very authentic experience. The high-tech training simulator (using very advanced software and computer graphics) saves bundles of money, which allows more Javelin units to be purchased, in this case by the Ukrainian army. It is estimated that in the first three weeks of the war, Ukrainian soldiers were able to destroy 550 Russian tanks and armored personnel carriers with these missiles, allowing the Ukrainians to win the Battle of Kyiv. By the end of March 2022 the remaining Russian columns in northern Ukraine retreated from the battlefield. These fairly inexpensive but incredibly powerful computer-guided shoulder-launched weapons saved the government of Ukraine from an early and ignominious defeat. High-tech weapons were decisive in the first phase of the war.

A second critical high-tech weapon in the war has been the HIMARS (High Mobility Artillery Rocket System), an "artillery rocket" system made by Lockheed Martin that launches fairly large precision-guided missiles at land-based targets. The HIMARS is the size of a medium-sized shipping container, and is pulled around by a truck cab. It is a "shoot and scoot" weapon. It launches one or more rockets, but then the operator quickly drives away so the enemy doesn't detect their location and counter with their own missiles. What HIMARS shares with the Javelin is that it is stuffed full of SCs. These allow the HIMARS rocket to be self-guided, but at a much longer range than the shoulder-launched anti-tank missiles. A HIMARS-launched missile can fly up to fifty miles and precisely hit a target, like an ammunition depot, an enemy command headquarters, or an army barracks. The HIMARS were critical in "softening up" the Russian defensive line in eastern Ukraine when, in September–October 2022 the Ukrainian army launched a successful counteroffensive and retook some 30 percent of the territory gained by the Russians at the beginning of the war, including the regional capital Kharkiv. Again, the Battle of Kharkiv could not have been won by the Ukrainians without high-tech precision weapons.

In the fall/winter of 2022–2023, when military ground operations decreased, Russia began a major campaign of firing missiles and drones into Ukraine to take out electrical and other utilities, but also to hit civilian apartments and community buildings (like museums) in order to try to break the spirit of Ukrainians—notwithstanding that firing weapons at nonmilitary targets constitutes a war crime. To defend against these illegal attacks, the Ukrainians deployed the Patriot (Phased Array Tracking Radar to Intercept on Target) air defense system (ADS), which is made by Raytheon (with Lockhead Martin making some advanced missiles for it). The Patriot is a very sophisticated multicomponent system that costs in the range of $1.1 billion for a typical configuration, consisting of $400 million for the general system and typically $700 million for the initial inventory of interception missiles. A radar unit detects and tracks incoming threats, and then sophisticated computers, and very complicated software, provide targeting direction for the launch of the intercept missiles.[1] While expensive, the user tends to get what they pay for, in that the Patriot has an about 95 percent success rate. In Ukraine they have even shot down Russian Kinzhal hypersonic missiles, which Putin had claimed previously was impervious to ADS intercept missiles.[2] The Patriot uses a lot of artificial intelligence capability, especially when it is in "automatic" mode.

A number of other high-tech weapons and devices have also proven to be very important in the Ukraine war. The Ukrainian army relies heavily on drones for reconnaissance, especially for targeting their own (non-smart) artillery fire. Traditional artillery, like 155 MM howitzer cannons, continue to play an important role in the war, repulsing Russian forces in the Battle of Kyiv. Some drones have also been rigged so they can drop a small bomb. Ukrainian troops are exhibiting superior innovation skills in crafting custom technology solutions that fit the needs of the battlefield. Ukraine's prewar strength in civilian information technology capacity is playing an important role during the war. Chapter 1, in discussing the sources of military and economic power, highlighted the increasing fusion of the civilian and the military realms when it comes to technology. Ukraine's use of drones in its war with Russia is a good example of this trend.

Simultaneously with military campaigns in the physical battle space in Ukraine, this war has seen a massive information war extending from the smartphones used by the troops on the front lines to various social media platforms (including the many Russian "military bloggers" on the Telegram channel), to television screens in apartments all around the world, but especially in Russia. Putin's autocratic propaganda purveyors spend enormous effort using television, social media, and even low-tech outdoor advertising to convince the Russian public of a range of mistruths justifying his brazen military campaign in Ukraine. At the beginning of the war, Putin labeled his full-scale invasion merely a "special military operation," so as not to frighten middle-class Russians. This is critical for Putin, because as an autocrat his core social compact with Russian citizens is that he will ensure a steadily improving lifestyle for them, and in return they will not concern themselves with Putin's personal corruption nor the general corruption of the government and military, and they will allow him to run domestic politics and Russian foreign and military policy as he sees fit. Therefore, Putin must continue to devise a positive narrative about the war, even if it doesn't reflect reality.

Putin's primary technology for propagating his domestic disinformation is television, which is very much an information channel that dates from Cold War 1. Nevertheless, it is a very effective communication medium for about 80 percent of Russians, especially seniors, who obtain most of their awareness of current affairs from evening TV news, which of course is crafted entirely by the Kremlin's propaganda department. Quite literally, every day around 3:00 P.M. the newsroom at *Russia Today* and other government-controlled news outlets get a notice from the Kremlin as to what Putin wants on the evening news and how it must be presented. The supine media outlets dutifully package the request into stories to be broadcast a few hours later. To be clear, a number of governments in the democracies fund publicly owned media properties, like the BBC in the United Kingdom, the CBC in Canada, NPR in the United States, and ABC in Australia, but in each of these (and similar) cases in the democracies there is a firm wall separating the government of the day from exercising any editorial control or influence over the reporters and other content creators at these media outlets, which is how they maintain editorial independence.

The role of television in an autocracy should not be underestimated. In Russia, almost two years into the Ukraine war, 80 percent of the population believes that Putin is working hard to de-Nazify Ukraine. Putin has also convinced a majority of Russians that NATO started the war in Ukraine. These results are not surprising—what else can be expected when a person's only information source is the evening news doled out by the Kremlin's disinformation department. The experience of other autocracies corresponds with this state of affairs in Russia. In North Korea, as a result of unrelenting disinformation by the autocratic regime in Pyongyang, seventy-four years after the brazen invasion of South Korea by the armies of North Korea under the leadership of the North's dictator Kim Il-Sung, the vast majority of North Koreans still believe that it was South Korea that attacked North Korea, and that North Korea was only fighting the three-year-long war in self-defense. (Strictly speaking, this war is still ongoing as a peace deal was never signed between North and South Korea.)

Putin is also well equipped to spread propaganda on more digitally oriented platforms. Since the start of the Internet revolution, Russia has invested in, and fostered, large troll-farm operations located within Russia that specialize in distributing massive amounts of disinformation to the Internet and social media users around the world, with specific messages and memes targeted at Western audiences, other messages at people living in the Global South, others in Asia, and so on. For instance, the Mueller report gives a good sense of how these Russian troll farms operate, and what they managed to achieve in respect of the 2016 presidential election in the United States. Therefore, when Putin started the war in Ukraine in 2014 it was simple to have these Internet troll businesses start propagating disinformation about the war, which has simply continued to the present day.

Using these information distribution channels, Putin has scored some big successes, such as when pollsters report that in countries like China, India, and South Africa a majority of the respective populations believe that it was actually Ukraine, propped up by NATO, that started the Russo-Ukrainian conflict. Equally, Putin has been very effective at spreading the lie that grain prices have increased worldwide because of Ukraine raising prices unilaterally, the reality being that grain prices rose because Russia's invasion of Ukraine cut off shipments from Ukraine (thereby tightening supply) as Russian naval vessels blocked the use of Ukraine's grain ports on its coast along the Black Sea.

At the same time, though, what is also fascinating about the new social media and related communications technologies and data dissemination techniques is how quickly they can be spun up from a standing start. For his part, President Zelenskyy did not have preexisting Internet troll farms to take advantage of, but he was equally keen to launch a major information campaign on social media. Indeed, given Ukraine's heavy, some would argue even existential, reliance on assistance (both military and financial) from the democracies, it was necessary for Zelenskyy to make a deep connection with tens of millions of citizens in the donor countries, and to keep them engaged, so that their politicians would see in their public opinion polls that support for Ukraine ran high. For the most part, President Zelenskyy has achieved this objective with impressive success.

Even though the Russo-Ukrainian War has not yet concluded, after one and a half years of fighting the huge Russian army, the excruciating toll on Ukraine is clear. Ukraine's economy is devastated. Roughly 14 million refugees (largely women and children) have fled the country's worst war zones, of which 6 million have left Ukraine altogether. Hundreds of thousands of Ukrainian children have been abducted by the Russian occupiers of eastern Ukraine. Hundreds of schools, hospitals, museums, and other places of Ukrainian culture have been specifically targeted by Russian missiles. Thousands of war crimes are being documented, including the senseless murder of noncombatant civilians in Ukrainian towns occupied by Russian troops. The vast horrors of modern warfare have been severely inflicted on Ukraine and its people by the invading Russians. Supported by military equipment, and financial and humanitarian assistance from the democracies, the Ukrainians have been able to fight back valiantly against the Russians, but at great cost—estimates of the number of dead and wounded Ukrainian soldiers hover in the range of 130,000. All of this murder and mayhem came in order to satisfy the whims of a Russian autocrat. Such is the awful, bloodstained calculus of Cold War 2.0, because autocrats feel threatened by the mere existence of democracies.

It is not surprising, therefore, that the Ukrainian leadership is united behind the position that they will only negotiate a peace deal once all Russian troops have left Ukraine as its borders were constituted before Putin's 2014 infiltration of the Donbas and annexation of Crimea (referred to as "1991 Ukraine"). Some influential commentators, including Henry Kissinger, have stated that it would be worth it for Ukraine to give up this territory—which, including the additional territory captured by the Russians in the 2022 invasion, comprises about 20 percent of 1991 Ukraine—in return for firm security guarantees from key democracies or even NATO membership. One suggestion: any politician in a democracy making a similar proposal should be prepared to voluntarily give up 20 percent of their own country to one or more neighbors before they are allowed to recommend that President Zelenskyy do the same for Ukraine. Does anyone think India's prime minister Modi would give up 20 percent of India (or even 20 percent of just the northwest province of Kashmir, or even the Ladakh portion of it) to get a lasting peace deal with China for the border dispute between the two Asian giants? And if that's not reasonable for India, why is it reasonable for Ukraine?

Even if the Russo-Ukrainian War has not ended, there are nevertheless a few important lessons to be drawn from it for Cold War 2.0. Digital and computer-based technologies, deployed in weapons systems but also in a myriad other ways, have come to play a significant role in this conflict. Moreover, the weapons systems resulting from innovation in the democracies are superior in their functionality and performance to those emanating from autocracies. Economic sanctions levied by the democracies on Russia as a result of the war have crimped Russia's war-fighting effort, but additional measures must be taken on sanctions to make them more compelling. Importantly, notwithstanding a pledge by China's paramount leader that China's friendship with Russia knows no limits, in practice the Chinese have circumscribed their assistance to Russia. For instance, the Chinese have not been willing to supply the Russians with weapons, presumably because they fear their economy being subject to broad-based sanctions by the democracies. These lessons will presumably be helpful to the democracies as Xi contemplates his own plans and timetable for attempting to bring Taiwan back into the Chinese fold.

THE NEAR WAR IN TAIWAN

To the extent Cold War 2.0 has another major current flashpoint, it is the island of Taiwan. China, the world's second-largest country by landmass (9.33 million square kilometers) and one of the two largest by population (with 1.4 billion people), considers Taiwan an indivisible part of China. For its part, Taiwan, 139th on the list of countries by size (Taiwan is

36,197 square kilometers, a bit bigger than the size of the Netherlands), with a population of 23.5 million, does not see itself as a part of China, and the vast majority of Taiwanese citizens do not wish to become citizens of China.

Taiwan, officially known as the Republic of China, has a fascinating history.[3] The island was first populated by aboriginals from islands in the South Pacific, not Han Chinese. The Dutch established a colony in the 1600s, when Han Chinese immigration picked up pace as well. Later in that eventful century Zheng Jing, a supporter of the Ming dynasty, escaped to the island when the Qing dynasty was establishing itself on the mainland under the influence of the Manchu. (Zheng couldn't abide by many of the practices of the Manchu.) Interestingly, the island was used as a sanctuary from social developments on the mainland—sound familiar? Two hundred years later Taiwan was under the control of the Qing dynasty. The Qing lost a disastrous war with the Japanese in 1885. Indicative of how little the mainland Chinese valued Taiwan, the Qing emperor ceded Taiwan to the Japanese as part of the peace treaty, though the local residents of the island refused to be ruled by the Japanese and they declared independence. The resulting six-month war of independence against the Japanese was bloody, but ultimately in vain due to Japan's superior army.[4] Again, while history doesn't repeat itself precisely, it sure does rhyme from time to time. The Japanese eventually crushed the resistance and ended up governing and colonizing the island for the next forty years.

Taiwan today is one of the most contested regions in the world because in 1949, when Mao's Communist forces completed taking over all of mainland China, Chiang Kai-shek and 2 million of his supporters (the Kuomintang, or KMT) fled to Taiwan. Chiang had ruled mainland China as an autocrat between 1928 and 1949, and was instrumental in dislodging the Japanese at the end of World War II, a fight in which he was joined by the Chinese Communist Party (CCP), led by Mao Zedong. After losing the civil war to Mao and fleeing to Taiwan in 1949, Chiang's intention was to regroup his forces on the island, and then eventually launch an attack against the communists and regain power in Beijing.

That never happened, but neither was the CCP successful taking over Taiwan. In 1949 the CCP landed three divisions on the Kinmen island group, which was part of Taiwan but very close to the mainland—only ten kilometers from the mainland's coastline. (The Chinese city of Xiamen can be seen clearly from Kinmen.) Taking Kinmen was seen by the CCP as a first step to taking the bigger island of Taiwan. This attack on Kinmen was repelled by the KMT forces. In 1950, though, the CCP and the PLA were successful in taking the large island of Hainan after an amphibious assault of some 100,000 troops. In late 1954 the CCP was also successful in capturing the Yijiangshan Islands from the Taiwanese. The Taiwanese also abandoned the Dachen Islands a little later. After these actions, which are collectively called the First Taiwan Strait Crisis, Taiwan consists of the main island of Taiwan and the smaller islands of Kinmen, Penghu, and Matsu.

The First Taiwan Strait Crisis was brought to an end when the United States sent the Seventh Fleet, including an aircraft carrier, into the Taiwan Strait to protect Taiwan, and to make sure the KMT didn't attack mainland China either. It must be remembered that between 1950 and 1953 the South Korean and US militaries (with a number of US allies under the banner of the United Nations) fought a bloody war to keep South Korea out of the hands of the North Korean communists, who were supported by about 700,000 Chinese communist soldiers fighting on behalf of North Korea. This US-led force eventually saved South Korea, just as the US navy saved Taiwan a few years later. And of course, all this conflict took place during a period where the US did not recognize the legitimacy of the CCP as the government of China.

In 1955 Taiwan and the United States signed a mutual defense treaty, which committed the US to defending the island if it were attacked by the CCP. Importantly, this treaty did not apply to the defense of the smaller islands closer to China, such as Kinmen and Matsu. This treaty also required the US to agree to any attack on the mainland by the KMT. In effect, the treaty froze the new status quo, which essentially secured Taiwan from CCP attack while restraining the KMT from doing anything rash to mainland China. By the mid-1950s the Eisenhower administration had concluded that there was no way the KMT could make a meaningful attempt at retaking mainland China.

At the height of the First Taiwan Strait Crisis, the US secretary of state publicly announced the US was considering using nuclear weapons against the PLA, though NATO allies, including Winston Churchill argued firmly against such action. Presumably this nuclear brinksmanship had some impact on Mao's decision to de-escalate from the crisis, as China did not yet have nuclear weapons at that time. Also playing a role was Moscow's unwillingness to agree to retaliate against the US with Russian nuclear missiles were the US to use nuclear weapons against China. This decision is the final impetus Mao needed to start developing his own nuclear weapons. In 1964 China successfully detonated its first atomic bomb, and three years later its first hydrogen bomb. The dynamics are reversed today. South Korea, Japan, the Philippines, and Australia each are under an American "nuclear weapons umbrella." Were the US to signal at some point that it was withdrawing this nuclear weapons guarantee, very likely one or more of these four countries would pursue its own nuclear weapons program. History's rhyming sometimes reverberates in a somewhat different key, but the core rhythm is the same.

Fighting between the PLA and the Taiwanese army broke out again in August 1958 when the PLA started firing artillery shells into Kinmen and Matsu islands. This is referred to as the Second Taiwan Strait Crisis. There were also serious aerial dogfights between the two air forces. The US-supplied AIM-9 Sidewinder air-to-air missiles proved superior, with the result that thirty-one PLA planes were blown out of the sky by these new weapons (which used heat-seeking technology to lock onto their target), while the Taiwanese lost only two planes. The US army also sent long-range M115 howitzers to Kinmen Island to give the Taiwanese the edge in their artillery duel. In October 1958 the PLA declared a unilateral ceasefire, largely because they had run out of ammunition for their artillery, though right up to 1979 the PLA and the Taiwanese exchanged artillery fire, usually on alternating days. (In June 1960, however, when President

Eisenhower visited Taiwan, the PLA lobbed over 100,000 artillery shells into Kinmen, killing thirteen and wounding seventy-four.) When Eisenhower departed Taiwan, the Taiwanese fired thousands of shells into mainland China.

There was yet a Third Taiwan Strait Crisis when, in May 1995 the US issued a visa to Taiwanese presidential candidate Lee Teng-hui to visit his alma mater, Cornell University in upstate New York. Beijing was very angry over this visit and during the summer of 1995 it conducted missile firings and naval procedures, including amphibious landing exercises, in the vicinity of Taiwan. Moreover, just days before Taiwan's presidential election in March 1996, Beijing decided to show the Taiwanese that voting for Mr. Lee would mean very difficult relations with China, possibly including military conflict. The PLA again conducted missile firings around Taiwan, this time sufficiently close to Taiwanese ports to disrupt merchant container shipping. The US responded by moving two aircraft carrier groups into the vicinity of Taiwan (one passing through the Taiwan Strait) in order to prove America's determination to defend Taiwan; the naval armada amounted to the largest show of American military strength in Asia since the Vietnam War. Ironically the Chinese missile firings and other flexing of military muscle backfired, given that the PLA intimidation actually increased Mr. Lee's support by about 5 percent and helped him win the election. Autocrats regularly shoot themselves in the foot when they roll out their stocks of weapons to scare the democracies. In this case the show of armed force by China also further strengthened the military alliance between the US and Japan, the latter country increasingly realizing that its own defense hinged on the successful defense of Taiwan.

Circumstances changed significantly, though, after Mao's death in 1976. In the late 1970s and early 1980s mainland China came out of its diplomatic hibernation, and reached out to the world, looking for diplomatic recognition and trading relationships. China, however, presented potential economic partners with an important condition: any country that wanted commercial relations with China had to agree with China's "One China Policy," whereby it recognized mainland, communist China as the only

China, and that country had to break off diplomatic relations with Taiwan. Like many countries desirous of doing business with China, in 1980 the US terminated its mutual defense treaty with Taiwan (under which it had been obligated to defend Taiwan), and instead adopted the Taiwan Relations Act (TRA). Under the TRA, the US is entitled to sell military equipment to Taiwan, but, importantly, under the TRA the US does not pledge to defend Taiwan, but it doesn't say that it cannot defend Taiwan either. It leaves this critical question unanswered, and therefore ambiguous.

The Chiang regime focused on developing Taiwan's economy. In the 1970s, the military government instituted a massive infrastructure-building program. This continued after Chiang's death in 1975, which also precipitated a loosening of political control, and a slow shift to democracy. Taiwan instituted a modernization program, building universities and new business parks. By the 1980s Taiwan had a prosperous middle class, and a middle-income economy. In a stroke of genius, the president of the day, Sun Yun-suan, managed to lure Morris Chang to Taiwan from his job in Silicon Valley, where he was president of General Instrument Corporation. Shortly after arriving in Taiwan, Chang started a new SC company, called Taiwan Semiconductor Manufacturing Company (TSMC). Based in the business park of Hsinchu, TSMC had modest beginnings, starting with only one facility.

TSMC's growth in the 1980s and 1990s (eventually building other fabs in Taichung, Tainan, and Kaohsiung) mirrored Taiwan's development. While not a full member of the OECD (China won't allow that under its One China Policy), Taiwan does participate on three OECD committees. Although Taiwan has diplomatic relations with only fourteen countries, it has informal trade offices in many more. Ranked by income per capita, Taiwan's is $33,907, slightly behind Japan ($35,385) and somewhat ahead of South Korea ($33,393). In July 1987, martial law was terminated. Importantly, in 1996 Taiwan had its first presidential elections, and in May 2000 it experienced its first peaceful transfer of power by political parties, when previous President Lee Teng-hui (of the KMT) handed the gavel of power to incoming President Chen Shui-bian (of the Democratic Progressive party, the DPP). Since that election, Taiwan has had five further peaceful elections, and two additional peaceful transfers of power. Democracy has become firmly entrenched in Taiwan.

Since Mao's death, China has not acted militarily to snuff out completely the reality of Taiwan, and Beijing has not indicated any specific timeline by which it expected Taiwan to be integrated back into China. Beijing has said, however, it would take military action if Taipei declared independence, and many actions could constitute such action, including another country selling arms to Taiwan (though, interestingly, the US sells huge quantities of weapons to Taiwan) or another country opening an embassy in Taipei (trade and cultural exchange offices are okay, etc.). There is a lot of nuance in the diplomatic language around the One China Policy as well. Beijing says most countries "oppose" Taiwan's claim to independence. Many countries, though, don't actually say they "oppose" it, they simply say they "don't support it." In other words, these countries don't take a view of the matter, so long as whatever transpires does so peacefully. China also views a referendum on the question within Taiwan as a declaration of independence, regardless of the outcome of such a vote. Again, it must be remembered that autocratic regimes don't believe in deciding anything through voting.

For the past several decades China's overall strategy toward Taiwan was premised on the expectation that eventually a mass movement of Taiwanese would form that would demand integration back into China, and that China could wait out the time required for this endgame to unfold peacefully. In turn, the US found the core ambiguous compromise between Taiwan and China acceptable (i.e., China would not invade Taiwan so long as Taiwan did not declare independence). Therefore, Washington never officially articulated whether it would protect Taiwan if China invaded it, all with a view to discouraging Taiwan from declaring independence. Taiwan would never be entirely certain that the US would come to its defense, so the tortured logic goes, if China invaded in response to a Taiwanese declaration of independence. Finally, for its part the ambiguous arrangement worked well enough for Taiwan as it could go on doing its own thing in the knowledge that the status quo allowed it to effectively do as it pleased on the world stage so long as it didn't declare independence. Taiwan's current president, Tsai Ing-wen, doesn't accept that Taiwan is part of China; moreover, she likely believes Taiwan is already "independent," which in many ways it already is, but she is careful not to articulate this in public.

This unorthodox and highly unusual arrangement could have carried on indefinitely, except that over the past few years a number of factors have been threatening its viability. First, China's waiting game (hoping that a government supporting integration would eventually come to power in Taipei) is not working. Over the last twenty years support in Taiwan for integration with China has been falling steadily. In a major tracking poll in June 2022 only 6.5 percent of Taiwanese supported integration with China, either immediately (1.3 percent) or eventually (5.2 percent).[5] This is bad news for Beijing, and is causing Xi to lose patience. Apparently he has told the senior officers of China's People Liberation Army (PLA) to prepare to take the island by force by 2027. In response, President Biden has on three separate occasions broken the "ambiguity protocol" by stating, in clear terms, that if China attacked Taiwan, the US would come to the defense of Taiwan. (Albeit after each such utterance, White House staff walked the statement back, "clarifying" that US official policy is still not to guarantee military support of Taiwan.)

Given that Xi presumably does not have unlimited patience, it is worth considering the technological dimensions of the various scenarios for how China's attempt to take over Taiwan might unfold. The most direct action would be an invasion by a large Chinese naval force with hundreds of amphibious craft carrying thousands of soldiers—think the D-Day landings in Normandy on June 6, 1944. It is likely that such an operation would be preceded by a vast naval and aerial bombardment, or a massive missile strike on Taiwan's defenses to "soften up the island" before the Chinese troops come in on their landing craft. (Such a missile attack scenario is depicted in the introduction.) Or, would the first wave of attacks be carried out by Chinese air forces almost exclusively, including by thousands of drones vying to establish air superiority?

In either of these direct, highly kinetic scenarios, the quantity and quality of Taiwan's air and missile defense systems will be key. The AI-enabled command and control systems used by Taiwan, either alone or along with the US (and other potential allies among the democracies), will be critical, perhaps even determinative of the outcome. The Strait of Taiwan is roughly 100 miles (160 kilometers) across, which means the average current cruise missile (flying at about 500 mph, or 800 km/h) will take about twelve minutes to cross the water and slam into a target on the island. The missile engagement zone, as far as Taiwan is concerned, is therefore about forty to sixty miles off shore Taiwan's west coast, which means Taiwan has only about six minutes to detect the launches of missiles from China's east coast, or only a couple of minutes for missiles launched from China's ships at sea or aircraft even closer to the island. Then they must decide on the specific countermeasures required for these Chinese missiles, and then launch intercept missiles quickly enough to give them sufficient time to hit the incoming missiles well over water. Human intelligence will simply be inadequate—and too slow—to take in all the streams of sensor and targeting information, decide what to do, and then respond quickly enough to achieve the goal of intercepting Chinese missiles at some distance away from the island. Incredibly reliable and high-performance AI and extremely powerful SC technology will be required, and at massive scale, likely bolstered by quantum computers if they are sufficiently advanced at that point. And then the process has to be repeated when the second, third, and subsequent waves of Chinese missiles are launched against the island. Not a job for the faint of heart—or for second-class armaments.

A second strategy that China might employ for taking Taiwan by force involves a more incremental use of military power. China would impose a blockade of the island, with Chinese naval vessels (including submarines) and aircraft enforcing a perimeter around Taiwan that no foreign or Taiwanese shipping or cargo aircraft would be allowed to cross (think the Berlin Blockade, but with a much more powerful military laying in the siege). The Chinese could also cut fiber-optic cables that connect Taiwan to the outside world. China might also take out those satellites detected to be assisting Taiwanese and American (and allied) troops. The Chinese goal would be to encircle Taiwan in a physical and digital noose, and then squeeze the island into submission. Presumably Taiwan (with the assistance of its allies) would respond by trying to break the embargo, by shooting down the offending aircraft, and sinking or disabling the relevant Chinese ships. This scenario would take longer to unfold, which might work in Taiwan's favor, as it would give the US (and potentially other allies, especially the Japanese and South Koreans) longer time to muster military support for Taiwan.

Both of these war scenarios have political and military thought leaders on Taiwan debating heavily what type of modern weaponry is best suited for the defense of the island. To date, emphasis has been placed on advanced fighter aircraft, such as the 4th generation F-16, and the 5th generation F-35. There is a strong argument, however, that rather than all the defense budget going for these very high-cost elite armaments, Taipei should buy more of the "hedgehog weapons" that are very robust when used in tight defensive situations in conjunction with excellent command and control systems, and especially those that use the latest AI software for operating or optimizing them, as well as AI systems for overall battle management.

The Taiwan standoff raises a further important issue related to TSMC, which is headquartered in Taiwan, and where most of its production facilities are still located, notwithstanding a number of TSMC plants in the US, China, and Europe. Put simply, TSMC is an indispensable player in the global semiconductor market. It would be devastating for the economies of the democracies if in any invasion of Taiwan the fabs operated by TSMC on the island were damaged or harmed. Even worse would be if in the course of the Battle of the Taiwan Strait hundreds of senior scientists and technologists (70,000 in total) that TSMC employs in Taiwan were injured, let alone killed in the hostilities. The market for high-end SCs can get incredibly tight—witness the massive SC shortages in the entire global economy in 2020 and 2021, especially in industries like the auto sector. It would be devastating not only for TSMC, but indeed the entire global economy, if China damaged, let alone completely destroyed, TSMC's SC plants—or its staff—in Taiwan. A technological winter would descend on the global economy that would make the SC shortages in 2021–2022 look like a walk in the park. Again, this concern might prompt China to use exclusively AI-based guided weapons in Taiwan, including only AI-enabled high-precision artillery shells and drones against Taiwanese targets.

There are a number of lessons to be drawn from the foregoing discussion about Taiwan. In the long run, the skill with which China and the democracies, respectively, integrate and deploy AI into their militaries will be determinative of success in any military conflagration over the island nation. At the same time, in an attempt to prevent such a hot war, during Cold War 2.0 it is imperative that the US make it clear that it will participate in the defense of Taiwan. Over time, it would be extremely helpful if the other principal democracies in the region, especially Japan, but eventually South Korea, the Philippines, and Australia, also pledged their commitment to come to Taiwan's defense in the event of a Chinese attack. Finally, at a minimum, the key European powers, namely the United Kingdom, Germany, and France, should clearly signal to Beijing that their economic relationship with China would decline precipitously—indeed, come to a halt—if China were to move against Taiwan. If these nine democracies cannot come together into a formal global "GATO," or at least an Asian-oriented "PATO," then a "built-for-Cold War 2.0 coalition" of these most powerful democracies needs to remind China—and themselves—in a more ad hoc manner that when it comes to Cold War 2.0, "none of us is as strong as all of us."

BUYOUT PEACE PLANS FOR TAIWAN

There may be another way to deal with the menace that China poses for Taiwan. Many on the island see their high-tech companies, and especially the jewel-in-the-crown TSMC and its 70,000 employees, as a "shield" against any Chinese invasion. "Surely," the reasoning goes, "China won't attack Taiwan militarily because it would not want to do any damage to

TSMC facilities or harm any of its staff." This argument seems very weak, particularly if China's missiles, drones, and artillery are made "smart" through AI, such that they only do damage to military targets. Indeed, the counterargument seems stronger, namely that the very presence of TSMC on Taiwan makes taking the island more attractive to China, because (1) with precision firing (missiles, drones, and smart artillery) the island can be taken without causing a lot of collateral damage, and (2) the day after securing control over the island China could embargo the shipment of high-performance SCs to the democracies, or at least they could extort enormous financial sums out of the democracies to keep the flow of SCs going to them. On the other hand, it is precisely the fact that 90 percent of the high-performance SCs in the world are made on Taiwan that will lead the US to fight fiercely to ensure that China does not take control of the island. In either scenario, however, the presence of TSMC fabs in Taiwan raises the stakes over Taiwan to a very dangerous level.

Therefore, what would happen if the democracies collectively offered asylum, right now, to millions of Taiwanese, and especially high-tech workers and their families? Entire fabs (of TSMC and other companies in Taiwan) and their staff could be relocated to the democracies. There is some recent precedent for this. In the decade before Hong Kong reverted to China (in 1997), about 1 million Hong Kong residents decamped to a number of other countries, including Canada, the US, Australia, and the United Kingdom, and another 200,000 residents of Hong Kong have left since China imposed its national security law in 2020. If the SC fabs are inexorably driving China to effect a violent military takeover of Taiwan, then remove the incentive for them to do so by denying them the crown jewels of the island before any war has broken out. The buildings would remain, but the people and critical equipment would be removed.

There is another precedent for this sort of responsible emigration from Taiwan. In 1895, when the Qing emperor ceded Taiwan to the Japanese, the new Japanese occupiers of the island gave every resident a two-year window in which to sell their land and move off the island; those that didn't exercise this option had to become Japanese citizens. The democracies would effectively facilitate such a process for the Taiwanese people. It is an attempt to find a peaceful solution to what otherwise appears to be a fairly bloody war to be fought, eventually, at China's insistence. The economic emigration plan is not perfect, but neither is the massive loss of life in a prospective Sino-Taiwan War, even if such a conflict were to unfold primarily with AI precision weapons.

The danger with the economic migration plan is that it precipitates a self-fulfilling prophecy. Once China gets wind of the plan to move the critical mass of some of Taiwan's leading companies off the island, China may well attack Taiwan to prevent the plan from moving forward. At the same time, though, the PLA has told Xi that the PLA will not be ready to carry out a successful campaign against the island until 2027 at the earliest. Therefore, this plan has a narrow window of opportunity, essentially the next few years. Time is of the essence.

There is yet one other scenario, related to the emigration option noted above, that might be intriguing for a solution to the democracy-autocracy impasse over Taiwan. The precedent for it is in the way the country of Czechoslovakia split up into the Czech Republic and Slovakia in 1993. Rather than a referendum, the leaders of the two communities within Czechoslovakia held a series of secret meetings, and simply decided to settle their various disagreements over social, political, and economic issues by agreeing to part company; one day the people of Czechoslovakia woke up and they now lived in either the Czech Republic or Slovakia.

In a somewhat similar vein, the leaders in Beijing and Taipei would secretly agree on the following. China and Taiwan would suddenly announce an agreement whereby Taiwan would revert to China on the fifth anniversary of the agreement, but upon the announcement of this deal China would offer to buy out the property and businesses of all citizens and companies that did not wish to stay in Taiwan after the reversion of the island to China. The price of homes, land, businesses, and other assets would be set as the greater of the price the day before the announcement or one year after the announcement. This would give Taiwanese one year to check out their prospects in other countries and to decide whether to leave.

During the second year after the announcement, the prices for the buyouts would be finalized, and by the end of that year Taiwanese citizens would have to give their decision whether they are leaving or staying. If they are leaving, China would have to deposit the purchase price for the buyouts in escrow (with a neutral country, like Switzerland) by the end of the second year. If China failed to do this, the deal would be off, and China would relinquish its claims to Taiwan in perpetuity—and Taiwan would be entitled to declare independence and enter into a mutual defense treaty with the United States (or join GATO or PATO if they were in effect then). If China did put the required funds into escrow by the end of the second year, the reversion of the island to China would go ahead on the fifth anniversary as originally contemplated, and the citizens who chose to leave would receive their payments from the escrow fund as they turned over their assets to the Chinese government. While not a perfect solution for the Taiwan challenge of Cold War 2.0, it would avoid a very bloody war.

CONVENTIONAL CONFLICTS WITH POTENTIAL NUCLEAR CHARACTERISTICS

The actual war in Ukraine, and the potential war over Taiwan, present a very delicate challenge because Russia, China, and the United States have nuclear weapons. The obvious question is how to avoid either of these conflicts escalating to the point where nuclear weapons are used. In the Ukraine war, the Biden administration did this by very early on signaling to Putin that neither American troops, nor soldiers from any other NATO country, would be deployed into the conflict. Put another way, while the US and NATO would supply Ukraine with weapons, intelligence, and other military, financial, and humanitarian assistance, US and NATO soldiers would not engage with Russian troops. This ban on direct participation would include US-NATO air forces; no US-NATO "no fly zones" would be implemented over Ukraine. Biden was widely criticized in some circles for this "signaling," with the criticism summed up in the question: "Why would we ever take any military option off the table? If we keep the Russians guessing, that might temper their behavior."

Biden did the right thing. Putin, and the rest of the world, needed to know what the rules of engagement were for the defense of Ukraine. In the result, Putin made threats to use his nuclear weapons, but the reasonableness of the US position made Russian nuclear saber-rattling appear only irresponsible (and downright desperate), especially to the Chinese, whose approval Putin (as China's junior partner) would have to secure for the release of nuclear weapons. In effect, Biden was able to construct and impose a model for the war in Ukraine where only conventional weapons were allowed to be used, thereby neutralizing the fact that of the two combatants, Ukraine and Russia, only the latter possessed nuclear weapons.

The Americans (and their allies in Japan, South Korea, the Philippines, and especially Taiwan) would need to arrive at some similar understanding with China regarding nuclear weapons if Cold War 2.0 turned hot over Taiwan. Given direct American involvement in such a war, constructing a "conventional weapons only" model will prove more difficult than in Ukraine, but not impossible. Washington could propose a deal along the following lines: neither China nor the US would use, nor threaten to use, nuclear weapons in the conflict so long as the other side adheres to the following "rules." No militaries of any of the combatants would target civilian assets of the opponent; if a combatant breached this rule the opposing force could target those military assets but would use reasonable efforts to avoid collateral civilian damage and civilian loss of life. Each combatant would agree to use only precision-guided firing, including smart artillery, and no traditional ("dumb") artillery would be allowed to be used.

There is a risk that signaling such a set of "terms of engagement" would have the effect of making war over Taiwan more likely, because nuclear deterrence is taken off the table by the Americans. This risk is very modest, however, because the Americans using nuclear weapons against China over a conflict involving only Taiwan is simply not a credible possibility. Therefore, it is worth giving up something not worth much for the much more important deterrence posture, namely: "We, the Americans, and several of our allies in the Pacific, will absolutely intervene directly militarily on behalf of Taiwan, albeit limiting our war-fighting to conventional weapons so long as China agrees to abide by the mutual restrictions in the model we propose." This has greater deterrent effect than the current "ambiguity" as to whether the US would intervene at all on behalf of Taiwan if China attacks the island. It is the current American ambiguity that increases the likelihood of a Chinese invasion of Taiwan because it encourages China to think there is still a scenario for attacking Taiwan where the Americans don't come to its defense. The Americans, by signaling this nuclear weapons posture on Taiwan, make it clear that China should disabuse itself of the thought that there is any scenario in Cold War 2.0 where the Americans leave the Taiwanese democracy to face the Chinese autocracy on its own.

A final word about the seeming absurdity of contemplating a scenario where China, Taiwan, and the US can work out rules of engagement for a war but seemingly cannot continue the same process to then work out a deal to avoid the war altogether. It seems perverse indeed. Unfortunately, Cold War 2.0 will be full of such ironic conundrums. Here, the risk of war looms over Taiwan because while the democracies argue, "Hey, let's just have a fair, free, and credible referendum by the people of Taiwan as to whether they want to be independent or a part of China, and everyone agrees to abide by the result," Chinese autocrats don't believe in citizens voting on anything. Rather, in their view, the CCP has determined that Taiwan is to return to be a part of China, and that's simply the end of the discussion. Period. Hence the high likelihood that this democracy-autocracy Cold War 2.0 impasse over the small island of Taiwan will be decided by force of arms.

THE FIGHT FOR THE HEARTS AND MINDS—AND POCKETBOOKS—OF THE GLOBAL SOUTH

In Cold War 1, Russia was active in the Global South (it was called the Third World in those days) making development loans for various projects like building dams to promote electricity generation, or roads or railroads. The democracies also extended this sort of financial, engineering, and construction assistance to countries in the Global South. The hope by both camps was to leverage this form of help into diplomatic support at the United Nations. In addition, the democracy or autocracy hoped that by providing such support their mining, agricultural, engineering, and construction companies would be better placed to exploit economic opportunities in the country receiving the aid.

This form of competition between the democracies and the autocracies still goes on during Cold War 2.0, but with two important differences. First, China is able to offer a great deal more of this assistance than Russia ever could simply because China's economy is fifteen times larger than Russia's. Also, China is much better at building physical infrastructure than Russia was (or is). It is no surprise, therefore, that under China's Belt and Road Initiative, Beijing has loaned more than $1 trillion to some 150 countries and international organizations in Asia, Central Asia, Africa, and Central and South America for major infrastructure projects ranging from railways to entire ports. Some of these deals have proven to be very controversial, because if the borrower goes into default, China can receive favorable access to the underlying infrastructure. (An example of such "debt trap diplomacy" is the loan China made to Sri Lanka, which, when it went into default, gave China favorable access to the Hambantota International Port in Sri Lanka through a ninety-nine-year lease.) But then again, the democracies are not that different in their lending terms for similar projects.

Where China in Cold War 2.0 is very different from Russia in Cold War 1 is with China's technology-oriented deals for communications and surveillance systems with customers in the Global South. The buyers for these systems are invariably autocracies themselves, and they really appreciate receiving state-of-the-art means for tracking and monitoring their citizens, and for suppressing democracy or any other movement that would potentially unseat the autocrat. The first objective for any and every autocratic ruler is to ensure they stay in power indefinitely. Therefore, any computer-based system that helps with this goal is very welcome.[6]

Moreover, the AI software supported by these surveillance systems allows autocrats to undertake a wide range of oppressive activities against their citizens. To date China has sold such systems to at least sixty countries.[7]

There is an added benefit to the buyers of these autocratic oppression systems from China. China doesn't ask questions about the state of human rights, or the rule of law, in the buyer's country. Indeed, the fact that the buyer is installing such a system without worrying about privacy norms tells China all it needs to know, namely that the buyer is as uninterested in human rights as China is. A similar system purchased from a democracy would elicit all sorts of probing queries about how and when the system would be used, and what legal, security, and other safeguards would be implemented in conjunction with the system. Then there could be a nosy press reporter or activist from an NGO gathering facts for a story on how the buyer misuses the system to monitor and harass citizens, or worse. With China there is none of this. There are some democracies in the Global South that would not buy such technology from China for just these reasons, and they end up purchasing a system from a fellow democracy that has controls and constraints built into it (is designed and operates according to "Standards of Democracy"). Still, there are many countries in Central and South America, the Middle East, Asia, and Africa ruled by strongmen who want an AI-based tech system useful for controlling citizens.

There is another dynamic in Cold War 2.0 that is playing out in the Global South that is new, namely the use of private mercenaries by Russia. Russia's Wagner Group has played a significant role in the Russian invasion of Ukraine. Wagner was a "private military company" (PMC) owned and operated by Yevgeny Prigozhin, who years ago was a convict in a Russian prison (serving nine years for armed robbery). He then became Putin's private caterer, and then talked his boss into hiring him to recruit and operate a private security company. In Ukraine he was notorious for recruiting 50,000 convicts from Russian prisons, offering them pardons for their crimes if they survived the war for more than six months. Another PMC used by Putin in Ukraine is the private militia operated by Chechen leader Ramzan Kadyrov.

Prior to the invasion of Ukraine, Wagner had been active in Syria, Libya, and a dozen other countries in Africa. Wagner benefits Russia because they allow Putin to disclaim knowledge and responsibility for their actions, not count their dead and wounded in the "official losses" of Russian military personnel, and maintain greater secrecy of Russian military activities. At the same time, though, the world, and especially Wagner's clients in the Global South, know that Putin and Prigozhin are coordinating efforts behind the scenes, and in particular Wagner group contractors (who are almost all ex–Russian military between the ages of thirty-five and fifty-five, except for the recent prison recruits for the Ukraine war). They share bases with the Russian military, are transported by them, use Russian military medical services, and are awarded Russian military medals. Wagner represents a model of private military contractors that Putin believes increases his options, and his effectiveness in many parts of the world; at least up until the dramatic falling-out between Prigozhin and Putin in June 2023 (and Prigozhin's untimely death, likely at the hands of the Kremlin).[8] Wagner also affords the kleptocratic tendencies of Putin and many of his oligarch enablers free rein, as Wagner often gets paid a percentage of the output from the mines and other facilities they capture or protect. It is modern privateering for serious profit—and as always, Putin and his Russian government enablers receive a material cut of the profits. Incidentally, it is not correct to compare Wagner to Blackwater (later Academi), the American security contractor, because Blackwater performed largely security details, like guarding the American ambassador in Iraq, and they didn't fight in frontline military operations.

These efforts by the two leading autocracies are having an impact on the hearts and minds of the 6.3 billion who live outside the world's democracies. In these countries of the Global South 70 percent and 66 percent feel positively toward China and Russia, respectively.[9] On the other hand, of the 1.2 billion people living in the democracies, 75 percent and 87 percent hold negative views of China and Russia, respectively. Moreover, the proportion of people living in the democracies who view Russia positively has fallen from 39 percent to 12 percent, a precipitous drop, indeed. This is reflected even in Hungary, the most pro-Russian country in the European Union, where support for Russia has fallen from 45 percent to 25 percent. Clearly Russian disinformation has its limits during Cold War 2.0.

Outside of the democracies, though, public opinion continues to be solid in favor of Russia, still at 75 percent in South Asia, 68 percent in Francophone Africa, and 62 percent in Southeast Asia. In these countries, and in many others, the democracies need to up their game if they hope to prevail in Cold War 2.0 in the Global South. One such channel of assistance is to provide sustained media coverage of world events through reputable international providers of news and information, such as the BBC World News (which has a program focused on Africa, *Africa Daily*) and the Voice of America (the VOA provides programming in many local languages in Africa). Here are other measures the leading democracies among the OECD need to be focusing on, especially in challenged democracies in the Global South:

- *Economic prosperity* has to be an important priority. If the pocketbooks of people in a struggling democracy are not growing, or indeed are getting slimmer, then very little else on this list will matter. When a solid majority of people are dissatisfied with the performance of their democracy, that same majority will feel more positively disposed toward Russia and China. The challenge for the democracies is very simple—either pull your people into a sustainable middle class or lose them to autocratic tendencies.

- *Anti-corruption* efforts are also very important. Corruption in fledgling democracies is hugely corrosive, and greatly reduces respect for other aspects of the rule of law. Financial transparency is also important. If the average citizen feels that the economic playing field is stacked against them, they will lose faith in the democracy project in their country. Technology, such as electronic payment systems, can help a great deal in bolstering transparency and fairness. India's electronic payment system, which ensures that government transfers go directly to the people they are intended for and are not reduced by exorbitant (or any) fees, is a wonderful example of how technology can help foster citizen confidence in democracy.[10]

- *Credible elections* are a very visible component of an effective democracy. People need to see the electoral process unfold in a fair, free, and credible manner. The electoral management body must be independent, and display solid expertise in running credible elections. Elections are another factor in people deciding whether their democracy can "get the job done," and whether it can deliver effective institutions and processes. A rigged election puts the entire democracy project in doubt.

- *Independent judges* play a key role in reinforcing the message that the rule of law is paramount in a democracy. If people, especially victims or survivors of abusive state organs, cannot get a fair hearing before an impartial judge, then the reputation of the democracy-building exercise will wilt.

- *Media freedom* is as important as freedom of personal speech, in some ways even more so, because individuals need to see their views, hopes, and opinions reflected in news outlets on paper, online, and in media such as television and radio. Human rights and freedom of expression cannot survive, let alone thrive, without independent media. In this regard, the personal safety of journalists is of paramount importance. The thuggish behavior of would-be autocrats within democracies (such as drug lords) intimidating journalists, or worse, physically harming them, including in some instances murdering them, can serve as a major impediment to the free circulation of ideas and especially criticism of the government in power.

- *Civil society* must be strengthened in all countries with fledgling democracies. The more independent sources of social interaction beyond state-sanctioned ones, the better. Especially important are unions in the workforce, to serve as an independent source of democracy training. Equally, small businesses are vital for training individuals in mobilizing workers and other resources to combine skills in building the economy, but always in keeping with reasonable environmental and health and safety practices.

- *Human equality* has to be ingrained in the educational, social, and political practices of the country. Gender equality is a good barometer of the overall state of democracy. If there aren't women in meaningful roles of power at every level of the country, then prospects for democracy are not good. Equally, diversity by ethnicity, race, religion, and sexual orientation is another yardstick for measuring the progress being made by the democracy. Essentially, if the society fails to be inclusive of a range of people in its power structures, the democracy will, at best, be greatly handicapped, and at worst will fail miserably.

- *Technology training* is the final piece in building a fully functioning democracy. As this book has already discussed at length, the world is in the midst of a technology revolution, and countries, institutions, and people need to have the proper technology tools and training to cope in this new environment, let alone thrive in it. Citizens need to know how to protect themselves from cyber criminals; at the same time, if some ministries in their own governments, or some businesses in their own country, are imposing technology restrictions on them, such as mass surveillance or large-scale censorship, they need to know how to push back these restrictions so that democracy can continue to function.

Just as the autocracies have created and deployed mercenary armies like the Wagner Group, the established leading democracies must take full advantage of their partners in supporting fledgling democracies, namely the philanthropies and NGOs such as Doctors Without Borders, the Bill and Melinda Gates Foundation, Open Society Foundations, Ford Foundation, Children's Investment Fund Foundation, Rockefeller Foundation, CARE, Oxfam International, Plan International, Rotary International, Lions Clubs International, Kiwanis International, and the Nature Conservancy.

Businesses in the democracies can also play important roles, such as the philanthropic arms of large pharmaceutical companies, or the similar group within Starlink, which makes Internet uplink devices available to low-income communities). If the leading democracies are going to compete effectively against the autocrats in the Global South during Cold War 2.0, they must bring a whole-of-society strategy to bear on the effort.

12

MANAGING COLD WAR 2.0

This chapter discusses the tools that are available—and that should be available—to the democracies to manage the challenges of Cold War 2.0. The discussion begins with some reform proposals for the United Nations and the collective security alliances of the democracies, because the current institutional frameworks that they have to rely on could be usefully bolstered with additional mechanisms. The UN is almost eighty years old. It needs an important overhaul, otherwise it will lose its relevance altogether, at least for geopolitical security matters. NATO, on the other hand, is a good news story, but one that during the course of Cold War 2.0 could be made great if it can undertake global expansion in a sensible manner.

Then the analysis shifts to sanctions, which are a useful mechanism for sure, but are also due for a rethink in some of the ways they are applied and enforced. The world is a more complex place than even thirty years ago when sanctions played a meaningful role in ending apartheid in South Africa. Creative anti-evasion solutions are particularly required when the items being denied to the autocracies are technology based. Cyberattacks also require a different response, including shutting down the Internet for some meaningful period for the entire country where a brazen hacker group is protected by an autocratic government—that will catch their attention. Then there are some tricky "people issues." These are important because, as noted earlier in this book, ultimately technology and innovation come down to the people who design, develop, and deploy technology. Making all these issues tougher for the democracies in Cold War 2.0 is the hard, cold fact that China is simply a far more formidable adversary than Russia ever was in Cold War 1.

REFORM THE UNITED NATIONS SECURITY COUNCIL

On February 24, 2022, Russia launched a full-scale military invasion of neighboring Ukraine in clear violation of the Charter of the United Nations. The next day the United Nations Security Council (UNSC), the body specifically tasked with keeping world peace, considered and voted on a resolution condemning Russia's unprovoked aggression and intending to end Russia's military violation of Ukraine's sovereignty. Of the fifteen members of the UNSC eleven voted in favor of the resolution, three (China, India, and the United Arab Emirates) abstained, and one country, Russia, voted against the resolution. The resolution did not pass, though, because Russia and four other members of the UNSC have a veto—if any one of them votes against a resolution it does not pass. Russia's lone vote against the resolution killed the resolution because it was also a veto. Ukraine's frustration with the uselessness of the UNSC was summed up when the Ukrainian representative told the chair of the UNSC that "Your words have less value than a hole in a New York pretzel."[1]

Clearly, the UNSC has to be reformed. The main objective of the UNSC, and indeed the United Nations generally, is to promote peace and prevent war. To this end, the UNSC has some very important and effective powers to take concrete actions against an aggressor state that attacks another country. In 1991 Saddam Hussein, the then Iraqi autocrat, invaded and took over Kuwait by force. The UNSC met, agreed it was an invasion that violated the Charter of the UN nations, and duly authorized a military campaign to push Hussein out of Kuwait, which is exactly what happened.

Illegal military might was countered successfully by the rule of international law (backed up by a large expeditionary force) because no UNSC member with a veto voted to block it. This didn't happen with Russia's invasion of Ukraine because the very invader also wielded a veto at the UNSC.

Obviously, the main institutional design defect with the UNSC is the veto wielded by each of its five permanent members. Currently China, France, Russia, the UK, and the US have a veto. In the case of Iraq's invasion of Kuwait in 1991, none of these five powers used its veto, and the UNSC was able to do its job properly, efficiently, and effectively. (Kuwait promptly had its full sovereignty restored as all Iraqi troops were either killed or ejected from Kuwait.) There are other similar cases, thankfully. But at the same time, Russia has used the veto 129 times, the United States 89 times, and the other three veto-wielding members of the UNSC many times as well. In effect, each holder of the veto uses it when it is in their interest to do so. Most egregiously this means if one of these five powers attacks another country (as Russia did with Ukraine), then the veto-wielding aggressor will use the veto to stymie any UNSC action against them. This structural, institutional defect greatly reduces the effectiveness of the UNSC.

This movie has been seen before. The predecessor to the UNSC (and the UN) was the League of Nations, set up after World War I to prevent any further wars. (World War I was supposed to be "the war to end all wars.") Four countries had a veto in respect of the League—France, Italy, Japan, and the UK—the United States did not because it refused to join the League altogether. When Imperial Japan invaded and annexed the Chinese province of Manchuria in 1931, literally everyone at the League voted in favor of ejecting Japan from Manchuria. The vote in the main League assembly was 42–1. The single vote against was Japan's, and they had a veto so the League could take no action against Japan. Instead, Japan left the League in a huff. A few years later, when the autocrat Benito Mussolini invaded Ethiopia, all League members (except Italy) voted again to have Italy stopped and the Italian army in Africa sent home. Italy exercised the veto and stomped out of the League in a huff. A pattern can be discerned. When Russia, in 1939, attacked Finland, Russia was expelled from the League.

Bottom line, the veto has to go and the UNSC has to be restructured. Here's what should be done. Currently the UNSC has fifteen members, five permanent (the big, nuclear weapon–wielding powers with the vetoes) and ten members made up of other countries on a rotating basis for two-year terms, but none of these ten has a veto. The membership of the UNSC should be recast as follows: reduce the number of members to thirteen, all of whom would be permanent. These would comprise the current five (China, France, Russia, UK, US) plus Brazil, Egypt, Germany, India, Indonesia, Japan, Nigeria, and South Africa. And remove the veto, so that none of them can block any matter, and certainly not a matter involving themselves.

Each resolution in the new thirteen-member UNSC would need seven votes to pass, in effect a simple majority. In practice, assuming the democracies voted together, and the autocracies voted together, each camp would have to find additional votes from the nonaligned countries. In effect Brazil, India, Indonesia, Nigeria, and South Africa would be the swing votes. It would be important to add one other very important procedural reform in respect of UNSC voting. Votes at the UNSC votes would be taken "secretly," such that the final vote tallies would never be made public. All that would be announced was that a resolution passed by the required majority, or failed to pass for not having the required majority. This way, all the countries on the UNSC could exercise their vote the way they really want to, and not just the way some other country is strong-arming or "bribing" them to.

There is useful precedent for such secret voting. Most citizen elections in democracies use secret ballots. The cardinals of the Catholic Church use secret ballots when electing the new pope. There is a lot to criticize about the Catholic Church—i.e., how can it be that toward the end of the first quarter of the 21st century women are still treated as second-class citizens in that church?—but they are steeped in wisdom when using secret ballots to elect their worldly leader. Knowing exactly which cardinal voted for which candidate for pope just serves to divide the College of Cardinals (and the new pope from those cardinals who didn't vote for him) once they come out of their conclave. This same reasoning applies for the expanded UNSC.

Secret voting in the UN will result in sensible, reasoned decisions, and not simply "might is right" results.

EXPAND NATO TO "GATO"

The democracies cannot leave their collective security solely in the hands of the United Nations, even if the UNSC reform advocated above were implemented. Moreover, NATO should expand to include all eligible democracies in the world, not just the states in Europe and North America. NATO should become GATO, the Global Alliance Treaty Organization. GATO would have a leadership structure and secretariat along the lines of NATO, with elements drawn from the OECD, an organization comprised of democracies committed to the rule of law, human rights, and an open market economy.[2] GATO would have strict criteria for membership. Before being admitted to GATO, each prospective member's political, legal, and related practices will be reviewed carefully to ensure only true democracies join GATO. Moreover, if a member fails to maintain these rigorous standards, the GATO assembly can expel a member by a simple majority vote. Membership in GATO will confer significant privileges, and therefore each member must continually meet its strict criteria around fair, free, and credible elections, personal rights for all citizens, and the rule of law enforced by independent judges. Certain members of NATO today wouldn't qualify for membership in GATO.

In addition, each member of GATO must spend an amount equal to at least 2 percent of their GDP on defense. For prospective members, they must attain this level of spending—and actually have spent it—during each of the two years before they join GATO. Any existing member can be expelled from GATO by a simple majority vote if their defense spending falls below this level in any year. Importantly, the GATO secretariat will have detailed criteria as to what constitutes eligible expenditures for meeting the 2 percent defense spending requirement. (For instance, pensions or extended health benefits for veterans don't count.) GATO will also have rules for how much of the country's defense spending must be on new, eligible weapons systems. GATO would be a high-performance organization with rigorous standards. It should not be otherwise, because its task is to defend the democracies from militarily threatening autocracies. It is not an overstatement that GATO would be the most important international institution on earth, just as NATO has been the most important international institution over the eighty years since its founding.

GATO's core function would be to operate a collective defense system, much as NATO does today. If a country attacks a GATO member, then a NATO Article 5–type mutual commitment will be triggered in the GATO treaty, and each member of GATO has to contribute troops and money to the GATO secretariat and military command commensurate with their size, to be used to defeat the unlawful invasion. Assuming Australia, Japan, New Zealand, the Philippines, South Korea, and Taiwan join GATO, they will each be protected against Chinese invasion under GATO's collective defense regime. If NATO's European members refuse to join GATO, then at a minimum these six Asian countries, the United States, and Canada (and possibly Chile, Colombia, and Costa Rica) should right away establish PATO, the Pacific Alliance Treaty Organization, a collective defense alliance comprised of democracies in or bordering on the Pacific Ocean. This structure is preferable to the current "hub and spoke" bilateral mutual defense treaty that the US has with each of them, because the alliance would continue even if the US pulled back from defending democracies in Asia because of isolationist sentiment in the US Senate or White House.

There will be many actions by autocrats, and possibly nonaligned countries, taken against GATO members that do not amount to war, but which require a firm response from GATO. Or an autocracy might attack one of the world's democracies that is not a member of GATO. One important role of GATO is to ensure that GATO members don't undermine one another's security by helping an autocracy "divide and conquer" them. For example, in 2021, after the appearance of COVID-19, Australia suggested that an investigation be undertaken by the World Health Organization in China to determine the origin of the virus, so that measures could be taken to prevent future outbreaks. China took exception to this suggestion, and promptly embargoed thirteen products from Australia. One of the products was wheat.

Upon hearing of this Chinese boycott of Australian wheat, Canada promptly contacted China to reassure them that Canada had sufficient surplus wheat with which to meet the forgone imports from Australia. This was a dark day in diplomacy among the democracies. Canada, a fellow democracy and a longtime partner of Australia in many security endeavors, should never have contacted China to sell them more wheat to make up for the embargoed Australian wheat. Indeed, if China had called the Canadians to ask them to sell China more wheat as a result of the Australian embargo, the Canadian response should have been a firm "no." Instead, the country being economically coerced by China should notify GATO. Then GATO should make a quick assessment of the situation, and if it finds that the member did not bring the autocracy's coercion upon itself, GATO would notify all members that they are not to backfill the product that has been banned by the autocracy. The point of this system is to deter the autocracy from implementing the ban in the first place.

What if a nonaligned country (not a member of GATO) picks up the slack instead? This raises an interesting opportunity for GATO to again improve the position of the democracies on the global stage. GATO would estimate the value of the additional exports made by the nonaligned country to the autocracy, and then GATO would require GATO members to block imports from the nonaligned country having a value roughly commensurate with that amount. Or it might be that GATO requires its members to embargo the shipment of certain high-tech products to the nonaligned country having the value of the substitute product provided to the autocracy by the nonaligned country. The rationale for this provision is, again, to convince the nonaligned country that the cost of backfilling products wrongfully banned from democracies is too high. The general objective is that through GATO the democracies will be able to push back on threats made against them by autocracies in the new Cold War 2.0 world. The democracies must always remember: none of us is as strong as all of us.

STRENGTHENING SANCTIONS

When a democracy is harmed by an autocracy (either through military action or economic coercion undertaken by the autocracy), one of the primary responses available to the democracy is levying economic sanctions on the autocracy. Sanctions have a long and uneven history in diplomacy. They are used to show displeasure where a response is required short of full-on military retaliation. They can also raise the cost to the wrongdoer of their actions, ideally serving as encouragement to have them stop or curtail their violent or economically harmful actions. Sanctions can be effective at disrupting the target country, even if they might not cause an aggressor to change its behavior altogether.[3]

It came as no surprise, therefore, that a number of democracies banded together to impose economic sanctions on Russia in response to its invasion of Ukraine. The depth and breadth of those sanctions surprised the Russians—and probably the democracies as well, given the relatively anemic sanctions effort after Russia annexed Crimea in 2014. Subsequent to the levying of these sanctions, Canada set a precedent by passing a law that allows the Canadian government to seize sanctioned assets located in Canada and to turn over the resulting financial proceeds to Ukrainian groups involved in rebuilding their war-torn country. Other democracies appear to be interested in following Canada's lead. Presumably China is taking into account the willingness of the democracies to engage in more extensive sanctions regarding Russia's full-scale invasion of Ukraine as China considers its options vis-à-vis Taiwan.

Still, several aspects of the sanctions on Russia need to be improved, some dramatically so. First, more than a year and a half after the invasion of Ukraine, there are still some 550 companies with head offices in democracies that are doing business in Russia. This is unacceptable. These companies have to be either convinced through "moral suasion" to leave behind their Russian operations or, at some point (presumably within a year of the commencement of hostilities), the companies should be forced by domestic legislation in the democracies to divest their Russian subsidiary or branch. The democracies cannot have commercial relations with autocracies that invade fellow democracies.

Second, when imposing sanctions on autocracies the democracies need to do much better on trade diversion. For example, a major focus for the sanctions on Russia since 2022 has been to block the Russian economy from getting SCs that are manufactured in democracies. The democracies have been quite successful in shutting down direct shipments of SCs to Russia. This is one of the reasons Russia was ripping SCs out of washing machines and repurposing them for use in precision-guided weapons, not an ideal solution to say the least. On the other hand, in 2022 companies in little Armenia bought 500 percent more SCs than in the previous year, and—surprise, surprise—97 percent of these SCs were exported from the country, the bulk of which went to Russia. The democracies have to be much tougher on this blatant form of trade diversion to avoid the sanctions regime. In effect, if sanctions are worth doing, they are worth doing well. Suitable staff and technical support must be given to regulators in the democracies to police these sorts of anomalies, so that importers in the sanctioned country cannot bring in products through the back door if they were prohibited through the front door. Sanctions are coming to play a very important role in Cold War 2.0 as the democracies improve their ability to collectively wield their economic clout. It is therefore imperative that they crack down hard on sanction-diversion tactics wherever they might occur.

A third proposed improvement relates to the personal sanctions that are levied on individuals associated with the Russian regime. Many of these people are "enablers" of the autocrat, and in turn many of them are known as "oligarchs," namely businesspeople in Russia who do very well from their connections to the Kremlin. A good number of these oligarchs actually don't like Putin, and would be willing to disassociate themselves from him if they had a safe path for doing so. The democracies, therefore, should give them such an avenue, particularly where they have assets and businesses outside of Russia. The democracies should make a deal with these oligarchs. The sanctions against the oligarch would be lifted if they do the following: First, in writing they must denounce the war in Ukraine and denounce Putin himself, with these statements being posted on a website accessible broadly on the Internet. Second, they must leave Russia, claim refugee status if required, and live permanently outside of Russia. Third, they must donate at least one-half of their personal wealth to Ukraine to help fund the massive rebuilding effort that will be required at the end of the war.[4] And finally, given Putin's rabid revenge tactics against those who he believes betray him, the oligarch might want to participate in a witness-protection program for as long as Putin runs Russia.

Where an autocracy invades a democracy militarily, as Russia has done with Ukraine, it would be expected that the democracies would implement a comprehensive set of sanctions, with the aim of making the autocracy a pariah state, not unlike North Korea for the last several decades. Since the beginning of Russia's invasion of Ukraine in February 2022, some fifty countries have sanctioned Russia, and it is running out of a number of key products, especially high-tech goods like SCs and spare parts for commercial aircraft. It is worth considering, therefore, how a sanctions regime would be implemented against China if Beijing were to order the PLA to invade Taiwan. For starters, China's economy is roughly fifteen times larger than Russia's. Most important, the economy of virtually every democracy in the world (and each sizable nonaligned country) is either very, or materially, dependent on exports to, imports from, and supply chains within China. Consider the following trade statistics that are very relevant to Cold War 2.0 and possible sanction scenarios:[5]

TABLE 1

China's top fifteen trading partners for 2022, by exports: i.e., how much China sells to these countries

1	United States	$582.8 billion	16.2 percent of China's total exports
2	Hong Kong	$297.5	8.3 percent (most intended for markets outside HK)
3	Japan	$297.5	8.3 percent
4	South Korea	$162.6	4.5 percent
5	Vietnam	$147	4.1 percent
6	India	$118.5	3.3 percent
7	Netherlands	$117.7	3.3 percent (most intended for EU generally)

8	Germany	$116.2	3.2 percent
9	Malaysia	$93.7	2.6 percent
10	Taiwan	$81.6	2.3 percent
11	United Kingdom	$81.5	2.3 percent
12	Singapore	$81.2	2.3 percent
13	Australia	$78.8	2.2 percent
14	Thailand	$78.5	2.2 percent
15	Mexico	$77.5	2.2 percent

TABLE 2

China's biggest bilateral trade surpluses (for 2022): i.e., how much more these countries buy from China than sell to China.

1	United States	$403.8 billion
2	Hong Kong	$289.7
3	Netherlands	$105.2
4	India	$101
5	Mexico	$60.1
6	United Kingdom	$59.7
7	Singapore	$47.2
8	Philippines	$41.6
9	Poland	$33.1

TABLE 3

China's biggest bilateral trade deficits (for 2022): i.e., how much more these countries sell to China than buy from China

1	Taiwan	$156.5 billion
2	Australia	$63.3
3	Brazil	$47.6
4	Switzerland	$42.2
5	Saudi Arabia	$40.1
6	Russia	$38
7	South Korea	$37
8	Oman	$32
9	Iraq	$25.4
10	Chile	$22

TABLE 4

China's top trade deficits by product (for 2021): i.e., how much more China buys of these products than sells of these products

1	Integrated circuits/ microassemblies	$250.5 billion	up 59.3 percent since 2014
2	Crude oil	$228.5	up 0.3 percent
3	Iron ores, concentrates	$169.9	up 81.9 percent
4	Petroleum gases	$59.7	up 114.9 percent
5	Copper ores, concentrates	$50.6	up 135.6 percent
6	Soya beans	$48.2	up 20.4 percent
7	Gold (unwrought)	$40.8	no 2014 data
8	Machinery for making SCs	$34.1	up 253.5 percent
9	Refined copper	$29.5	up 24.9 percent
10	Cars	$26.4	down 52.2 percent

TABLE 5

China's top trade surpluses by product (for 2021): i.e., how much more China sells of these products than buys of these products

1	Phones, including smartphones	$176.8 billion	up 16 percent since 2014
2	Computers	$145.2	up 7.8 percent
3	Lamps/lighting/ illuminated signs	$44.2	up 44.5 percent
4	Models/puzzles/misc. toys	$41.1	up 198.3 percent
5	Televisions/monitors/ projectors	$35.4	up 19 percent
6	Furniture	$33.6	up 22.5 percent
7	Seats	$32.8	up 49.2 percent
8	Plastic items	$28.2	up 78.7 percent
9	Electric water heaters/ hair dryers	$27.6	up 48.9 percent
10	Electric storage batteries	$25.2	up 442.5 percent

As these tables vividly show, trade relationships can be an asset or a liability or both, depending on the circumstances. Astoundingly, China is the largest trading partner for 152 countries (these tables show just the largest relationships). For instance, it was not shown on the above tables that

China is the largest trading partner of Germany, and Volkswagen makes 60 percent of its global profit from its huge operations in China, where the German automaker has forty plants and sells 2 million cars a year. Or consider that the European company Airbus assembles smaller "regional commercial jets" in China, because it sells more of these types of planes to Chinese buyers than in any other market, particularly in the past few years since China-US trade relations (and therefore Boeing's prospects in China) have deteriorated. This is likely why French president Emmanuel Macron, flying back from Beijing in April 2023 after a three-day sojourn with China's paramount leader Xi, said to reporters that he didn't think Europe ought to follow America into a war with China over Taiwan.

These tables explain certain current sanctions already in place. Chapter 5 included a discussion of the American sanctions on SCs, and equipment for making SCs, that Japan and the Netherlands have agreed to honor as well. Table 4 above answers the question: Why SCs? The answer is that for the simple reason that "integrated circuits and microassemblies," which comprise SCs for the most part, are the product category in which China is the most deficient. (Notice also item 8, machinery for making SCs.) The next product on the list is oil, but China has significant supply of crude from Saudi Arabia, Iraq, and more recently Russia, so that commodity is not a good candidate for sanctions, except to cut off purchases from China. Having iron ore next on the list shows that China desperately requires it from abroad to keep its steel mills running, and this is why Australia and Canada, if they acted in unison, could exert some pressure on China courtesy of their combined iron ore exports. And if you were wondering how soya beans got on the list of President Trump's trade war against China in 2017, the answer is row 6 in Table 4. In China, soya beans are necessary to feed pigs as 60 percent of the meat consumed in China is pork.

This all raises an important question: What kind of a sanctions regime might be expected from the democracies were China to invade Taiwan? If the Americans participate in the defense of Taiwan, which President Biden has said on several occasions he would do, then certainly complete US sanctions would apply to trade with China, and a large number of allied democracies would participate in these American sanctions, even if they didn't supply troops or ships for the military operations, including, very importantly, Japan, South Korea, the Philippines, Poland, the United Kingdom, and Australia. Just those countries would represent, collectively 28 percent of China's exports in 2022 (see Table 2 above), creating a massive hole in China's economy. If the entire EU joined the sanctions, that would absolutely devastate the Chinese economy, which in turn would cause significant unemployment in China, likely followed by widespread social dislocation, especially in its industrial cities. That in turn would then invariably trigger Xi's worst fear, namely street protests (reminiscent of the Tiananmen Square demonstrations) that would threaten the very survival of the CCP regime in China.

This is a very different picture from what followed Russia's 2022 invasion of Ukraine, because when the democracies laid on the sanctions against Russia, Putin had the fallback of redirecting a lot of his commodity exports to China. Xi doesn't have that security blanket. For China, there is simply no market (nor markets) in the world that could replace the democracies taken together. Moreover, it's not just the loss of export markets that will start to bite. When the spare parts for Airbus planes run out (assuming France participates in the sanctions), and when the SCs from TSMC are used up, then China will really start to feel economic stress, a condition that neither Russia nor any nonaligned country could alleviate. In this regard, consider that Taiwan sits at the top of Table 3 above, and Australia right behind it. Moreover, it should be noted that items 1 and 2 in Table 5 are somewhat misleading, because thousands of components for the high-tech devices covered by these two categories in fact are sourced from outside China, and then the final products are largely only assembled in China. Therefore, a major sanctions regime against China, following China's commencement of hostilities against Taiwan, would crater the two export domains that bring the biggest surpluses to China.

This sanctions scenario of course strikes abject fear into the hearts of many businesspeople in the democracies as well, because it represents "mutual economic destruction" on a global scale. As a result, many CEOs of companies based in the democracies are hurriedly adopting a "China plus 1" supply chain strategy; that is, in addition to their source of supply in China, they establish a second, and sometimes even third, source of supply outside China. This is why Tim Cook, the CEO of Apple, has shifted the production of AirPods to Vietnam, and he has (through his contact manufacturer Foxconn, also headquartered in Taiwan) begun to move production of iPhones, laptops, and iPads to India and Vietnam. At a macro level, Xi's saber-rattling over Taiwan is already starting to weaken the Chinese economy.[6] At the same time, though, three weeks before meeting India's prime minister, Cook was in Beijing trying to calm fears of economic decoupling, telling an audience in Beijing that the "symbiotic" relationship between China and the US over the past thirty years has been mutually beneficial.[7] Cold War 2.0 will see a great deal of diplomatic juggling, both by diplomats as well as company bosses. More important than what CEOs say will be what their companies actually do.

In a rational world, driven only by economic dynamics, the interdependence illustrated by Tables 1–5 above would drive both China and the democracies to continually uphold the status quo—China refrains from invading Taiwan, and Taiwan stops short of declaring independence. In effect, the ambiguous yet peaceful arrangement of the last forty-plus years would simply continue. Mutual assured economic destruction would argue a long-lasting—indeed indefinite—deterrence that keeps both sides focused on building wealth and prosperity and avoiding armed conflict. Moreover, Russia's difficult experience in Ukraine would seem to amplify the wisdom of China leaving Taiwan alone. And yet, despite all these sensible reasons, China's near war in the airspace and waters around Taiwan continue apace, and have even been escalated in the past couple of years. (When Nancy Pelosi, the speaker of the US House of Representatives, visited Taiwan in the summer of 2022, China effectively blockaded Taiwan with rockets and planes for a full three days, a new apogee of military violence in the cross-strait relationship. In short, in Chinese politics it should be the case that economics wins out over national reunification, but that is by no means a certainty. It would not be a big surprise if Xi Jinping decided (and it is solely his decision in autocratic Beijing) to turn his Cold War 2.0 near war with Taiwan into a hot war.

DEALING WITH PEOPLE FROM SANCTIONED AUTOCRACIES

Sanctions generally deal with goods and information crossing borders. What about people who want to move across a border from a sanctioned state to a democracy? Within several months after Russia's invasion of Ukraine in 2022, some 500,000 members of Russia's "innovation cohort" fled their homeland to other countries. This group of Russians included journalists, writers, media types, entrepreneurs, and especially workers in high-tech firms. Their destination of choice was a democracy because of the freedom it afforded them. Some seven months after the start of the war, when Russia called up hundreds of thousands of conscripts to fight, another wave of young Russians, mainly men, fled Russia. Their main destinations were Georgia, Armenia, and the Central Asian countries; relatively fewer of this cohort went to democracies because their jobs didn't require the values found in states practicing the rule of law.

Should democracies allow these sorts of emigrants to come into their countries? On the one hand, humanitarian instincts argue for admitting them into democracies; they are fleeing a brutal autocratic regime, and what could be more consistent with the liberal values that animate democracies than to provide refuge for those fleeing tyranny? The counterargument, though, is that if democracies want to encourage autocrats to change their behavior, then democracies should not let people into their countries who are fleeing autocratic societies. While counterfactuals are usually not that helpful, imagine what would have happened in Russia if just half of the innovation cohort (say, 250,000 of them) and half of the conscript dodgers (another 250,000 men) had stood their ground and protested Putin's war by taking to the streets, perhaps three days a week, every week?

As it was, domestic protest against Russia's war in Ukraine has been anemic. There have been relatively few demonstrations against the war, and those that have occurred see tiny numbers of protesters, generally in the ten-to-thirty range. These were broken up easily by Russia's state security services and police forces. By contrast, if there had been 250,000 to 500,000 protesters, on a weekly basis, would that have altered Putin's view of the war? Perhaps not, if China's methodical oppression of democracy protesters in Hong Kong in 2019 is any indication. Nevertheless, protests in these numbers would certainly give autocratic leaders cause to pause, and it definitely increases their costs of commencing and conducting an unjustified war. It would also make them think twice about next time. Even in China, the protests at the end of 2022 over the COVID-19 lockdowns ultimately had the effect of convincing Beijing to entirely change its approach to fighting the virus. People power matters, and democracies undermine their own interests when they allow themselves to be used by the autocrats as dumping grounds for unwanted dissidents and outspoken critics of the autocratic regime.

This has happened in Cuba, for example, when both in 1965 (the Camarioca exodus) and 1980 (the Mariel boat lift) the autocratic Cuban government allowed tens of thousands of Cubans to travel to and find a permanent home in the United States. These emigrants comprised mainly economic migrants, but also included some political prisoners, and common criminals. As such, Fidel Castro, Cuba's longtime autocrat, was delighted to get rid of thousands of Cuban citizens who opposed his regime. Putin's reaction was the same toward the innovation cohort that left Russia in reaction to his war: a source of weakness for Putin was removed by the democracies themselves; how useful that is to the autocrat-in-chief!

Democracies need to be more muscular on these sorts of issues vis-à-vis the autocracies. For inspiration, consider the decision of the Ukrainian government to not allow Ukrainian men between the ages of seventeen and twenty-seven to leave Ukraine in the wake of the Russian invasion. Generally speaking, the right to travel across borders is an important right of citizens in a democracy. Ukrainian president Zelenskyy, however, suspended this right because he needed all able men to stay and join the Ukrainian army. He took some criticism for this decision, but it was the right one. Had the departure of some men initially turned into a flood, the very existence of Ukraine might have hung in the balance. Zelenskyy, incidentally, was very critical of democracies allowing entry to Russians fleeing Russia after the Putin started his full-scale invasion, or for allowing draft dodgers to escape to the democracies.

A similar set of considerations applies to Russian athletes, entertainers, and other high-profile people working in democracies (such as the fifty-seven Russian hockey players in the US National Hockey League, which is 5.4 percent of the total). The sanctions that democracies brought against Russia certainly hurt average Russians living in Russia; they were denied the economic and other benefits of certain goods and services previously sourced from democracies. It is not right that the Russian celebrities could go on earning a living in a democracy as if no war was being waged by their government.

Accordingly, governments in democracies should institute the following program for the Russian celebrities, or any other famous figures from autocratic countries that have been sanctioned for waging war against a democracy. Where the celebrity's country is sanctioned by a democracy for waging war, if the celebrity wishes to continue working in the democracy then they must do two things to decouple themselves personally from the autocratic regime that started the unjustified war. First, they must make a clear, unequivocal, and widely available written statement (including being posted on the celebrity's own website) that they oppose the war waged by the autocrat, and that they stand in solidarity with the victims of the war. Second, the celebrity must physically sever ties with the autocracy and continue residing only outside of it. Only if these two conditions are met would the celebrity be allowed to compete, perform, or in any other way earn income in the democracy.

A third category of individual from an autocracy is the university student, typically having completed an undergraduate degree in a STEM subject, who wishes to pursue graduate studies at a university in a democracy. For example, each year about 300,000 students from China attend colleges and universities in the United States. Generally nothing should be done to curb the flows of highly qualified students into democracies from autocracies that are not under war-related sanctions. (If their country has been sanctioned, then the foregoing discussion applies.) Although there are a few cautionary notes to be sounded in respect to students from China and the other autocratic countries, particularly in respect to those students wanting to study in technical domains where the democracy has levied specific sanctions.

Broadly speaking, the host democracy should not take any action to stem the flow of these students. Based on past performance, around 60 percent of these students will want to stay in on the country they studied in. In terms of students from China this percentage drops somewhat, to 40 percent. Moreover, most of the students who stay want to immediately get on in a workplace, and so they are an important resource for the countries that hosted them for their advanced university degree. Indeed, there is a vibrant competition among the democracies with leading universities (typically the US, UK, Canada, and Australia) for landing these students in graduate programs in their country.

One concern with these students, especially those from certain autocracies—namely China or any other autocracy that has been sanctioned by the democracies over technology matters—is that they are receiving too much information from academic scientists in the democracies. The concern is heightened in respect of those students who do not stay on after finishing their degrees, as they could return to their home country and share sensitive information gleaned during their studies in the democracy with their next employer or public research institution in the autocracy. While this risk exists, it is arguably small, especially when compared to the large added value for the host democracy from those students who decide not to return to their autocratic countries. Moreover, relative to the returning students, all professors should be coached to be careful that classified or sensitive research information and data not be shared with any graduate students from autocracies, even if they're simply working in the professor's laboratory in order to meet their degree requirement. In effect, the somewhat higher risk profile presented by some of these foreign students is still not that great and can be adequately managed, especially when weighed against the oversized benefits derived from those students who come to the democracies to study and then stay to lay down multi-decade careers.

RESPONDING TO CYBERATTACKS

The autocracies have been very active in inflicting harm on the democracies over the last several decades through various operations undertaken over the Internet. These cyberattacks take many forms, and generally the response of the democracies has been weak and inadequate. The limp response has invariably emboldened the state and near-state actors in the autocracies who perpetrate these cyberattacks; clearly, appeasement never works in these matters. At the same time, the heightened response of the democracies should not be capricious or over the top. The democracies don't want to cease being democracies in the way they respond to the cyberattacks of the autocracies.

Some of the cyber activity conducted by the Russians and the Chinese can be termed digital, remote espionage. Espionage of the traditional variety, using humans to infiltrate the opponent's government and military in order to garner intelligence, including photos taken by small cameras, has always been tolerated by governments—to a degree—in peacetime as part of "diplomacy." Presumably a "reasonable amount" of such activity, albeit undertaken by computers over the Internet, will also be tolerated by all governments. There is even an argument that some of this covert intelligence-gathering activity helps to maintain international peace to the extent it allows a government, especially a significant military power, to glean a better sense of what the other side is up to. (For example, allowing a military power to avoid a major kinetic operation given that through espionage it understands that the true nature of a particular risk is less than originally contemplated.) Ironically, truth obtained through a certain limited type of espionage is not a bad thing, especially given how opaque autocracies can be to outsiders.

On the other hand, it is something else again when espionage morphs into a wholesale infiltration of the computers of the entire government, as was the case in the SolarWinds attack in 2020, in which 18,000 computer systems worldwide were infiltrated by a Russian cyber espionage group (APT29, or "Cozy Bear," which is affiliated with the Russian state security police, the FSB).[8] Such a case requires a forceful countermeasure. The key is proportionality in the response. Therefore, the democracy—or, depending on the extent of the original attack, NATO, or if established by then, GATO or PATO—should craft an action that is commensurate to the original cyberattack launched by the autocracy. In the case of SolarWinds, that would be a return hack that hits Russian private-sector and public-sector entities in a fashion similar to what the US experienced.

At the same time there should also be delivered a warning from the highest levels of the US government—the White House and the Pentagon—that this type of widespread cyberattack "first-strike" is simply unacceptable, and if it continues a disproportionate response would also be forthcoming. That could include, at some point, a kinetic response, but there are several interim escalation points. One would be to cause a shutdown of the entire Internet in Russia, for perhaps fifteen minutes. This can be done, technically speaking. It would be coupled with a message that indicated that longer outages would be forthcoming if the large, state-sanctioned or organized Russian hacks continue. Presumably such an Internet shutdown would only be undertaken once the Internet nodes and infrastructure in the US are sufficiently hardened so that a retaliatory response by Russia would stand little chance of success.

Similar considerations should apply to what is often referred to as "digital propaganda" dispensed by the autocracies. The practice of propaganda has been around for a long time. As with espionage, it is propagated by the democracies as well, as exemplified by the Voice of America radio service in the 1950s. (There is still such a group, but today it operates digitally as much as over radio.) Therefore, today, a certain amount of state-originated propaganda by Russia and China is to be expected, and can be tolerated, such as when ads extolling the virtues of China appear on TikTok screens in America or another democracy.

It is another matter altogether, though, when Internet trolls from Russia and China, such as the Internet Research Authority, ingratiate themselves into American Facebook chat discussions for several weeks or months, and then begin to make comments that are divisive and eventually incendiary (even inciting violence), all in an effort to sow dissension, distrust, and ultimately social conflict in the US or some other democracy. Another red flag is triggered when this type of behavior, or something similar, is deployed into a political discussion in the democracy, especially in the run-up to an election—all with a view to helping a certain candidate get elected who is presumably more favorably disposed to one particular autocracy. This is full-on interference with an election in a democracy, and that crosses the line into completely unacceptable behavior by the autocracy. The response has to be swift and firm—perhaps shutting down the Internet in the autocracy for thirty minutes—something very significant to make sure the message isn't lost.

The final level of escalation can be contemplated when the autocracy, directly through its own personnel—such as members of the Russian military intelligence, the GRU, or the Federal Security Service, the FSB, or through agents retained and paid by the autocratic government—carry out hacking attacks that through so-called wipers destroy data on corporate or government websites in the democracy, or unleash malware software that blocks use of a computer until a ransom is paid. One such malware attack is described in some detail in chapter 4 (the Colonial Pipeline attack), but there are literally hundreds of these attacks a year in each democracy, invariably coming mainly from Russia and China. Serious pushback is required on this cyber front from the affected democracy or democracies. The reciprocal, proportionate response here would be immediate counter-cyberattacks that levy roughly the same harm on Russia or China. But again, there should be a warning that at some point, fairly soon, the volume of attacks will become unacceptable, and when that point is reached the democracy reserves the right to respond in a more muscular manner, eventually including, but not limited to, a kinetic response. (For instance, in response to the Colonial Pipeline hack, an American response that shut down a Russian pipeline for an equivalent time would be commensurate.)

STEMMING FENTANYL PRECURSORS FROM CHINA

Chapter 3 touched upon the "Opium Wars" in the 1800s, where Britain traded opium (grown at the time in British India) to China in consideration for the various unique goods that only China had in quantity, such as silk, tea, and porcelain. Ultimately, the opium was extremely damaging to China's population, with about 30 percent of its people becoming opium addicts. Paramount leader Xi Jinping talks about the Opium Wars as a humiliating period in Chinese history.

Ironically, today the tables are reversed. There is a crisis in America of illicit fentanyl use. Each year about 100,000 Americans die of an illicit fentanyl overdose. Fentanyl is a synthetic drug, the product of biotechnology engineering. The fentanyl comes from Mexico, where it is produced in illegal labs operated by two large drug cartels. The ingredients for the fentanyl, the so-called precursors, are "dual-use" chemicals manufactured in China. China does a roaring trade supplying the precursors to the drug cartels in Mexico; it is estimated to be worth in the tens of billions of dollars a year.

Fentanyl is a synthetic drug resulting from the biotechnology revolution. It is made when ANPP (4-anilino-N-phenethyl-4-piperidine) and NPP (N-phenethyl-4-piperidone) are combined in very precise amounts. The resulting fentanyl is up to fifty times stronger than heroin, and up to one hundred times stronger than morphine. It is a perfect drug for trafficking. It is so potent that only tiny amounts of it are required to get suitably high. Therefore it is easy to transport relatively small amounts over the Mexico–US border but still make huge amounts of money on the illegal importation.

At the same time, though, fentanyl's very potency makes it extremely dangerous for users. When it is prescribed by a doctor and dispensed by a pharmacist, it is contained on a patch that controls precisely the amount of fentanyl released into the patient's bloodstream. When a small packet is purchased from an illicit drug dealer, the user has to carefully count out 5–7 grains of it—each the size of a grain of salt, sometimes a little smaller. Pity the user with poor eyesight, or someone who can't focus while ingesting the drug, or someone trying to count out the correct dosage in a dimly lit alley. Remember, 5–7 grains, and the user gets high. If the user, though, takes 7–12 grains or more, then they stand a very good chance of dying of an overdose. Or, the dealer puts too many grains into the fentanyl pill that he is selling. These are the reasons why each year about 100,000 Americans die of an illicit fentanyl overdose.

The US government has negotiated with the Chinese government to have the latter block the Chinese chemical companies that make the precursors for fentanyl from selling them to the Mexican drug cartels. These interdiction efforts of the Chinese government have diminished as the diplomatic relationship between China and the US has deteriorated over the past few years. Intense corruption among the CCP officials who administer the relevant regulations in China also contributes to the failure of China's counter-narcotic activities. The Chinese government also allows organized crime groups within China to facilitate transactions in fentanyl precursors.

As part of a new agenda for Cold War 2.0, the US should increase pressure on China to step up enforcement efforts against these Chinese chemical companies. This is not rocket science. When Beijing wanted to outlaw cryptocurrencies in China, it did so with a single decree in 2021 and the threat of very significant jail time for any transgressors. Illegal cryptocurrency stopped circulating in China within a few months. China could do the same with the companies that produce the fentanyl precursors, but it chooses not to. The drug companies that make the precursors are widely known. The Chinese authorities simply have to want to get serious with them. To date the US government has not given Beijing enough incentive to want to do this. And so the carnage of fatal fentanyl overdoses continues on the streets of American cities. Convincing China to take this problem seriously should be an American priority for managing Cold War 2.0. If

China won't cooperate, additional sanctions should be levied on Chinese exports to the US. In all likelihood, though, if Chinese precursors are cut off from reaching Mexico, the large drug cartels will look elsewhere for their fentanyl ingredients. What is really required is that the biotechnology expertise has to be harnessed to innovate another solution to getting fentanyl addicts to a better place. This solution is one of the ways democracies need to strengthen themselves.

13

STRENGTHENING
DEMOCRACIES

The ability to project geopolitical hard and soft power around the world begins at home. Democracies should take some very muscular actions to protect themselves and extend their power and influence in a number of ways that play to their strengths in technology and innovation. These measures, however, require that the democracies be strong enough themselves to be able to take and sustain these actions. Put in the vernacular, the democracies cannot run the long Cold War 2.0 marathon, and certainly not against the Chinese, unless they are in good physical, mental, and emotional shape.

The democracies need to spend more money on defense, but at the same time governments must resist corporate interests who argue unreasonably an "AI gap" or "biotech gap" just to get more government money. In order to effectively fend off the autocracies in Cold War 2.0, the democracies need to help their citizens become more digitally resilient. This was useful for a social media–saturated world, but it is now absolutely imperative for an AI-infused world. Moreover, AI should be regulated, but with a light touch that doesn't dampen the tempo and volume of research and development or build a digital moat around today's leading AI behemoths. This will be one of the most consequential legislative interventions in the economy in the history of the United States—Congress and the White House, with the help of the courts, should be prepared to course-correct a few times before they get it right. And not to end on an ominous note, but the democracies need to better protect themselves internally from the autocrat apologists and autocrat appeasers—and would-be autocrats—all mingling among their own citizens. Given the assessment of the state of global technology innovation undertaken in this book, it is highly unlikely that the autocracies can win Cold War 2.0 on their own, but their chances improve markedly if it becomes an inside job.

DEFENSE SPENDING BY DEMOCRACIES

There are several very sobering lessons to be learned from Russia's annexation of Crimea in 2014, its unjustified invasion of Ukraine in 2022, and the resulting Russo-Ukrainian War. Some are big, macro lessons, while others operate at the more specific, micro level. Most fundamental is the realization that the autocracies are willing, in the current era, to pursue territorial conquest by military invasion. Prior to 2014 it was thought in the democracies that this form of state aggression went out of fashion in 1945 with the defeat of Hitler, the Nazi autocrat. Clearly that was wishful thinking. Pursuing territorial conquest by military force, contrary to the UN Charter,[1] is again something, practiced and condoned by the autocracies. This expansionist behavior underlies much of the tension and anxiety inherent in Cold War 2.0.

The previous chapter proposed, among other changes, refashioning NATO (which currently comprises only countries in Europe and North America) into GATO, the Global Alliance Treaty Organization, an international collective defense community of democracies. This would bring together a number of democracies in the Asia-Pacific with their counterparts in North America and Europe into a formidable global collective security pact. Whether or not GATO can be made a reality, there remains the critical question of whether, and by how much, GATO members, or existing NATO members and those other democracies, should increase their defense spending in light of Russia's invasion of Ukraine, and China's stated intention to take back Taiwan, including by military force if necessary.

Table 1 in chapter 10 sets out the size of the economy of each major democracy, and the relative size of their respective defense budgets. Just focusing on the countries that are NATO members, only seven spend the NATO-required 2 percent of domestic GDP on national security, and of these countries four have small militaries in absolute terms: Greece, Lithuania, Estonia, and Latvia. The three larger countries that do meet the 2 percent threshold include, thankfully, the United States, which has a very large military budget (the two others are the United Kingdom and Poland). Still, that leaves twenty-four NATO members who do not meet the 2 percent requirement.[2] This has to change, and immediately. Helpful statements have been made in this direction by several governments, including in Germany, but actually turning a pledge into real military equipment ready to deploy in case of conflict is quite a task, and currently many democracies are failing this important test.[3] Canada, for example, can and should do more for defense preparedness. Canada is a G7 country, and an important member of the G20, and yet Canada spends on defense only 1.3 percent of GDP. That is just not good enough. For far too long Canadian governments have been content to outsource their defense to the United States. That cannot go on. If Canada hopes to be taken seriously around the world on matters of Cold War 2.0, it has to step up its defense preparedness. (I specifically call out Canada because I am Canadian.)

REBUILDING MILITARY-INDUSTRIAL
CAPACITY IN THE DEMOCRACIES

Even if all the laggard countries (like Canada) stepped up with additional financial commitments for defense spending, currently many of them would be unable to procure new equipment because the most compelling weapons systems are on back order. In short, even if the demand side were corrected, there would remain serious challenges on the supply side.

During World War II the factories of the United States (with important support from Canada's industrial concerns) became the "arsenal of democracy." In 1943, at peak production of that war, the industrial base in North America was producing 8,000 planes and 700 tanks each *month*, and three "Liberty" naval vessel every *two days*. The cost was high, including in foregone cars for civilians that were postponed until later in the 1940s. The stakes, though, were even higher, and so it made sense to repurpose industrial capacity to the war effort in this high-tempo, urgent manner.

Since the end of Cold War 1 the military-industrial base of the democracies has atrophied. When the East Bloc gained its freedom in 1989, and Soviet Russia collapsed in 1991, the democracies believed they had earned a "peace dividend." They were delighted that huge sums of money that henceforth didn't have to be invested in national defense could instead be spent on healthcare, education, and pensions. No one seemed to notice that the factories that used to produce military assets like ammunition were downsized dramatically, and in some cases shut down.

The result is that today in the United States, for instance, only one factory makes 155 mm artillery shells. The plant dates from the 1930s. It can produce 460 shells a day. At the peak of the Russo-Ukrainian War, Ukraine was firing about ten times that in order to match the Russians shell for shell. As a result, Ukraine at various times in that war experienced a dire shortage of artillery shells. There are ten (smallish) factories in Europe that produce 155 mm artillery shells, and they are working hard to backfill Ukraine's requirements, but it will take some time. Bottom line, the military-industrial base in the democracies for the nuts and bolts of war fighting needs to be rebuilt.

In some respects, the lack of capacity in the democracies in manufacturing high-end weapons systems like Patriot air defense systems, F-35 fighters, and tanks is even more pronounced. Take the Patriot ADS, the high-performance system that has made such a difference defending

Ukraine, including against the Russian Kinzhal hypersonic ballistic missile—that's the great news. The bad news is that building a new Patriot system takes two years. That is simply unacceptable. The two US defense contractors responsible for manufacturing it can only produce eighteen of them a year. This is also unacceptable. And the cost is an eye-popping $1 billion for each one. Again, unacceptable. And each intercept missile that it shoots at incoming missiles costs $4 million. That's on the border of unacceptable, but still needs to be much cheaper. The weapon, or its successor, needs to be redesigned to make it less expensive. And its supply chain needs to be able to produce many more of them much more quickly.

In the meantime, the current production dynamics (even at the grotesque costs) have to be massively improved, and fast. Taiwan put in an order for $19 billion worth of Patriots and other high-end weapons from the United States in 2019, and (five years later) is still waiting for deliveries to begin. Poland is in the same position. It has recently signed agreements to buy 18 HIMARS, 32 F-35 fighters, 96 Apache helicopters, 250 Abrams tanks, and 6 Patriot systems. But it must get in line behind Taiwan, which in turn is now behind Ukraine, which is of course the customer in the most pressing need at the moment. Clearly American military-industrial capacity is not where it needs to be. Supremacy in high-technology innovation, especially in AI and high-performance SCs, will be necessary for the democracies to prevail in Cold War 2.0, but will not be sufficient if the industrial capacity of the democracies is inadequate to build in a timely manner the physical weapons systems into which all that high-tech innovation excellence is integrated.

BEWARE THE FALSE TECHNOLOGY GAP

When it comes to the procurement of weapons systems, the democracies should not underreact to the Russian full-scale invasion of Ukraine. At the same time, however, notwithstanding the two previous sections of this chapter, neither should the democracies overreact. US president Dwight

Eisenhower in 1960 (fifteen years after he stepped down as the supreme commander of allied forces at the successful conclusion of World War II), when leaving office after eight years, warned of the "military-industrial complex," and the danger in simply deferring to defense companies on the critical question of how much of the government budget to allocate to national security. Arms manufacturers will always argue that the democracies are behind the autocracies in military capability because these companies are always striving to receive yet more government spending on military equipment. In democracies, though, governments cannot allow the fox to take the hens to market.

This has happened numerous times since World War II. In the 1950s (when Eisenhower was president) some proponents who wanted more military spending argued there was a "bomber gap," namely that the Soviet air force had many more large bomber aircraft than the US, thereby allowing Russia to deliver atomic bombs against targets in America more effectively than the Americans could do against Russia. A decade later it was the "missile gap" that had many arguing for increased US military spending. (The "missiles" referred to the intercontinental ballistic rockets that were used to deliver nuclear warheads to their targets half a world away.) In both cases, though, when the facts were looked at clearly and dispassionately, there was neither a bomber gap nor a missile gap.

Currently, some commentators argue that the Chinese have surpassed or will soon surpass the US in artificial intelligence technology and innovation.[4] These claims should always be carefully considered and tested. Currently if there is a "technology gap" (including in AI) it is in the favor of the democracies, especially if the contributions of all the major democracies are considered in the aggregate (and not just those of the United States). Accordingly, as long as all NATO members manage to spend their 2 percent of GDP target amount, that should be sufficient to pay for defense for the foreseeable future. Poland, perhaps not surprisingly because it is so close to Russia, is calling for this spending target to be increased to 3 percent of GDP. This should not be required, so long as the industrial capacity blockages referred to above can be fixed. If all NATO members hit their 2 percent requirement, an additional $200 to $700 billion will flow into military spending in the near term,[5] and that should be plenty to deal with the threats posed in Cold War 2.0.

In other words, government decision makers should not simply take as gospel the claims about optimal spending on the military made by certain persons in the relevant industry who are under severe conflicts of interest. Rather, governments must always be prepared to make their own assessments of the facts on their own merits. This process begins by determining what objective threats actually face a democracy, and then deciding how best to counter them. Then and only then can a sensible defense budget be prepared. For example, if each leg of the American nuclear triad (bombers, submarines, land-based missiles) were simply reduced, serious financial savings could be achieved without sacrificing operational effectiveness.[6] For smaller democracies, should the emphasis be on procuring very expensive fighter jets, like the F-35, or are they better off buying more missiles and drones? At the end of the day, they might be able to perform virtually all of the functions of the fighter jet required by the smaller country, particularly when deployed in a predominantly defensive capacity. This is precisely the debate currently being waged in Taiwan about its defense spending plans, particularly as the small island nation considers the wisdom of implementing a "hedgehog" approach to fending off a likely Chinese attack. This debate in Taiwan has been turbocharged by the war in Ukraine, where early on, after the invasion by massive Russian forces, the smaller country (Ukraine), to everyone's amazement, was able to perform well against the behemoth Russian army using just such hedgehog tactics.

A further, somewhat related lesson can be gleaned from the Russo-Ukrainian War. Notwithstanding Putin's multiple threatening statements about the potential use of nuclear weapons, at the end of the day the Russian autocrat has not used them. It appears China's leader Xi Jinping reinforced with Putin a policy of no first use of nuclear weapons. Perhaps for any armed confrontation over Taiwan a similar understanding will be reached, namely that the US will not bring nuclear weapons to that battle, nor will China use them against Taiwanese or American (and allied) forces, so long as the defenders use their conventional missiles only against Chinese military installations. It appears the modus operandi is developing that nuclear weapons, even so-called tactical ones (intended to be used on a battlefield against troops rather than against civilians in a city), are to be contemplated only as second-strike weapons, essentially in response to an enemy that has violated the no-first-strike rule. That would be a useful doctrine coming out of the Russo-Ukrainian War, and would help ensure deterrence through mutual assured destruction (but no other use of nuclear weapons). Confirming such an understanding between both sides of the Cold War 2.0 conflict, or realizing that logic simply compels such a conclusion, would allow democracies and autocracies with nuclear weapons to spend less money on them over the years to come.

BEWARE THE NONOPTIMAL WAR

Collectively, the NATO countries can field the largest military force on the globe, particularly if properly funded by all its members (see above). With the poor performance of Russia's army on the fields of Ukraine, there may be a temptation on the part of NATO to deploy its much stronger military forces into theaters where they should not be sent. For example, there is a terrible civil war unfolding in Sudan. International journalists based in Khartoum generate a constant stream of awful images of the fighting and the vast suffering of civilians. As terrible as these pictures and videos are, the democracies should resist intervening in Sudan. If anyone decides to send in peacekeepers once there is a reasonable hope that the belligerents have had enough of the fighting, it should be the African Union. This is a civil war between two autocratically oriented camps and is no place for troops from democracies. On the other hand, Botswana is a democracy in Africa that is situated in a very dangerous neighborhood. Were Botswana to ask for help, including military assistance, from the democracies, they should respond favorably. Democracies everywhere should assist other democracies, wherever they might be. Other democracies in Africa are threatened by al-Qaeda and other militant Islamist militias. Again, these countries deserve military support from democracies.

By contrast, the US and certain other democracies should not have invaded Iraq in 2003, notwithstanding that Saddam Hussein, Iraq's autocrat, was odious in the extreme. In a similar vein, the US and other democracies were justified in going into Afghanistan in 2001 to clear out al-Qaeda training camps, but this took only about ten months to accomplish. After achieving this goal, the armed forces of the democracies should have left Afghanistan. Instead, they stayed on to attempt to "bring democracy" to this country. After eighteen years, sacrificing much blood and spending huge amounts of treasure, the democracies in August 2021 pulled out ignominiously. Incidentally, the embarrassing manner of their exit invariably factored into Putin's decision to launch his invasion of Ukraine six months later.

In short, the democracies should not try to "bring" democracy to another country or region that has not previously been a democracy. That is an incredibly daunting, high-risk task. In an appropriate case, the democracies might send some help that can "amplify" the efforts of a large group fighting for democracy, but it cannot supplant them. Put another way, if only a small group of local people want democracy enough to die fighting for it, then most likely sending troops from the established democracies cannot do much to help the campaign. This seems like a harsh conclusion, but the alternative is worse, namely the quagmire in Afghanistan. Ironic as it sounds, democracies should not be in the business of planting the tree of democracy in some foreign land. What the democracies can do, though, is help water and nourish a democracy tree for a limited period that was previously planted by a solid majority of the local population. Ultimately, though, it is up to the local population to take over the care and maintenance of that democracy, and if they fail, that will be a sad day, but not one that should prompt the intervention of armed forces from the democracies.

At the same time, though, while extreme care must be taken not to send troops from the democracies into war zones where only a bloody quagmire awaits them, neither should the democracies shy away from using military force where clearly it is called for and it can be dispatched with relatively low cost, both in treasure and blood. In 2013, the US government made it clear to the ultra-autocratic Syrian regime that use by Damascus of chemical weapons against its own people would be a redline for Washington and would result in a military response by the US armed forces. When the Assad dictatorship nevertheless dropped chemical bombs on its own people, the Obama administration failed to follow through on its prior redline warning. This was a major mistake, and gave the Syrian dictator even more rein to sow deplorable violence on his own people.

RESILIENT DIGITAL DEMOCRACIES

One of the great strengths of democracies is their openness. That very openness, alas, is also one of their principal weaknesses. The openness allows the autocracies to pump social media into the democracies that is full of disinformation. The Mueller report described in great detail how Internet troll farms in Russia conducted a concerted campaign to undermine the 2016 elections in the US. Moreover, the quality of the disinformation propagated by the autocracies is getting increasingly more sophisticated. The Mueller report makes the point that many of the messages from the disinformationists didn't simply say "vote for Trump." (Putin did not want Hillary Clinton to win the election, as she was very tough on the autocrats, especially him, when she was US secretary of state.) The tactics of the autocrats on social media are more devious, but highly effective. A Russian operator would sign up to, say, a Facebook group, and over the course of months he would slowly, but surely, insert messages into the conversation that turned members of the group very anti–Hillary Clinton. What can be done about this and related problems where the autocrats, as a core strategy of Cold War 2.0, steadily work to undermine democracy in the digital space of the United States, Canada, and other democracies?

One answer is not to become a closed society (as autocracies are doing), but rather to remain open, but then to become very resilient. Two avenues compel themselves. First, the social media companies must step up and delete social media accounts of the most obvious nefarious foreign agents. They have started to do this, but much more effort has to be expended on this. The social media companies in the democracies have significant financial resources, and more of that wealth, generated from their online services (including related advertising), has to be reinvested in making them safer.

An interesting analogy can be drawn with the meat processing industry 120 years ago. When they were first operating in America, large, unhygienic meat factories shipped a great deal of tainted meat.[7] Many consumers of this bad meat were getting sick, and some were dying. The government finally decided to step in and impose standards on the meat-packers, coupled with inspections of their operations by government regulators. The meat processors responded that it was unreasonable on the part of the government—simply too onerous—to require that no meat leaving the plants could be tainted. The government remained firm. It effectively said, "If you are making profit from a slice of meat leaving your plant, you have to make sure no one eating it will get sick from it." Within a few years, the US meat-packing industry cleaned up its act, and the rate of sickness and death from tainted meat dropped dramatically. Today, tainted meat in the US consumer market is very rare indeed. This is what needs to be done with disinformation. American social media companies are very profitable. Apple, Google, Meta, and Microsoft together had combined profits of $255.7 billion in 2022.[8] Clearly, more of these earnings must be reinvested in the safety of their products or services.

Governments in the democracies, including through their schools, colleges, and universities, must also educate their public to identify and handle disinformation. To push the meat analogy a little further, when a consumer is shopping for a steak or a pork chop at the grocery store, they need to be able to spot at least the visible signs of tainted meat by taking a good hard look at the package they take out of the cooler. Is it discolored in any way? Is it past its best-before date? Does the cellophane wrapping have a rip in it? Yes, the meat processor, and the grocery store must take their measures as well, but so should the consumer. With disinformation, there are many artificial intelligence filters that need to be applied by social media companies to remove problematic accounts and false or problematic content. Certain sophisticated disinformation has to be reviewed by human content moderators employed by these companies. Still, some disinformation will get through these filters, and that's why a discerning content-consuming public is required as well.

Taiwan and Estonia are democracies that have been particularly successful at educating their citizens about disinformation. Both live beside huge autocracies that deluge their smaller neighbors with waves of problematic messages over the Internet, as well as large-volume hacking and malware attacks. Taiwan and Estonia have done a good job of defending their computer systems against the professional hackers that China and Russia, respectively, either employ, enable, or condone. Estonia's expertise has been recognized by having it host NATO's permanent anti-disinformation and cyber-hacking center. Impressively, Taiwan and Estonia have also coached their citizenry, including children, to recognize disinformation so they are not as easily duped as millions of citizens are in other democracies. All students in elementary and secondary school in all democracies should be taken through the training that these two countries give their students. It is important that the democracies inoculate their people at a young age against pernicious social media tactics and other software-based attacks on their country, including the various ways that autocracies try to debase the truth. In Cold War 2.0 all the citizens of the democracies are frontline troops in the struggle against disinformation and weapons of hacking destruction, and citizens of all ages need to be given the proper weapons and training so they become resilient against them.

There is a further challenge for the democracies in the digital world of disinformation dissemination: high-quality journalism must be saved in many information markets, especially some cities and smaller centers where currently there simply is no local journalism. Different funding models need to be explored, and they may well include some financial assistance from the social media companies calibrated to the number of users they have in any given region, particularly if its efforts at minimizing disinformation are not working very well. In that case, the more money the social media platform makes from the disinformation the more it should pay to fund independent journalism in that region, so that at least some of the worst effects of the disinformation that it enables can be countered by the high-quality journalism (which presumably would be made available for citizens in the region at no cost rather than only behind a forbidding paywall).

STANDARDS OF DEMOCRACY:
TECHNOLOGY REGULATION

The four accelerator technologies profiled in chapters 5 to 8 are so powerful that their use, and certain aspects of their development, will require some government regulation and oversight. For example, the owner of a concert venue in New York City is using facial recognition software to ban entry to people to events simply because the owner doesn't like them.[9] This, and similar use of digital technology that offends a broad sense of morality and ethics in the democracies, must be regulated. How this is done in the democracies will be very different from how it is attempted in the autocracies. Importantly, the mechanisms employed in the democracies for ensuring suitable protection of the public through regulation must be sensitive to the dynamic of competitive displacement. Regulations must not become barriers to entry that make it practically impossible for smaller, late-to-the-game "improvers" from competing against larger "first movers" in the marketplace. When large tech companies with virtual monopolies in the marketplace lobby governments for specific types of regulation, proponents of open markets should start to worry.

Mindful of the foregoing admonition about the need to regulate carefully, three sets of rules should be contemplated. First, the democracies need a privacy law that protects the reasonable expectations of users of technology regarding their own personal information, whether provided for some online transaction, or collected by a service supplier as part of a service or product, or provided to a medical center as part of a biotech procedure, just to name three of the literally hundreds of ways personal information is increasingly being collected, stored, used, and shared in a modern tech-oriented society.

The democracies around the world now have enough experience with privacy and technology that under the auspices of the OECD all the democracies should come together and agree on a single format for such a privacy law. The starting point would likely be the European Union's privacy rules, the so-called General Data Privacy Regulation (GDPR) as they have been adopted by all twenty-seven countries of the EU, but then they would be tailored to allow the United States, Canada, and other democracies to adopt them as well. The result would be a single set of common privacy laws that would apply wherever an individual happens to interact with an online or offline service based in a democracy. The law's enforcement, though, would be done locally by the data privacy regulator in that specific country.

Two other laws would be required, one for artificial intelligence (AI) and one for biotechnology (BT). The privacy aspects of these two domains would be governed by the privacy law discussed in the previous paragraph. Several other laws found generally in democracies that set out norms of behavior for the entire society would also cover these two technologies. For example, suppliers of products and services who advertise to consumers cannot make false claims for their offerings. This general law would already apply if a merchant used an AI that wrote a misleading advertisement.

The specific laws for AI and BT, by contrast, would address risk aspects unique to these two novel domains of technology. On AI, the European Parliament is ahead of the rest of the democracies in this regard and as of June 2023 adopted legislation on AI that regulates with a fairly light touch, at least initially, and only those AI applications that present material risk to users or the public at large. The logic here is that it makes a big difference whether the AI software is being used to generate fan fiction among a club of writers (a low-risk activity), or if it is being used to fly a plane in autonomous mode without a human pilot (high-risk). Only the latter software would have to go through rigorous testing, and possibly even certification, before it is allowed to be released into the stream of commerce.

A similar risk-based approach could be taken relative to BT, but presumably just about any BT application that touched human health would have to be preapproved by a regulatory body for at least safety and possibly efficacy (like pharmaceutical drugs), especially if its supplier would be making claims about the ability of the BT to achieve specific medical results. Services related to human reproduction, especially anything along the lines of an artificial uterus, would require very extensive testing by the relevant government medical device regulatory agency. The ectogenesis machine will also attract broader scrutiny. For example, the prospective parents of the EGM baby might be screened for "suitability," just as if they were parents adopting a child, but there is a counterargument as well, given that "natural parents" are not screened in such a manner. There is some precedent to build on here in the medical field when it comes to ethics for in vitro fertilization, but there will also be some uncharted territory to explore in respect of EGM babies, in which case revisiting "the first principles of democracy" will be important.

Most contentious will be the rules surrounding "designer babies." There might be the threshold issue whether the particular democracy even wants to allow prospective parents to have the option of requesting the health care system to attempt genetic changes that could impact personal traits, particularly if they can only be effected in a manner that makes them inheritable. Assuming the answer is in the affirmative, the really heavy ethical lifting will be to scope out the parameters of what traits are permitted to be modified and which are not. This area will be contentious, for sure, but the way democracies approach these questions will be superior to that adopted by the autocracies, at least in terms of matching technological progress with human values and ethics at each phase of the scientific/ technological journey.

The goal with these three legal regimes is to construct for the new technologies of the Cold War 2.0 era a set of values, ethics, and norms that people in democracies will be comfortable with and proud of. These "Standards of Democracy" technology norms will be consistent with the underlying principles of democracy itself: the importance of significant input from everyday citizens in their formulation, the role of personal freedom, the operation of the rule of law, and press and media scrutiny as the process unfolds, to name some of the major ones. The objective is to build in each democracy a consensus in the big middle of the social spectrum; presumably persons at the two margins will not be able to be accommodated. (Some left-wing pundits will argue for a complete ban on the particular activity, and some right-wing pundits will argue for "anything goes.") The sensible middle ideally will result in "moving ahead steadily, but always working to minimize unreasonable risks and personal and social harm."

This prudent approach to mitigating technology risk with sensible ethical norms should become the hallmark of technology innovation and deployment in an advanced democracy throughout Cold War 2.0. If designed and managed with standards of democracy always animating the exercise, it will be far more attractive to individuals exposed to these new technologies than what is on offer in the autocracies, namely anything goes that a particular enabler is capable of sliding past the autocrat on any particular day. Over time, the superior culture for developing *and regulating* technological progress in the democracies will prove itself, particularly as the technological horror stories seep out of the autocracies. This distinction, between technology regulation in the democracies that assists people in their daily lives, as opposed to the less humane technology environment in the autocracies, will be an important positive differentiator of the democracies in Cold War 2.0.

STANDARDS OF DEMOCRACY:
IMMIGRATION

Democracies derive strength from openness. This is true across many fronts, including open debate and criticism (this is why freedom of speech and press are so important) and an open market economy that allows competitive displacement to flourish. A further area where openness is of paramount importance is immigration, combined with proper controls and rules.

Openness always has limits. Freedom of speech does not include shouting "fire" maliciously in a packed theater when there is no actual fire. The open economy operates in an environment of public regulation that establishes rules that all business owners must observe concerning employment, protection of the environment, the payment of taxes, etc. Likewise for immigration. Each democracy requires a firm border, and entry into the democracy is not a right. The border, though, must also have gates through which certain people (including bona fide refugees, entrepreneurs, and other designated categories of legal immigrants) can pass, if and when they qualify, as determined by the rule of law. Immigrants, like all citizens of democracies, also have obligations and duties, one of which should be to relinquish their former citizenship when they become citizens of their newly adopted country (i.e., dual citizenship should not be allowed in democracies).

Democracies profit immensely from immigration. This is particularly true in the domain of high-tech innovation, for the simple reason that literally hundreds of perspectives on science and technology are required to achieve broad progress across today's multitude of disciplines in modern science and technology. This is certainly true in the domains of the four accelerator technologies (artificial intelligence, semiconductor chips, quantum computers, and biotechnology). Considering the computer industry for a moment, it is a stunning reminder of the value of immigration that the current CEOs of IBM, Google, and Microsoft were each born in India. Or, going back to the invention of the semiconductor chip (SC), consider that the MOSFET (metal-oxide semiconductor field-effect transistor) version of the SC, the one most commonly used currently, was invented by Mohamed Martin Atalla and David Kahng in 1959. Atalla was born, raised, and received his first degree in Egypt, and then went to the United States for graduate work at Purdue. He then joined Bell Labs, where with Kahng, he invented the MOSFET in 1959. As for Kahng, he was born, raised, and earned his first degree in South Korea, immigrated to the United States, where he earned his doctorate in 1959 from Ohio State University, then joined Bell Labs, where he collaborated with fellow first-generation American Atalla.

The list of immigrant contributors to American technology supremacy is a long one. Kahng later invented the floating-gate MOSFET with Simon Min Sze, who was born in Nanjing, raised in Taiwan, and educated at the National University of Taiwan; immigrated to the US for his masters degree in 1960 at Washington State and doctorate in 1963 at Stanford; and then joined Bell Labs, where he collaborated with Kahng. Or consider David K. Lam, who made his immense contribution in another phase of the SC value chain. Lam was born in China; his family moved to Vietnam and then to Hong Kong. As a student Lam moved to Canada to attend the University of Toronto (engineering physics, 1967), then on to MIT in Boston for his masters and doctorate. He worked at Texas Instruments and Hewlett-Packard before striking out on his own, founding Lam Research Corporation in 1980, which went public in 1984 and today is one of the world's leading producers of etching machines used for making high-end SCs. It is also the second-largest manufacturing company in the San Francisco Bay Area after Tesla. And speaking of Tesla, Elon Musk was born in South Africa, spent a couple of years as an undergrad in Canada at Queen's University, then on to MIT, and then Tesla, SpaceX, Starlink, Neurogenesis, Twitter, etc., etc.

All democracies, not only the United States, benefit hugely from immigration. With respect to AI, Geoffrey Hinton is a professor at the University of Toronto and is often referred to as the founder of the current model of AI technology. He was born in the United Kingdom and emigrated to Canada in 1987. Or consider the two key principal researchers who developed mRNA vaccine, Ugur Sahin (who was born in Turkey) and Özlem Türeci, born in Germany but whose father had immigrated to Germany from Turkey. Drs. Sahin and Türeci's company BioNTech developed the leading mRNA vaccine for the COVID-19 virus, then did a deal with Albert Bourla (a Greek immigrant living in the United States and CEO of the pharmaceutical giant Pfizer) to distribute BioNTech's vaccines worldwide.[10] The fact that Sahin and Türeci are of Turkish origin and Bourla is of Greek origin is somewhat ironic because of the historic enmity between Turkey and Greece. The joint venture between BioNTech and Pfizer illustrates what wonderful collaboration can happen in a democracy when people look forward to a bright future aware of but not mired in the dark moments of the past.

This list could go on for an entire book of its own, focusing just on immigrants to the democracies in the tech sector. I'm particularly sensitive to this open dynamic because in Toronto, 50 percent of residents were born outside of Canada. Currently, with a population of just over 40 million, Canada is taking in 500,000 immigrants a year. About 10 percent of the newcomers are refugees, and the rest come in under a very discerning system where potential applicants have to meet specific criteria. They are allotted "points" for different skills and attributes, and they have to achieve a certain point level to be considered for entry. Another route is to come to Canada as a university graduate student (like Atalla, Kahng, and Lam mentioned above, vis-à-vis the United States). Then, if the student is successful, they can apply to remain in Canada permanently, and eventually apply for citizenship.

Some newcomers find themselves in the new world because of romance. Tobi Lütke met his future Canadian wife while the two were snowboarding in Europe. He followed her back to Ottawa, where she lived. He started making snowboards, and when he went to sell them on the Internet he found that there really wasn't an easy way to do that, so he developed some e-commerce software himself. After a while he noticed other merchants had an interest in using his software, and he started selling the software instead of snowboards. Today, his company Shopify has sales over $5 billion and a market capitalization of $82 billion. Toby and his wife still live in Ottawa, and they still enjoy snowboarding.

While controlled immigration under a rules-based system is a true asset and strength of democracies, very large-scale uncontrolled economic migration is not. It is simply not viable to have an unlimited number of migrants approach the gate and force entry without any limits, vetting, or controls. Democracies do themselves and their citizens a disservice if they allow this sort of mass immigration. At the same time, with low fertility rates and declining populations, most democracies will require significant levels of immigration across a broad range of people with very diverse skills, including personal support workers for the health care system, construction workers, service workers, and technology entrepreneurs as previously high-lighted. Still, democracies must be on the lookout for autocracies that try to destabilize democracies by encouraging illegal migrants to flood into one or other democracy, as when Belarus's autocratic leader flew migrants from the Middle East into Belarus only to then force them to cross into Poland (a democracy), in an effort to cause political tension within a neighboring country. This is one of the more outlandish geopolitical tactics used by an autocrat in Cold War 2.0.

At the same time, the inability of autocracies to be open and inviting to potential newcomers is a huge handicap for them. The unwillingness of China and Russia to explore meaningful levels of immigration as a response to their declining population numbers will eventually impact their economies significantly. Already millions of job vacancies are going unfilled in both countries. They might consider the ectogenesis machine (EGM) concept, but at best that technology is ten years away, and then the early EGM cohorts would not appear in the workforce for another twenty years; between now and then the population declines in both countries will be severe. Controlled, planned immigration is the only immediate to midterm solution for them, short of forcing on women a totalitarian *Handmaid's Tale*-type fertility system,[11] but presumably even the autocracies will find that a nonstarter. But then many people in democracies thought another major land war for territory in Europe was unthinkable, too, and then Russia invaded Ukraine. Therefore, the ability to craft immigration systems that work both for immigrants and host countries will be a net plus for the democracies in Cold War 2.0, so long as governments in the democracies approach immigration with resolve, compassion, and a rules-based system of selection, screening, and entry.

DEMOCRACY DAY

Democracies have any number of major public holidays, where some form of remembrance is celebrated by giving the populace a day off work, typically a Monday or a Friday, so that people get a three-day weekend. Thanksgiving, Memorial Day, and Labor Day are good examples in the US. There are many others. In the UK they are called "bank holidays." There will be a number of new ones made over the next decade or so as the workweek continues to shrink—perhaps one of the finer benefits of enhanced productivity brought about by the deployment of enterprise-level AI in the economy. One of those new Fridays or Monday holidays should be designated "Democracy Day." Or, better yet, and showing some urgency, why not relabel New Year's Day as Democracy Day? After all, what is the point of calling the first day of the new year New Year's Day? Sounds like it is just stating the obvious. Feels like this day is just waiting to be rechristened to a moniker of more import.

The United Nations has dozens of "international days" designated by the General Assembly. [12] June alone has thirty of them, including Global Day of Parents (June 1), International Day of Yoga (June 21), and International Asteroid Day (June 30). The UN celebrates International Day of Democracy on September 15 each year. As with so many other things emanating from the UN, the intent is laudable, but the execution is poor. That day needs to be repositioned as a real holiday, and some excellent, meaningful programming should be created to commemorate and reinforce a foundational institution. It will also highlight a deep asymmetrical advantage of the democracies over the autocracies. Presumably not even Putin and Xi, as brazen as they are, will rev up a holiday called Autocracy Day.

If New Year's Day were rebranded, not much would happen on the morning of Democracy Day given the revelry from the night before. A Democracy Day brunch, though, would generally kick off the day's activities. There is nothing like sharing a marvelous meal with friends and family, and then weaving in some discussion about what makes democracy special, and what the current threats are to the continued vibrancy, perhaps even survival, of our greatest political institution and its many necessary constituent components, like freedom of expression, freedom of the press (including the protection of journalists), and the rule of law (including the independence of judges). For the more competitive around the table, quizzes could be crafted from sources like *The Economist*'s "Global Democracy Index": name the top ten democracies in the world, which democracies fell into the "flawed democracy" category the year before, which are the top twenty (i.e., worst) autocracies in the world (spoiler alert, this all-star sublist of the most awful autocracies includes China and Russia). And so on.

If there are kids around the Democracy Day brunch table, this might be when some civic education gets imparted to them. School-based learning about democracy can be a hit-and-miss thing. Simple but thoughtful booklets aimed at children could be circulated by their school or the local government. Reading these together after brunch would be a good way to spend thirty minutes. Democracies don't do enough (anything?) to commemorate the heroes of democracy, past and present. The democracies are all in Cold War 2.0 together. It would be a good idea to get everyone in a democracy up to speed as to why it's a contest worth fighting, and winning.

THE AUTOCRATS AMONG US

Sadly, not all leaders in democracies are committed to the ideals of democracy. Some of them actually would prefer to be autocrats themselves. A prime recent example of an autocrat within a democracy is former US president Donald Trump. In or out of the White House, he never cared for the rule of law. Many of Trump's actions showed little or no regard or respect for the United States Constitution, although at his inauguration as the 45th president of the United States on January 20, 2017, he swore an oath to uphold it. His contempt for democracy and its norms and rules became apparent early in the primaries for the Republican nominee for president in 2016. Trump was asked to disclose his tax records, as has been customary in US presidential electoral politics in the previous fifty years, and as all other Republican primary candidates had done in 2016. Trump refused to do so, and he never did disclose them voluntarily. Later, as the GOP's nominee for president, he was asked in one of the candidate debates whether, if he lost the election, he would accept the result. He said he wasn't sure, thereby putting in doubt one of the most sacred practices in democracies, the peaceful transition of power.

A similar autocratic posture was repeated when, as president, he was running for reelection in 2020. He crafted a canny autocratic narrative, arguing that the only way his opponent could win is if there was election fraud, and when he clearly lost the vote, voilà, he rolled out the big lie, that the election had been stolen from him. This was an incredibly brazen move, and one that shook the American democratic system to its core. If voters do not believe their election was run fairly, then the legitimacy of the entire system of democracy can come into question. It was telling that in the sixty court cases that Trump's team brought alleging voter fraud, they were not successful in a single one. Judge after judge threw out the fabricated claims for a complete lack of evidence. And still, even after sixty defeats in court, Trump continued to appeal to his base, propagating the big lie that the election was stolen, and asking for money. Between his election day loss in November 2020 and the removal of his account from Twitter (for inciting the attack on the US Capitol on January 6, 2021), Trump raised a total of $200 million from his malleable fans who, it seems, would believe anything spouting from Trump's mouth or social media posts.[13]

Trump's encouragement of members of his base to attack the Capitol on January 6, 2021, and his other efforts to subvert the election of 2020 are the clearest evidence of his autocratic tendencies. Trump kept insisting that Vice President Mike Pence overturn the election results in a few states, and thus allow the House of Representatives to vote to retain Trump in power. Thankfully, Pence had the backbone to stand up to this craven attempt at an autocratic coup. A week earlier, another politician, Brad Raffensperger, the Georgia secretary of state, also showed great courage in the face of enormous pressure from Trump and threats (including against his life from Trump supporters). Trump lost the electoral college vote in Georgia by about 11,000 votes. On January 2, 2021, in what is now an infamous telephone call, Trump was recorded demanding of Raffensperger, who had overall responsibility for the conduct of the presidential election in Georgia (including recounts), "I just want to find 11,780 votes." To his great credit, Raffensperger refused to give in to Trump's illegal demands; he subsequently also ran successfully for reelection against another candidate strongly endorsed by Trump. His rationale for running again and having to put up with threats to his life: "If the good walk off the field and leave the field to the bad, then the bad wins."[14] This statement sums up the courage required of people when they stand up to the autocrats among us.

What then should have happened to prevent Trump's autocratic attack on the US electoral process and democracy more broadly? Right at the very beginning, during the 2016 primaries, when Trump didn't release his tax returns voluntarily, the Republican Party should have insisted he do so. If he continued to refuse, he should not have been allowed to continue in the Republican Party contest. The GOP should have kept his name off primary ballots. Likewise, in the 2020 election, once Trump exhausted his sixty legal challenges, and it was crystal clear there was no fraud at the level Trump was arguing (i.e., enough to change the outcome of the election), Twitter and all other social media should have terminated his accounts right then and there if he continued perpetrating what at that point was clearly a massive fraud. (His lawyer for a number of these cases has since been censured by a Colorado judge after she admitted to making false claims in these cases—she said they could show there was fraud in the election results when the Trump legal team knew there was no such fraud.)[15] Equally, Trump should have been prevented by the legal process, presumably criminal prosecution, from raising money based on a fraudulent claim that he now (after the results of the court cases) knew to be false. At that point, his continuing to spout lies about his losing the election through fraud should have been dealt with as the Department of Justice and Federal Trade Commission deal with any other misrepresentation used to make money: prosecute the con man for earning money on the strength of false claims.

At the same time, the Republican Party leadership should have come out loud and clear to condemn Trump and deliver him into the custody of Washington, DC police. When the full history of the Trump presidency and the 2020 election is written, including the dangerous and disgraceful attack on the US Capitol, a significant portion of the blame will be heaped upon the leadership of the Republican Party. Leaders like Mitch McConnell and Lindsey Graham will be judged as "enablers," men who refused to stand up and push back on the autocrat. We have seen this movie before. There was a coterie of businesspeople and other respectable establishment figures in Germany who thought Adolf Hitler would serve as a useful implementer of many of the objectives of the enablers. And Trump did deliver a massive tax cut for McConnell, Graham, and the other Republican Party stalwarts. Then, as happened with Hitler, the GOP grandees lost control of Trump, and unconstrained, he nearly single-handedly brought down the federal government system in the United States. Next time when an autocrat or a would-be autocrat appears on the US scene, those of both parties who believe in democracy must step up and fight for immediate expulsion of the would-be autocrat. Luckily Joe Biden's winning margin in 2020 was sizeable enough to dissuade most GOP foot soldiers from joining the insurrection; will the US be so lucky next time?

The Democratic Party became seized with a somewhat similar problem when Robert Kennedy Jr. entered that party's primary race in June 2023. Kennedy's basis for running is his belief in a series of conspiracy theories that he peddles on social media.[16] Many of these theories have been debunked, such that Instagram had deplatformed him. The Democratic Party should do the same. Kennedy can run for president as a third-party candidate, but the Democratic Party should not allow candidates whose primary occupation is to traffic in disinformation to do so under the Democratic Party banner.

THE APPEASERS AMONG US

Trump shows his autocratic tendencies in many different ways. In the 2024 primaries for the Republican Party nomination for president, Trump is calling for the United States to stop providing assistance to Ukraine, which country, having been the victim of a heinous invasion by the Russians, is fighting for its very existence. Although Ukraine receives assistance from some fifty nations, the military equipment and financial support from the United States is key, and without it Ukraine would have ceased to exist in the spring of 2022. Trump is of the view that this support for Ukraine serves no American interest, and that, effectively, Putin can have his sphere of influence in the countries surrounding Russia even if it means extinguishing a democracy of 38 million people to get it. The other leading candidate in these Republican primaries, Florida governor Ron DeSantis, echoes this Trumpian view, and then goes even further. In a statement DeSantis released in March 2023, he argued that Russia's war in Ukraine was simply about a "territorial dispute." In sync with Trump, DeSantis argues there is simply no American interest served by supporting Ukraine.

This position of these two candidates for the Republican nomination for the presidential election in November 2024 is reminiscent of the way two great democracies of the 1930s, namely France and the United Kingdom, tried to deal with the autocrat extraordinaire of the day, Adolf Hitler. Hitler came to power legally in Germany in an election in 1933; but once in power, he immediately went about dismantling the checks and balances first of the German state, and then of the European security system. By 1936, Hitler's autocratic powers within Germany were virtually complete. He then proceeded to take over Austria, and then parts of Czechoslovakia. The French and British governments were terrified of what Hitler was doing, and they met with him in March 1938. They got Hitler to sign a written agreement that after digesting Czechoslovakia, the Nazi leader would pursue no further designs on his neighbors. British prime minister Neville Chamberlain thought this a great result, and when he returned to England he proudly waved the document signed by Hitler in front of the press and stated that he (Chamberlain) had secured "peace in our time."

Chamberlain was (understandably) channeling a huge desire on the part of the people in Europe (outside of Germany) to avoid a war in Europe, which would actually be *another war*, given that essentially the same nations had been engulfed in World War I just twenty years previous. (That war was referred to at the time as the "war to end all wars" because it was so horrendous, with some 10 million soldiers having died fighting in it.) Chamberlain was hailed as a hero for negotiating a deal that would (apparently) keep Hitler in his place. As events would later prove, Chamberlain was fundamentally wrong about Hitler, who proceeded to invade first Poland, then France, and then bombed England and a dozen other countries in Europe before the end of 1940. This new war, World War II, would ultimately claim the lives of 70 million people. So much for "peace in out time."

Autocrats like Hitler, and today Putin and Xi, know that their success in growing their physical empire, and imposing their autocratic regime on others, relies heavily on there being plenty of appeasers talking up "peace in out time" within the democracies. If the appeaser comes to power, then the autocrats can easily bully him into a bad deal because politicians like Chamberlain, and Trump and DeSantis today, are willing to trade away the political independence and freedom of a small democracy such as Ukraine (like a sacrificial offering of tribute to the autocrat) in return for getting a plush position in the new order. Therefore, if the democracies don't support Ukraine now in defending themselves against the Russians, Putin will continue his crazed plan to rebuild the Russian Empire, country by conquered country, even though decades ago all relevant parties signed agreements confirming the various former republics of the Soviet Union (including Ukraine, Moldova, Belarus, Estonia, Latvia, and Lithuania) were independent countries with inviolable borders.

As for what the Chinese think about peace agreements, treaties, and other niceties of democracies like the rule of law, in April 2023 the Chinese ambassador to France Lu Shaye was interviewed on French television. In response to the question whether he thought the Crimean peninsula was wrongfully annexed in 2014—when Russian troops forcefully yanked it from Ukraine, and since then populated it with 600,000 Russian colonists—the ambassador replied that not only did Crimea belong to Russia, but all the territories of the "new" countries created back in 1989–1991 out of Soviet Russia were not recognized in international law, and hence they were open to having Russia retake them, presumably by force, as Putin was doing with Ukraine. It was astounding to see the mask slip just for a moment and to see the real, visceral view of the world as exercised by the autocrats: "We can basically do anything we want because we are stronger than you." In effect, the appeasers among the democracies who supported Putin's false narrative that the Baltic states should never have been allowed to join NATO should finally have the scales fall from their eyes. These three countries (Latvia, Estonia, and Lithuania), Poland, Hungary, East Germany, Czechoslovakia, Bulgaria, Romania, and most recently Finland, in 2023, have joined NATO because it is only through collective self-defense that the democracies can keep the rapacious autocrats at bay, including Xi Jinping, the boss of Ambassador Lu Shaye, when he looks to extend the Chinese empire to include the small island of Taiwan.

From a practical perspective, the narrow answer to Trump and DeSantis and others of their ilk of appeasement is that if the United States and the forty-nine other democracies stopped supporting their fellow democracy, Ukraine, then no democracy on earth would be safe from the rapacious appetites of Russia and China, least of all Taiwan. In essence, the fight against the autocracies in Ukraine, in Taiwan, in the South China Sea, in Xinjiang (against China's using sophisticated technology to oppress the Uighurs), against Chinese geopolitical and economic coercion, and the many other violations that the autocracies make against the rules-based international order are certainly matters for all democracies to take very seriously. It's why the democracies are supporting Ukraine, Taiwan, and the rules-based international order wherever the autocrats start a new front in Cold War 2.0.

14

A WORLD
TECHNOLOGICALLY
DECOUPLED

I t remains, as a final task, to sketch out how a world buffeted by Cold
War 2.0 should function satisfactorily from the perspective of the democracies. In essence, the democracies would decouple some of their technology from the autocracies, but largely only for the four accelerator technologies (artificial intelligence, high-performance semiconductor chips, quantum computing, and biotechnology) and certain other important technologies. The total volume of trade impacted would be about 25 to 35 percent of the current mix of trade between the democracies and China, though there would be some broader strategic, political, and even cultural geopolitical and security implications, especially for the autocracies.

The reason for the tech decoupling is simple—the democracies should not give the autocracies the rope then used to hang the democracies. Moreover, this suspicion that the autocrats want to "hang the democracies" is reasonably held so long as the autocracies refuse to live in a global community animated by their adherence to a rules-based international order. The second rationale for tech decoupling is so that the democracies do not contribute to the technology that the autocrats use to hang their own citizens. The world's most insidious digital system of human surveillance, control, and oppression should not include AI software written in Silicon Valley or semiconductor chips designed in the United States and fabricated in Taiwan. How does Cold War 2.0 end? One of three ways. China decides to emulate Japan, South Korea, and Taiwan; becomes a responsible global citizen and a domestic democracy; and gives up its designs on Taiwan. Or China attacks Taiwan and the democracies win that war. Or the current bifurcated world of technology and innovation continues indefinitely, with the democracies enjoying an ever-superior standard of living relative to the increasingly isolated and technologically stunted autocracies. Then when Putin and Xi leave power, their successors effect economic *and* political regime change in order to catch up to the democracies.

The core framework for technological decoupling in Cold War 2.0 would operate as follows. The world would be divided into three main groups of countries. The democracies will encompass the United States, the other major democracies listed in Table 1 of chapter 10, and a number of smaller democracies. The major democracies ideally would band together into a GATO (Global Alliance Treaty Organization) or perhaps more likely they will stay somewhat more loosely associated on the world stage as they currently are, though with a strong regional NATO in Europe and an "Asian NATO" in the Pacific, called PATO (Pacific Alliance Treaty Organization). However their global or regional alliance structure unfolds, the democracies will be recognized for holding free, fair, and credible elections; upholding the rule of law, overseen by independent judges; ensuring personal political freedoms and gender and social equality; fostering a free and independent media environment; and promoting an open market economy with effective public oversight and regulation, including promoting the use of the four accelerator technologies (AI, SC, QC, and BT), and certain other technologies, in a manner consistent with human rights, consumer choice, and consumer protection (the so-called standards of democracy).

By contrast, the autocracies—principally China and Russia, but also Cuba, Iran, Nicaragua, North Korea, Saudi Arabia, Syria, and Venezuela—will continue to be identified in Cold War 2.0 by the fact that each of them has a single political party, and if they have elections at all, they are manipulated by the single political party to predictable outcomes. In autocracies there is no rule of law, the judiciary is a cog in the autocrat's social control machine, only limited personal freedoms are permitted at the whim of the autocrat, the autocrat employs thousands of state security police to keep the autocrat in power by use of force and violence, and the autocrat also relies on a state-of-the-art technological monitoring/surveillance/propaganda dissemination system (which uses AI, SCs, QC, and BT, as well as complete control over media outlets) to cement his position in power. There is no oversight of the autocrat's behavior, including whatever economic benefits he bestows upon himself and his enablers, especially the state security police and the military. The citizens for the most part accept this arrangement because the autocrat cements his legitimacy by ensuring that some of the wealth of the country will be shared sufficiently with them (through better pensions, higher minimum wages, and the like).

The third group of nations in a tech-decoupled world are the so-called nonaligned countries. Some of the nonaligned countries are democracies with some strong elements of autocratic practices, but they do not wish to join a group like GATO, or even a regional alliance of democracies, largely because they see their economic success closely bound up with autocratic China. Similarly, the autocratic nonaligned countries usually want to be closer to Russia (in order to get weapons and, often for African nations, mercenaries from Moscow) and sometimes China, but not so close as to be in a formal alliance with either of them. In effect, the nonaligned states are driven mainly by *interests* rather than *values* in their geopolitical dealings, and they are constantly looking for transactional opportunities to advance their national interests. Expect democracies and autocracies to continually bid for their favor. This is the "kasbah geopolitics" dimension of Cold War 2.0.

TECHNOLOGIES AND OTHER IMPORTANT
ASSETS—COMPOSITE SCORE TABLE

In order to understand how a global geopolitical technology decoupling would work as part of Cold War 2.0, it is first necessary to assess at the aggregate, macro level the overall technological and innovation strength of the democracies, the autocracies, and the nonaligned countries relative to the data about the various technologies referred to in chapter 5 to 8 (in terms of the accelerator technologies) and chapter 9 (in terms of the other important technologies). This is done in Table 1 below by weighting different technologies and innovation-related assets into a single, manageable "Technology—Composite Scores" schema.

TABLE 1

Technology Composite Scores	US	Other Dem	China	Russia	Non-Aligned	Total Dem	Total Auto
Artificial Intelligence (6x)	36	12	12	0	0	48	12
Semiconductor Chips (6x)	18	30	12	0	0	48	12
Quantum Computing (6x)	30	6	24	0	0	36	24
Biotechnology (6x)	24	18	12	6	0	42	18
Universities (6x)	36	18	6	0	0	54	6
Subtotal	**144**	**84**	**66**	**6**	**0**	**228**	**72**
Defense Industries (3x)	18	3	6	3	0	21	9
Nuclear Power (3x)	6	6	9	9	0	12	18
Space/Satellite (3x)	15	6	6	3	0	21	9
Cloud Computing (3x)	12	3	9	3	3	15	12
Jet Engines (3x)	15	9	3	3	0	24	6
Critical Minerals (3x)	3	9	13.5	3	7.5	12	16.5
Subtotal	**69**	**36**	**48.5**	**24**	**10.5**	**105**	**72.5**
Fusion Power (1x)	8	1	1	0	0	9	1
Telecom	3	3	4	4	0	6	8

Internet Platforms (1x)	6	0	4	0	0	6	4
Software (1x)	7	2	1	0	0	9	2
IT Services (1x)	5	2	2	0	1	7	2
Automobiles (1x)	3	5	3	0	0	8	3
Shipbuilders (1x)	1	5	4	0	0	6	4
Commercial Aircraft (1x)	4	4	1	.5	.5	8	1.5
Robotics (1x)	2	7	1	0	0	9	1
Financial Services (1x)	5	2	2	1	1	7	3
Subtotal	**44**	**31**	**23**	**5.5**	**2.5**	**75**	**29.5**
Total	**257**	**151**	**137.5**	**35.5**	**13**	**408**	**174**

These figures track the categories of technologies and other items in chapters 5 to 9, and then apply some weightings. The accelerator technologies and the university rankings are worth six times more than the next category of important technologies, which in turn are weighted three times more heavily than the final group of technologies. Then through the exercise of additional judgment, final figures are given to each item, which are then multiplied by the weightings to achieve the composite scores. It's not rocket science, and some readers will quibble about the respective weightings assigned to various line items, but the overall conclusion is sound (even if some figures are adjusted, etc.): the United States alone is materially stronger than China when it comes to technology and innovation, and if the US and the other leading democracies are taken together, then their collective advantage over China and Russia increases dramatically (i.e., the democracies together wield more than twice the technological/innovation heft of China/Russia, 366 to 154.5). Some lesser takeaways are also important, including that the technology/innovation assets of the nonaligned countries, and even Russia, are very modest indeed.

For the foreseeable future the democracies will be the center of gravity for technology and innovation in the world. China will make important discoveries as well, but not nearly of the quantity or especially quality as will come from the universities, companies, and research institutes located in the democracies. If there will be efficient fusion energy or workable high-energy beam weapons in the next twenty years, as well as cures for cancer, dementia, and diabetes, these game-changing advances in innovation will be made in the democracies and not the autocracies. Moreover, the lead that the democracies currently have over the autocracies will not be relinquished any time soon. Bottom line: the democracies will be the primary engine of technological progress in the world. The democracies, through their open economies that allow competitive displacement to work its productivity enhancing magic, also will be able to benefit from these innovations far more than the autocracies. The democracies also are more adept at transforming these paradigm-changing technologies into instruments of military power, an exercise that enough democracies—and especially the United States—are willing to fund with a material portion of their surplus national wealth to produce the leading weapons of our time. This conclusion, and the figures found in the table above, make clear what the democracies have to do in Cold War 2.0 to effect a sensible strategy of decoupling technologically from China.

THE CENTRAL ROLE OF THE AMERICAN DEMOCRACY

Before discussing technology decoupling in some detail, it must first be acknowledged that while generally the following talks in terms of "the democracies," one simply cannot meaningfully discuss the strengths (and weaknesses) of the democracies without first analyzing the prime position of the United States in the constellation of democracies. As seen in Table 1 above, the United States plays the central, leading role among the democracies when it comes to innovation and technology development. The American secret sauce begins with its world-beating universities. These institutions then attract the world's smartest people, both domestically (from a US population of 330 million, which is large by global standards) and, very importantly, internationally. In the contest that is Cold War 2.0, the US doesn't need to have a population of 1.4 billion like each of the two most populous countries on earth if, at the end of the day, it attracts the best and brightest 200,000 non–US university STEM undergraduates every year to US universities where they will pursue graduate degrees, most of whom who will then stay on and become US citizens.

The other ingredient in the American secret sauce of innovation and technology development is the outsize role of private investment, in particular venture capital and private equity investment directed by people who are deeply versed in science and engineering, and who have previously operated entrepreneurial companies themselves. The biggest shortcoming in the Chinese model of technology development is the oversize role of government in the funding of early- and mid-stage technology companies. Public bureaucrats, especially ones beholden to an autocratic system of political power, are unable to make sufficiently knowledgeable capital allocation decisions for an entire sector such as artificial intelligence, high-performance semiconductor chips, quantum computers, and biotechnology; even if they could, they dare not allow the dynamic of competitive displacement to operate as it would bring down on them the wrath of incumbent investors, mainly regional governments that have forked out billions of dollars on the old technology and are anxiously waiting for solid returns from it. Governments and agencies also give some financial support to technology companies in the US, but typically these funds are used only to *amplify* private investment decisions, and not to make the core, threshold technological and business model decisions regarding the direction and pace of development, and funding, of a particular promising innovation initiative.

The distinction between the American innovation funding model and the autocratic one was striking during the last three decades of Cold War 1, especially in the domain of computers. The Soviet Russian model of tech development finally collapsed in a great heap in the late 1970s and early 1980s, leading to the demise of the entire regime a short time later. The Chinese, especially under supreme leader Deng Xiaoping, remedied some of the failings of the autocratic economic model after Mao Zedong's death. While these changes resulted in a fairly low-tech economic unleashing that was still quite extraordinary in its macro effect (pulling hundreds of millions of Chinese out of poverty), for the most part the resulting investment and operational model for doing innovation and technology development in China was still too government oriented, too top-down, and too dependent on scientists and technology entrepreneurs currying favor with the autocrat and his coterie of enablers—including regional "princes" of the CCP, who to this day play an important role in handing out all sorts of subsidies to tech companies, but who typically have never actually run a high-tech company before. The dramatic failure of China's "Big Fund I" to finance and develop meaningful high-end semiconductor manufacturing equipment makers in China that could make up for today's embargo of such machines from the democracies is the ultimate example of this failure, but by no means the only one.

The exceptional American funding and development model for innovation has allowed the United States to create by far the wealthiest country in the world. This national economic preeminence then allows the US to play the other critical American geopolitical role, which is to fund, sustain, and deploy internationally a military that is large and extremely technologically driven. The US defense budget dwarfs all others in the world. This in turn allows the US to provide vast amounts of business to the five largest defense contractors in the world, all of whom, importantly, are private sector players. These US companies dwarf the five largest Chinese defense contractors, all of whom are publicly owned, and Russia's defense contractors are smaller still. It is no wonder that dozens of countries look to the United States for technological and innovation leadership in the military sphere. This trend, an important element in Cold War 2.0, will only accelerate given that Russia has displayed its incompetence on the battlefield in Ukraine, including when its hypersonic missiles, which Putin previously said were invincible, were in fact routinely shot down by America's Patriot antimissile system over Ukraine in 2023. (It appeared that some of the missile's inventors were arrested for treason partly as a result, because every such setback in an autocracy requires a scapegoat.)[1]

Since the end of World War II, American preeminence in the technology and military domains has been accompanied by American politicians and opinion leaders generally holding a global outlook, such that American diplomats and forward-deployed military units have been the primary bulwark against autocratic regimes around the world, including during Cold War 1. The current war in Ukraine, where the world's second most powerful autocracy, Russia, is attempting to destroy a much smaller democracy, would have ended soon after Russia's full-scale invasion in February 2022 but for American leadership in rallying NATO partners to supply weapons and a financial lifeline to Ukraine—by far the biggest portion of which has come from the United States itself. Without the US, there would not be an independent Ukraine today. A similar narrative has unfolded in the Pacific region. Without US support for Taiwan, a small democracy menaced by the world's leading autocracy, the island nation just off the coast of China would have long ago been swallowed by its huge mainland neighbor. Bottom line, there is no path to a soft landing in Cold War 2.0 without the United States playing a major leadership role. Indeed, without US engagement in Europe and Asia, Cold War 2.0 has a very different, and likely very bleak, ending for the democracies in these two regions.

Beyond Ukraine and Taiwan, though, it is astounding how central the US is to the preservation of democracies in many other regions as well. In North America, it pains me to say (because I'm Canadian), but the Liberal Canadian government has simply stopped taking defense seriously, presumably because it believes the US will defend it from the Russians and the Chinese regardless of the size of the Canadian defense budget, which is well below the NATO minimum of 2 percent of GDP. In the Middle East, Israel's survival depends, at least in part, on the US. Even India, long the unofficial leader of the nonaligned countries, is now happy to have a closer security relationship with the US, including through the Quad (Australia, India, Japan, and the United States), given New Delhi's fraught relations with the Chinese (though there are certainly limits to India-US friendship; see below).

In Asia, the countries of Japan, South Korea, the Philippines, and Australia have asked the US to help them backstop their defense, primarily against an expansionist China. The history of the Philippines over the last twenty-five years illustrates well the crucial role of the US in helping to preserve the sovereignty of its allies in the region. In 1999 the Philippine Senate voted not to renew the leases for America's large naval (Subic Bay) and air (Clark) bases in the Philippines, and the US military effectively left the country. Seeing an opening, soon thereafter the Chinese began their assertive diplomacy in the South China Sea, including their island-building in waters clearly belonging to the Philippines. More recently, for six years the Rodrigo Duterte government cozied up to China, and numerous Chinese firms began investing in Luzon, the country's main northern island—the one that would be particularly relevant if China launched an attack on Taiwan. The current Philippine government, alarmed by China's growing influence, has reengaged with the US, and now allows the American military to use nonpermanent sites in the Philippines to store munitions, especially on Luzon, in the province of Cagayan. Unfortunately, the damage is done, as it will be difficult to dislodge the Chinese from the territorial gains it has already made in the South China Sea not far from the mainland of the Philippines. The stark reality is, no democracy in the world is currently able to stand up to China or Russia in anything approximating a military or quasi-military confrontation without having the United States firmly committed on the side of that democracy.

Beyond global security, the role of America on the world stage is critical and multifaceted. There is simply no path to a solution on global climate change without American technology, diplomacy, and money. There is no meaningful international preparation for the next global pandemic without American vaccine know-how and pharmaceutical distribution channels. There is no realistic regime of regulation of the high seas (whether for overfishing or irresponsible seabed mining) without American satellites and naval vessels. And the list goes on to include world hunger and poverty, international terrorism, and international crime. Of course, other democracies (especially those comprising the European Union) and one of the autocracies (China) have to be a part of these solutions, but only one country—the leading democracy—is indispensable to their success; the United States of America.

It is precisely because Cold War 2.0 requires the US to play such a linchpin role as the leading democracy in the world that the rise of autocratic and isolationist tendencies in the US are so disconcerting. There is no sugarcoating the immense risk. Donald Trump has said he would withdraw support from Ukraine. This would embolden Putin, cause a crisis of confidence within NATO, and cause shock waves through the foreign ministries in Seoul, Tokyo, and Canberra. If Trump wins the 2024 election, it would not come as a surprise if the president of Poland, the president of Taiwan, and the prime ministers of Japan and Australia immediately begin discussions with Britain and France to acquire nuclear weapons from them on an expedited basis.

In a perfect world, American isolationism is an option. In the wildly imperfect world that actually exists, where autocrats constantly strive to expand their physical and digital spheres of empire and oppression, American isolationism cannot become an option. In the early 1920s, after a terrible World War I, America retreated back to the Western Hemisphere and refused to join the League of Nations, not wanting to get entangled in "old world" conflicts anymore. America's departure from the world stage virtually ensured an even bloodier World War II. Thankfully, America decided to help build a world governed by a rules-based international order after World War II. The result (helped along by deterrence afforded by nuclear weapons, to be sure) has been a lasting peace among the great powers since then. It would be absolute folly for the Republican Party to try again the 1920s geopolitical strategy of isolation, especially when the world is in the midst of Cold War 2.0. Americans need to do the right thing on November 5, 2024, not just for the other democracies of the world, but for themselves.

What about Europe taking more responsibility for its own defense? Perhaps one day during Cold War 2.0, but certainly not for the next few years. The British, who now understand the threat from the autocracies very well, self-immolated when they Brexited out of the European Union.

(It is estimated Great Britain lost between 1.2 and 4.5 percent of their GDP since they left the EU.) Plus, for years they not only tolerated Russian oligarchs in "Londongrad"; they positively encouraged them to come and settle there. To be sure, since Russia's full-scale invasion of Ukraine the British have tightened their rules about Russian oligarchs buying up British assets, including football (soccer) clubs, but a lot of damage has already been done.

The Germans for decades also wore rose-colored glasses about the Russians, building not one but two gas pipelines from Russia, causing them and many others in Europe to become overly reliant on energy from the autocratic nation. The Americans warned them, and the Germans steadfastly ignored the warnings. On February 24, 2022, when Russia invaded Ukraine, the Germans were in shock. Thankfully, though, the scales have now fallen from the eyes of the Germans, and they are plowing serious tens of new billions of euros into defense. Nevertheless, it will take a number of years before Germany is ready to defend itself, let alone meaningfully help in the overall defense of Europe.

As for the French, they certainly have the military muscle. They are a nuclear-armed state—one of only two in Europe, the other being Britain. And France is part of NATO, but they like to walk a fairly idiosyncratic path. In the 1960s they were angry with the Americans and pulled out of the integrated command of NATO for a few years. Soon after Putin's invasion, France's president Emmanuel Macron made a trip to Moscow to see if a deal could be done with Putin. Putin sent him packing. In April 2023 Macron made a trip to Beijing to see if he could get Xi to bring Putin to his senses. Xi sent Macron packing, but not before Macron sold a bunch more Airbus planes to the Chinese. Which prompted Macron to tell a reporter on the way back to Paris that the Europeans would not support the Americans in their defense of Taiwan. So, the answer to the question "Can the Europeans defend themselves yet?" has to be a resounding no. For the foreseeable future the US is the indispensable military anchor of NATO. Period. This is simply one of the truths governing relations in Cold War 2.0 for the next decade or so.

TECHNOLOGICAL DECOUPLING

Before turning to what a technologically decoupled world will look like (indeed, is already looking like), it is worth recalling why Cold War 2.0 requires such a technology bifurcation in the first place. There are two main reasons. First, it has been the sensible policy of the democracies not to sell weapons and munitions to autocracies that are hostile to the democracies. This is done so that the democracies never face a situation where autocracies use weapons made in the democracies against those very democracies. Call this a policy of straightforward self-preservation. What has evolved in this policy over the decades, though, is that computer-based technologies are increasingly being embedded into weapons systems. (Recall the "dual-use" discussion, where the same high-tech device can be used for civilian or military purposes.) Therefore, the democracies currently don't just block the sale to autocracies of weapons, but also of technologies that could be integrated into weapons by the autocracies. And still some deals along these lines get through the multiple regulatory screens, as when it came to light in June 2023 that a university professor in Britain was helping an Iranian scientist with research on drones. (Remember that Iran has sold Russia hundreds of drones that have then all been launched against targets in Ukraine.) It is precisely this sort of behavior in the democracies that the export ban on weapons and dual-use technologies (and technological know-how) is intended to curtail.

The second reason for democracies decoupling technologically from the autocracies is that autocracies make intensive use of high-tech goods to oppress their citizens. China in particular has developed a number of tech products that implement continuous, intrusive, and relentless surveillance of Chinese citizens—especially the 13 million in the Uighur community in Xinjiang—using facial recognition software, DNA testing kits, video recordings along every inch of many streets, voice recordings made from telephone calls, and all forms of digital messages. All of this material is then analyzed, sorted, and processed in real time by massive supercomputers so that authoritarian tactics can be used, and oppressive punishments inflicted, upon wholly innocent people. In light of this behavior by the Chinese government, the democracies have decided to block the export of any technologies that China could integrate into these systems of mass surveillance and oppression. Bottom line: the democracies don't want to be implicated in this sort of inhumane technology model that completely violates the human rights of privacy and dignity as set out in the United Nations Universal Declaration of Human Rights, a document that is binding on all members of the UN, including China and Russia. Moreover, having perfected this grotesque system of digital citizen surveillance and oppression, China sold has sold such systems to some sixty other eager autocracies around the world. China is the leader by far in technology with nefarious autocratic characteristics.

Furthermore—with respect to the question "Why technological decoupling?"—it is important to recall that the Chinese have been decoupling technologically from the democracies for decades. Soon after the Internet came on the scene, China built the so-called Great Firewall of China, which in electronic form tries, and usually succeeds, in replicating the ancient physical Great Wall built across large swaths of Chinese northern territory centuries ago in order to keep attackers out of the country. This is why a typical computer or smartphone user in China cannot access Google, Facebook, or a number of other American Internet services. Equally, the Chinese government has cut off entire domains of economic and social activity from investment by people and companies residing in the democracies. Therefore, while it sounds childish, when the question "Why should the democracies decouple from China technologically?" is posed, a partial answer is "China long ago started the technology decoupling! The democracies are just taking to a logical conclusion a process started by the Chinese." Therefore, the Chinese should not be up in arms that TikTok may one day be banned from the US, given that similar American services have been banned from China.

It should also be noted, along this same vector, that China is far from done decoupling from the democracies. China wants to decouple from quite a lot of the networks and systems put in place by the global community.

China strives desperately to get off the US dollar as the world's reserve and payments currency; it requires more of its counterparties to pay in Chinese renminbi—including telling (not asking) Russia to take renminbi in payment for Russian oil and gas shipped to China. China would also dearly love to replace the SWIFT (Society for Worldwide Interbank Financial Telecommunication) financial payments system with a Chinese version. China is also concerned that many of the fiber-optic communications cables that stitch the world's countries together are owned and operated by companies in democracies, and therefore their national security organizations can tap these cables to monitor data and voice conversations. The Chinese are already putting their own communications satellites into orbit so that they don't have to rely on ones operated by the democracies. Technical decoupling is not a new thing; it's just becoming more urgent given Cold War 2.0.

Two overarching thoughts about technological decoupling are worth keeping in mind at all times. First, doing it will be fiendishly difficult. The degree of intertwining of the Chinese economy with those of the major democracies is so extensive that unraveling the two, even partially, will be a complex and arduous task. That's why it's important to remind businesses and others in democracies (as in the previous paragraphs) of the rationale for doing it when phases of the process prove to be extremely challenging and expensive.

The second general point pertains to nomenclature. The Americans started using the word "decoupling," and it spooked a lot of people. The Europeans have countered with the word "de-risking." At the G7 meeting in May 2023 the Americans tried to win some points with the Europeans by dropping "decoupling" and switching to "de-risking," another example of the Biden administration's alliance-maintenance skills being second to none.

The best phrase, however, is "technological decoupling," for several reasons. "De-risking" lacks urgency. Prudent commercial actors will always be looking to reduce risk in their dealings, so the word "de-risking" just labels a best practice that presumably has been happening in global business for decades. It does not inspire or prod companies and governments to go beyond "business as usual" thinking and action.

"De-coupling" alone, though, while it conveys the right degree of seriousness, if left unqualified is overly broad. Hence the right balance is achieved with the phrase "technological decoupling." It's still urgent, but also limited to the pinnacles of technology and some other assets necessary for tech-related activities (such as rare earth exploration, mining, and processing). As such, "technological decoupling" is better suited to an era of Cold War 2.0 that is driven by digital and other hyper-innovative processes.

The focus of the tech decoupling contemplated by the democracies will be products that comprise or include the four accelerator technologies. The US government should block the export of these items to China under sanctions laws, resembling the kind of sanctions passed in October 2022 to prevent the shipment of high-end SCs to China. In addition, though, it can be expected that the US also eventually passes a law preventing American investors from putting money into Chinese companies involved in these technologies, and American university professors will be barred from collaborating with Chinese counterparts in the areas of these technologies.

Most products, though, traded between the democracies and the autocracies will not be impacted by these sanctions; that is, roughly two-thirds to three-quarters of products from China will remain unaffected by such sanctions. For example, the hundreds of goods that can be purchased in a Walmart that are made in China will not be impacted by the technology decoupling, subject to one very significant exception. China might undertake some behavior so egregious that the democracies decide they need to prevent all trade between themselves and China. This is exactly what the democracies did when Russia launched its invasion of Ukraine in 2022. Therefore, if China were to attack Taiwan, many democracies will likely sanction all trade between those democracies and China. In that case, even low-tech goods would be caught in the embargo, as China will assume the status of a pariah state.

Consider the following scenario. China attacks Taiwan. The US comes to the defense of Taiwan, as the Biden administration has said it would.

This means not only that the US provides weapons to Taiwan (as it did to Ukraine), but also that US soldiers actively participate in the fight against China, which the US did not do against Russia in the Russo-Ukrainian War.

Within a few days of after the prospective Chinese attack against Taiwan, a Chinese missile strike on a US aircraft carrier in the Pacific is successful—just as a Ukrainian cruise missile sank the *Moskva*, Russia's leading ship in the Black Sea—and 350 American sailors die in the attack. The gruesome videos of death and destruction from the disabled ship circulate all over American social media. Some weeks later the body bags containing slain young American men and women begin arriving back in small towns across the United States. If after this attack Tesla continues to make cars in its factory in China, and Tesla continues to sell its cars from its showrooms in China, there is a very strong likelihood that not a single Tesla car will be sold in America for the duration of the Taiwan War and for months, perhaps years, afterward. Moreover, when the first American missiles take out a Chinese warship, and 350 young Chinese sailors die, it is likely that no Chinese consumer will thereafter buy a Tesla—and those who own Teslas in China will likely be too worried to drive them anymore, given that mobs of Chinese nationalists had already torched Tesla's show-rooms. Social media in both America and China would have implemented the most far-reaching trade embargo in human history.

Elon Musk, Tesla's boss (and the world's richest person), is hoping that such a scenario never comes to pass. He was in China in June 2023 telling his hosts that China and the US were "conjoined twins" with commercial interests that are completely aligned.[2] This may well be, but Beijing behaves as if its desire to take over Taiwan trumps its economic relationship with America. It is also interesting to see the Chinese use Musk's visit to trumpet how open Beijing is to foreign investors when Musk's Twitter company is not allowed to do business in China and neither is Musk's Starlink satellite business, because both offend China's restrictive policies of censorship and complete social control. And it was fascinating how Musk, perhaps the most outspoken business executive in the world, is not so much when he is in

China—he did not dare post a single tweet while he was in China, lest he upset his hosts. It's easy being for free speech when you're in America, the bastion of free speech in the world; true character and courage are better judged when you support free speech where the government is an autocracy. Musk failed this test miserably.

Musk is not alone. Starbucks CEO Laxman Narasimhan was also in China in the spring of 2023, proclaiming that he would like Starbucks to grow to 9,000 outlets in China from 6,000 today. Fair enough, but those plans will be dashed if the US supports Taiwan militarily in defending the island nation from a Chinese attack, because mobs of Chinese will likely destroy every Starbucks outlet they can get their hands on. This isn't simply conjecture. Recall the social media outrage against Swedish clothing retailer H&M in 2021 when H&M was critical of Chinese labor practices in Xinjiang, and the Chinese government unleashed the Communist Party youth wing against H&M.[3] A hot war over Taiwan, where Chinese soldiers are dying because of American missiles fired from American naval vessels, aircraft, and land bases in Guam, Okinawa, and the Philippines, would be a much worse scenario. Chinese social media outrage would inevitably spill over into the physical world, and American-owned retail outlets in China would be the obvious target.

To prepare proactively in case of such a scenario, companies in the democracies can be expected to reorganize their supply chains in order to mitigate their potential risk. Assume an American furniture retailer has an important supplier in China that manufactures 80 percent of all the furniture they sell in the United States. They would be prudent, at a minimum, to contract with another supplier as a second source of products, perhaps a factory in Mexico. That way, if its China supply is blocked at some point, it can have the Mexican plant keep producing and ideally increase its production to make up for the lost production from the Chinese factory. Or it may opt for a second source factory in Mexico and a third source factory in Vietnam. The key objective is to diversify, or "de-risk," supply chains from non-tech goods to be ready for any contingency. Even in the tech space, Apple is implementing such de-risking by having Foxconn, its major assembler of iPhones in China, shift some production to India, and a lesser amount to Vietnam as well. Better safe than sorry, even if this strategy will cost more in the short to medium term.

As for retail outlets like Starbucks or Tesla dealerships, they need to have contingency plans for responding to extreme blowback in the Chinese market. It might be that the Chinese government keeps a lid on protest and consumer reaction, but if things do turn ugly (particularly where the Chinese government pushes consumers in that direction), these and similarly placed companies need contingency plans to deal with worst-case scenarios. Ideally the companies created these plans some time ago, as just another cost of doing business in the world's largest consumer market. And presumably the profits from such businesses are significant enough that even if a complete exit from the market is the ultimate result (due to a hot war over Taiwan), the companies still made sufficient rate of return on their (albeit truncated) investment while the going was good.

As for the tech goods from the democracies that will no longer be traded with the autocracies due to tech developing, they will become more "democracy friendly" than the equivalent goods made in the autocracies. For instance, facial recognition technology made in the democracies will have many more controls against possible abuse by unscrupulous system operators or hackers who penetrate the system. They will have much stronger security features than the equivalent products emanating from the autocracies. In short, they will be built to the "standards of democracy." And presumably they will be used by governments and businesses in democracies in a manner very different than in autocratic China, but this remains to be seen.

Trade relationships between democracies and nonaligned countries will be similar in one respect to those between democracies and autocracies. Low-tech goods, including agricultural products, processed foodstuffs, and the thousands of items found in a Walmart, will all pass both ways across borders with little concern (except, as noted above, in case of the general trade embargo following a Chinese attack on Taiwan). Trade in technology products will have a different and much more nuanced strategy, as between democracies and nonaligned countries. Nonaligned countries that are democracies will presumably want to acquire high-technology products only from other democracies because they will be made in accordance with the "standards of democracy."

On the other hand, the nonaligned country, even a long-standing democracy, will not like the idea of getting locked into a long-term technology supply arrangement with any country, whether it is an autocracy or democracy, if it can avoid it. In order to remain attractive as a trading partner to the autocratic camp, the nonaligned country will not want to be perceived as too close to the democracy camp. The autocracies may even make their continued purchases of large volumes of commodities from the nonaligned country contingent on the nonaligned country buying certain types of high-tech goods from the autocracy. If these types of tech goods do not comport to the nonaligned country's norms of democracy, a fairly important impediment will arise between these two potential trading nations. Democracies that can assist nonaligned countries navigate these difficult shoals of global trade policy will be well received in the capitals of the nonaligned; those that cannot thread these delicate needles will lose market share among the nonaligned. Some nonaligned countries will try to make more of their technology goods, as India is doing with some of its digital identity and payment systems software.[4]

One area of "partial decoupling" that will be particularly fraught concerns the situation where services (rather than goods) are supplied from an entity in an autocracy to customers in a democracy (including a nonaligned democracy). The case of TikTok is illustrative. TikTok is a hugely popular app, particularly among teenagers (and even tweens). It has some 150 million users in the United States. What complicates matters is that it is owned by a Chinese company, and the video sharing/streaming service collects personal data from users. A core problem arises because under Chinese law, the Chinese government has the right to access all user data collected by companies like TikTok. TikTok says it has never been asked by Beijing to give up customer data, but of course that doesn't mean Beijing couldn't exercise its right of access tomorrow.

No democracy should allow a digital (or any other) service to collect personal data from its citizens if there is a risk of that personal data being shared with a foreign government. One solution for the TikTok situation is for the Chinese owner of TikTok simply to divest the American TikTok business to a non-Chinese buyer, presumably an American company. This idea is attractive because it is a neat and tidy solution. In effect, companies in autocracies should not be entitled to operate businesses in the democracies where data from consumers in the democracy either flows back to the autocracy in the ordinary course of daily operations, or the company ultimately has to transfer such data to the autocratic government at the government's request. Indeed, a lot of tech decoupling has already gone on in this regard in terms of the big Internet companies, with the impetus for decoupling coming from the autocracies. This is why Google and Facebook, as noted above, are unavailable to consumers in China. Therefore, so long as ByteDance owns TikTok, governments in the democracies should ensure the service is not made available to consumers in the democracies. Such a restriction would simply be a reciprocal limitation similar to the one China has for decades levied on American suppliers of digital services.

This doesn't mean all foreign investment by Chinese firms in democracies should be prohibited, just as there are a lot of entities in the democracies that are permitted to invest in Chinese businesses—though all these businesses have greater risk now that there could be a wholesale embargo on trade between their respective countries, in which case the foreign investor will face the major hurdle of pulling out of the other's market. On the other hand, Chinese companies should not be able to invest in companies in a democracy that make high-end tech products in the domains of the four accelerator technologies, and even investments in the less sensitive, but still important, industries listed in chapter 9 need to be reviewed carefully by governments in the democracies.

Technological decoupling, as part of Cold War 2.0, is a structural solution to the risk posed by autocracies to the democracies in the globalized era defined by high tech. In addition to dealing with the problems posed by technology, however, it should not be forgotten that the democracies must also respond to certain low-tech behaviors of the autocracies that are also unacceptable. When an autocracy exercises economic coercion against a democracy—or China conducts or condones cyberattacks against entities in democracies, or attempts to influence lawmakers in democracies through intimidation—ideally the entire community of democracies will respond in the manner outlined in chapter 12, with a collective response that is muscular and economically proportionate. Most important, the democracies must act in unison; otherwise, the massive economic leverage of China will prevail relative to any single democracy (perhaps with the exception of the US). The democracies must remember the admonition: "none of us is as strong as all of us." This is extremely useful advice when the democracies consider how to respond to economic threats (let alone political or military ones) from the large autocracies, especially China.

THE AUTOCRACIES AFTER TECHNOLOGY DECOUPLING

Within the world's autocracies it is clear that for the foreseeable future only China will be able to innovate meaningful new technologies on a sustained basis. There will be, therefore, an ongoing continual tightening of the economic orbits of all autocratic countries around China. This is already happening even between Russia and China, partly as a function of the economic sanctions levied on Russia by the democracies as a result of Russia' invasion of Ukraine. It is an open question whether Russia, once the Ukraine War is over, will continue to accept its new role as junior partner to China. Recall that in Cold War 1 the roles were very much reversed; plus, in the 1960s Russia and China experienced a schism, and even a low-grade military conflict along their mutual border. Will Russia be content to play second fiddle to China for the balance of Cold War 2.0?

Still, while Russia is a much smaller country than China in terms of its economy and population, Russia nevertheless punches above its weight on the world scene because for the last twenty-five years its autocrat, Vladimir Putin, has liked to punch. Putin has absolutely no hesitation to put young

Russian men in harm's way, so long as their deaths and maiming advance his vision of a restored Russian Empire—recreated under Tsar Putin, who earns fabulous wealth from this enterprise, of course. This is the major reason why Putin has been so successful in military terms, at least up to his invasion of Ukraine. Most citizens in the democracies no longer find it acceptable to have soldiers come back from a war zone in body bags unless the war was genuinely unavoidable and very limited in scope and duration. Presidents of the United States and leaders in many other democracies have learned the lessons of Afghanistan and Iraq, and have deployed boots on the ground very sparingly ever since. Russia, by contrast, has no reservations, and it also uses private mercenary groups aligned to the Russian government, like the Wagner Group, to carry out military and security missions in places like Africa, so that these soldiers (almost all being ex–Russian military) can undertake distasteful missions that even Putin doesn't want to be associated with in the global press. These mercenary forays into the Global South in support of local autocracies are also extremely lucrative, both for the mercenary group and for Putin, as they often take payment in the commodities produced by the facilities they are protecting, such as gold mines.

Although China will be the leading technology innovator of the autocracies, technological progress there will invariably fall behind what is achieved in the democracies (led by the United States), given the lead in innovation built up by researchers and companies in the democracies over the past fifty years. Over the coming decades, as the accelerator technologies speed innovation in the democracies across all domains of the economy and the military, the deficiencies inherent in the Chinese top-down tech industrial strategy model will become visible for all to see. Ultimately, falling behind the democracies may lead Xi to consider whether it makes sense to attack Taiwan sooner than later—but it might also lead Xi, or more likely Xi's successor, to propose a "grand bargain" whereby China gives up its claim to Taiwan, and in return the democracies drop all trade embargoes.

Given that China will be tasked with innovating the bulk of technology used by the autocracies going forward, it is useful to ask whether

China will continue to allow hundreds of thousands of China's best young minds, especially in the STEM disciplines, to leave China to study in the democracies, principally for graduate degrees in the STEM subjects. Of these students, about 80 percent return to China, but that means tens of thousands stay in the democracies. Will a Cold War 2.0 global innovation model allow this brain drain from China to continue? And if China wants to stem this emigration, presumably it will have to offer its homegrown talent compelling opportunities and lucrative employment to stay put in China. This will put a strain on the Chinese economic system. The lure of California's Silicon Valley for young engineers is great, as they want to work on the coolest tech going and make a small fortune along the way. If this dual opportunity is not available to them in China, but at the same time they cannot emigrate to a democracy, the resulting tension inside China will grow. Will Cold War 2.0 (with its tighter controls on technology and people flowing between the two camps) lead inevitably to a Tiananmen Square 2? This is one very significant risk factor worth watching for in a technologically decoupled world.

The converse of this issue for the democracies is this: even if China continues to allow its best and brightest STEM students to study in the democracies, should the democracies continue to take them in? On the one hand, a very high-performing 20 percent will stay in the democracy and contribute materially to the technological progress of the democracies. On the other hand, the 80 percent that return to China pose some security risk in that they may well have had access to information and material that the democracies would prefer not to share with the autocracies. This second risk can be managed, though, through some prudent oversight of university graduate students from autocracies.

The main question, then, in allowing so many fine grad students to study, and then stay, in the democracies, is whether the democracies are thereby depriving the autocracies of just the type of minds that, if they remained in the autocracy, would very well be leaders of the revolution in favor of democracy. Put another way, how can the democracies reasonably expect a Tiananmen Square 2 freedom movement (but this time with more success) if the democracies siphon off the crème of the student population. Put in these terms, the immigration policy that favors bringing to democracies the world's best and brightest from the autocracies is somewhat selfish and shortsighted.

THE NONALIGNED COUNTRIES AFTER TECHNOLOGY DECOUPLING

The principal nonaligned countries that are democracies are listed in Table 4 of chapter 10. In the aggregate they have a population of 2.717 billion people (but a combined GDP of only $8.27 trillion). Nevertheless, the nonaligned countries will be able to punch above their economic weight because both the democracies and the autocracies will be wooing them furiously during Cold War 2.0. China, in particular, will absolutely require the natural resources and foodstuffs grown by the nonaligned countries, in particular those of Brazil, South Africa, and Mozambique. For their part, the democracies will keep reminding the major nonaligned democracies that, at the end of the day, they are democracies themselves.

Blood, however, will not often be thicker than water in this relationship between aligned and nonaligned democracies. The nonaligned countries will invariably purchase a great deal of technology from the democracies, and in return they will want to export a lot of products to the democracies, but in terms of overall economic value, a country like Brazil earns much more from its sales to autocratic China than it does to all the democracies combined. Consider these statistics: Brazil's five leading exports in 2022 were iron ore ($46.2 billion), soybeans ($39 B), crude petroleum ($30.7 B), raw sugar ($10 B), and poultry ($7.6 B), while its five leading export markets were China ($88.3 billion), the United States ($30.2 B), Argentina ($12 B), Netherlands ($9.3 B), and Chile ($7.1 B). The hearts of the non-aligned democracies might be in the camp of the democracies, but their heads are certainly engaged with the autocrats.

The nonaligned countries, though, need modern weapons systems. They are nonaligned, but they are certainly not immune from regional security risks, and they all tend to be in very rough neighborhoods. Take India, for instance. It is certainly in a difficult region in terms of security challenges. Table 15 in chapter 9, though, reveals that India has only two small weapons manufacturers, and the other nonaligned countries have none. Therefore, whichever arms manufacturer India (and others among the nonaligned) buys from creates a long period of tech dependency on a foreign power, up to thirty years for a complex system like a modern jet fighter, but even twenty years for a state-of-the-art tank. Which camp they choose such strategic technology from may in effect cancel their nonaligned status, at least for military preparedness purposes. In today's technologically infused world, maintaining nonaligned status is not a simple exercise.

Several nonaligned countries will play important roles in Cold War 2.0, in particular India, Brazil, and South Africa. India, though, will be extremely important. With China's population shrinking, India is now the world's most populous country (though this fact alone can be a blessing or a curse). It is also a democracy, though some of the nationalist, sectarian programs of Prime Minister Narendra Modi reflect a somewhat autocratic bent. Economically speaking, there has long been a sense that India's full potential in the domains of manufacturing, finance, and commerce is being thwarted by very cumbersome bureaucratic government procedures, and in some cases by state-fueled corruption. Modi, however, is clearly signaling that he wants India to move up the value chain in advanced manufacturing, and he is working hard to attract iPhone assembler Foxconn[5] to India; he is even taking a stab at establishing a semiconductor chip (SC) manufacturing plant.[6]

India has had some meaningful success in the information technology outsourcing domain. Companies like Infosys, Wipro, Tata Consultancy Services, and Cognizant have modern computer-equipped campuses in Bangalore, Chennai, and Pune that would not be out of place in Silicon Valley. These companies, though, should not be mistaken for what they are not. They don't produce world-class innovation and constantly release new products and services like AWS, Microsoft, and Google. Which is one of the reasons there continues to be a massive flow of India's best and brightest

STEM university graduates to the US, Canada, the UK, and a number of other democracies. This Indian diaspora has done very well for themselves, and for the new countries they now call home. As noted in the introduction, hundreds of CEOs of North American tech companies were born in India, including the current CEOs at Google, Microsoft, and IBM. India has also fairly recently implemented a digital ID system, to which they then added payments and other features; India is now selling this successful "Made in India" technology to other members of the Global South.

Nevertheless, a review of the league tables in the four accelerator technologies and the other important technologies confirms that India is still a net importer of innovation. Indeed, today 70 percent of the weapons systems used by India's air force were designed in Russia, and a whopping 90 percent of the weapons systems used by India's army were sourced from Russia. With this sort of reliance on Russia, can one even meaningfully talk about India as "nonaligned"? Recently India has been warming up to the United States in order to counterbalance the serious threat India sees from China—and yet India still purchased its new antimissile system from Russia (the S-400), rather than procure the Patriot system from the US, much to the consternation of the Americans.

At the same time, though, India has discomfort about Russia's increasing dependence on China because, as noted above, India is very nervous about China. India and China share a disputed border, and in 1962 they fought a war over that border, a war that India lost in a humiliating manner. They had a skirmish along the contested frontier as recently as December 2022, but without any deaths as they have an agreement not to allow weapons into the area. Moreover, India's ongoing distrust of China has led India to join the Quad, a loose strategic security dialogue group made up of the United States, Japan, Australia, and India, focused on countering China's aggressive tactics in the Indo-Pacific region. The Quad also undertakes the largest joint military exercises in the region. India is also a member of the I2U2, a group somewhat similar to the Quad but comprising India, Israel, the United Arab Emirates, and the United States. And on the military technology front, India has just recently agreed to buy fighter jets from

France, and engines for fighter jets from an American company, with the happy blessing of the American government. Clearly India's military procurement plans are in a state of flux.

At the same time, though, when Russian energy sales to Europe were phased out by the Europeans in 2022 in response to the invasion of Ukraine, India agreed to buy much of Russia's oil, which was previously being sold to the Europeans. (In 2022, India's imports from Russia rose 400 percent.) Again, the Americans were perturbed and the Ukrainians were livid. In Cold War 2.0, the democracies will find managing their relations with the nonaligned countries a challenge, if India is any indication. During cold wars, the world becomes bipolar in terms of geopolitics. From the perspective of the nonaligned countries, bipolarity gives them options and opportunities, particularly because they have weak technology innovation capabilities. They are, when all is said and done, nonaligned as a matter of choice, not chance. Notwithstanding their challenges, the democracies have a reasonably good hand to play vis-à-vis the nonaligned, but again it is one best played when the major democracies deploy their cards in a somewhat coordinated fashion.

MUTUAL COOPERATION—OR NOT?

Some commentators argue that even if relations between China and the United States become fraught, as would certainly be the case in a full-blown Cold War 2.0 world, there will still be plenty of scope for them, their allies, and their partners to collaborate on internationally relevant projects where it is clearly in the interests of the entire global community. Issues that fall into this domain of potential cooperation include climate change, combating terrorism, pandemic preparedness, food security, regulation of the high seas, nuclear arms controls, international crime, and illicit drugs—and this is just a partial list.

In theory there is no reason why countries in a generally partially technologically decoupled world couldn't cooperate on noncontentious matters that benefit them all. At least that's the theory. In the real world, though, with technology underpinning virtually all pressing global issues, and technology being the very sensitive linchpin matter between democracies and autocracies, there will indeed be some very difficult challenges confronting cooperation across the camps.

Suppose the United States invents a new battery technology that absolutely revolutionizes electricity storage, a device desperately required for renewable energy from solar and wind power to work at scale on major national electricity grids. This innovation could seriously move the dial on combating climate change. The US offers China a license for the technology, but would China accept it? What if there is a subsequent embargo against China using any technology from the US because of a dispute over Taiwan? Even if there isn't that problem, will China be willing to be beholden to the US for a long time for updates to the technology? All told, it's much easier for China to simply go about building its own batteries, even if they're not quite as good as the new one from the US. Then there's the question of China losing face in the global community, especially among the nonaligned countries, if it uses technology from the democracies. Recall that China is still not buying mRNA COVID vaccines from the democracies even though they have proven far superior to the (non-mRNA) ones made in China.

Another area urgently calling out for cooperation among the US, Russia, and China is putting some limits and processes around nuclear weapons. There is solid precedence for this between the US and Russia between the early 1970s and the late 2010s. Over that period, this form of international cooperation, even during the height of Cold War 1, made progress between the two nuclear superpowers. After the US and Soviet Russia came fairly close to an exchange of nuclear weapons during the Cuban Missile Crisis in 1963, negotiators from both governments began discussions about placing limits on their respective nuclear arsenals. The result was the signing by the US and Soviet Russia of the Strategic Arms Limitation Talks in 1972. Other treaties followed, dealing with nuclear nonproliferation, nuclear weapons testing, and intermediate-range nuclear weapons.

Then, after Russia annexed Crimea in 2014, nuclear weapons discussions between the US and Russia came to a halt, and one after another the various treaties between them expired without renewal, or one side or the other pulled out of them. Currently only one treaty still is in force. The atmosphere for negotiations has not been improved by the fact that Russia has not been able to prevail over Ukraine in the war launched by Putin, largely because of the high-tech weapons provided to Ukraine by America and other democracies. In short, it is not a very propitious moment to resume negotiations on nuclear weapons treaties, particularly as the US will want to add China's nuclear weapons to the mix, as it certainly makes sense for the US to treat the two autocracies together when tackling the finicky question of nuclear weapons control. Again, as with climate change, the players intellectually know what needs to be done, but there is simply precious little goodwill among them to get a meaningful deal done. Cold War 2.0 could very well be a lean period for negotiating and concluding such international arrangements.

A final question on democracy/autocracy cooperation concerns international sports competitions, such as the Olympic Games and the football World Cup. The privilege to host these major sporting events, or to sponsor a golf league like the PGA, should never be awarded to autocracies. Russia made a mockery of the Olympics when it hosted the 2014 Winter Games at Sochi. First, the government ran the most elaborate and extensive illegal doping system ever conceived for an international competition, including secret compartments cut into the walls where samples were collected from Russian athletes so they could pass illegal substitutes to the testers. And then, mindful that one major purpose for such sporting competitions is to bring the world together in peace and harmony, within two weeks of the final ceremony at Sochi, Putin invaded Ukraine and annexed Crimea illegally. Eight years later, Putin traveled to Beijing to meet with Xi as the 2022 Olympics are wrapping up in China—and then two weeks later Putin launched his full-scale invasion of Ukraine. Again, autocrats simply don't care about the true meaning of sporting events such as the Olympic Games and World Cup football (soccer) matches; their only interest in these globally important events is to try to scrape together some patina of legitimacy for themselves and their people.

Whether athletes from autocracies should be entitled to participate in such international competitions hosted in democracies is addressed in chapter 12. Here, the point is that autocracies should never be allowed to host them. For example, Saudi Arabia desperately wants to host the 2030 football World Cup. The Saudis also want to "sportswash" their autocratic behavior by, for example, buying off professional golfers with huge sums of money, thereby allowing the Saudis to host the PGA as their own, in effect. The response to the Saudis should be a resolute "no" on both counts.

These are sporting events that were first established in democracies, and the democracies therefore should "repatriate them" and once again make them their own, exclusively. Moreover, they would have an easier time making a "clean version" of the decoupled games competitions, for the simple reason that the most prolific cheaters (when it comes to doping), namely the Russians, will be eliminated from the version of the games that caters only to participants from democracies.

Of course the autocracies might host their own versions of these competitions. They would have to be held in their own countries, and presumably athletes from the democracies could attend them in their individual capacities, presumably something attractive to them because the organizers will offer enormous cash prizes to the athletes who do well. They could be marketed as the "Money Games." Presumably the sums involved would be high enough that many (most?) athletes from the democracies who would compete would be willing to undergo a doping regimen, like their counterparts in the autocracies, notwithstanding the adverse impact on their health in the longer term. In effect, another tech decoupling would be achieved—a clean form of sport with reasonable compensation in the democracies, or a dope-filled competition for lots of money in the autocracies. Sadly, the latter will likely get higher television ratings, even in the democracies.

Incidentally, the cultural decoupling that this proposal about sports events would represent was started, in a fashion, by the autocracies. In 1970 the Russian author Aleksandr Solzhenitsyn was awarded the Nobel

Prize for Literature for his book *The Gulag Archipelago*. He did not attend the award ceremony because the Russian government made it clear it was very unhappy with his winning the prize, given that the book described in detail the forced labor camps in Siberia run by the Russian government. Similarly, in 2010 China slapped a partial trade embargo on Norway for six years because the Nobel Committee awarded the Nobel Peace Prize to Chinese dissident Liu Xiaobo, who was languishing in a Chinese jail. A bifurcated world of sporting competitions would fit nicely into this cultural decoupling paradigm, and would be wholly consistent with Cold War 2.0 trends.

THE DURATION OF COLD WAR 2.0

The final question worth asking about Cold War 2.0 is "How long will this technology bifurcated global system continue?" This is a natural question because wars tend to come to an end. Cold War 1 certainly terminated when the East Bloc countries left the orbit of Soviet Russia in 1989, an ending further confirmed a couple of years later when Soviet Russia itself collapsed. This was such a momentous culmination that a leading historian even ventured the thought that history had ended, in the sense that the contest of political systems was over and the clear winner was democracy. [7]

Could there be such a determinative end to Cold War 2.0? There is certainly precedent for an autocracy to make the transition to democracy and responsible membership in the international community. Germany and Japan were the leading warmongering autocracies in the first half of the 20th century. After World War II, with some coaching, direction, and much economic subvention from the democracies, both nations became democracies themselves, to the point where today it is inconceivable that either will revert to autocratic ways. Both Germany and Japan have also learned that commercial and financial success don't actually require physical colonies, and that financial trading is more effective than military raiding. Japan is the third-largest economy in the world, while Germany is the third-largest exporter in the world. Both have done fabulously well throwing their lot in with the democracies.

There is plenty of precedent, therefore, for a country making the transformation from autocracy to democracy. Many other countries (besides Germany and Japan) have taken the same transformative path (think Italy, Spain, Portugal, South Korea, or Taiwan, to name a few).

In effect, what would it take for Russia and China to become democracies? There are two scenarios. In one, the current Cold War 2.0 technology/ innovation gap in favor of the democracies over the autocracies, grows steadily over time. Starved of the fruits of innovation emanating from the democracies, Russia and China try to keep up to the democracies, but inevitably their relative pace of innovation decreases, and their standard of living compared to the democracies declines commensurately, gradually in the short term, and then significantly in the midterm. Eventually, the gap becomes a chasm obvious for all to see (including their own populations), as both Russia and China become, in essence, large North Koreas.

What the populations of Russia and China see is that the cure for cancer, dementia, drug dependency, and diabetes are developed in the democracies; completely clean fusion energy is made to work in the democracies; aircraft in the democracies run on nonpolluting aviation fuel; wheat that can withstand blistering heat is grown in the democracies; and the democracies collectively launch the first crewed mission to Mars. In twenty years, when both Putin and Xi step down, the new leaders of Russia and China could craft a transformation not unlike what Deng Xiaoping accomplished when he succeeded Mao and what Boris Yeltsin did when he came after Gorbachev—except this time the successors of Putin and Xi transform both the economy *and* politics, and bring real democracy to Moscow and Beijing. Cold War 2.0 would be over.

The second scenario essentially plays out like the first, with one major difference. China, prompted by the forecast of its future decline, makes a grab for Taiwan and attacks the island nation. Ironically, just as the Russian full-scale invasion of Ukraine steeled the democracies against Putin, Xi's reckless war against Taiwan and the US further galvanizes the democracies. Whether Xi is actually able to conquer Taiwan or not, the net effect of his act of hubris is that the isolation of China, and Russia, becomes more complete than under scenario 1, with the result that the two leading autocracies become large North Koreas even sooner. The unintended result is that regime change in both countries is hastened; democracy comes to them in a decade rather than in a twenty-year timeframe.

Obviously such predictions, complete with timelines, are subject to many conditions and inevitable twists and turns in possible permutations. Still, one indispensable requirement for the democracies to prevail over the autocracies is as certain as night follows day: the democracies will only win Cold War 2.0 if they all continue to move forward together under the leadership of the United States, but their success is assured if they continue to increase their cooperation and joint action on a host of fronts, including technology innovation and military preparedness.

Therefore, the most serious threat to these two scenarios becoming reality is if sometime over the coming decade someone became president of the United States who led that country to an isolationist retreat from Europe and Asia. That scenario ends in catastrophe for the democracies, including the United States.

CODA

Recent events in the domains of technology and innovation, and in geopolitics, confirm the main themes discussed in this book. Artificial intelligence (AI) continues to power global markets in finance and weapons systems. OpenAI is raising funds at a company valuation of $90 billion (on sales of only $1 billion). The leading supplier of SCs for high-end AI applications, Nvidia, has achieved a market valuation of $1 trillion. Amazon has invested $4 billion in a small early-stage AI company called Anthropic. In our Cold War 2.0 era, AI is rapidly insinuating itself into every nook and cranny of society, including the military.

Drones, both air-based and more recently naval ones deployed in the Black Sea, have become indispensable to both sides in the Russian-Ukrainian War. Mindful of this new battlefield reality, the United States military recently announced the "Replicator Program," which will respond to the pacing threat posed by China in the Indo-Pacific by building in a matter of eighteen months literally thousands of AI-driven drones that will operate under the sea, on the water's surface, on land, and in the air. The Pentagon has for some time used AI in intelligence gathering and reconnaissance, with the help of companies like Palantir. The new emphasis is on using AI for active war-fighting operations, relying on a new generation of

AI companies like Shield AI, Skydio, Anduril, and Kratos, which will team up with established defense contractors like Lockheed Martin and RTX (formerly Raytheon) to build lethal weapons infused with AI capabilities, including autonomy.

Once the new AI weapons systems are developed, their production at scale will be the critical challenge—in 2022, Shield AI made only 38 drones. This level of unit output won't suffice even for a day when the Ukrainians are burning through about 10,000 drones a month. A core lesson of the war in Ukraine is that kinetic military conflicts involving major powers don't end quickly, and once they continue for more than a month, then industrial capacity to produce sufficient ongoing weapons re-supply becomes a critical factor between success or failure of the campaign.

The Russians are also feeling the squeeze of insufficient weapon-making capacity, and are turning to two lesser, but important, autocratic partners for assistance. Moscow has rekindled its relationship with North Korea, which began sending the Russians large volumes of artillery ammunition, even though what Russia will give in return will likely breach the UN sanctions on North Korea that Russia itself agreed to. When the chips are down, autocrats ignore the rules-based international order with even greater impunity. Russia has also come to rely heavily on Iran for drones, both buying them from the theocratic autocracy and having Tehran help Moscow build a factory in Russia to produce them in greater volume. Iran's role in the Axis of Autocracies is increasing in other important ways as well. For example, Iran supplies weapons and military tech expertise, and significant financial resources to Hamas, all of which was evident when Hamas attacked Israel in October 2023. Hamas runs the Gaza territory (from which it launched the attack on Israel) as its autocratic fiefdom, having driven the Palestinian Authority from the enclave years ago. The senior political leadership of Hamas also had three meetings with senior Russian officials prior to the attack. Cold War 2.0 is a global conflict indeed.

The geopolitical contours of Cold War 2.0 also became clearer when China recently hosted the autocrat of Syria for a state visit. Moreover, neither Putin nor Xi attended the G20 meeting in New Delhi, nor the

United Nations in New York for the annual leaders summit, which indicates where their priorities are nowadays. The essential battle of Cold War 2.0 is the push by the autocrats to topple the rules-based international order, and the ability—and hopefully willingness, resolve, and stamina—of democracies to resist this dangerous effort by the autocracies. The new reality of Cold War 2.0 and what needs to be done was captured well by Japan's Prime Minister Fumio Kishida when he stated that: (A) the rules-based, free and open international order based on international law is in grave crisis, with Russia in Ukraine, Hamas in the Middle East, China openly trying to deny the international order in the East China Sea and the South China Sea, and with authoritarian narratives penetrating some democracies; and (B) that as the two largest democracies, the United States and Japan must demonstrate that democracy offers the best model for prosperity, stability, and security. Well said by one of the stalwarts of the globe's democracies!

Xi Jingping is staying close to home partly because of China's domestic difficulties. The Chinese economy is in the doldrums, beset with major structural challenges. When recently youth unemployment in China began to exceed 20 percent, Beijing promptly stopped putting out further statistics on this metric. The Chinese government has also criminalized the disclosure of certain basic data about the Chinese economy, essentially making investment in China by foreign companies very difficult. On a recent visit to Beijing, the US Secretary of Commerce, Gina Raimondo, noted that American companies now consider the Chinese market as "uninvestable." This amplifies the technological decoupling that is ongoing between the world's leading autocracy and the democracies.

Similar information and freedom-suppressing autocratic tactics also characterize Putin's domestic information space, where the opposition activist Vladimir Kara-Murza was given a twenty-five-year sentence in a Siberian labor camp for daring to question Russia's military actions in Ukraine. Russia's months-long unlawful detainment of *Wall Street Journal* reporter Evan Gershkovich continues, without a single shred of evidence of wrongdoing being revealed to the outside world. Many of the infamous

Russian practices against dissidents implemented during Cold War 1 have been revived with gusto for the current one.

For the democracies, a very important Cold War 2.0 diplomatic breakthrough was registered recently when US president Biden hosted the leaders of Japan and South Korea at a precedent-setting summit in the US, in order to build a powerful tripartite common front in the face of Chinese, Russian, and North Korean threats in the Eastern Pacific. It's not quite a PATO, at least not yet, but closer cooperation between Washington, Tokyo, and Seoul will advance the cause of deterrence in East Asia, including indirectly on behalf of Taiwan, a very important objective of Cold War 2.0. Industrial capacity in weapons production, though, is an important question for these four democracies, as the Japanese announced they will jointly produce a sixth-generation jet fighter with the United Kingdom and Italy (and not with the United States). This aircraft is the one that will follow the largely American-made F-35 fifth-generation fighter aircraft, of which the Japanese have bought about 150. The Japanese want more industrial benefits from their next large (and very expensive) fighter aircraft program, and they want to be much more self-sufficient in case the US takes an isolationist turn in the coming years or decades.

Isolationism is indeed raising its ugly, unhelpful head in the bowels of the US Republican Party. Leading candidates for the Republican nomination for the November 2024 presidential election are calling for the US to cut off support for Ukraine and Taiwan. The most callous position argues that the US should cease support for Taiwan in 2028 just after the US becomes self-sufficient in advanced SC production capacity. This strategy is flawed in multiple ways, including the fact that TSMC, although it is building advanced SC production capacity in the US, is not building its most advanced SC capacity in the US—that technology is staying firmly in Taiwan.

More to the point, though, Taiwan's multi-party politics, vibrant press freedom, adherence to the rule of law, and civil society with liberal values makes it among the strongest democracies in the world. It is entirely in the national interest of the United States, and other democracies, that Taiwan continue to be free of occupation by China, just as supplying weapons and financial aid to Ukraine directly supports US American national interest by helping Ukraine serve as a bulwark against a revanchist, expansionist Russia. Nevertheless, the core question on Taiwan remains: if China attacks the small island nation, will the US come to Taiwan's defense, not merely by supplying weapons, but by sending in American land, sea and air forces?

In a recent poll taken in the US, only 37 percent of persons polled said they supported such an action, while 22 percent said no, and a whopping 41 percent answered they did not know enough about the topic to voice an opinion. This is extremely problematic, given that American kinetic military action against China in support of Taiwan will cost the deaths of tens of thousands of American lives in the first few weeks of the conflict (a publicly analyzed war game predicts two aircraft carriers and up to twenty other US naval vessels would be destroyed by Chinese missiles in the opening weeks of the war, notwithstanding the best air defense systems the US can muster in response). These poll results show how important it is for the leaders of the democracies, including in the United States and Europe, to explain to their publics the qualities of Taiwan, and why that amazing island nation deserves the support of democracies everywhere.

Moreover, people like Elon Musk are now chiming into the debate, in his case with the hugely uninformed comment that Taiwan is to China essentially what Hawaii is to the US. Musk's technological and innovation bravado and success (with Tesla electric cars, SpaceX rockets and satellites, Neuralink brain/computer interface technology, and the X social media platform, formerly known as Twitter) make him arguably the most successful technology entrepreneur of our present time. Still, these outstanding tech credentials clearly do not automatically confer wisdom in geopolitics. Presumably Musk's position on Taiwan is driven by the fact that Tesla runs a giant factory in Shanghai. Indeed, the normally omni-vocal Musk has not said a word, ever, against the Chinese Communist Party (even when Beijing caused the shutdown of the Tesla plant during Covid), though Musk rails against heavy-handed politics in America all the time. This confirms, yet again, that enablers of autocrats can be found in every country, even the

United States. The democracies have their work cut out for them—including within their own borders—if they hope to prevail in Cold War 2.0.

The most significant threat to US national security, though, and indeed to America remaining a democracy, is the continued participation of Donald Trump in the nation's political process. He now stands accused of ninety-one counts of criminal activity in four separate proceedings. While he is presumed innocent until proven guilty, a true supporter of democracy would stand aside from partisan politics while contesting these charges. Instead, he barrels ahead, seemingly hell-bent on throwing the country into political chaos in the run-up to the next presidential election. He has even implied on social media that the outgoing top officer of the US military, the chairman of the Joint Chiefs of Staff, ought to be executed. Responsibility for the immense democracy wrecking ball that is Donald Trump rests not only on Trump's own shoulders, but also on the many enablers within the Republican Party who speak nary a word against this autocrat wannabe while he attempts to break every institution of domestic and global democracy he possibly can. In truth, the greatest battle to date of Cold War 2.0 will not be fought in Ukraine, or in the Taiwan Strait, but at the American ballot box in November 2024.

ACKNOWLEDGMENTS

While writing a book is a solitary journey, I am delighted to recognize and thank a number of people who have helped me at various times along this particular route.

My agent, Don Fehr (Trident Media), has been unstinting and invaluable in sharing his wisdom about the book publishing business. Don also had the good judgment to connect me with the fine people at Pegasus Books.

The team at Pegasus—Claiborne Hancock, Jessica Case, Julia Romero, and Maria Fernandez—have all been professionals of the first order, and they continue to be a joy to work with. Drew Wesley Wheeler has copy edited the manuscript with a light but firm touch—the ideal combination for an author.

The following people read an early draft of the manuscript and provided useful comments: Parham Aarabi, John Black, Ronald Blank, Daniel Eustache, John Gruetzner, Konrad Mech, Ramon Nissan, Jonathan Rose, Frank Svatousek, and a particular call out to John Black for his literary, business, and professional acumen—for the past thirty years we have been not quite Boswell and Johnson, and vice versa, but pretty close.

Most importantly, to my spouse, Barbara Anderson, a deeply heartfelt thank you for being a constant moral compass. You have made our journey a wonderful adventure.

NOTES

Chapter 1: Technology and National Power

1   Mao Zedong, "Problems of War and Strategy," *Selected Works Vol. II* (Oxford, UK: Pergamon Press, 1965), 131.

2   "'Whoever Leads in AI Will Rule the World,' Putin to Russian children on Knowledge Day," *RT*, Sept. 1, 2017.

3   companiesmarketcap.com.

4   Ilaria Mazzocco, "How Inequality Is Undermining China's Prosperity," Center for Strategic & International Studies, May 26, 2022.

5   "GDP, current prices (List 2022)," International Monetary Fund, imf.org.

6   "GDP, current prices (selection 2022)," International Monetary Fund, imf.org.

7   This 9:33-minute excerpt from the movie can be found on YouTube: "*2001: A Space Odyssey*—The Dawn of Man."

8   Morris Rossabi, "All the Khan's Horses," *Natural History*, Oct. 1994.

9   Linda Davies, "Why the Battle of Agincourt Is Still Important Today," *Guardian*, Oct. 25, 2015.

10   "World's Best Hospitals 2023," *Newsweek*, October 7, 2022.

11   *The Convention on the Prohibition of the Development, Production, Stockpiling and Use of Chemical Weapons and on Their Destruction*, Jan. 13, 1993.

12   Diego Cerdeiro, "Sizing Up the Effects of Technological Decoupling," IMF Working Paper—WP/21/69, 2021, imf.org.

Chapter 2: Cold War 1: Autocracy, Democracy, and Technology

1   Jonah Crane, "DeFi World Faces Jarring Transition to Proper Oversight," *Financial Times*, May 17, 2023.

2   "The World's Most, and Least, Democratic Countries in 2022," *The Economist*, Feb. 1, 2023.

3   Dexter Filkins, "A Dangerous Game over Taiwan," *New Yorker*, Nov. 14, 2022.

4   Mary O'Grady, "Evan Gershkovich and Our Brave New World," *Wall Street Journal*, June 5, 2023.

5   Chun Han Wong, "China Accuses Newspaper Editor of Espionage after Meeting with Diplomat," *Wall Street Journal*, April 24, 2023.

6   Alyssa Lukpat, "A Record Number of Journalists Were Detained Worldwide Prior to Evan Gershkovich's Arrest," *Wall Street Journal*, April 20, 2023.

7   Jennifer Dunham, "Deadly Year for Journalists as Killings Rose Sharply in 2022," *Committee to Protect Journalists*, Jan. 24, 2023, cpj.org.

8   Orla Ryan, "The Joke Can Be on Hong Kong Comedians If They Cross the Line," *Financial Times*, June 1, 2023.

9   Alexandr Solzhenitsyn, *The Gulag Archipelago* (New York: Harper, 1976).

10   Jamie Dettmer, "Hitler's 'War of Annihilation' Caught Stalin by Surprise," *VOA*, June 22, 2021, voanews.com.

11   Anne Applebaum, *Iron Curtain* (New York: Doubleday, 2012).

12   Winston Churchill, "The Sinews of Peace," International Churchill Society, winstonchurchill.org.

13   Full disclosure: the author's parents fled Hungary as political refugees in November 1956, and the author was born in Toronto in August 1957.

14   See transparency.org.

15   Kelly McLaughlin, "Is Putin the World's Real Richest Man?" *Daily Mail.com*, Feb. 20, 2017.

16   Pjotr Sauer, "Kremlin Critic Alexie Navalny Says He Faces Life in Jail over Terror Charges," *Guardian*, April 26, 2023.

17   James Titus, "Soviet Computers: A Giant Awakes," *Datamation*, Dec. 15, 1971.

Chapter 3: The Emergence of China

1   Margaret Macmillan, *Paris 1919* (New York: Random House, 2001), 322–344.

2   Tania Branigan, *Red Memory* (New York: W. W. Norton, 2023).

3   Valerie Strauss, "How Many Died? New Evidence Suggests Far Higher Numbers for the Victims of Mao Zedong's Era," *Washington Post*, July 17, 1994.

4   Scott Kennedy, "*Data Dive: The Private Sector Drives Growth in China's High-Tech Exports,*" Center for Strategic & International Studies, April 28, 2022.

5   Evan Feigenbaum, *China's Techno-Warriors: National Security and Strategic Competition from the Nuclear to the Information Age* (Stanford, CA: Stanford University Press, 2003).

6   "Essay: The Crack-Up by F. Scott Fitzgerald," PBS, *American Masters*, Aug. 31, 2005, pbs.org.

7   "China's Faltering Outlook for Growth," *Financial Times*, June 1, 2023.

8   Alexandra Stevenson, "What to Know about China Evergrande, the Troubled Property Giant," *New York Times*, Dec. 9, 2019.

9   Michael E. O'Hanlon, "China's Shrinking Population and Constraints on Its Future Power," Brookings, April 24, 2023.

Chapter 4: Storm Clouds and Near Wars

1   Nicholas Kristof, "Crackdown in Beijing; Troops Arrest and Crush Beijing Protest; Thousands Fight Back, Scores Are Killed," *New York Times*, June 4, 1989.

2   "Communiqué on the Current State of the Ideological Sphere (Document No. 9)," April 22, 2013, published by Rogier Creemers, digichina.stanford.edu.

3   Josh Chin, *Surveillance State* (New York: St. Martin's Press, 2022).

4   Shoshana Zuboff, *Surveillance Capitalism* (New York: Public Affairs, 2019).

5   Elizabeth C. Economy, "The Great Firewall of China: Xi Jinping's Internet Shutdown," *Guardian*, June 29, 2018.

6   Adam Taylor, "Is Vladimir Putin Hiding a $200 Billion Fortune? (And If So, Does It Matter?)," *Washington Post*, Feb. 20, 2015.

7   Former US ambassador to Russia Michael McFaul describes Vladimir Putin's descent into the depths of autocracy in "Russia's Road to Autocracy," *Journal of Democracy* 32, no. 4 (Oct. 2021), journalofdemocracy.org.

8   Andrew Osborn, "Putin Critic Jailed in Treason Case for 25 Years," Reuters, April 17, 2023.

9   "Department of Justice Seizes $2.3 Million in Cryptocurrency Paid to the Ransomware Extortionists Darkside," press release, U.S. Department of Justice, June 7, 2021.

10   Special Counsel Robert S. Mueller III, *Report on the Investigation into Russian Interference in the 2016 Presidential Election*, Washington, March 2019, Vol. 1, 1.

11   Ibid., Vol. 1, 4.

12   PCA (Permanent Court of Arbitration) Case No 2013-19, In the Matter of the South China Sea Arbitration, before An Arbitral Tribunal Constituted Under Annex VII to the 1982 United Nations Convention on the Law of the Sea, between the Republic of the Philippines and the People's Republic of China, Award, July 12, 2016, pcacases.com.

13   Suresht Bald, ed., Thucydides, *The Peloponnesian War* (New York: Random House, 1951), "Melian Dialogue," nku.edu.

Chapter 5: The Contest for Artificial Intelligence Supremacy

1   For a layperson's explanation of AI and its implications for the world, see Henry Kissinger, Eric Schmidt, and Daniel Huttenlocher, *The Age of AI: And Our Human Future* (New York: Little, Brown, 2022).

2   Geoffrey Hinton et al., "Learning Representations by Back-Propagating Errors," *Nature* 323, no. 6088 (1986).

3   Kai-Fu Lee, *AI Superpowers* (New York: Mariner/Harper Collins, 2021).

4   Zeyi Yang, "The Bearable Mediocrity of Baidu's ChatGPT Competitor," *MIT Technology Review*, March 22, 2023.

5   Mykhaylo Zabrodskyi, "Lessons in Conventional Warfighting: Russia's Invasion of Ukraine: February–July 2022," *Royal United Services Institute*, Nov. 30, 2022.

6   Stephen Chen, "China Tests AI-Powered Long-Range Artillery That Can Hit a Person 16 km Away," *South China Morning Post*, April 17, 2023.

7   Emily Branson et al., *Digital Future Index 2021–2022*, digitalcatapult.org.uk, 33.

8   Ibid., 34 (original figures in pounds converted into US dollars).

9   See materials at stopkillerrobots.org.

10   "Pause Giant AI Experiments: An Open Letter," futureoflife.org.

11   Cade Metz, "Elon Musk Ramps Up A.I. Efforts, Even as He Warns of Dangers," *New York Times*, April 27, 2023.

Chapter 6: The Contest for Semiconductor Chip Supremacy

1   For statistics on the semiconductor industry in the US and in the rest of the world see the Semiconductor Industry Association, semiconductors.org.

2   Ryan Smith, "Samsung and AMD Renew GPU Architecture Licensing
        Agreement: More RDNA Exynos Chips to Come," April 6, 2023, AnandTech,
        anandtech.com.
3   To hear the story firsthand from ASML, see Sander Hofman, "Making EUV:
        From Lab to Fab," March 30, 2022, asml.com.
4   Remarks by national security advisor Jake Sullivan at the Special Competitive
        Studies Project Global Emerging Technologies Summit, Sept. 16, 2022,
        whitehouse.gov.
5   For a good overview of the supply chain in the SC industry, see Jan-Peter
        Kleinhans, "The Global Semiconductor Value Chain," Stiftung Neue
        Verantwortung, Oct. 2020, stiftung-nv.de.
6   Synopsis.com, "Strategic Acquisitions."
7   Zeyi Yang, "Corruption Is Sending Shockwaves through China's Chipmaking
        Industry," *MIT Review*, Aug. 5, 2022.

Chapter 7: The Contest for Quantum Computing Supremacy

1   Kenneth Chang, "Quantum Computing Advance Begins New Era, IBM Says,"
        New York Times, June 19, 2023.
2   Stephen Witt, "The World-Changing Race to Develop the Quantum
        Computer," *New Yorker*, December 12, 2022.
3   Others, involving the IBM QC, can be found at ibm.q.com.
4   Yudong Cao, "Quantum Chemistry in the Age of Quantum Computing,"
        Chemical Reviews 119, no. 19 (2019).
5   Ibid.
6   Dylan Tokar, "Alphabet Launches Bank AI Tool," *Wall Street Journal*, June 22,
        2023.
7   Amine Zeguendry, "Quantum Machine Learning: A Review and Case Studies,"
        Entropy 25, no. 2 (Feb. 2023).
8   See *Pressure*, a play by David Haig, 2014.
9   Stephen Chen, "Post-Snowden China Looks to 'Hack-Proof' Quantum
        Communications," *South China Morning Post*, June 13, 2014.

Chapter 8: The Contest for Biotechnology Supremacy

1   Rob Stein, "First Sickle Cell Patient Treated with CRSIPR Gene-Editing Still
        Thriving," Dec. 31, 2021, NPR, npr.org.
2   Dennis Meadows, *Limits to Growth* (Falls Church, VA: Potomac Associates, 1972).
3   Paul Ehrlich, *The Population Bomb* (New York: Ballantine Books, 1968).
4   US4259444A, "Microorganisms Having Multiple Compatible Degradative
        Energy-Generating Plasmids and Preparation Thereof."
5   Emily Partridge et al., "An Extra-uterine System to Physiologically Support the
        Extreme Premature Lamb," *Nature Communications*, April 25, 2017.
6   Rob Stein, "*Scientists Create Artificial Womb That Could Help Prematurely Born
        Babies,*" NPR, npr.org, April 25, 2017.
7   Shuo Xia et al., "A Microfluidic Culture Model of the Human Reproductive
        Tract and 28-Day Menstrual Cycle," *Nature Communications*, March 28,
        2017.
8   Julian Savulescu, "First Synthetic Embryos: The Scientific Breakthrough Raises
        Serious Ethical Questions," *Phys Org*, Aug. 12, 2022, phys.org.

9   Xiujian Peng, "China's Population Is Now Inexorably Shrinking, Bringing
         Forward the Day the Planet's Population Turns Down," *The Conversation*,
         Jan. 18, 2023, theconversation.com.
10   Valentine Faure, "The Children of the Nazis' Genetic Project," *The Atlantic*,
         Feb. 22, 2023.
11   Roni Rabin, "Many Women Have an Intense Fear of Childbirth, Survey
         Suggests," *New York Times*, May 16, 2023.
12   Talya Minsberg, "Track Star Tori Bowie Died in Childbirth," *New York Times*,
         June 13, 2023.
13   Antonio Regelado, "The World's First Gattaca Baby Tests Are Finally Here,"
         New York Times, Nov. 8, 2019.
14   Sui-Lee Wee, "China's Ill, and Wealthy, Look Abroad for Medical Treatment,"
         New York Times, May 29, 2017.
15   As ranked by QS Top Universities, topuniversities.com.
16   As presented at companiesmarketcap.com.

Chapter 9: Other Important Technologies

1   Jared Malsin, "Kremlin Extends Global Influence with Russian Nuclear-Power
         Juggernaut," *Wall Street Journal*, April 27, 2023.
2   Fusion Industry Association, fia.org.
3   Jennifer Hiller, "Tech Billionaires Bet on Fusion as Holy Grail for Business,"
         Wall Street Journal, April 23, 2023.
4   SIPRI Arms Industry Database, sipri.org.

Chapter 10: Other Powerful Assets

1   worldpopulationreview.com.
2   World Bank, data.worldbank.org.
3   World Population Review, at worldpopulationreview.com; only "active duty,"
         and excluding "paramilitary" and "reserves."
4   Junhua Zhang, "Failing Aircraft Venture Highlights Strains in Chinese-Russian
         Relations," *GIS*, Aug. 17, 2022, gisreportsonline.com.
5   Agathe Demarais, "Why China Hasn't Come to Russia's Rescue," *Foreign
         Affairs*, April 28, 2023.
6   U.S. Geological Survey, *Mineral Commodity Summaries*, Jan. 2023,
         pubs.usgs.gov; information for Uranium: Melissa Pistilli, "Top 10
         Uranium-Producing Countries," *Investing News*, Sept. 5, 2022,
         investingnews.com.
7   The US Geological Survey doesn't give figures for actual production in order "to
         avoid disclosing company proprietary data."
8   As ranked by QS Top Universities, topuniversities.com.
9   Geoffrey Hinton et al., "Deep Neural Networks for Acoustic Modeling in
         Speech Recognition," *IEEE Xplore*, Nov. 2012.

Chapter 11: Cold War 2.0 Flashpoints

1   *Patriot* (updated report), by the Center for Strategic & International Studies,
         Missile Defense Project, missilethreat.csis.org.
2   Marc Santora, "Ukraine Claims It Shot Down Russia's Most Sophisticated
         Missile for the First Time," *New York Times*, May 6, 2023.

3   For an interesting read with lots of local color, see James Wheeler Davidson,
      The Island of Formosa, Past and Present (New York: Macmillan & Co., 1903),
      accessed in Google's digital archive.
4   Ibid.; Davidson gives great detail about how the Japanese campaign started with
      a landing in the north, and then methodically worked its way south. Is this the
      path Xi Jinping would have his PLA take were he to attack the island?
5   "Changes in the Unification-Independence Stances of Taiwanese as Tracked
      in Surveys by Election Study Center, NCCU; John Feng, "Taiwan's Desire for
      Unification with China Near Record Low as Tensions Rise," *Newsweek*, July 14,
      2022, newsweek.com.
6   Paul Mozur, "Made in China, Exported to the World: The Surveillance State,"
      New York Times, April 24, 2019.
7   Steven Feldstein, "The Global Expansion of AI Surveillance," Carnegie
      Endowment for International Peace, Sept. 17, 2019.
8   Asli Aydintasbas, "What Is the Fallout of Russia's Wagner Rebellion?"
      Brookings, June 27, 2023.
9   Roberto S. Foa et al., "A World Divided: Russia, China, and the West,"
      Oct. 2022, Centre for the Future of Democracy, University of Cambridge,
      bennettinstitute.cam.ac.uk.
10   "How India Is Using Digital Technology to Project Power," *The Economist*,
      June 4, 2023.

Chapter 12: Managing Cold War 2.0

1   "Security Council Fails to Adopt Draft Resolution on Ending Ukraine Crisis, as
      Russian Federation Wields Veto," United Nations, meetings coverage and press
      releases, SC/14808, press.un.org.
2   "Framework for the Consideration of Prospective Members," OECD, June 7,
      2017.
3   Costas Paris, "Russian Shipbuilders Are Running Out of Parts," *Wall Street
      Journal*, April 24, 2024.
4   Canadian finance minister Chrystia Freeland has proposed a program along
      these lines at the G7 meeting in Germany in 2022, but to date neither the US
      nor the EU has adopted anything like it.
5   World's Top Exports, worldstopexports.com.
6   Yang Jie, "Apple CEO Tim Cook Meets Prime Minister Modi, as Tech Giant
      Looks to Expand in India," *Wall Street Journal*, April 19, 2023.
7   "America's Commercial Sanctions on China Could Get Much Worse," *The
      Economist*, March 30, 2023.
8   Dan Goodin, "18,000 Organizations Downloaded Backdoor Planted by Cozy
      Bear Hackers," *Ars Technica*, Dec. 14, 2020, arstechnica.com.

Chapter 13: Strengthening Democracies

1   "WE THE PEOPLES OF THE UNITED NATIONS DETERMINED to
      save succeeding generations from the scourge of war, which twice in our lifetime
      has brought untold sorrow to mankind . . .", preamble, United Nations Charter;
      "All Members shall refrain in their international relations from the threat or use
      of force against the territorial integrity or political independence of any state. . . .",
      Article 2.4, United Nations Charter, un.org.

2   "Funding NATO," April 14, 2023, nato.int.

3   "Europe Is Struggling to Rebuild Its Military Clout," *The Economist*, May 7,
       2023.

4   Kai-Fu Lee, *AI Superpowers: China, Silicon Valley and the New World Order* (New
       York: First Mariner Books/Harper Collins, 2018).

5   "How to Get More Bang for the Buck in Western Defence Budgets," *The
       Economist*, May 25, 2023.

6   "How to Save $48 Billion from the US Nuclear Triad over the Next 10
       Years—While Still Keeping It," Center for Arms Control and Non-
       Proliferation, Nov. 20, 2013, armscontrolcenter.org.

7   Upton Sinclair, *The Jungle* (New York: Barnes & Noble Classics, 2005; original
       edition 1906).

8   Will Daniel, "4 Tech Giants Accounted for More Than 16 Percent of Fortune
       500 Earnings—Even in a Down Year," *Fortune*, June 6, 2023.

9   Kashmir Hill, "Madison Square Garden Uses Facial Recognition to Ban Its
       Owner's Enemies," *New York Times*, December 22, 2022.

10   David Gelles, "The Husband-and-Wife Team behind the Leading Vaccine to
       Solve COVID-19," *New York Times*, Nov. 10, 2020.

11   Margaret Atwood, *The Handmaid's Tale* (Toronto: McClelland & Stewart, 1985).

12   "List of International Days and Weeks," United Nations, un.org.

13   Chris McGreal, "Trump Raised $200 m from False Election Claims. What
       Happens to the Money Now?" *Guardian*, Dec. 19, 2020.

14   Sam Levine, "He Became a Hero for Halting Trump's Efforts to Overturn the
       Election. Will Voters Now Punish Him?" *Guardian*, May 19, 2022.

15   Jacqueline Thomson, "Trump Lawyer Jenna Ellis Censured over 2020 Election
       Fraud 'Misrepresentations,'" *Reuters*, March 9, 2023.

16   John Hendrickson, "The First MAGA Democrat," *The Atlantic*, June 26, 2023.

Chapter 14: A World Technologically Decoupled

1   Francesca Ebel, "Russian Scientists, Experts in Hypersonic Technology,
       Arrested for Treason," *Washington Post*, May 17, 2023.

2   Christian Shepherd, "China Gives Elon Musk a Hero's Welcome—and a
       Message for the U.S.," *Washington Post*, June 2, 2023.

3   Raymond Zhong, "How China's Outrage Machine Kicked Up a Storm over
       H&M," *New York Times*, March 29, 2021.

4   "How India Is Using Digital Technology to Project Power," *The Economist*, June 4,
       2023.

5   Assembling the iPhone outside of the Chinese ecosystem of Foxconn's 150
       suppliers will be a challenge in India (where Foxconn has only eleven suppliers,
       and even in Vietnam it has only twenty-six, so far at least); Rajesh Roy, "Top
       Apple Supplier Foxconn Plans Major India Expansion," *Wall Street Journal*,
       March 4, 2023.

6   Philip Wen, "India's Manufacturing Push Takes an Audacious Gamble on
       Chips," *Wall Street Journal*, Dec. 13, 2022.

7   Francis Fukuyama, *The End of History and the Last Man* (New York: Free Press,
       1992).

INDEX

C

Cadence, 141, 144, 154, 192
Canada
 aircraft manufacturers and, 214
 artificial intelligence and, 131
 biotechnology and, 185
 competitive displacement and, 2–4
 democracies and, 226
 early-stage AI companies, 128
 financing sources and, 222–223
 fusion technology and, 209
 military defense contractors and, 221
 nuclear industries and, 204, 206
 relations with, 96
 software companies and, 192
 telecommunications and, 196
 universities and, 242–243
 vertical AI companies, 128
 weapons systems and, 20
 women leaders and, xxii
Canadian Association of Defence and Security
 Industries, xxii
Canon, 143, 146
Capella Space, 199, 201
Capgemini, 193
CARE, 275
Carrefour, 79
Castro, Fidel, 293
Catherine II, Tsarina, 57
CBC, 251
CERN, 158–159, 208
Ceva, 144
CGI, 193
Chakrabarty, Ananda, 176
Chamberlain, Neville, 327–328
Chang, Morris, 259
ChatGPT, 112, 118, 120–121, 132–133
Cheka, ix, 41
Chelomey, Vladimir, 61
chemical weapons, 17–18, 28–29, 181
Chen Shui-bian, 259–260
Chiang Kai-shek, 255, 259
Chicago Daily Tribune, 47
Children's Investment Fund Foundation, 275
Chile, 100, 226, 282, 287, 354
China
 aircraft manufacturers and, 213–217
 artificial intelligence and, 82, 86, 93–94, 96,
  119–123, 126–128, 134
 autocracies and, 228
 automobile manufacturers and, 211
 biotechnology and, ix, 61, 82, 93, 178–179, 181–187
 cloud computing, 189–190
 competitive displacement and, 16–17, 31–32
 composite score and, 333–335
 early-stage AI companies, 128
 economic status of, 65–70, 75–86
 emergence of, xxx–xxxi, 65–86
 financing sources and, 222–223
 flashpoints, 246–247, 252–273

 fusion technology and, 207–209
 global industry and, 77–78, 144–147
 horizontal AI companies, 127
 innovation and, 66–86
 Internet platforms and, 194
 jet engine manufacturers and, 215–217
 military defense contractors and, 219–221
 near wars and, 87–109, 255
 nuclear industries and, 206–207, 257
 nuclear warheads and, 232
 population declines, 84–85, 178–179, 321
 propaganda and, 93, 297–298, 322
 quantum computers and, 9, 82, 93, 157–161,
  166–172
 relations with, xi–xxxviii, xl, 31–32, 50–51,
  65–86, 278, 366–368
 robotics industry and, 218
 semiconductor chips and, 9, 82, 86, 93, 135–139,
  143–156
 shipbuilders and, 212
 software companies and, 192
 space technology and, 199–201
 strategic minerals and, 237–241
 technology and, 1, 3–4, 8–10, 66–86
 technology decoupling and, 330–363
 telecommunications and, 195–197
 trade deficits, 287–288
 trade surpluses, 77, 287–288
 trading partners, xxvii, 228, 236, 286–289
 universities and, 242
 vertical AI companies, 128
China Aerospace Science and Industry Corporation
 (CASIC), 199–200, 220
China Aerospace Science and Technology
 Corporation (CASC), 199–200, 220
China Electronics and Technology Group
 Corporation (CETC), 200
China Electronics Corporation (CEC), 200
China General Nuclear Power Group, 206
China Integrated Circuit Industry Investment Fund,
 152
China National Nuclear Corporation (CNNC),
 206–207
China Satellite Networks Limited (CSCN), 200
China State Shipbuilding Corporation, 212
China Telecom, 195
Chinese Communist Party (CCP), ix, xi–xii, xxix,
 1, 42–43, 72–73, 79–81, 87–95, 127, 218–219,
 255–256, 337, 369
Chinese Institute of Computing Technology, 120
Chips Act, 151
Chrysler, 210
Chugai, 186
Churchill, Winston, 19, 34, 45–47
Cianfarani, Christyn, xxii
Cisco, 195, 197
Civil War, 7–8
civilian artificial intelligence, 126–128
civilian technology, 2–5, 29–32. *See also* technology
Clinton, Hillary, 105, 311

ABOUT THE AUTHOR

George S. Takach holds a first degree in history, political economy, and philosophy from the University of Toronto; a graduate degree from the Norman Paterson School of International Relations at Carleton University; and a law degree from the University of Toronto. For forty years, he practiced technology law at McCarthy Tétrault. He has written three books on technology law/tech commercial subjects—this is his first book for a general audience.